Agrippina the Younger

WOMEN IN ANTIQUITY

Series Editors: Ronnie Ancona and Sarah B. Pomeroy

This book series provides compact and accessible introductions to the life and historical times of women from the ancient world. Approaching ancient history and culture broadly, the series selects figures from the earliest of times to late antiquity.

Turia
A Roman Woman's Civil War
Josiah Osgood

Monica
An Ordinary Saint
Gillian Clark

Theodora
Actress, Empress, Saint
David Potter

Hypatia
The Life and Legend of an Ancient Philosopher
Edward Watts

Boudica
Warrior Woman of Roman Britain
Caitlin C. Gillespie

Sabina Augusta
An Imperial Journey
T. Corey Brennan

Cleopatra's Daughter
And Other Royal Woman of the Augustan Era
Duane W. Roller

Perpetua
Athlete of God
Barbara K. Gold

Zenobia
Shooting Star of Palmyra
Nathanael Andrade

Eurydice and the Birth of Macedonian Power
Elizabeth Donnelly Carney

Melania the Younger
From Rome to Jerusalem
Elizabeth A. Clark

Sosipatra of Pergamum:
Philosopher and Oracle
Heidi Marx

Helena Augusta:
Mother of the Empire
Julia Hillner

Radegund:
The Trials and Triumphs of a Merovingian Queen
E.T. Dailey

Fulvia
Playing for Power at the End of the Roman Republic
Celia E. Schultz

Bathild of Francia
Anglo-Saxon Slave, Merovingian Queen, and Abolitionist Saint
Isabel Moreira

Poppaea Sabina
The Life and Afterlife of a Roman Empress
Neil W. Bernstein

Octavia
The Life of a Roman Matron Between Antony and Augustus
Beth Andrea Severy-Hoven

Sulpicia
Life, Love, and Literature in Ancient Rome
Alison Keith

Agrippina the Younger

A Dangerous Woman in Rome's Early Empire

MARY T. BOATWRIGHT

OXFORD
UNIVERSITY PRESS

OXFORD
UNIVERSITY PRESS

Oxford University Press is a department of the University of Oxford. It furthers the University's objective of excellence in research, scholarship, and education by publishing worldwide. Oxford is a registered trade mark of Oxford University Press in the UK and in certain other countries.

Published in the United States of America by Oxford University Press
546 Fifth Avenue, New York, NY 10036, United States of America.

CIP data is on file at the Library of Congress.

ISBN 9780190945824 (hbk)
ISBN 9780197857151 (pbk)

DOI: 10.1093/9780190945855.001.0001

Printed by Integrated Books International, United States of America

The manufacturer's authorized representative in the EU for product safety is Oxford University Press España S.A. of Parque Empresarial San Fernando de Henares, Avenida de Castilla, 2 – 28830 Madrid (www.oup.es/en or product.safety@oup.com). OUP España S.A. also acts as importer into Spain of products made by the manufacturer.

MIX
Paper
FSC FSC® C183721

To all my sisters, mothers, and daughters, through the generations by blood, marriage, adoption, love, and solidarity. May each of your stories be told.

Acknowledgments

Agrippina the Younger might seem the natural sequel to my *Imperial Women of Rome* (2021), but this biography has been peculiarly challenging for me. Trained to drill down on positivistic evidence, I began the biography in earnest just as the Covid epidemic and my retirement isolated me even from libraries. The unflagging interest and encouragement of many helped pull the project through those days and now to its completion. Whatever errors or infelicities remain in my book, however, are due to me alone.

Special thanks here go to my "sister," Tia Lombardi, and my husband, Paul Feldblum: you cannot know how much you mean to me and have meant for this book. Insights and inspiration have also come from innumerable graduate and undergraduate students, notably Molly Pryzwansky in 2008, the fearless students in my 2019 seminar on imperial women, and David Mellgard, my last honors thesis student. Daily progress often relied on my writing groups over the years, which included not only fellow classicists like Clare Woods and Lauren Ginsberg but also Duke faculty in medicine and other disciplines. Eve D'Ambra, Michael Maas, Francis L. Newton, Kent Rigsby, Rose Mary Sheldon, and Richard Talbert furnished particularly important insights and information. Rex Crews has been my invaluable interlocutor about Latin. Equally significant support came from farther afield. A talk, "Agrippina the Younger: 'I, Me, Mine?,'" presented at the University of Michigan while I was first formulating the project in 2019, allowed me to explore—tentatively!—Agrippina's psychology through a "stress inventory." (David Halperin's advice there to see Handel's *Agrippina* was life changing.) Another presentation, "What Would Agrippina Do?," given as I ended my presidency of the Society for Classical Studies early in 2020, had me lean into Agrippina's relevance to current concerns and introduced me to Anise Strong. At the University of Washington in 2025 I presented "The Afterlife of Agrippina," clarifying my work for Chapter 6 of this book. Earlier, as I began actual writing, Lynne Lancaster was central to my invitation to be a resident at the American Academy in Rome (AAR) in spring 2021. There, even Covid's restrictions could not repress AAR's encouragement of new knowledge and thinking. My section on Agrippina's autopsy came from that happy time and conversations with Rebecca Messbarger. Werner Eck's kind invitation to contribute to a volume honoring the late Tony Birley—whose own work continues to be a lodestar—spurred my investigation of Agrippina's enslaved and freed dependents, research that reminded me of the need for rigorous objectivity, even—especially?—when analyzing problematic subjects. Just around the same time, Keith Bradley provided compelling guidance on how to write a sympathetic biography without losing sight of a person's life, times, and reception. Lucrezia Ungaro has been an inspiration for my forays into sculpture. Cathy Keane helped me with Juvenal, a sore spot for me, and Peter Keegan generously corresponded with me about female "biography." The outstanding Stefan Vranka and far-sighted editors of OUP's Women in Antiquity series have been reassuringly patient, and an anonymous reader provided essential direction when I most needed it. All these individuals, and many more, have helped me craft something I hope does justice to Agrippina and to my readers.

Tolly Boatwright

Durham, NC
April 2025

Contents

List of Illustrations xi
List of Abbreviations and Notes for the Reader xv
Agrippina's Genealogy and Relations xvii
Timeline for Agrippina the Younger xix

Introduction: Agrippina's Contexts and Impacts 1

1. Agrippina's Youth (15–37 CE) 12
2. Life under Caligula (37–41) 35
3. Betwixt and Between (41–48) 51
4. At Last, at the Center (49–54 CE) 70
5. Best of Mothers—or Nero's Nemesis (54–59) 99
6. Agrippina's Afterlife and Legacy: Conclusions 135

Notes 159
Bibliography 207
Index 217

List of Illustrations

Ill. Intro.1. Gemma Claudia cameo, depicting (left) the emperor Claudius and his wife Agrippina the Younger face-to-face with (right) Germanicus, Claudius' brother, and his wife Agrippina the Elder, Agrippina the Younger's father and mother. 12.0 × 15.2 cm. Vienna, Kunsthistorisches Museum (inv. IX a 63). © KHM-Museumsverband. 5

Ill. Intro.2. Portrait head of Agrippina the Younger, ca. 50 CE. Marble, 32 × 27 × 28 cm. Getty Villa (obj. no. 70.AA.101). Open Content photo courtesy of the Getty Museum. 6

Ill. Intro.3. Bust of Agrippina the Younger (Ancona type; late Claudian/early Neronian). Marble, 36 cm H. Ny Carlsberg Glyptotek, Copenhagen (inv. no. 755). © Ny Carlsberg Glyptotek, Copenhagen/Jo Selsing. 7

Ill. 1.1. Rome's Palatine Hill during Agrippina the Younger's youth. The House of Germanicus was once that of Julia the Elder and Marcellus; that of Antonia the Younger perhaps belonged to Octavia before passing to Antonia and Drusus the Elder, and then to Claudius after Antonia's death in 27 CE. Where exactly Julia Augusta dwelled over the years is unclear. Plan by author and MossMaps Cartography, after Carandini 2018, tav. 4 and Carandini and Carafa 2017, Tab. 70. 28

Ill. 2.1. Agrippina and her sisters Drusilla and Julia (Livilla) guised as Security, Harmony, and Good Fortune, on the reverse of a centrally struck *sestertius* of Caligula from 37/38 CE. © The Trustees of the British Museum. 40

Ill. 4.1. Agrippina Augusta with Nero, *Princeps Iuventutis*, on a centrally struck *denarius* from 50–54. © The Trustees of the British Museum. 79

Ill. 4.2. Bronze bust of Agrippina with traces of gilding, found in Alba Fucens (Italy). 12.7 cm H × 10 W × 6 D. Now in MUSE'Nuovo Museo Paludi di Celano (AQ). Image courtesy of the Ministero della Cultura, MAN Chieti—DRMN Abruzzo. (Reproduction and duplication forbidden.) 90

Ill. 4.3. Oversized marble relief of Agrippina clasping the right hand of Claudius. From the Sebasteion at Aphrodisias. © New York University Excavations at Aphrodisias (G. Petruccioli). 91

Ill. 4.4. Plan of Rome during Agrippina's lifetime, including monuments relating to her and discussed in the text. © Ancient World Mapping Center. 92

Ill. 5.1. Agrippina face-to-face with the new emperor Nero on an *aureus* from Rome struck 54–55. © The Trustees of the British Museum. 103

Ill. 5.2. Agrippina and Nero, jugate, on an *aureus* from Rome struck 54–55. © The Trustees of the British Museum. 104

Ill. 5.3. Oversized marble relief of Agrippina crowning Nero, from the Sebasteion at Aphrodisias. © New York University Excavations at Aphrodisias (G. Petruccioli). 105

Ill. 5.4. Agrippina crowning Nero on a cameo, 8.04 × 6.41 cm. Cathedral of Cologne, Shrine of the Three Kings (Dreikönigsschrein), front Epiphany side, trapezoid plate, right side (cameo Catalogue 1, position number 55). © The High Cathedral of Cologne, Cathedral Office (Photo: Matz and Schenk). 107

Ill. 5.5. Reconstruction of the phases of the dedications to the imperial family in the Shrine of the Aenatores Romani. The final two phases indicate honor for Agrippina and its subsequent obliteration. Material now in the Museo Nazionale Romano delle Terme di Diocleziano. Image from Morizio in Panella 1996, Fig. 180; courtesy of C. Panella and the Archivio Fotografico Scavo Meta Sudans, Dipartimento di Scienze dell'Antichità, Sapienza Università di Roma. 117

Ill. 5.6. Head of Agrippina from the Caelian statue. Graywacke, 30 cm H. Ny Carlsberg Glyptotek, Copenhagen (inv. no. 753). © Ny Carlsberg Glyptotek, Copenhagen/Ole Haupt. 120

Ill. 5.7. Reconstructed phases of graywacke head of Agrippina from the Caelian. The second phase includes recutting of lips to more closely resemble those of the young Nero. The final phase includes recutting of the diadem to accommodate inset gems. Drawings of Ny Carlsberg Glyptotek inv. no. 753 by Thora Fisker (kindness of M. Moltesen). 121

Ill. 5.8. Statue of Agrippina (graywacke; body 180 cm H) from the Caelian Hill, as reassembled in the Musei Capitolini, Centrale Montemartini, Rome (inv. no. MC1882), with a cast of the portrait head now in the Ny Glyptotek, Copenhagen (inv. no. 753). © Sovrintendenza di Roma Capitale—Foto in Comune. 122

Ill. 5.9. The topography of Agrippina's murder in 59 in Baiae in the Bay of Naples. Key: 1 = Claudian nymphaeum; 2 = Villa of the Pisones; 3 = bath complexes; 4 = modern monumental park; 5 = Castello di Baia; 6 = Cento Camerelle. (Keppie 2011, 38; drawn by L. Keppie and used with his permission.) © The Classical Association 2011. 129

Ill. 6.1. Standing portrait of Agrippina the Younger, Milan-Florence type. From the Metroon at Olympia, Greece, probably 54–59. Marble, 203 cm H, (head) 26.5 cm. Olympia, Archaeological Museum A 143. Carine Vaissiere/Alamy Stock Photo. 141

Ill. 6.2. Detail of head of marble standing portrait of Agrippina the Younger (203 cm H), Parma-Naples type, from imperial family installation at Velleia. From the Museo Nazionale di Antichità, Parma, inv. no. 830. With the permission of the Ministero della Cultura—Soprintendenza Archeologia, Belle Arti e Paesaggio per la città metropolitana di Bologna e le province di Modena, Reggio Emilia e Ferrara. Reproduction prohibited for profit, even indirect. 142

Ill. 6.3. Head of Agrippina the Younger, Stuttgart type, 54–59 CE, marble, 40.5 cm H. Stuttgart, Landesmuseum Württemberg, Arch. 68/2. Landesmuseum Württemberg, Hendrik Zwietasch CC BY 4.0 https://creativecommons.org/licenses/by/4.0/deed.de. 142

Ill. 6.4. Standing female statue now in the Minneapolis Institute of Art. Once identified as Agrippina the Younger, this is now titled "Roman Matron, 50–60 CE." Marble, 128.27 × 33.02 × 26.67 cm. Accession number 32.16. Photo: Minneapolis Institute of Art. 144

Ill. 6.5. Colossal marble head from the Forum of Trajan (106–112 CE), 80 cm H (head 62 cm from chin to vertex). Rome, Museo dei Fori Imperiali, Mercati di Traiano (inv. FT 6116)—Archivio Fotografico del Museo dei Fori Imperiali. © Roma, Sovrintendenza Capitolina ai Beni Culturali. 145

Ill. 6.6. "Nero Pauses for a Drink during the Mutilation of His Mother's Body," French manuscript illumination in *Des cas des nobles hommes et femmes.* Getty Ms. 63 (96.MR.17), fol. 224v, Boucicaut Master, ca. 1413–1415, Paris. Open Content image courtesy of the Getty Museum. 149

Ill. 6.7. "Nero and Agrippina," illumination from the late 15th-century manuscript *Roman de la Rose* by Jean de Meun and Guillaume de Lorris. © British Library Board, Harley 4425, f. 59r, Bruges, ca. 1490 to ca. 1500. 149

Ill. 6.8. Antonio Rizzi, "Nero and Agrippina" (1894; now in the Museo Civico "Ala Ponzone" in Cremona, Italy). Courtesy of the Musei Civici di Cremona. 151

List of Abbreviations and Notes for the Reader

For ancient literary works I follow the abbreviations of the most recent edition of *Oxford Classical Dictionary*. Cassius Dio poses special challenges because of the fragmented status of his text, and for convenience I use the book, chapter, and section numbering of the Loeb edition by E. Cary, *Dio's Roman History* (London and Cambridge, MA, 1914–1927). For references to journals, I follow the abbreviations of *L'Année philologique*.

Throughout the text I provide full praenomina for Roman men, but in endnotes, "Agrippina's Genealogy and Relations," and the timeline I use the common Latin abbreviations (e.g., Titus Statilius Taurus; T. Statilius Taurus). Similarly, consonantal I appears as J in the narrative but as I in references (e.g., Julia; Iulia). Rome's third *princeps*, Gaius Caesar Augustus Germanicus, is referred to as Caligula other than in references to coins from his reign in *Roman Imperial Coinage*, which appear as *RIC*² I, Gaius and the appropriate entry number.

Capitalized "Republic/an" refers to the period from Rome's overthrow of its monarchy (traditionally dated to 509 BCE) to Augustus' consolidation of power in 27 BCE, as well as the system of government during that era. I generally use "principate" to refer to the political system that evolved to replace it, when civil administration, the military, and religion were dominated by a princeps—a man, first among equals, who ruled by ratified rights and indeterminate authority.

Object dimensions are given as length × width × height in centimeters, unless otherwise noted.

AE	*L'Année épigraphique*, published in *Revue Archéologique* and separately. Paris 1888–.
b.	born.
CFA	Acta of the Arval Brethren; cited as *CFA* and document number as they appear in the authoritative edition of J. Scheid (ed.), *Commentarii fratrum Arvalium qui supersunt. Les copies épigraphiques des protocoles annuels de la confrérie arvale (21 av.-304 ap. J.-C.)*. Rome 1998.
CIL	*Corpus Inscriptionum Latinarum*. 16 vols. Berlin 1863–.
EDCS	Epigraphik-Datenbank Clauss-Slaby, http://www.manfredclauss.de/
EDR	Epigraphic Database Rome, http://www.edr-edr.it/en/present_en.php

FOS	Raepsaet-Charlier, M.-T. 1987. *Prosopographie des femmes de l'ordre sénatorial (Ier–IIe siècles)*. Louvain. References to individuals are by their entry number in the catalogue.
FGrH	Jacoby, F. 1923–. *Die Fragmente der griechischen Historiker.* Leiden.
Furneaux	Furneaux, H., ed. 1896. *The Annals of Tacitus.* 2 vols. (Vol. I: Books 1–6. 2nd ed., with H. F. Pelham and C. D. Fisher. Oxford; and Furneaux, H., ed. 1907. *The Annals of Tacitus.* Vol. II: Books 11–16. 2nd ed., with H. F. Pelham and C. D. Fisher. Oxford.) Cited by volume number and page (in Arabic numbers), referring to specific passages or general commentary.
HS	*Sestertius, sesterii* (pl.), a Roman mid-value coin and monetary unit. English renders the plural as sesterces.
IG	*Inscriptiones Graecae.* Berlin 1873–.
IGRR	*Inscriptiones Graecae ad res Romanas pertinentes*, ed. R. Cagnat. Vols. 1, 3, 4. Paris 1901–1927.
I. I.	*Inscriptiones Italiae.* Rome 1931–.
IK	*Inschriften griechischer Städte aus Kleinasien.* Bonn 1972–.
ILS	*Inscriptiones Latinae Selectae*, ed. H. Dessau. Berlin 1892–1916.
Koestermann	Koestermann, E. 1963–1968. *Cornelius Tacitus, Annalen.* 4 vols. Heidelberg. Cited by volume number and page (in Arabic numbers), referring to specific passages.
LTUR	*Lexicon Topographicum Urbis Romae*, ed. E. Steinby. 6 vols. Rome 1993–2000. Citations to this are followed by volume number and page, entry, and author of entry.
OCRE	Online Coins of the Roman Empire, http://numismatics.org/ocre/
Phlegon	*Phlegon of Tralles, Book of Marvels*, tr. W. Hansen with introduction and commentary. Exeter, UK 1996.
PIR^2	*Prosopographia Imperii Romani saeculi I, II, III.* 2nd edition by E. Groag et al. Berlin 1933–.
RGDA	*Res Gestae Divi Augusti.*
RE	*Paulys Real-Encyclopädie der Classischen Altertumswissenschaft*, ed. A. Pauly, G. Wissowa, and W. Kroll. Berlin 1893–1980.
RIC^2	*Roman Imperial Coinage.* Vol. 1 *(31 BC–AD 69).* Revised 2nd edition by C. H. V. Sutherland and R. A. G. Carson. London 1984.
SCPP	*Das Senatus Consultum de Cn. Pisone patre, CIL* II^2/5, 900 = EDCS-46400001, cited according to the text as established by W. Eck, A. Caballos, and F. Fernández. Munich 1996.
SEG	*Supplementum Epigraphicum Graecum*, ed. A. Chaniotis et al. Leiden 1926–.
Smallwood	E. M. Smallwood, *Documents Illustrating the Principates of Gaius, Claudius and Nero.* London 1967.

Agrippina's Genealogy and Relations

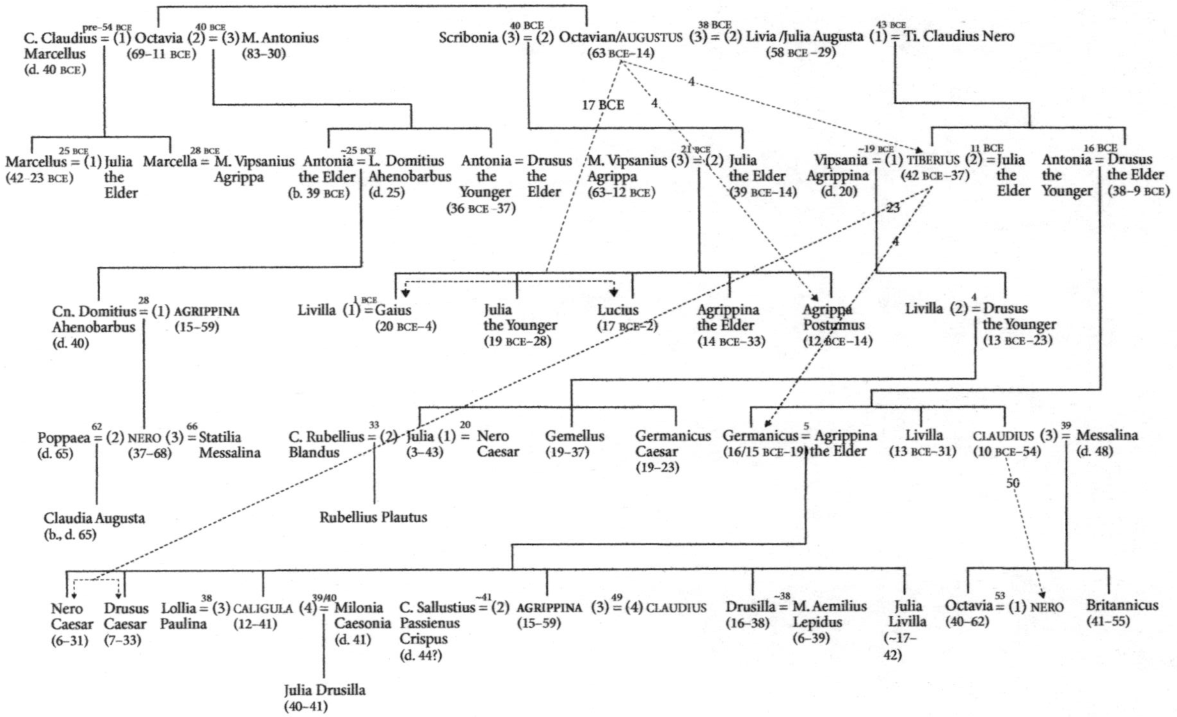

Key: (i) Agrippina the Younger appears as AGRIPPINA, but other names are those used in book; (ii) Unless otherwise stated, dates are CE; (iii) Emperors' names are in SMALL CAPS.

(iv) Dashed lines indicate adoption; (v) Not all biographical detail is indicated for each of Agrippina's relatives.

Timeline for Agrippina the Younger

(Agrippina the Younger is identified simply as Agrippina after the death of her mother in 33 CE.)

27 BCE–14 CE	***Principate of Augustus***, Agrippina the Younger's maternal great-grandfather.
4 CE	Adoption of Tiberius (and Agrippa Postumus) by Augustus; adoption of Germanicus (later father of Agrippina the Younger) by Tiberius.
5	Agrippina the Elder and Germanicus (Agrippina the Younger's parents) wed.
14–37	***Principate of Tiberius***
14–17	Agrippina the Elder with Germanicus in the Three Gauls; son Caligula joins 18 May 14.
15 (6 November)	Birth of Agrippina the Younger in Oppidum Ubiorum.
17 (26 May)	Triumph of Germanicus in Rome. Five children ride in his chariot, including Agrippina the Younger.
19 (10 October)	Germanicus dies in Antioch while overseeing Rome's affairs in the East (accompanied by Agrippina the Elder, Caligula, and Julia Livilla).
20 (early January)	Agrippina the Elder reaches Rome with Germanicus' ashes (and children) and moves into house of Antonia the Younger, Germanicus' mother.
23	Tiberius adopts Agrippina the Younger's brothers Nero Caesar (17 y.o.) and Drusus Caesar (15 y.o.).
27(?)	Agrippina the Younger and siblings move from house of Antonia the Younger to house of Julia Augusta. Tiberius moves to Capri.
27	Agrippina the Younger's mother and brother, Agrippina the Elder and Nero Caesar, move to Herculaneum.
28	Agrippina the Younger weds Cn. Domitius Ahenobarbus.
28	Julia the Younger (Agrippina the Younger's maternal aunt) dies in exile.
29	Agrippina the Elder is exiled to Pandateria, Nero Caesar to Pontia.
29	Julia Augusta (Livia) dies; Caligula delivers eulogy in Forum Romanum.
30	Drusus Caesar is indicted.

31	Caligula moves to Capri (after 31 Aug.). Fall of Sejanus (18 October). Nero Caesar commits suicide on Pontia (uncertain day).
32	Ahenobarbus *cos. ord.* for entire year.
33	Agrippina the Elder commits suicide; Drusus Caesar dies in Rome.
33	Agrippina's sisters, Drusilla and Julia Livilla, wed L. Cassius Longinus and M. Vinicius.
37	Agrippina's husband, Ahenobarbus, charged with treason, adultery, and incest with sister Domitia Lepida.
37–41	***Principate of Caligula***, Agrippina's older brother
37	Caligula ratified as princeps (18 March) two days after Tiberius' death at Misenum; arrives in Rome (28 March).
37	Unprecedented honors for Caligula's three sisters, including inclusion of their names in official oaths and on coins.
37 (15 December)	Agrippina births L. Domitius Ahenobarbus (the later Nero) at Antium.
37–38	Caligula acutely sick, probably late October 37 through January 38.
37/38	Death of Antonia the Younger, Agrippina's paternal grandmother.
38	Death (10 June) and consecration as *diva Panthea* (?23 September) of Drusilla, Agrippina's sister.
39	Conspiracy of Cn. Cornelius Lentulus Gaetulicus (before 27 October). Conspiracy of Agrippina, Julia Livilla, and others. Agrippina banished to Pontia, Julia Livilla to Pandateria.
40(?)	Death of Ahenobarbus; estate seized by Caligula; Nero placed with Domitia Lepida to be raised.
41 (24 January)	Caligula, Milonia Caesonia, and daughter Julia Drusilla killed.
41–54	***Principate of Claudius***, Agrippina's uncle (and husband after 49).
41	Claudius acclaimed as princeps by praetorians (25 January). Recall of Caligula's exiles, including Agrippina and Julia Livilla.
41(?)	Agrippina weds C. Sallustius Crispus Passienus.
41	Agrippina's sister, Julia Livilla, charged with conspiracy and adultery, banished to Pandateria, and dies.
42–43	Kos honors Agrippina.
42	Revolt of Scribonianus in Dalmatia.
43	Claudius travels to war in Britain (late July/early August).
44	Roman triumph of Claudius, in which Messalina participates.
44? (late January?)	Death of Passienus, Agrippina's second husband.

47–48	Messalina's "marriage" with C. Silius ends in death of both (autumn 48).
49	Marriage of Agrippina to Claudius.
49–54	Agrippina appears often with Claudius in public.
49	Betrothal of Octavia to Nero. Seneca appointed tutor of Nero.
50 (25 February)	Claudius adopts L. Domitius as Nero Claudius Caesar Drusus Germanicus.
50	Agrippina receives honorific "Augusta." Colonia Claudia Ara Agrippinensium established.
51/52	Submission of Briton Caratacus to Claudius and Agrippina in Rome.
51	Acceleration of Nero's *toga virilis* and other honors.
51	Substitution of two praetorian prefects by Afranius Burrus alone.
51	Agrippina enters Capitolium in a *carpentum*.
51/52	Agrippina, Claudius, and Nero at attempted drainage of Fucine Lake.
52	Praetorian insignia and HS 15M decreed to Pallas.
52	Agrippina mediates with Claudius on behalf of Agrippa II and the Jews.
53	Wedding of Nero to Octavia. Domitia Lepida sentenced.
54	Announcement of death of Claudius. Nero acclaimed princeps (13 October).
54–68	***Principate of Nero***, Agrippina's son
54	Death of M. Junius Silanus and Narcissus (after 13 October).
54	*Funus censorius* of Claudius. Agrippina priestess of *divus* Claudius.
54	Praetorian watchword "Best of Mothers." Agrippina covertly attends senate meeting. She attempts to join Nero with Armenian embassy.
54/55	Nero has an affair with Acte. Agrippina promotes Britannicus.
55	Pallas removed (January). Britannicus poisoned at banquet (11 February).
55	Agrippina charged for treasonably supporting Rubellius Plautus.
56	Games in Puteoli dedicated by Augustales to Nero, Agrippina Augusta, Jupiter Optimus Maximus, and the Genius of the Colony.
57	Arval Brethren celebrate Agrippina's birthday in Rome (6 November).
58	Trial of P. Suillius; Agrippina and Seneca defamed as sexually involved.

58	Arval Brethren celebrate Agrippina's birthday in Rome (6 November).
58	Arval Brethren honor Agrippina at Nero's birthday (15 December).
59	Plots, encouraged by Poppaea, begin for removal of Agrippina (January).
59	Agrippina invited to feast with Nero for Festival of Minerva Quinquatrus (19–23 March). Agrippina killed (23 March)
68	Nero kills himself (9 June).

Introduction: Agrippina's Contexts and Impacts

How can we understand Agrippina the Younger, the extraordinary Roman woman declared "unique" by the historian Tacitus both for her own political standing in 51 CE and as the daughter of a triumphing general and the sister, wife, and mother of emperors?[1] The second-century author's appraisal underlines not only her roles and activities but also her connections to those who ruled Rome. As we will see in this biography, Agrippina is remarkably prominent not only in Tacitus and other literary sources but also in sculpture, on coins, and in inscriptions relating to her. Her distinction is the more remarkable in light of her gender: Roman women, considered inherently weak and incapable, were subject to age-old laws and norms restricting their behavior and choices. In Agrippina's case, however, her familial connections made her central in the newly important yet unofficial group of imperial women—women with marriage, blood, or adoptive relations to Rome's emperors in what is known of as the Julio-Claudian period (see the Genealogy in the frontmatter). Such women had ill-defined positions and duties during Agrippina's lifetime of 15 to 59 CE. This is not surprising. The very nature of Rome's new regime—now called the principate, after *princeps*, the term for its male rulers—was in flux under its founder Augustus (r. 27 BCE–14 CE; Agrippina's great-grandfather) and his successors Tiberius (r. 14–37; her adoptive grandfather), Caligula (r. 37–41; her brother), Claudius (r. 41–54; her husband from 49 to 54), and Nero (r. 54–68; her son).[2] Any attempt to understand Agrippina the Younger must investigate her own attainments and setbacks, as well as her wider contexts in this formative period of the Roman empire.

Agrippina garnered more honors, reportedly involved herself in greater political maneuvering, and was more visible in person and imaging in Rome and its environs than other imperial women, even the prototypical Livia, wife of Augustus.[3] The major ancient historians, especially Tacitus, whose *Annals* dates some 60 years after Agrippina died at Nero's orders, were intensely interested in her. Tacitus' account is unforgettably clever and sustained for the years from 49 to 59, her years with Claudius and Nero (covered in my Chapter 4 and Chapter 5). But his forceful interpretation reduces her to a morality tale: she appears as a power-hungry and transgressive woman who got what she deserved when killed in 59 by the son she had deviously brought to supreme imperial power.

Viewing her from the end of her life, Tacitus' version is usually followed by modern historians and biographers who, with greater amounts of documentary and other evidence, evaluate her political power and influence in ways that are condemnatory or revisionary. But such a construct flattens the complexity and brilliance of her life and choices. It also obscures the shifting nature of the many norms and practices assayed, cast aside, modified, or adopted as Rome's principate evolved. Agrippina the Younger was from a family of unprecedented wealth and power, and she lived during an extraordinarily fluid time of changing rules and expectations. My biography aims to center this woman as she grew up and made her way, avoiding or escaping—until the end—the numerous perils that destroyed so many of her female relatives. I hope to illuminate her within the background of the society and structures she accepted, exploited, and resisted during her 44 years.

In my attempt to portray Agrippina the Younger, I turn to all types of available evidence, but also occasionally to informed speculation. The documentation for Agrippina spans numerous sources even though women, including those of the imperial family, are less fully recorded than others in the Roman world. Only the compilation of all relevant data enables the Timeline in the frontmatter, as skeletal as it may appear.

Many significant lacunae complicate Agrippina's biography. For instance, the year of her birth is uncertain, although her actual birthday was 6 November, the day on which the fragmentary Acts of Rome's prestigious Arval Brethren record its celebration in 57 and 58.[4] Other evidence also has lamentably disappeared: mere oblique references, for example, attest that Agrippina herself wrote memoirs about her life and the misfortunes of her family.[5] Such a first-hand account would be invaluable to any biography, all the more so for Agrippina, who is the only imperial woman who wrote such memoirs.[6] Yet the difficulties of the ancient evidence, which I sketch out in this introduction, should not overshadow Agrippina the Younger's indubitable political acumen and personal force. Nor should we focus exclusively on her notorious disruptions to Rome's traditional and evolving political structures, for they—and she—are more comprehensible and interesting within the larger background of her personal life and settings.

Other than in the major historians, literary references to Agrippina are spotty or tendentious (see especially Chapter 6). Authors writing within a few generations of her death, like Pliny the Elder and Josephus, stress her death at her ungrateful son's doing as retribution for her reprehensible life, as does her brief but sensational appearance in the anonymous drama *Octavia*, which was likely written soon after Nero's suicide in 68 CE.[7] Further, although the historian Josephus does not dwell on Agrippina herself, his extensive treatment of the conspiracy against her brother Caligula in 41 significantly contributes to my biography (Chapter 3). Agrippina is mostly absent from "occasional" literature of her era, even the *Apocolocyntosis*, which, shortly after Claudius' death, celebrated the accession of her son Nero (see Chapter 5).

The elaborated historical works of Tacitus, Suetonius, and Cassius Dio are more instrumental for modern interpretations of Agrippina. They broadly concur in depicting her as decisive and "almost manlike" (*quasi virile*) in her self-control and inventive handling of resources and openings to power.[8] They assess her mostly in her imperial decade of 49–59 CE, when she is portrayed first as wife to a weak and uxorious Claudius and then as mother to a deceptive and perverse Nero.[9] (The extant *Annals* now lacks coverage of much of 29 through the first nine and a half months of 31, and again from 37 to mid-47.) The presentation can be especially cunning in Tacitus' *Annals* where, for example, the description of the downfall of Claudius' third wife, Messalina, in 48 opens, "Claudius was driven to recognize and punish the outrages of his wife—so that he would thereupon burn for an incestuous wedding" (with Agrippina; Chapter 3).[10] Although indebted to Tacitus' insightful and captivating text, especially in Chapters 4 and 5, I hope to have successfully kept my focus on Agrippina herself.

Suetonius furnishes a few sensational, usually undated vignettes concerning Agrippina in his imperial biographies from the early second century. She is mostly peripheral, however, in this collection that seeks to elucidate the morals and behavior of the emperors.[11] Agrippina as maleficent wife appears in *De vita Passieni Crispi*, an incomplete biography of her second husband, Crispus Passienus: this is one of two *Lives* from a book Suetonius presumably wrote on non-imperial orators.[12] Cassius Dio's *Roman History*, from a century later, contains more, and more nuanced, information about Agrippina than do Suetonius' works. Yet for most of the years of Agrippina's ascendancy as Claudius' wife (49–54) and as the mother of the emperor Nero (54 and following), the majority of Cassius Dio's history has been reconstituted from excerpts and summaries by later Byzantine scholars and now lacks precise chronology.[13]

The three ancient historians depict Agrippina the Younger as an imperious, ambitious woman who achieved her political aims—most obviously the accession of her son—by employing all her resources, including her sexuality, regardless of the cost to others or herself.[14] Her transgressive nature, her "frenzied female rage and overweening presumptions" as Tacitus puts it, is a keynote of the major authors' presentation.[15] Their *animus* against Agrippina is particularly strong, as we see in the following. Tacitus and Suetonius, both writing some 60 years after her death, apparently turned to the same first-century sources for information: Cluvius Rufus, a prominent member of the imperial court in the fraught reigns from Caligula's to Nero's; Fabius Rusticus; and Pliny the Elder.[16] Cassius Dio, whose now-abridged Roman History dates to the early third century, may have used the same sources and/or turned directly to Tacitus and Suetonius.[17] But the first-century historians are now lost, leaving us wondering whether Tacitus, Suetonius, and Cassius Dio constructed or greatly elaborated a patently hostile understanding of Agrippina the Younger, and if so, why.

The historians' appalled, even fearful, view of Agrippina ignores the long stretches of her life when she presumably lived unremarkably, or at least unremarked, like the legendarily virtuous, compliant, and docile women of Rome. Traditionally, elite women in Rome were to produce children and raise sons for public service and daughters to marry such men: they themselves were to stay far from politics.[18] Agrippina brazenly broke with the second expectation, or so Roman historians write. Their political focus, however, neglects her personal life, which might now be described as a lonely one. In contrast to the meaningful female friendships Livia and Agrippina the Elder maintained,[19] for instance, Agrippina notably turned against her friends and had only one named female companion at the end of her life (Acerronia; see Chapter 5).[20] No ancient author attempts anything close to a biography for Agrippina the Younger. Very little attention is paid to her life before her marriage to Claudius in 49, and any analysis offered centers on her purported lust for power.[21] Despite Agrippina's vividness in the narratives of Tacitus, Suetonius, and Cassius Dio, theirs is a one-sided presentation of her life.

We might assume that Agrippina's portraits offer understanding of her as a person, her "soul" so to speak, even while admitting that no extant author describes her physically other than Pliny the Elder—and he notes only that she had an extra, and lucky, canine tooth.[22] As illustrated in this biography, her relatively numerous likenesses are found in different media, including oversized sculptures like the graywacke standing statue from the Caelian Hill (Ill. 5.8), exquisitely detailed cameos like the double portrait cameo now in Vienna (Ill. Intro.1), and coins struck in Rome from 37 to 55, that is, during the reigns of Caligula, Claudius, and Nero (e.g., Ill. 5.1). The finest and best-preserved of such images, such as the Getty head of Agrippina with its apparently self-assured, open, and harmonious face with full and slightly smiling lips, seem beguilingly accessible (Ill. Intro.2). The Getty, however, is but one of many different images now identified as our Agrippina. Its somewhat uncertain background excluded it from A. Alexandridis' catalog of portraits of imperial women with fairly secure provenances and adequate diagnostic remains, although in that catalog Agrippina is the second most frequently represented woman (20 likenesses, compared to 36 for Livia; see Chapter 6).[23]

C. B. Rose and others have explored the varied original settings of such imperial portraits as far as they are now detectible, some of which will be seen in following discussions. These include group installations of the imperial family in family galleries or clustered in public settings or shrines,

Ill. Intro.1 Gemma Claudia cameo, depicting (left) the emperor Claudius and his wife Agrippina the Younger face-to-face with (right) Germanicus, Claudius' brother, and his wife Agrippina the Elder, Agrippina the Younger's father and mother. 12.0 × 15.2 cm. Vienna, Kunsthistorisches Museum (inv. IX a 63). © KHM-Museumsverband.

Ill. Intro.2 Portrait head of Agrippina the Younger, ca. 50 CE. Marble, 32 × 27 × 28 cm. Getty Villa (obj. no. 70.AA.101). Open Content photo courtesy of the Getty Museum.

a phenomenon in Italy and elsewhere from the Tiberian period and increasing noticeably in the Claudian one (Chapters 4 and 5).[24] But portraits were also displayed in individual villas and palaces of the imperial family and of the elite as busts and full-sized statues, and such wealthy individuals also owned and exchanged precious cameos that incorporated images of Agrippina. Likenesses were additionally seen more frequently on coins, which could pass from hand to hand or be hoarded, especially if of higher worth (Chapters 3–5).

The high number of extant portraits of Agrippina the Younger and her many years of active connection to Rome's rulers, which Tacitus remarks as unique, ensure that hundreds of images commemorated her during her lifetime.[25] Scholars classify those still extant into four distinct types primarily by coin images, a project helped by the fact that the singular Agrippina is the first woman portrayed and identified by name on coins centrally struck during her lifetime[26] (see, e.g., Ill. 5.1.) The critical taxonomic element is Agrippina's hairstyles on the coins.[27] (Deeper discussion can be found in Chapter 6.) Centrally struck coins, which can be generally dated, were an official medium under the general supervision of the emperor and his functionaries and probably with some input from the court. Nonetheless, there is no evidence that any imperial woman of the Julio-Claudian period, even Agrippina the Younger herself, determined her numismatic portraiture.[28] Further, and despite the undeniable importance in ancient Rome of women's hair and hairstyles,[29] it would be speculative to construct a person's life on the basis of her hair. Portraits often identified as Agrippina the Younger may in fact have depicted her sisters Drusilla and Julia Livilla, her distant relative Messalina (Claudius' wife before Agrippina), or another imperial or private woman of the era who favored the same curly hairstyle.[30]

Comparison of various established portraits of Agrippina the Younger, moreover, reveals inconsistencies not easily attributable to aging or another

Ill. Intro.3 Bust of Agrippina the Younger (Ancona type; late Claudian/early Neronian). Marble, 36 cm H. Ny Carlsberg Glyptotek, Copenhagen (inv. no. 755). © Ny Carlsberg Glyptotek, Copenhagen/Jo Selsing.

natural change. The Getty (Ill. Intro.2), for example, does not neatly fit any accepted type for Agrippina, as shown by its juxtaposition with the fine portrait bust now in the Ny Carlsberg Glyptotek in Copenhagen (Ill. Intro.3), assigned to the Ancona type from the late Claudian/early Neronian period.[31] The Getty piece has a looser treatment of the massed pin curls and lacks the usual two side curls falling down the neck from behind each ear. The faces differ as well. The Copenhagen portrait has a low brow; the eyebrows flare out rather than curve around the somewhat closely set eyes; and the lips suggest an overbite. The Getty face, in contrast, is broader at the bottom and top, with a wider and higher brow; the eyes are less closely set; and lips are fuller and longer than on other portraits.[32] Such distinctions may be due to factors such as artisans' skills and/or the verisimilitude of available models, the final display context, and the desires of the patrons, who were not always the imperial family.

Other discrepancies seem due to artists' tendency to portray members of Rome's imperial family as identifiably similar.[33] We see this especially clearly in the two representations of Agrippina found at the Sebasteion in Aphrodisias (discussed in Chapters 4 and 5): in the relief depicting her with Claudius she resembles Claudius, but in the slightly later one of her with Nero she resembles her son (see Ill. 4.3, Ill. 5.3). Such resemblances, apparently echoing the will of the imperial court, emphasize the difficulties in discerning Agrippina or, indeed, any individual imperial woman. In sum, the great variety of Agrippina's portraiture, together with the slight evidence we have for the creation and dissemination of imperial images, suggests that rarely, if at all, did Agrippina control her own image. (One might contrast the official portraits of the British royal family and of US presidents and their spouses.) The more closely we look at Agrippina's portraits—as seen in detail in Chapter 6—the less they seem to represent or explain the "real" Agrippina. Yet the undeniable appeal of the Getty head and many other images influenced me to study the person they once purportedly represented.

Epigraphy offers another type of evidence for Agrippina the Younger in its records of honors to her, her patronage, and her dependents and functionaries. Inscriptions have been particularly valuable for exploring the visibility and activity of Agrippina from 49 to 59, the last decade of her life. Epigraphic information for Agrippina is usually of a more official nature, often referring to her as the emperor's wife during her marriage to Claudius from 49 to 54 and the emperor's mother during the first five years of Nero's rule. This resource, however, is skewed by the circumstances of Agrippina's murder in 59 and the ensuing clampdown of her memory. Although there seems not to have been an official memory sanction against Agrippina, the infamy Nero encouraged apparently suppressed much epigraphic evidence relating to her (see Chapters 5 and 6). In particular, I once hoped that epitaphs and other data about the *familia Agrippinae minoris*, the enslaved and freed dependents of Agrippina, could fill in details of her personal life: who could know her more intimately than the dependents who attended her every need night and day? But after her death those individuals were incorporated into the *familia Caesaris*, the enormous ranks of enslaved and freedpersons owned by the emperor and serving at his command,[34] and they lost their former identity with Agrippina.[35] The milieu of the imperial residences,[36] however, is important for understanding how and where Agrippina grew and flourished. Filling in the background of life in the court, such material helps sketch out Agrippina's early life (see Chapter 1).

Finally, in my attempt to "know" Agrippina, I turn to evidence sometimes scanted in biographies of ancient figures: the locales in which she spent her days and nights. Since first visiting Rome in 1972 I have been fascinated with Roman remains, leaders, peoples, and systems. For this project I explored Rome again as well as other spots associated with Agrippina, such as her birthplace, Cologne (Germany), her exile island, Ponza (Italy), and the site of her murder on the Bay of Naples. Admittedly, nothing now looks like it did two millennia ago. The ruins of the imperial residences on Rome's Palatine Hill, despite the most recent excavations that opened in 2023, are only the barest bones of the magnificent palaces A. Carandini and others have suggested from archaeological remains and literary and documentary references.[37] Nonetheless, to experience the hills, seas, and cityscapes Agrippina experienced made me feel more in touch with her as a living person, not simply a literary construct. I have dared to imagine her pain, hopes, and fears; disappointments; and gratifications—even her privileged indifference and her cruelties. My hope has been to animate her life and times.

Previous scholars have welcomed the challenges of piecing together Agrippina the Younger's life and teasing out her "truth" from innuendo and outright falsehoods. Rigorously surveying the documentary and literary evidence and with an unparalleled understanding of imperial Rome, W. Eck analyzed her life and political milieu in *Agrippina, die Stadtgründerin Kölns; Eine Frau in der frühkaiserzeitlichen Politik* ("Agrippina, Founder of

Cologne: A Woman in Early Imperial Politics," 1993). This was updated and expanded by a volume of collected short essays by various authors, *Agrippina: Kaiserin aus Köln* ("Agrippina: Empress from Cologne," 2015), similarly radiating from her connection with the city in which she was born.[38] Three years after Eck's 1993 monograph, A. Barrett published a biography of Agrippina for the English-speaking world. Despite its sensational title in the United States, *Agrippina: Sex, Power, and Politics in the Early Empire*, Barrett argued for her generally positive effect on the developing empire.[39]

Representing Agrippina: Constructions of Female Power in the Early Roman Empire, by J. Ginsburg (2006), is especially insightful on the rhetorical tactics Tacitus and other ancient authors use in their largely misogynistic presentation of our subject. Ginsburg's focus on the authors and other evidence, which sometimes overshadows Agrippina herself, is largely exculpatory.[40] In 2007 appeared *Agrippina Minor. Life and Afterlife*, edited by M. Moltesen and A. M. Nielsen, a volume of essays spurred by the "join" of the head and body of a graywacke, over-life-size standing statue of Agrippina (see Ill. 5.8; Chapter 5).[41] More recently, A. Carandini has stressed Agrippina's physical surroundings, particularly her residences, in his *Io, Agrippina* ("I, Agrippina," 2018), which purports to be Agrippina's memoirs from 55 until her death in 59. Invaluable as an archaeological resource, *Io, Agrippina* largely parrots the hostile presentation of Agrippina and other members of the imperial family found in ancient histories.[42] An even newer contribution is E. Southon, *Agrippina: The Most Extraordinary Woman of the Roman World* (2019). This delightfully sly biography, aimed at a general audience and representative of most current interest in our subject, archly presents Agrippina as a clever proto-feminist misrepresented by ancient (and many modern) sources.[43]

The dramatic detail of Agrippina's ancient depictions, and her relative longevity and centrality in early imperial Rome, have ensured that she figures also in analyses of power structures and women overall.[44] In 2000 T. Späth analyzed all references to her in Tacitus' *Annals*, to conclude both that her reported activity was not outside the norm for aristocratic Roman women of her time and that Agrippina herself is now perceptible only as a literary construct.[45] Edited works such as H. Temporini-Gräfin Vitzthum's *Die Kaiserinnen Roms: von Livia bis Theodora* ("The Empresses of Rome: From Livia to Theodora," 2002), A. Kolb's *Augustae: Machtbewusste Frauen am römischen Kaiserhof? Herrschaftsstrukturen und Herrschaftspraxis II* ("Augustae: Power-Conscious Women in the Roman Imperial Court? Power Structures and Power Practices II," 2010), and my own *Imperial Women of*

Rome: Power, Gender, Context (2021), help contextualize Agrippina within Rome's varied and often overlapping hierarchies, conventions, and legal systems while avoiding the biases of ancient and modern approaches. Related to so many men who ruled Rome, Agrippina can also be elucidated by the prolific scholarship on the emperors from Augustus through Nero and on particular issues of their reigns. Other insights into her actions and contexts can be gained through research on less elevated topics and contemporary individuals: for instance, her protégé, early ally, and eventual defector Seneca the Younger wrote two jarring pieces we investigate in Chapters 3 and 5, the *Consolatio ad Polybium* and the *Apocolocyntosis*. A recent resurgence of interest in Nero has also turned attention to her.[46] My notes, copious as they are, cannot reflect how truly indebted I am to previous scholars who have explored Agrippina and her times.

Nonetheless, the time is right for a clear-eyed biography that, without judgment and over her lifetime, will center on Agrippina the Younger herself. Much separates her from us, particularly her enslavement of many now voiceless individuals, her disproportionate privilege within the ruling family of a brutally extractive empire, and her compliance in, and commission of, abusive misuse of power up to death. Only the latter set of events get play in the ancient historians' works. Although those authors may certainly exaggerate, Agrippina was a woman who could easily turn nasty, who pursued power and control, and who considered such domination as her birthright. Other parts of Agrippina the Younger's life and activities might resonate more easily with readers. All too many in our modern world have experienced oppressive treatment and setbacks because of traditional gender roles, and we are now seeing a violent backlash against whatever feminist gains were made in the last half century. Agrippina, repeatedly restricted and coerced by patriarchal structures, was determined to have authority over her body and her finances. Her trajectory reveals many instances of rule breaking. As is clear in this introduction, her resistance of conventional constraints, including about her sexuality and body,[47] is one source of ancient historians' criticisms and modern historians' fascination. But feminism, of whatever "wave," was unimaginable in her life and milieu. May this book contribute to the understanding of the circumstances and choices of Agrippina, born to Rome's most powerful family and persistent in her attempts to be more than a pawn of the men around her.

Agrippina the Younger: A Dangerous Woman in Rome's Early Empire. Mary T. Boatwright, Oxford University Press.
 DOI: 10.1093/9780190945855.003.0001

1

Agrippina's Youth (15–37 CE)

Introduction

Agrippina the Younger is from the third generation of the wide family connected by blood and marriage to Augustus, Julius Caesar's posthumously adopted son who by 27 BCE decidedly controlled Rome. Augustus had come to power through vicious civil wars that tore apart Rome, Italy, and Rome's dominion after Julius Caesar's assassination in 44. Known in this volatile period as Octavian, Augustus had schemed, made and broken treaties and promises, and gone into battle until 30 BCE and the deaths of his last rival, Mark Antony, and his backer Cleopatra VII, Egypt's queen. Augustus' consolidation of power rested not only on his supreme control of Rome's military and his dominance of its civil and religious structures but also on his appeal to age-old traditions such as respect for family.[1] From a shaky start—Augustus and his third wife Livia never had a child together—the princeps' own family had grown through multiple marriages and generations even while suffering numerous suspicious deaths and exiles (see Genealogy and the following sections).[2]

As a member of the *domus Augusta* (imperial house) Agrippina the Younger was among the most privileged individuals of the Roman empire. She grew up in unimaginable splendor in the imperial residences on Rome's Palatine Hill and in villas outside the city, constantly attended by countless dependents of the *familia Caesaris*. Like her relatives and siblings, she was raised with great expectations as well as privilege. The expectations were much less clear for girls than boys in the imperial family, however. Agrippina the Younger, born in Germany in 15 CE to Agrippina the Elder and Germanicus, was one of these girls and the first daughter of Augustus' granddaughter. The *domus Augusta* and her natal family seemed stable and fortunate. Agrippina the Elder, dear to her grandfather Augustus, had already born at least five sons to Germanicus, whom she had married in 5 CE. In 14, the year before Agrippina the Younger's birth, Germanicus helped, as Tiberius' adoptive son and one of the heirs apparent, in the rocky imperial transition to Tiberius after the death of Augustus, Rome's princeps or "first among equals" for more than 40 years. No one could have imagined the suspicious death of Germanicus four years hence or the downfall of most others in Agrippina the Younger's family before she was twenty-two.

The *Domus Augusta* of Agrippina the Younger

By the time our Agrippina was in her early twenties, *domus Augusta*, *domus divina*, and other designations for the extended imperial family had come into use. The variety reveals shifting notions of who belonged in that family, underscoring the evolving nature of the new principate. Although it is impossible to determine whether the names originated at an emperor's initiative, in the court, or locally,[3] the imperial house or household—no matter how designated—was never legally or constitutionally demarcated.[4] On the other hand, the terms reveal the family's distinct eminence in the Roman world. We discuss the terms before individual family members.

Gens Iulia and *gens Augusta*, both found on provincial dedications to the family, are marked by the use of the traditional *gens* for a family group. The first designates the Julian *gens* that Augustus headed as Julius Caesar's adopted son.[5] The more unusual second expression, documented in Carthage and Corinth, derives from traditional ideas of family as established by Augustus.[6] It has been proposed that Augustus developed the idea of the *gens Augusta* after welcoming into his family and his grand Mausoleum in Rome members such as the men married to Julia (the Elder), his sole child. First was Marcus Claudius Marcellus, the son of his sister Octavia and her first husband Marcellus; then came Marcus Vipsanius Agrippa, Augustus' (second) son-in-law who would be Agrippina the Younger's maternal grandfather.[7] *Augusta* connected the whole group to Augustus, imparting an air of sanctity much as did the term *Augustus* itself, which the senate had conferred on Octavian in 27 BCE as a mark of respect. Use of both *gens Iulia* and *gens Augusta* petered out after the Julio-Claudian period.

But wider designations then developed for the increasingly important and visible imperial family. Tacitus refers to it as the *domus Iuliorum Claudiorumque* and *Claudia et Iulia domus*, "the house of the Julii and the Claudii" and "the Claudian and Julian house."[8] Tacitus' terms, which use the more capacious term *domus* ("house" or "household") rather than *gens*,[9] include cognatic kin, that is Livia and her relatives who belonged to the Claudian *gens*, as well as Augustus' Julian relatives. The idea of "the family" was further complicated in 14 CE by Augustus' posthumous adoption of Livia, whose transferal into the Julian *gens* was marked by her changed name Julia Augusta. By then the term *domus Augusta* had developed to refer to Augustus' agnate, cognate, and distant relatives.[10] In Ovid's exile poetry (13 CE and thereafter) "the Augustan house" includes "daughters-in-law and grand-daughters and sons of grandsons and other members of the Augustan house" as well as, by name, Augustus, Tiberius, Germanicus, Drusus, and Livia.[11] Livia's pivotal role was clear, as Tacitus later implied in *domus Iuliorum Claudiorumque* and *Claudia et Iulia domus*: her Claudian son Tiberius inherited the *domus Augusta*, synecdoche for imperial power. In any case, by the time Agrippina the Younger was born in 15 CE, her extended family was the most distinctive in the Roman world.

Domus Augusta also appears in official and documentary contexts in Tiberius' reign, the time of Agrippina the Younger's childhood, promoting the unity of the family. An inscription of 19 CE incidentally records a "statue," dedicated by Gaius Norbanus Flaccus, to *divus* Augustus and the *domus Augusta* near a projected arch that would honor Germanicus at the Circus Flaminius in Rome.[12] The *domus Augusta* statuary, now lost, arguably was installed in early 15 CE and included Augustus, Livia, Tiberius, and Germanicus. The arch projected in 19 CE, now also lost, was to feature statues of Germanicus in triumph; his "natural father Drusus [the Elder], the brother of Tiberius Caesar Augustus"; his mother Antonia (the Younger), his wife Agrippina (the Elder), his sister Livia (Livilla), his brother Claudius (the future emperor), and Germanicus' (unnamed) sons and daughters.[13] The latter group surely included Agrippina the Younger, although our only reference to the arch does not identify her individually.[14] The decree elsewhere vaunts the devotion of all orders to Rome's *domus Augusta*.[15] And in the following year, 20 CE, the *Senatus Consultum de Cn. Pisone patre* ("Senatorial Decree Concerning Gnaeus Piso the Elder," or SCPP) cited the *domus Augusta* and emphasized a unified imperial family that specifically comprised even those, like Livilla the wife of Drusus the Younger, not properly belonging to Augustus' "house" or Julian clan.[16] Agrippina the Younger grew up in a distinct and special family. Its close ties had helped smooth the transition of power from Augustus to his stepson Tiberius in 14 CE. The family's unified image concealed numerous cracks within it, such as the concerns Augustus, Livia, and Antonia the Younger had about Claudius' health and mental acuity,[17] and more serious rifts we will see while assessing Agrippina the Younger's life.

Agrippina's singular family was enhanced by religious awe during her lifetime. From Italy come building dedications "in honor of the Augustan house."[18] Even more obvious marks of reverence are the use of "divine house" to designate the family and the record of municipal priests and priestesses of the Augustan house. By the time of Tiberius' death and the accession of her brother Caligula in 37, the family had been termed the *domus divina*, or divine house, on various inscriptions.[19] The earliest, dated to 33, was raised in Lucus Feroniae, 30 km north of Rome.[20] Inscriptions from Spain and elsewhere record, for example, priestesses of the Augustan house (*flaminica domus Augustae*).[21] By the end of Agrippina's life she and Nero, then emperor, had as their joint procurator Gaius Julius Spartiaticus, priest of the *domus Augusta* in Corinth and a man honored for his virtue and spirited and expansive munificence toward Corinth and the Divine House (*domus divina*).[22]

Did Agrippina understand such marks of adulation even while young? Surely. As intimated above in the discussion of the Arch of Germanicus decreed in 20, Rome was increasingly distinguished by stunning monuments built by or honoring members of the *domus Augusta* or celebrating the "house" as an entity; many of these—such as the Ara Pacis—served periodic religious rites. The imperial residences housed shrines to Augustus and large representations of family members; recurrent celebrations like the *ludi Palatini* and the Saturnalia invited members of the elite who were not in the imperial family.[23] An illuminating story from Tacitus, discussed later in this chapter, reveals the inherent tensions of the situation. In 26 and on behalf of a relative, Agrippina the Elder appealed to Tiberius while he sacrificed for his father Augustus. Desperate for her indicted cousin Claudia Pulchra, whom she saw as a proxy for herself, Agrippina the Elder charged that it was improper for someone to sacrifice for *divus* Augustus yet simultaneously persecute his relatives; further, *she* (Agrippina the Elder) was the true image of Augustus, born with his divine blood. Tiberius curtly retorted in Greek that she suffered no harm simply because she did not rule.[24] The tense interchange occurred at a shrine, undoubtedly graced with a statue and icons of Augustus, within the palace. But with that I turn to the imperial residences themselves and their inhabitants, among whom was the little Agrippina.

Agrippina in the "House"

As *primus inter pares*, "first among equals," Augustus projected an image of modesty and approachability now known as *civilitas*, or accessibility. This extended to his household and physical surroundings, as Suetonius is keen to point out.[25] The archaeological and epigraphic evidence for the Augustan and Julio-Claudian imperial "house," however, reveals that the family's habitations were anything but modest by the time of Agrippina's youth there. Perhaps in the Augustan period, when the princeps and his wife Livia lived on Rome's Palatine Hill near their relatives and friends, the architectural layout, furnishings, and service staff they enjoyed were not so different from those of other members of Rome's elite.[26] But just as the concept of the Augustan house became more distinct, the physical circumstances of its members became more opulent. By the time of Agrippina the Younger's death in 59, the scale of the imperial house was almost unimaginable. The continuous rebuilding of the Palatine has blurred the exact chronology of this growth, including in the Claudian period.[27] Nonetheless, a quick sketch can illustrate the privilege in which Agrippina grew up, helping us understand the entitlement she embodied and is said to have claimed and inverted.

It was not only Augustus' house on the Palatine Hill that was important, but other structures near it. The whole became known as the "Palatium," from which derives the modern word "palace."[28] Augustus' abode may itself have been "exceptional neither in size nor decoration,"[29] but it gained great splendor and cachet from its location. Near or adjoining it Augustus reconstructed some of Rome's most archaic sites, such as the Hut of Romulus, and constructed new shrines like the Temple of Palatine Apollo. His living quarters, enhanced by the Apollo shrine and other temples, were used for public functions like meetings of the senate, and the nearby Circus Maximus added a popular element. He and his relatives bought up older houses and constructed new dwellings, so that the Palatine Hill became filled with large and lavish houses belonging to the family.[30] Although individual dwellings cannot be definitively identified, literary and other evidence shows that at Agrippina's birth in 15, the Palatine held the former home of Augustus, which had passed to Tiberius as part of his inheritance, and others: those of Livia; Antonia the Younger, Augustus' niece and the mother of Germanicus, Livilla, and Claudius (the later emperor);[31] and

Germanicus.[32] Drusus the Younger, Tiberius' son who married Germanicus' sister Livilla, may also have had his dwelling there.

Excavations on the Palatine over more than four centuries have unearthed some of the astonishingly fine furnishings and adornments of these imperial residences, as well as inscriptions that illuminate the workings of the whole.[33] The reach and depth of Rome's power and imperial resources are clear in the site's white and polychrome marble statues as well as archaistic ceramic ones; inlaid marble decorations for walls, ceilings, and floors; and exquisite frescoes. Augustus made a show of not appropriating land for the Forum of Augustus he sponsored near the Forum Romanum and the Forum of Julius Caesar. But archaeology indicates no modesty regarding the fine appointments of his home or those of his relatives.[34] Upon Agrippina the Younger's arrival in Rome at age two (see next section), she would have grown up surrounded by the finest and most recherché objects in the Roman world. This was true also in the suburban villas of members of the imperial house: in her villa at Bauli, for example, Antonia the Younger (Agrippina's paternal grandmother) reportedly adorned a pet moray eel with earrings.[35] It took veritable troops of enslaved and freed dependents of Augustus, Livia, and other family members to maintain such opulent residences and serve their inhabitants.[36] Although at first such dependents were known by individual owners, such as those connected with Julia Augusta (i.e., Livia) or the individuals dependent on Antonia the Younger, over time they became subsumed into the *familia Caesaris*. Their specialized functions and complex organization are known mainly from their epitaphs, which in the early empire were often located in *columbaria* or subterranean communal tombs.[37]

The imperial residences, like the grand Republican houses from which they developed, were the locus of political and social life during the principate: they were never simply "private" homes.[38] Augustus met with the senate and greeted embassies in his; just as important for the functioning of Rome's elite, the Palatine imperial complex housed banquets and other social occasions, including theatrical performances such as the one at which Caligula was assassinated in 41 (see Chapter 2). One quintessential Roman practice held in the residences was the *salutatio*, the emperor's morning greeting of his friends and the public.[39] The social and political dominance of Augustus and subsequent emperors meant that the *salutatio* became ever more elaborate and demanding: for instance, all senators and elite equites were expected daily unless the senate was in session.[40] By the time of Tiberius' reign—when the child Agrippina the Younger lived on the Palatine—even Livia was formally granted the right to hold *salutationes* in her home. This evident mark of her influence as intermediary between elite and emperor was entered into the public registers.[41] Agrippina the Younger would later have the same right.[42]

Banquets were another occasion for competition of status and visibility and for the performance of power, as repeatedly shown in this biography.[43] They were held not only in the residences on the Palatine and imperial villas outside Rome but also in more public spots like the courtyards of temples.[44] Imperial banquets were not only for adults; noble children attended them and could thereby gain an understanding of the unwritten protocols regulating the evolving regime. The custom of having such children at feasts, albeit at their own, less lavish table or sitting at the ends of their parents' couches, is attested for the Claudian period.[45] It seems to date back to Augustus, however. Besides Suetonius' reference to the first princeps always dining with his grandchildren, the enslaved servant Anthus, who was responsible for the silver drinking cups of Augustus' grandson and adopted son Lucius Caesar, suggests that from early on imperial children were often at banquets.[46] Agrippina the Younger surely participated in numerous adult feasts as a child, essential upbringing for one living in the *domus Augusta*.

The Dramatis Personae: Agrippina's Relatives

Agrippina the Younger's family was extensive and deeply intertwined (see Genealogy). The first princeps, the long-lived Augustus, died at age 75 a year before Agrippina was born in Oppidum Ubiorum on the Rhine. He was Agrippina's maternal great-grandfather through his only natural child Julia the Elder (b. 39 BCE from Scribonia), who had born to her second husband, Agrippa, five children who included Agrippina the Elder, Agrippina the Younger's mother (b. 14 BCE). Tiberius, 56 when he became princeps in 14 CE, was Agrippina the Younger's paternal great uncle as well as her adoptive grandfather (through his adoption of Germanicus in 4 CE). Born in 42 BCE, Tiberius was the elder of the two sons of Livia and her first husband, Tiberius Claudius Nero. Livia's younger son, Drusus the Elder (b. 38 BCE), married Antonia the Younger. Before his untimely death in 9 BCE that younger couple had Germanicus (b. 24 May 16 or 15 BCE), Livilla (ca. 13 BCE), and Claudius (b. 10 BCE), later emperor and Agrippina's third husband. As mentioned, Germanicus was adopted by Tiberius in 4.[47] Such intricate relations are part of the endogamy characteristic of the extended Julio-Claudian family.[48]

Perhaps just as significant for the young Agrippina, who moved into the Palatine residences about age two, were the elder women of the *domus Augusta*. First and foremost was Livia (b. 58 BCE), her paternal great-grandmother (and maternal step-great-grandmother). Augustus' widow and Tiberius' mother, Livia became known as Julia Augusta after the death of her husband Augustus in 14. She lived for 15 more years in Rome, and her prominence and influence were openly acknowledged. Although in 14 Tiberius denied or decried most of the honors offered his mother other than adoption into Augustus' Julian *gens*, grant of the honorific "Augusta," and selection as priest of *divus* Augustus in Rome, their unprecedented nature and number left an enormous impression.[49] During Tiberius' reign Julia Augusta was more visible than she had been while Augustus was alive. Despite her advanced age (72 years in 14 CE), she engaged in building patronage, dedications, feasts, and other public activities in the capital city, as well as in more informal encouragement of select men and women of the elite.[50] The buildings with her name, such as the Porticus Liviae and the Macellum Liviae, and the dedications permanently installed by her or in her honor, embody the ties between the first and second emperor: often her feasts or other patronage celebrated her husband or son.

Agrippina the Younger is said to have consciously emulated Julia Augusta's magnificence when arranging obsequies for Claudius in 54;[51] further, she apparently followed the first imperial woman's lead in her formal *salutationes*, her presence alongside Claudius fighting fires, and other activities while she was an imperial wife (49–54). Another inspiration may have been Antonia the Younger, Agrippina the Younger's paternal grandmother, with whom the girl apparently lived first as a toddler and then later as a young teen (from 17 to 19 CE and from 27 to 28).[52] Antonia the Younger (b. 36 BCE) was more retiring than Livia. Nonetheless, she exerted great political influence behind the scenes. Sometime after 27 she interceded with Tiberius for Herod Agrippa, who went on to be king of Judaea in 41–44.[53] More significant for the *domus Augusta*, Antonia the Younger was involved in the downfall of Tiberius' deceitful praetorian prefect Sejanus in 31, reportedly sending Tiberius a letter denouncing this seducer of Tiberius' daughter-in-law, her own daughter Livilla,[54] and was rumored to have been personally responsible for Livilla's execution by starvation.[55]

Agrippina the Younger's Birth and First Two Years in Germany. Agrippina the Elder

Agrippina the Younger was born to a "nuclear" family that at her birth in 15 must have seemed charmed within the larger Julio-Claudian *gens*,[56] which—despite its envied position at the head of the Roman world—had already endured multiple premature deaths, exiles, and disgraces. Her parents Germanicus and Agrippina the Elder, never divorced, symbolized the ideal stability and fecundity essential to Rome,[57] and Agrippina was the fourth of their six children who lived to adulthood.[58]

Agrippina the Elder (b. ~14 BCE) was the daughter of Julia the Elder, Augustus' sole daughter, and Agrippa, Augustus' loyal friend and helper. Agrippina the Elder was a strong and steady individual who survived numerous tragedies and shocks in her youth. When Agrippa died in 12 BCE while she was but a toddler, her mother, Julia the Elder, married her own stepmother's eldest son, Tiberius.[59] This marriage was not a happy one. Despite bearing a short-lived son to Tiberius, Julia the Elder was spectacularly disgraced, divorced from him, and exiled in 2 BCE to the tiny island of Pandateria (modern Ventotene, Italy). Five years later (3 CE) she was moved to Rhegium (Reggio Calabria), where she died in 14. There was no public inquiry into the events leading to Julia's exile, and the charges may never have been clear, but they certainly involved charges of adultery and promiscuity that circulated during the lifetimes of her children and grandchildren.[60] Julia the Elder, whose mother, Scribonia, accompanied her in exile, was forbidden wine, fine foods, and male visitors.[61] In 8 CE her daughter Julia the Younger, the presumably older sister of Agrippina the Elder, would suffer exile like that of their mother, again without a trial and again with rumors of adultery. Julia the Younger was relegated to the even more distant island of Trimerus at the heel of Italy (in the Isole Tremiti, Italy), where she died in 28.[62] Besides these scandalous exiles, numerous male relatives died mysteriously: Germanicus' father, Drusus the Elder, in 9 BCE, and not long afterward the two favored brothers of Agrippina the Elder, Gaius Caesar (20 BCE to 4 CE) and Lucius Caesar (17 BCE to 2 CE). Gaius and Lucius had been adopted by their grandfather Augustus and raised as the heirs apparent,[63] but both perished before the age of 25, reportedly devastating Augustus. Their discredited brother, Agrippa Postumus—Agrippina the Elder's remaining brother—was killed after Augustus' death in 14.[64]

In such horrendous personal circumstances Agrippina the Elder married Germanicus in 5 CE.[65] Germanicus (b. 16/15 BCE)[66] was the eldest of the three children of Antonia the Younger, an archetypal maternal figure in the Julio-Claudian *domus*,[67] and Drusus the Elder, the beloved younger son of Livia and Augustus' stepson who had died in 9 BCE.[68] The family connections of Agrippina the Elder and Germanicus were close. She was Augustus' granddaughter; he, Livia's grandson. They must have grown up together on Rome's Palatine Hill. They became engaged in 4 after the deaths of Gaius and Lucius Caesar as, to make for a smooth imperial succession, Augustus adopted Tiberius and had Tiberius adopt Germanicus.[69] Such larger political aims for marriage alliances were standard, especially within the extended family of Augustus and Livia. More unusual for the time, given the frequency of divorce and remarriage, was the apparent strength of the young couple's union once they wed in 5 CE.[70] Germanicus' ties to his adoptive father would intensify when he valiantly served under Tiberius during combat in 7 CE and again in 12.[71]

Agrippina the Elder was exemplarily fecund, as well as being part of Rome's preeminent family.[72] She bore nine children to Germanicus in some 15 years, a remarkably large number in Augustus' and Livia's extended family.[73] The first three of the six children who survived to adulthood are now known as Nero Caesar (b. 6), Drusus Caesar (b. 8), and Caligula (b. 12). To this early period seem also to belong three boys who died as babies or toddlers.[74] The series of boys gratified the male-dominated world of Rome and the Julio-Claudian house, which desperately lacked sons.[75] It must be to these boys that Augustus gestured at a gladiatorial game while urging all Romans to have many children.[76] The boy who died as a toddler so charmed Livia and Augustus that Livia dedicated an image of him as Cupid in the Temple of Capitoline Venus, and Augustus put the child's statuette in his bedroom and kissed it every evening upon entering.[77] The three surviving daughters then born are now called Agrippina the Younger (b. 6 Nov. 15), Drusilla (b. 16), and Julia Livilla (b. 18).[78]

The children were living proof of the success of Germanicus and Agrippina the Elder's marriage (*pignora*, SCPP l. 139). Marriage harmony was a Roman ideal, although rates of divorce may have reached about 50 percent among the elite; in cases of divorce—which was not stigmatized—children remained with the father. Rome's imperative of marriage for the sake of procreating future citizens did not include the expectation that parents spend time with their young children,[79] especially among the elite, where childrearing was usually entrusted to dependents, and fathers often served Rome in the provinces. Yet this young, large, and cohesive imperial family offered the image of stability and hope for the future.

Agrippina the Elder was part of a shift in gender expectations about wives accompanying their husbands in the field,[80] a shift apparently spearheaded by the imperial family. From 14 CE at the latest she accompanied her husband Germanicus in his overseas duties. All three daughters were born overseas: Agrippina the Younger and Drusilla in Germany and Julia Livilla on the Greek island of Lesbos. Agrippina's birth site, on 6 November 15, was Oppidum Ubiorum, a provincial town on Rome's frontier with the German tribes.[81] In the last century of the Republic few wives and children of Roman administrators and generals had joined their husbands and fathers abroad. Travel was dangerous in general and particularly for pregnant women, even if attended by personal physicians as was Agrippina the Elder at least once (see next page).[82] But Augustus, and later Tiberius, displayed the new regime through members of the imperial family. The family's presence manifested the princeps' omnipresence and the promise of a secure future even more than statues, largesse, and other manifestations of imperial beneficence and local coins figuring Julio-Claudian individuals.[83] Julio-Claudian men and women often traveled together, even if the woman was or became pregnant: in 10 BCE Antonia the Younger bore to Drusus the Elder a son, Claudius, Germanicus' brother, in Lugdunum (now Lyon, France), and around the same time Julia the Elder delivered to Tiberius in Aquileia (at the head of the Adriatic in northern Italy) a boy who did not survive.[84]

Agrippina the Elder similarly attended her husband when he was abroad. The couple was accompanied by one or more children and, as seen above, she had at least three live births abroad.[85] She was with Germanicus from 14 to 17 when he governed the Three Gauls and commanded eight legions on the Rhine.[86] In their first year north, Gaius, their third surviving son who would later be called Caligula, was sent from Rome to join them. Suetonius cites a letter of 18 May 14 from Augustus to the young mother in which the emperor reports that he is sending the boy as well as a doctor whom Germanicus could keep in his service. Although in Rome's northern reaches, at that moment she was not with her husband as he conducted a census of the three Gallic provinces.[87]

The young couple, with Agrippina the Elder pregnant again, were north with their son when news of Augustus' death reached the German troops in

September or October of 14. During the unrest that led to outright mutiny, Germanicus persuaded Agrippina the Elder to retreat to the lands of the Treviri (around modern Trier, Germany). Tacitus uses the occasion to sketch out Agrippina's character by reporting, indirectly, Germanicus' pleas to his wife to leave for safety and her proud retort that she was "sprung from *divus* Augustus and no less able to face perils than he."[88] The historian emphasizes her physical condition by showing the weeping Germanicus embracing her belly (*uterus*) and their son as he begs her to leave.[89] She finally withdraws, carrying the little boy and attended by a crowd of tearful women. The mutiny is quelled.[90] Mother and child appear in another version of the difficulties, with less personally revealing details: Cassius Dio reports that the seditious soldiers actually seized the pregnant woman and boy, letting Agrippina go only after recognizing her pregnant state and releasing her son only when his use as a bargaining chip seemed moot.[91]

Agrippina the Elder did not retreat into obscurity after the critical incident of 14. In early 15 she stopped a desertion of Roman soldiers by physically barring their flight across a bridge of the Rhine. In Tacitus' report of this memorable event, which he credits to Pliny the Elder, he notes Agrippina the Elder as a "woman, great in spirit, who at that time assumed the duties of a male leader."[92] Tacitus underscores Tiberius' unease with Agrippina, recounting that the princeps fretted, "Nothing was now left for the real rulers when a woman was among the rank and file, approached the standards, attempted distributions; as if it was not grandstanding enough that she carried around her young son in a soldier's outfit and wanted him to be called Caesar Caligula!" The emperor also griped, "An insurrection, which the name of the princeps had not succeeded in checking, had been quelled by a woman." His worries were intensified by his ambitious confidant Sejanus, who as praetorian prefect was then the sole commander of the imperial troops of Rome.[93] The historian thus establishes Agrippina the Elder in Germany as transgressive, acting like a man as she competed in male spheres.[94] Such criticism will be aimed at her daughter Agrippina the Younger, as shown in Chapters 4 and 5.[95] The two women were also likened visually, as we saw in Ill. Intro.1: in retrospect, Agrippina the Elder was the precursor and model for her eponymous daughter.

The crisis in Germany passed, but Agrippina the Elder remained with at least some of her family in the unsettled northern area. Agrippina the Younger was born in Oppidum Ubiorum (now Cologne, Germany), on 6

November 15.[96] Her sister, Drusilla, also saw the light first in Germany, at Abitarvium (now Koblenz, Germany, some 80 km, or 50 miles, up the Rhine) on 16 September; the year is uncertain, but it was probably 16.[97] By this time Germanicus was campaigning north of the Rhine. His alleged intent to extend Roman domination to the Albis River (now the Elbe) was never achieved,[98] and in 17 the family returned to Rome to mark his German victories in a celebrated triumph.

Their travel abroad exposed the young family to more obvious dangers than mother and children would have ever met in Rome, something Tacitus' account stresses after the mutinous night in the camps in 14.[99] The family's presence in the restless border province must have habituated the children, no matter their young age, to troops and military life: one obvious example is the creation of the nickname Caligula, or "little boots," for the boy Gaius. At the same time, as sources for that pet name suggest, the familiarity of the troops with the young family particularly enamored the rank and file to its members.[100] The German troops and the praetorians famously continued to be loyal to Germanicus and his family, including his daughter Agrippina the Younger (see Chapter 5).[101]

Back in Rome, 17–

In Germanicus' great triumph over the Germans on 26 May 17 in Rome, Agrippina and her siblings—his "five children"—rode in his chariot.[102] This is the first time Roman children appeared in a Roman triumph.[103] Others in the "brilliant" triumphal procession were the most renowned men, women, and children of the Germanic peoples Germanicus had subdued. They were surely labeled with identifying placards, but perhaps the young Caligula and Agrippina recognized some of them.[104] Large floats carried the war spoils and the likenesses of mountains, rivers, and battles associated with Germanicus' exploits,[105] emphasizing the exoticism of Rome's conquests. The young Agrippina, in the capital for the first time, must have marveled at the city's dense polyglot crowds, multistory housing, and close-set monumental buildings, so different from the frontier towns and encampments she had seen so far. Her position on her father's triumphal chariot in this vivid and noisy triumphal procession gave her a taste of being at the center of attention.

Rome was to remain her home for the rest of her childhood. She and her siblings, other than Caligula (and Julia Livilla, born on the island Lesbos in late 17 or early 18),[106] stayed in the capital rather than accompanying their parents to the East. They presumably lived in their grandmother Antonia's dwelling, which had housed their uncle Claudius.[107] Their presence on the Palatine connected them to others of the Julio-Claudian family.[108] The most important was, of course, the emperor Tiberius, although the hostile literary tradition about this suspicious and unpredictable old man suggests he was not very welcoming to his young relatives.[109]

In Rome Agrippina the Younger and her siblings were taught letters, literature, and the cultivated arts by a phalanx of pedagogues and teachers whose names are now mostly lost. Augustus had emphasized the education of his grandchildren by personally teaching them writing fundamentals, swimming, and even his own handwriting (Suet. *Aug.* 64), and both Germanicus and Agrippina the Elder were markedly cultured. In 4 CE Germanicus had finished a popular Latin version of the astronomical treatise of Aratus' *Phaenomena*; Germanicus' work, now known as the *Aratea*, survives in numerous manuscripts and reveals both his scientific mind and his frank devotion to the imperial house.[110] At some unknown date Agrippina the Elder received praise—and a warning—from Augustus about her literary and speaking abilities, an indication of her own culture.[111] Children of the *domus Augusta* were to excel in their studies, females as well as males.[112] Agrippina the Younger's later exile in 39 was tied to allegedly treasonable letters in her own handwriting, suggesting that she was a prolific correspondent even in her early 20s. Further, she is famous for writing her own memoirs (see Introduction).[113]

In autumn 17 Germanicus, Agrippina the Elder, and Caligula went East so Germanicus could oversee matters with a special military command.[114] Germanicus was also intrigued by storied locales from Asia to Egypt, many of which he visited.[115] But his most importunate task was to settle Rome's shaky relations with the Parthian empire concerning the border region of Armenia. During most of his trip he clashed with Gnaeus Calpurnius Piso, the new governor of Syria. The friction assumed special significance because Piso was a mature and trusted confidant of Tiberius, and his wife Plancina was a close friend of Julia Augusta (Livia).[116] In Rome the child Agrippina would have been at most but dimly aware of these conflicts. In any case, she never saw her father alive again.

Germanicus' Death and Legacy

Before Agrippina the Younger turned five Germanicus mysteriously sickened and died on 10 October 19 in Antioch (modern Antayka, Turkey). Rumors held that he had been poisoned.[117] Carrying his ashes, Agrippina the Elder and two children[118]—presumably Caligula and Julia Livilla—made a slow and dramatic return to Italy.[119] Disembarking at Brundisium (modern Brindisi, Italy), the cortège made its way up the Via Appia, finally reaching Rome in early January 20. The way was filled with public lamentation and display, and at Tarracina (modern Terracina, some 90 km/55 miles southeast of Rome) the procession was joined by Germanicus' other children accompanied by Tiberius' son Drusus the Younger and Germanicus' brother Claudius.[120] In the autumn of 19 the city had been filled with despair and rumors about Germanicus' sickness; once his death was accepted as fact, innumerable honors were decreed in Rome and throughout the empire.[121] The senate installed an honorary arch for him at the Circus Flaminius on which were to be placed statues of Germanicus in triumph, his "natural father Drusus (the Elder), the brother of Tiberius Caesar Augustus," his mother Antonia (the Younger), Agrippina (the Elder), his sister Livilla, his brother Claudius (the future emperor), and Germanicus' (unnamed) sons and daughters.[122] The many memorials and images of Germanicus decreed in this mourning period remained as permanent reminders of the great general and his family. Agrippina the Younger would continue to be identified as the daughter of Germanicus throughout her life.[123]

The procession of Germanicus' family with his ashes found the capital city in a paroxysm of grief. Agrippina the Younger and others in Italy had missed Germanicus' cremation and first funeral in Antioch, when he had been praised for his many virtues and likened to Alexander the Great as a glorious leader taken much too young.[124] She would have heard much similar talk, however, during the sorrowful procession from Tarracina and then Germanicus' obsequies in Rome, which ended with the interment of his ashes in the Mausoleum of Augustus.[125] She may have been too young to understand the invidious comments Tacitus relates, which emphasized the inadequacy of Germanicus' honors, especially from his uncle and emperor Tiberius.[126] Tiberius and Julia Augusta stayed away from the proceedings, reportedly because public lamentation would be beneath their dignity;

Germanicus' own mother Antonia the Younger also did not show.[127] How did the children take these absences, especially that of their home's matriarch?

In Rome Germanicus' death was followed by a senatorial investigation into charges that Piso and his wife Plancina had committed treason and were complicit in his death. The case gripped Rome, to judge from its description in Tacitus' *Annals*, which is echoed in the *Senatus Consultum de Cn. Pisone Patre* (SCPP), the senatorial decree passed at its conclusion and discovered in fragments in Spain some thirty years ago.[128] Plancina was found guilty but exonerated through the influence of her friend Julia Augusta.[129] Piso killed himself. Germanicus and his family are key in the SCPP and in Tacitus' rendition of the trial, much more than they would be in a modern trial about poisoning and treason. Besides the painful exposé of the lamented leader's loss we find praise of Agrippina the Elder for having been in Augustus' high regard and for her harmonious and fertile marriage with Germanicus (SCPP lines 136–39).[130] The children, who lost "such a father," are publicly lauded for having restrained their grief within a commendable limit thanks to the discipline of their grandfather, paternal uncle, and Julia Augusta (SCPP lines 146–50).[131] The decree was to be inscribed on bronze and exhibited in multiple places, including in the busiest part of the most frequented city of every province and in the winter quarters of each legion, near the standards (SCPP lines 169–73). Despite such honors, the family was desolate.

The fatherless young family regrouped in Germanicus' home in Rome, with the two older boys, Nero Caesar and Drusus Caesar, placed under the guardianship of Drusus the Younger, Tiberius' son who was married to Germanicus' sister Livilla.[132] Josephus indicates that the home was one of many adjoining houses on the Palatine inhabited by members of the imperial family. The whole included the house of Germanicus' mother, Antonia the Younger.[133]

Visiting between the individual "homes" must have been frequent. The most recent recreations of the Palatine during the Julio-Claudian period show the proximity of homes, which were embellished by many porticoes, and the many connecting passageways that we may speculatively fill with the sounds of running children and their attendants (see Ill. 1.1).[134] Constant interaction among the various homes on the Palatine is also implied in the stories of worsening relations between Agrippina the

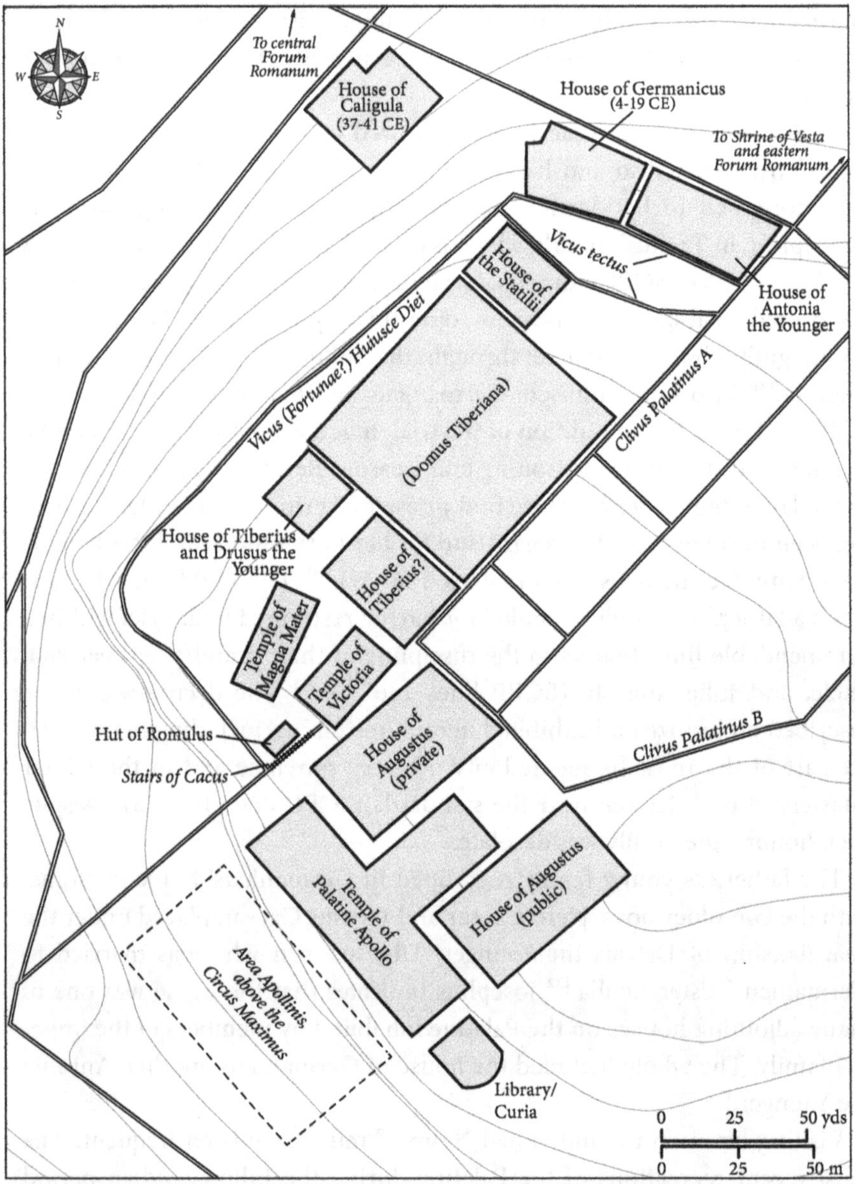

Ill. 1.1 Rome's Palatine Hill during Agrippina the Younger's youth. The House of Germanicus was once that of Julia the Elder and Marcellus; that of Antonia the Younger perhaps belonged to Octavia before passing to Antonia and Drusus the Elder, and then to Claudius after Antonia's death in 27 CE. Where exactly Julia Augusta dwelled over the years is unclear. Plan by author and MossMaps Cartography, after Carandini 2018, tav. 4 and Carandini and Carafa 2017, Tab. 70.

Younger's mother and Tiberius.[135] We mentioned, for example, Agrippina the Elder's fruitless intercession for her indicted cousin Claudia Pulchra in 26.[136] She appealed to Tiberius while he sacrificed for his father Augustus, surely in the palace. Tacitus' vignette opens by characterizing the woman as "always truculent and formidable, and at that time further provoked by her relative's danger" and her imprudent claim that *she* was the true image and living representation of Augustus' divine blood.[137]

Later that year of 26, in tears rather than indignant pride, Agrippina the Elder begged Tiberius for permission to remarry. He spurned her without a word or acknowledgment of her virtuously maintained *pudicitia*, or chastity.[138] In another note, which incidentally attests to the frequency of family feasts, Sejanus suborned Agrippina's acquaintances to warn her against dining with Tiberius. This further damaged the relationship. At one meal, which also included Julia Augusta, the younger woman ate nothing at all. When Tiberius noticed and offered Agrippina the Elder an apple from his own hand, she passed it untasted to her enslaved attendants.[139] Besides the stories' suggestion of Tiberius' increasingly tyranny are the indubitable daily contacts of the imperial family. Agrippina the Younger and other imperial children may not have attended all such meals but were certainly invited to some, as we saw above. This exposed them to court etiquette. But at the banquets attentive children could also learn dissimulation, false praise, and other tricks useful for survival.[140]

The Downfall of Agrippina the Elder, and Other Losses Beginning in 27

The literary sources, although vague about the chronology of Agrippina the Elder's worsening troubles that culminated in her exile and death,[141] unmistakably point to swelling resentment and suspicion within the imperial house. This continued even after Tiberius left Rome, first for Campania (late 26) and then Capri (in 27). Sejanus, who remained in Rome, is usually identified as the catalyst. Tacitus and others depict the conflict as between Agrippina the Elder, struggling to secure her sons' political eminence, and Tiberius' praetorian prefect Sejanus, intent on advancing himself. Agrippina the Younger is never noted in the discord, although it must have been palpable to her as she entered her teens.[142] Tension had increased notably at the death of Tiberius' son Drusus the Younger in 23, a year after a special grant of tribunician power had marked him out as the heir apparent to his father and emperor.[143] Tiberius had subsequently adopted as his successors the two eldest brothers of Agrippina the Younger, Nero Caesar and Drusus Caesar (then 17 and 15), since his own grandson, Gemellus (son of Drusus the Younger and Livilla), was only four.[144] The two sons of Germanicus and Agrippina the Elder were openly promoted and trained for their political future in Rome. Tensions grew, however, as Sejanus apparently furthered his own cause. According to Tacitus, in 25 Sejanus asked Tiberius for the hand of Livilla, Drusus the Younger's widow and the mother of Tiberius' only grandson, Gemellus. Sejanus was checked by the emperor's haughty refusal. Reportedly, however, his illicit relationship with Livilla continued, as did his undermining of Germanicus' sons and widow.[145]

By 27 Agrippina the Younger and her siblings seem to have moved from the house of Germanicus to that of Julia Augusta in the midst of intensifying difficulties for their mother and eldest brother, Nero Caesar.[146] Agrippina the Elder's relationship with Tiberius was quickly deteriorating. Among swirling rumors said to be instigated by Sejanus were that mother and son were considering flight to the German armies, appeal to the People and the Senate of Rome, and public embrace of the image of *divus* Augustus in the Forum Romanum: actions credible for the family of the popular Germanicus, and especially for his widow, Augustus' direct descendant.[147] In 27 mother and son were put under armed supervision in a villa near Herculaneum.[148] Two years later, after Julia Augusta's death in 29, the senate condemned them on charges brought by Tiberius. They were indicted as public enemies. Tiberius also alleged immorality (homosexuality) in Nero Caesar's case and arrogance and obstinacy in Agrippina the Elder's.[149] Agrippina was exiled to Pandateria and Nero Caesar to Pontia (modern Ventotene and Ponza, respectively, two small islands some 40–50 km south of S. Felice Circeo, Italy).

The marriage of Agrippina the Younger to Gnaeus Domitius Ahenobarbus in 28, when she was 13 (discussed in the next section), shows her own life was not derailed by such hellish difficulties. But other family members were affected. In 30 Drusus Caesar, Agrippina the Elder's second son, was indicted on unknown charges, sent to the emperor at Capri for judgment, and convicted. The 22-year-old was returned to a miserable cell in the imperial residence in Rome, where he starved to death a few years later.[150] The toxic situation of the young family is also reflected in the rumor that Caligula raped his sister Drusilla while they lived in Antonia the Younger's house, where the dwindling family moved after the death of Julia Augusta in 29. If the rumor is true, Drusilla was 11 or even younger.[151] The murkiness of the charges, punishments, and deaths of Agrippina the Elder and her two eldest sons may date back to these years,[152] as well as to the patchy understanding that Agrippina the Younger and her sisters were given about events. They were not even in their upper teens by the late 20s and early 30s. Although Agrippina the Younger was considered mature enough to marry in 28, her two younger sisters would not be wed until 33, when they were around 16.[153] It is no surprise that Agrippina the Younger wrote memoirs about her family: they were a way for her to recapture memories and "fix" facts.[154] The loss of these memoirs deprives us of her understanding of these difficult days as well as her own voice.[155]

The convictions of Agrippina the Elder, Nero Caesar, and Drusus Caesar coincided with other troubles for the family in the late 20s. In 28 Agrippina the Younger's aunt Julia the Younger died in exile:[156] although the young woman had probably never met this Julia who was in exile before Agrippina was born, the loss of her mother's sister resonated ominously with her mother's widening difficulties. In Rome itself the death in 29 of Julia Augusta, Tiberius' steely mother, was another significant blow. The longevity of this impressive woman, who had become much more visible and forceful in the 15 years after Augustus' death, was a stabilizing element for those connected to her. She had exhibited kindness on and off to members of her imperial family, and Agrippina the Younger, Caligula, and their sisters had moved into her house after 27. When in 29 Caligula, then 17, proclaimed Julia Augusta's eulogy in the Forum Romanum, his sisters must have watched. And then, sometime in 31 but before the fall of Sejanus that year,[157] Caligula moved to Capri to live in Tiberius' villa. He was now the only brother of Agrippina the Younger not in exile, imprisoned, or dead.

Marriage to Ahenobarbus

But long before 31 Agrippina the Younger herself had left the imperial residences, having married Gnaeus Domitius Ahenobarbus in 28.[158] The young bride was about 13; he, perhaps 30. The nuptials were held in Tiberius' presence in Campania and also celebrated in Rome.[159] His paternal line reached back to the earliest days of the Republic, establishing him as one of the highest born in Rome: Suetonius and others call him "most noble," "most renowned," and "prominent," although also accusing him of a violent and deceitful nature.[160] Further, he shared blood with the imperial family as the son of Lucius Domitius Ahenobarbus and Antonia the Elder: his maternal grandmother Octavia was Augustus' sole sister.[161] The Domitii family were also very wealthy,[162] and Ahenobarbus himself owned a large house on the Velia on the eastern Sacra Via, putting him in the center of Rome.[163] Especially if his negative tendencies (if true) were still hidden, Ahenobarbus was a good match for this young imperial woman beset with increasing familial difficulties.

The wedding ushered in a confusing and dark time for Agrippina. We have no evidence relating to her individually,[164] but it is clear that her husband's rising political career coincided with more devastating blows to her family.[165] On the one hand, Ahenobarbus experienced an apparently unbroken series of political successes, even during the horrendous aftermath of Sejanus' downfall in 31, which lingered into 33.[166] Ahenobarbus had been a member of the prestigious Roman confraternity of the Arval Brethren from before his marriage to Agrippina, and their official records (*acta*) record his participation in their rites in 33, 38, and 39, and perhaps 27 as well.[167] He served as one of the two consuls, traditionally Rome's most important magistrates, for the entire year of 32, an uncommonly long tenure for the consulship at this time;[168] further, as this was the year following the Sejanus crisis, the unusual honor indicates Tiberius' trust in him.[169] In 36, after a devastating fire consumed the southern side of the Circus Maximus and the Aventine in Rome, Ahenobarbus was part of the small group Tiberius established to evaluate the fire damage. Three of the other four members similarly had been husbands of imperial women since 33: Cassius Longinus, wed to Drusilla; Marcus Vinicius, to Julia Livilla; and Gaius Rubellius Blandus, to Julia, the eldest daughter of Drusus the Younger and thus the granddaughter of Tiberius.[170] The committee was a signal imperial benefaction both to Rome and to the individuals appointed to it.

Yet Ahenobarbus' political successes were more than offset for his young wife Agrippina by her personal losses during these unpredictable and distrustful years when the emperor ruled from an island retreat far from the capital city. The deaths of her aunt Julia the Younger and great-grandmother Julia Augusta, mentioned above, were apparently natural. The deaths after 31 were not. In 31 her eldest brother Nero Caesar killed himself while in exile on Pontia.[171] Her mother Agrippina the Elder suffered terribly in her exile on Pandateria, where—according to Suetonius—she lost an eye in a beating by a centurion and in 33 finally starved herself to death after being force-fed at least once. That same year, 33, saw the starvation death of the young Agrippina's second brother Drusus Caesar, whose deprivation compelled him to eat the stuffing of his mattress in his dungeon in the imperial palace. The remains of both brothers were scattered so that they could not be properly interred,[172] depriving Agrippina and her siblings of what is now called "closure" as well as one of the important funerary rituals for Roman women.

The cruel contradictions of Agrippina's young married life may have been particularly apparent in 33. That year, when her mother and second brother died so horribly, Tiberius also arranged the weddings of her two sisters. For Drusilla Tiberius chose Lucius Cassius Longinus; for Julia Livilla, Marcus Vinicius.[173] Both men had served together in 30 as the prestigious consuls taking power at the beginning of a year (*cos. ord.*, or eponymous consuls) and later survived the crisis of Sejanus' downfall. The dissonance of the young women's lives is revealed in the note that Cassius Longinus had been a witness against Drusus Caesar,[174] their brother who died of starvation that very year. Whatever the young women's feelings about the disgrace, torture, and deaths of their mother and brothers, it was much safer to keep their heads down and dissimulate.[175] They were the last of their nuclear family other than Caligula, whose move to Capri in 31 had separated them from him.

The three sisters probably spent time together as their husbands collaborated on the fire committee of 36. Such companionship may have helped soothe grief for their family members. Now that Drusilla and Julia Livilla were also married but still childless, Agrippina may have turned to them to commiserate about their common lack of children that contrasted their mother's celebrated fecundity. As yet, Agrippina the Younger had no known pregnancy, despite being wed since 28.

Agrippina the Younger and her sisters had myriad other distractions. They surely attended feasts, literary recitations, and private and public ceremonies, from birthday celebrations to Rome's periodic public games and festivals.[176] Some events, such as the celebration of an imperial youth's coming of age by his assumption of the *toga virilis*, were undertaken with great fanfare, usually in Rome.[177] Others might be staged in suburban villas, especially during the late summer and early autumn months when malaria and other diseases caused the rich to flee the crowded urban environment. The sisters' pastimes were presumably in the company not only of their husbands but of other young women of their age and status, such as Ahenobarbus' two sisters, Domitia Lepida and Domitia.

The fates of some companions, however, were forceful reminders of the young women's fundamental powerlessness. Junia Claudilla, the daughter of a consul elected in 15, married Caligula in 33 and moved to Capri to live with him. There, she died in childbirth sometime before 37.[178] Earlier, Aelia Paetina, who was related to Sejanus, had married Claudius (as his second wife) in 28 and bore him (Claudia) Antonia, a child Claudius cherished (see Chapter 4). But the fall of Sejanus in 31 dragged down his relatives, and that year Claudius divorced Aelia Paetina for "trivial offenses."[179] (Her fate, however momentous for her, was trifling compared to the brutal and publicized deaths of Sejanus' sons and young daughter.[180]) Despite innumerable privileges and august lineage, Agrippina and her sisters had little control over their fates. In that they resembled women of equal and of lesser status in Rome's world.

This must have seemed particularly apparent in early 37, when Agrippina's husband Ahenobarbus was charged with treason, adultery, and incest with his sister Domitia Lepida. The charges were allegedly made by the praetorian prefect Macro, who had succeeded to Sejanus' position and trust with Tiberius after 31. They clearly display Tiberius' displeasure with his former helpmeet.[181] The emperor's suspicious nature had become more unpredictable with age and distance from Rome. The charges must have struck terror into Agrippina as well as her husband: she would lose the buffer and protection she had enjoyed since 28.

To her great luck, the death of Tiberius on 16 March 37 freed Ahenobarbus from his charges.[182] The emperor's death brought a close to the long and ambiguous period in which Agrippina the Younger was in the shadows and apparently without agency of her own. Among the many other coming changes was that she was now the sister of the newly sanctioned princeps. On 18 March 37 Caligula was catapulted to Rome's supreme power. The young ruler, who would turn 25 only in August, immediately launched an effusive demonstration of familial piety. This swept up Agrippina and her sisters, and it opens our next chapter.

Agrippina the Younger: A Dangerous Woman in Rome's Early Empire. Mary T. Boatwright, Oxford University Press.
 DOI: 10.1093/9780190945855.003.0002

2
Life under Caligula (37–41)

Introduction

Agrippina the Younger could not have been overly surprised by the death of Tiberius in Misenum on 16 March 37. Since his retreat to Campania in 26 she had probably seen her reclusive great-uncle only sporadically—for instance, during the weddings he arranged for her and her two sisters in 28 and 33, respectively. By 37, however, the 77-year-old Tiberius was clearly ailing. We can be less sure that she knew of the rumors attributing Tiberius' death to her brother Caligula in cahoots with the praetorian prefect Macro and his wife Ennia Thrasylla.[1] In any case, Agrippina and all of Rome would have learned almost immediately of Caligula's imperial acclamation in Misenum by the praetorians on the day of Tiberius' death.[2] She and Caligula's other sisters must have personally rejoiced when the senate confirmed the acclamation on 18 March 37.[3] The family could now claim the position at Rome's center that was so tantalizingly augured first when Germanicus was promoted as Tiberius' adopted son (4 CE) and a generation later when Nero Caesar and Drusus Caesar were adopted by Tiberius at the death of his own son in 23 (Chapter 1).

The new roles that Agrippina and her sisters were given, however, were inconceivable. Hitherto important imperial women of the evolving principate, although certainly influential behind the scenes, mostly had been relegated to supporting positions. Octavia had been accommodating sister and then private maternal figure; Livia, dutiful wife and then barely tolerated "dowager"; and Antonia the Younger, caretaker and chaste matron respectably married only once (a *univira*).[4] In contrast, Agrippina and her sisters gained hitherto unimaginable visibility and ostensible power at the beginning of their brother's reign. Within two years, however, they were unequivocally demoted back to supporting roles or worse. Although information about Agrippina herself in this period is deficient especially in details, as we see in this chapter, review of the honors, privileges, and positions initiated by Caligula helps us understand the trajectory of her life.

Caligula's Family, March 37

Agrippina may not have grasped her brother's situation and prospects immediately in March 37. She could have seen Caligula only rarely since his move to Capri in mid-31. Presumably, she attended his coming-of-age ceremony, the assumption of his *toga virilis* (toga of manhood), on Capri in 31 and his wedding to Junia Claudilla at Antium in 33; presumably, he was at Drusilla's and Julia Livilla's weddings in 33. But Caligula's and Junia's married life on Capri curtailed further social interaction, and Junia's death in childbirth sometime before 37 would have lessened opportunities even more.[5] Caligula was advanced politically by being appointed *quaestor designatus* in 33 and marked out by the privilege of applying for all offices five years early,[6] but he never returned to Rome to undertake duties. Further, his designation as Tiberius' successor was not clear. The principate was not yet an institution: as we see in the next chapter, after Caligula's assassination just four years later (January 41) the senate considered re-establishing the Republic or choosing a leader not from the Julio-Claudian family.[7] In 35 Tiberius had further complicated the succession question by naming, on an equal basis to his estate, his own grandson Tiberius Gemellus coheir with Caligula.[8] In 37 Gemellus, similarly raised in the imperial court at Capri but seven years Caligula's junior, was only 17 or 18 and had even less political experience than Caligula.[9] In fact, neither young man was prepared to take on the principate, a task for which, even at the age of 56 in 14 CE, Tiberius had declared himself underprepared despite his many years in the field and the senate.[10]

But Caligula had an impressive and popular family in addition to the drive and cunning credited him in planning Tiberius' death, and he would effectively parade that family to consolidate support.[11] In 37 Agrippina, Drusilla, and Julia Livilla were made extraordinarily visible on coinage and in public life and the court (see next section). This innovation was momentous, especially for the three young women themselves, even if their promotion came alongside that of other relatives of Caligula—Germanicus, Agrippina the Elder, and others—and their own time in the limelight lasted only a year or two. The following discussion looks for Agrippina in Caligula's initial, very public commendation and recommendation of his sisters and other female relatives and in his retreat from such activity after the middle of 38. The exact chronology is hard to come by, since much of our information derives from Suetonius or from coins and documentary evidence that cannot be dated more precisely than within a year or two.[12] The fuzzy dates, however, cannot obscure the novel promotion of Agrippina the Younger and her sisters.

Caligula's Arrival in Rome in 37

Suetonius describes the fervor with which Rome greeted the 24-year-old Caligula on his arrival in the capital city on 28 March 37.[13] The ratification of his imperial position in the senate came that day or the next, making Caligula's precedence over Gemellus obvious. The younger boy would not receive Tiberius' legacy to him of half his estate: with Macro as intermediary, Caligula had the senate annul that part of Tiberius' will on the grounds that the aged princeps was not in full command of his facilities while writing it. Nonetheless, Caligula's public encouragement of Gemellus and bestowal on him of the title *Princeps Iuventutis* (Leader of the Youth) did imply that Gemellus was next in line for the succession.[14] In Suetonius' account, written almost a century after the events, Caligula's accession seemed like a blessing to the Roman people, "one might say the entire world," as well as to the majority of provincials and soldiers because "many" had known him as a baby. Rome's entire urban populace emotionally recalled Germanicus and extravagantly pitied "a family that had been practically wiped out by successive murders."[15]

Suetonius devotes a long chapter to the new emperor's actions, typifying them as Caligula's attempt to gain popularity by any means.[16] Numerous public ceremonies capitalized on Caligula's family while praising Tiberius and the smooth transmission of imperial power from Augustus through Tiberius to Caligula.[17] Tiberius' public funeral was celebrated on 3 April.[18] The young princeps honored many legacies Tiberius had made and, perhaps more surprisingly, ones his great-grandmother Julia Augusta had intended before Tiberius suppressed her will in 29.[19] Although some modern scholars puzzle over the latter distributions,[20] they fit other instances of Caligula's promotion of his female relatives, as well as male ones, dead and alive. Caligula left Rome to showily retrieve the ashes of his mother and brother Nero Caesar from Pandateria and Pontia: he sailed to the islands in a terrible storm, placed the remains in urns with his own hands, and brought them to Ostia in a specially ornamented warship.[21] He had Rome's most eminent equestrians carry the vessels, after they were barged up the

Tiber, through the crowded noon-time city to the Mausoleum of Augustus.[22] He then established yearly public rites for his mother and brother and accorded special honor to his mother with annual circus games and a special carriage (a *carpentum*) on which her image would be carried in a procession. That latter honor was commemorated by coinage,[23] rendering less ephemeral his mother's use of this two-wheeled carriage that traditionally marked out Rome's most eminent matrons, Vestal Virgins, and a select few male priests. In 22 CE Julia Augusta had received the honor during a grave sickness, and the *carpentum* would become ever more associated with imperial women.[24]

Caligula intensified the tributes and memorialization of his relatives.[25] He had the month of September renamed "Germanicus" after his father. Coins, centrally struck in precious metal as well as lower denominations, individually portrayed Germanicus and Agrippina, the latter identified as "Mother of Gaius Caesar Augustus Germanicus."[26] Those for his mother were the first centrally struck coins devoted, both in obverse and in reverse type, to a woman.[27] Issues also appeared honoring his two older brothers, Nero Caesar and Drusus Caesar, shown galloping on horseback like the divine twins Castor and Pollux.[28] Installation of statues to both deceased brothers was entrusted to Caligula's paternal uncle Claudius, whom the new emperor also chose as co-consul, although the elder man had never previously held a senatorial office.[29] But other than Claudius' promotion, this set of honors went to family members who were dead—arguably unjustly.[30]

Others exalted at the beginning of Caligula's reign were very much alive, and their acclamation was especially unusual if they were female. Indeed, Caligula's attention to the women of his family was particularly marked.[31] He sponsored a senatorial degree granting his paternal grandmother Antonia all of the honors ever awarded Julia Augusta (Livia).[32] The "first" imperial woman, Livia had a fairly low profile during Augustus' life but a higher one after her son Tiberius took power in 14.[33] With a deep network among Rome's matrons and many connections among the rising elite, Augustus' wife evidently worked mostly behind the scenes.[34] The court may have recognized her influence as Augustus' trusted advisor, but that influence was not signified widely by public sculptures or identifiable coin portraits.[35] Even the numerous public honors proposed after Augustus' death and posthumous adoption of her, when she was granted the name Julia Augusta, were largely curtailed by Tiberius (who had suppressed her legacies at her death in 29).[36] The honors he grudgingly permitted, such as her use of a *lictor* (civil servant and bodyguard) as priest of *divus* Augustus, the right to use a *carpentum*, and the right to sit in special, lower seats at spectacles, gave her public standing equal to that of Vestal Virgins.[37] It was these distinctions that Caligula sponsored for his grandmother Antonia the Younger, as well as the title of Augusta and the priesthood of *divus* Augustus. Antonia, who had never assumed even the visibility of Livia/Julia Augusta, refused the title of Augusta and died soon afterward in Caligula's first year.[38]

Agrippina, Drusilla, and Julia Livilla seem less reluctant to accept honors their brother encouraged for them. Some, those akin to Vestal Virgins' privileges they received along with Antonia, were not unprecedented. The sisters' prominence went further, however. Caligula also got them the right of witnessing the games in the Circus with him from the imperial seats.[39] Much more unusual was their new right of having uttered in their behalf the prayers annually offered by the magistrates and priests for the princeps' welfare and that of the state, and the oaths of allegiance that were sworn to his rule.[40] Suetonius specifies that hereafter in the annual loyalty oath, everyone had to vow, "I will not value my life or that of my children less highly than I do the safety of Gaius and his sisters!" Consular motions had to include "Good fortune attend Gaius Caesar and his sisters!"[41]

This was a radical change. Only 13 years earlier Tiberius had squashed the inclusion of Drusus Caesar and Nero Caesar in such vows, allegedly resenting the comparison of their youth to his proven capabilities, their evocation of Agrippina the Elder, and the offer to them of such great rewards (*praemia*) despite their lack of experience.[42] In 37 Agrippina, then 22, and her 21- and 19-year-old sisters were not much older than their 18- and 17-year-old brothers had been in 24, 13 years earlier. More shockingly, they were women who could never access the requisite military and political experience considered fundamental to Rome. Tiberius had been particularly adamant that women should be kept far from the state. He was notorious in the case of Agrippina the Elder, and he repeatedly warned his mother to stay away from great affairs, especially those not suitable for a woman.[43] No recorded oath or prayer corroborates Caligula's innovation,[44] but scholars generally accept Suetonius' and Cassius Dio's reports.[45]

Agrippina the Younger and her sisters had undeniably high visibility in Rome. Two coin issues—*sestertii* and *dupondii*—struck early in Caligula's reign depict and identify them, for the first time representing living women on official coins. The issue backs Caligula's portrait, name, and titles on the coins' obverse to an illustration of three females standing close together on

Ill. 2.1 Agrippina and her sisters Drusilla and Julia (Livilla) guised as Security, Harmony, and Good Fortune, on the reverse of a centrally struck *sestertius* of Caligula from 37/38 CE. © The Trustees of the British Museum.

the reverse. Dress, attributes, and postures assimilate the three, who are labeled AGRIPPINA, DRUSILLA, and IULIA (Julia Livilla), to *Securitas*, *Concordia*, and *Fortuna* (Freedom from Care; Harmony; Good Fortune)[46] (see Ill. 2.1). The young women's new privilege of special seating at spectacles also brought them before the public's eye. In August 37 they sat with Caligula and priests of the Augustan order at the long-delayed dedication of the Temple of *divus* Augustus;[47] they surely sat with him at various games celebrating Agrippina the Elder. Images of his sisters began to be included in the outpouring of sculptural groups honoring Caligula's family in Italy and elsewhere.[48]

Agrippina in Caligula's New Court

Rome's elite and the court were in great flux in 37, but it was obvious that Agrippina and her sisters would have important roles. Much of the state's business had been directed from Capri for the last decade.[49] In Rome itself many senators and others were said to have been worn down by interminable duties; many others had lost their lives to the aging Tiberius' suspicions.[50] Urged by his praetorian prefect Macro, Tiberius had turned even against Ahenobarbus, Agrippina's husband and his own close associate, although the old emperor's death freed the charged man.[51] Other senators not targeted by Tiberius had their own worries, particularly those who had voted to condemn Caligula's brothers Nero Caesar and Drusus Caesar as public enemies in 29 and 30.[52] Caligula showily burned the records of those events and his mother's condemnation in 29, although it would later emerge that he kept copies that he used to destroy select individuals.[53] The new princeps recruited men from throughout the empire to enter the depleted equestrian order, even allowing some senatorial dress and the promise of entering that more illustrious rank.[54] Caligula, who had been fairly isolated on Capri since 31, could use advice in this challenging time.

Agrippina and her sisters thus could play important roles in 37. Their continued life in Rome since childhood, albeit with presumable brief sojourns in suburban villas, contrasted with Caligula's absence from the capital city for the last six years. Agrippina had the most experience: the eldest of the three, she had been married since 28 CE to Ahenobarbus with his stellar political career in Rome until 37. In the last nine years her acquaintance with Rome's elite must have deepened as, for example, Ahenobarbus reported the inevitable conflicts he encountered as consul in 32 or shared the gossip he heard during the rites of the Arval Brethren (Chapter 1). She could impart knowledge about individuals' political leanings, dependability, and wealth. Agrippina's and Caligula's sisters Drusilla and Julia Livilla (since 33 similarly married to eminent senators, although Drusilla's marriage to Cassius Longinus was now ending) could corroborate or complement her information. Caligula himself was currently without a wife: his marriage to Junia Claudilla in 33 had ended when she died giving birth to an infant who also did not survive.[55] At the very least, Caligula probably turned to Agrippina and her sisters for a list of marriage prospects.

The Rise—and Death—of Drusilla, 37–38

Caligula's short reign is notable for the number and scandals of his marriages and semi-marriages, befitting his general presentation as a tyrant, and his first two years were notorious for his preference for his sisters.[56] After his first wife Junia Claudilla he married three more times, and he was also charged with open and sustained incest with his sister Drusilla.[57] In any case the three sisters, and especially Drusilla, clearly ranked higher than the women Caligula officially married and divorced in his first two years. In 37 Caligula "seized" Cornelia Orestina, reportedly during her wedding ceremony to her intended husband, only to abandon her soon after.[58] After Drusilla's death in 38 Caligula took Lollia Paulina from her husband Gaius Memmius Regulus, then governor of Achaia. Lollia Paulina boasted an unusually beautiful grandmother and had personally inherited prodigious wealth. Nonetheless, Caligula hastily divorced her, additionally forbidding her further sexual relations with men.[59] Despite his wives' resources and accomplishments, Caligula openly preferred his sisters: during banquets he would put his sisters in turn in the place of honor while demeaning the seating of his own wife.[60] Among these impulsive acts is Caligula's even more scandalous intimacy with his sister Drusilla, whom—according to Suetonius—the young princeps "carried off" from her husband Cassius Longinus so he could treat her as a "proper wife" (*abduxit... iusta uxor*).[61]

A serious and lingering illness afflicted Caligula in his first two years as princeps, complicating our understanding of these and other turbulent events.[62] Philo, who actually saw Caligula when he represented the Jews of Alexandria in a delegation to Rome in 39/40, dates the sickness' onset to the eighth month of the new emperor's reign—that is, after 18 October 37. Symptoms apparently lasted into January 38.[63] Among its signs was that Caligula had his cousin Gemellus forced to suicide on suspicions of conspiracy, with the specific charge that the younger man had prayed for and expected the ailing Caligula's death (in December 37 or slightly thereafter).[64] In 37 other previously close associates of Caligula were likewise forced to suicide: his former father-in-law Marcus Junius Silanus (father of Junia Claudilla), Macro, and Macro's wife Ennia Thrasylla, with whom Caligula had an affair on Capri.[65] By early 38 Caligula arranged a second marriage for Drusilla, now 21 or so, to Marcus Aemilius Lepidus.[66] Lepidus was the son of a great confidant of Tiberius and distantly linked to Augustus, but in 38 he was young and inexperienced.[67] On the other hand, he was rumored to be the lover of Caligula himself,[68] and he would later also be linked sexually with Agrippina and Julia Livilla.[69]

The young princeps exalted Drusilla in other ways. While ill, he reportedly designated Drusilla as heir to his goods and the whole empire.[70] This was not possible in Rome, where women were barred from holding the *imperium* that was essential to rule. Some interpret this as Caligula's hope she would bear to Aemilius Lepidus a son who would guarantee a Julian successor on the throne.[71] However construed, it was a sign of unprecedented confidence in a woman's capacity to rule. It could not have escaped Agrippina that the woman so designated was her own less experienced sister. Drusilla's sudden but apparently natural death on 10 June 38 was followed by a public funeral at which her husband Lepidus spoke—commemoration that was by now customary for respected female members of the imperial family.[72] Other tributes for Drusilla were more unusual, such as her posthumous grant of all honors Julia Augusta had ever received.[73]

Most extraordinary of all was Drusilla's official consecration, the first such distinction for a Roman woman. This was decreed by the senate on 23 September 38, presumably on Caligula's prompting.[74] The senator Livius Geminus swore, under oath, that he had seen her ascend to the heavens and speak with the gods.[75] Drusilla, now called "Panthea," was represented by a golden statue in the senate house, by another statue in the Temple of Venus in the Forum at the same size as that temple's icon of Venus (and attended by the same rites), and at a shrine of her own at which twenty female and male priests were to conduct worship. Women were to swear by Drusilla's name whenever they offered testimony, and on her birthday a free two-day festival, as splendid as Rome's venerable six-day Ludi Megalenses held in April, would be celebrated with the people feasting and senators and equestrians enjoying presents and public banquets.[76] Panthea's rites were enjoined for all Rome's cities.

Independent evidence verifies some of these honors, at least during Caligula's reign. A few inscriptions from throughout the empire attest priests of Drusilla/Panthea, or dedications to *diva Drusilla*.[77] The divinization was also felt in the court: Rubellius Blandus, who had married their cousin Julia in 33, made a dedication to *diva Drusilla* in Tibur.[78] Even Claudius publicly acknowledged his niece's "divine" status, if the common interpretation is correct of an anomalous dedication of 38 from Avennio (Avignon, France). Honoring Drusilla, *parens* (close relative), it was raised by "Tiberius" (Claudius) because of the "conferred honor of her divinity."[79] But the reactions of Agrippina and Julia Livilla to these innovations are not recorded.

Drusilla was the first woman, and only the third individual, to be consecrated by the Roman state. Livia, Julia Livilla, and some other imperial women had been honored by association with deities in the East, but that was spontaneous and not officially promoted.[80] Drusilla's worship in imperial cult was something different. In contrast to her predecessors in imperial cult, Julius Caesar and Augustus, Drusilla had performed no traditionally great deeds: she had not led Romans successfully against foreign foes, settled internal conflicts, or sponsored socially impactful legislation. Rather, she was simply one of Caligula's three supportive sisters, albeit his favorite. Early in his reign she was but one of a harmonious triad identified on central coinage and honored equally in seating during banquets.[81] Drusilla may have offered Caligula advice about politics in court or farther afield, but little experience informed the young woman's opinions.[82]

Agrippina the Matron

In contrast, by 38, Agrippina the Younger had achieved what was traditionally a Roman woman's most significant accomplishment: she gave birth successfully, thus rising to the ranks of Roman matrons.[83] As seen above, the death of Tiberius on 16 March 37 had freed her husband Ahenobarbus from treason and other charges.[84] He must have rejoined his young wife, now basking in the glory of her brother's ascent. Nine months later their son, who is now known as Nero, was born. No details of the twenty-two-year-old's pregnancy are recorded until the actual birth on 15 December 37 CE at Antium (now Anzio, Italy).[85] After more than eight years of marriage, Agrippina had brought a pregnancy to term. Was her pregnancy a physical obstacle to her activities as imperial sister?[86] Many pregnant women experience sickness, especially during their first trimester, and numerous illnesses were rife in the crowded metropolis of Rome during summer and fall. To sustain her pregnancy—becoming a mother was especially prized in the Julio-Claudian family—Agrippina may not have been able to participate fully in Caligula's new court. Yet the reported accord of the siblings at Caligula's accession, reflected on coins and by special seating at banquets, might argue for Agrippina's presence in Rome at least during the first few months of Caligula's reign. Intriguingly in light of her pregnancy and marital status, on the coins identifying her and her sisters, their repeated image is not that of a respectable Roman *matrona*, but of a nubile young woman in Greek chiton, himation, and diadem.

Agrippina's delivery of her child was accompanied by numerous omens, a frequent aspect of imperial births.[87] On the authority of Agrippina the Younger's own memoirs, Pliny the Elder reports, in a section on difficult parturitions and ones "against nature," that Nero was born feet first.[88] To facilitate such a perilous birth the infant was usually manipulated in utero in a painful procedure that was dangerous for both mother and child without antiseptics and anesthesia.[89] Other portents included inauspicious remarks of Ahenobarbus at the congratulatory news of his son's arrival: "Nothing could be born from [myself] and Agrippina except a thing loathsome and destined to harm the public." Less ill-omened was the report that the rays of the rising sun touched the baby even before it was laid on the earth itself.[90] Cassius Dio gives another, more famous, portent, which Tacitus places not at Nero's birth but at the death of his mother at his orders: when an astrologer predicted, from the apparently heavenly light and stars shining at the birth, that the child would rule and would murder his mother, Agrippina actually cried out: "Let him kill me, only let him rule!"[91] (We return to this in Chapter 5 at Agrippina's death.[92])

Omens are also associated with the baby's *dies lustricus*, the ninth day after birth when a male child was purified and received his name. They reveal Agrippina's focus on her natal family. Suetonius holds that the young mother, at this ceremony that probably took place at Antium,[93] deferentially asked her older brother Caligula to give whatever name he wanted to the child.[94] The new emperor sarcastically responded, "Claudius" while regarding his, and Agrippina's, paternal uncle, Tiberius Claudius Nero Germanicus. Agrippina spurned the suggestion, for Claudius was considered a laughingstock in the court at the time. The infant received the *trinomina* Lucius Domitius Ahenobarbus, traditionally named after his grandfather.[95] In Suetonius the exchange foreshadows the future: when in 50 Agrippina's son was adopted by Claudius, then emperor, he assumed the name Nero Claudius Caesar Drusus Germanicus.[96] Nonetheless, Agrippina's deference to Caligula underscores her clear preference for her imperial family.

That family was unmistakably falling apart. Caligula had already shown signs of his mysterious and disturbing illness that continued with the forced suicide of his cousin Gemellus around this time, among other impulsive acts. Caligula's clear preference for Drusilla marginalized Agrippina the Younger and Julia Livilla, who were further excluded by the subsequent threesome of Caligula, Drusilla, and Aemilius Lepidus, Drusilla's new husband and Caligula's reputed lover.[97] How Agrippina reacted to Caligula's extravagant grief when Drusilla died on 10 June 38 cannot be ascertained. She must have realized at that point, however, that her young son had now become the only member of the next generation with direct lineage to Augustus. Caligula's quick marriage and divorce from Lollia Paulina emphasized the low chance that this increasingly volatile young princeps would have offspring of his own.

Agrippina's Murky Downfall in Late 39

No evidence attests Agrippina from the *dies lustricus* of her son until her purported involvement in some sort of plot against her brother in 39.[98] We may assume that she was at the soirée sometime in 38 during which Caligula's (third) wife Lollia Paulina appalled Pliny the Elder, who later railed against her ostentatious display of pearl and emerald jewelry worth 40,000,000 sesterces, "the plunder of an entire province."[99] Tacitus' *Annals*, with its keen political analysis that might have noted Agrippina in Caligula's court, is missing for this period, rendering the more opaque her involvement in whatever plot(s) against her brother that resulted in her banishment from Rome.

The plot (or plots) is so poorly documented that some doubt that an actual conspiracy took place at all.[100] Some references speak hyperbolically of "many" trials, including those of high-ranking city magistrates like aediles and praetors,[101] but most attend to individuals reputedly closest to Caligula: his sisters Agrippina and Julia Livilla along with Aemilius Lepidus, Drusilla's widower and allegedly once Caligula's lover. Independent but undatable evidence of a conspiracy involving Gnaeus Cornelius Lentulus Gaetulicus, the commander of four legions in Upper Germany, has also been associated with the plot of 39. If so, the conspiracy was detected by 27 October of that year, when the Arval Brethren gave thanks that Gaetulicus' nefarious plans had been detected.[102] Agrippina's husband Ahenobarbus is not mentioned at all.[103] To modern eyes this seems odd, especially if Gaetulicus was part of a larger group of adherents of the old Tiberian regime who were unhappy with Caligula.[104] A further consideration is that Ahenobarbus was the father of Nero, at the time the only potential heir of the Julian line.

Agrippina's own involvement is hard to pin down. Cassius Dio stresses the emperor's mounting instability, focusing on Aemilius Lepidus as a "victim" of Caligula's growing abuses. His version explains the sisters' deportation to the Pontine Islands as due to their "improper relations" with Lepidus and "many impious and immoral acts," with which Caligula angrily charged them in the senate.[105] Suetonius' packed chapter on Caligula's sexual crimes notes that his incest with all three sisters made it the easier at Lepidus' trial to condemn Agrippina and Julia Livilla as adulteresses plotting against their brother.[106] Suetonius' skepticism about the cited proof, however, letters in the sisters' handwriting that he claims were obtained by trickery and sexual favors, weakens the charge of conspiracy.[107] In his Neronian books Tacitus makes a remark often taken to confirm Agrippina's plotting against Caligula. When alleging that in 59 Agrippina committed incest with Nero to retain influence over her son, he states, "The idea of deviant lust seemed the more believable in the case of one who, in her girlhood years, had allowed illegal sex with Lepidus in the hope of power."[108] The remark, presented as an anonymous judgment, is part of Tacitus' relentless depiction of an obsessively power-hungry Agrippina. Nonetheless, it is weak evidence for her involvement in a plot in 39: "girlhood years" (*puellaribus annis*) does not fit Agrippina's status as a married 24-year-old matron with a two-year-old child.[109]

The evidence is frustratingly vague for a conspiracy in 39 that involved Agrippina and her sister Julia Livilla. Where and how did the conspirators meet, and what were their goals? Did they communicate from the start with Gaetulicus, then in Upper Germany, or is his a separate plot? In particular, what could Agrippina and her sister have gained from removing their brother from supreme power? Perhaps if Agrippina were indeed having an (adulterous) affair with Lepidus and the plotters succeeded in killing Caligula, she hoped that her lover would become her husband (after divorce from Ahenobarbus?), rule Rome in an interregnum, and then designate Nero as successor.[110] But this conjecture overlooks Agrippina's husband Ahenobarbus and Julia Livilla, who was also banished in 39, and it does not address other questions.

Despite the ambiguities now riddling the plot, reaction was prompt and severe. Gaetulicus' uprising was quickly put down. As for Aemilius Lepidus, Agrippina, and Julia Livilla, Caligula informed the senate about their misdeeds as though they constituted a great conspiracy.[111] Lepidus had his throat cut by a tribune, and the senate decreed that his remains could not be dutifully buried.[112] After further humiliation by their brother, Agrippina and Julia Livilla were banished to Pontia and Pandateria, tiny islands far from the coast of southern Latium.[113] During his expedition to Gaul and Germany in 39 Caligula auctioned off his condemned sisters' goods, stressing their imperial pedigrees to inflate the prices; he is said to have sold even their freedmen clientage.[114] Although this has suggested to some that Agrippina and Julia Livilla were accompanying their brother and thus condemned outside Rome, as was Lepidus,[115] Caligula's apparently limitless desire for publicity in Rome makes this improbable. He made sure to denounce Agrippina and Julia Livilla in the senate for many impious and immoral acts, and at Lepidus' trial the two were cited for incest with their brother. Their intimate lives were exaggerated and publicized to their peers in the senate, undoubtedly including their own husbands, who of necessity divorced them before the charge of adultery was officially made.[116] The only named adulterer for Agrippina other than Lepidus, however, is the low-born Ofonius Tigellinus, and his sentence was milder than Agrippina's own.[117]

Before deportation, Agrippina was further shamed by being forced to carry Lepidus' bones to Rome in an urn clasped to her bosom,[118] staging a cruel parody of her mother's trip from Brundisium to Rome with Germanicus' ashes 20 years earlier.[119] The journey linked her with Lepidus' failure more clearly than did Caligula's public dedication, at the Temple of Mars Ultor in Rome, of the three daggers that presumably referenced Agrippina, Julia Livilla, and Lepidus.[120] Further, it seems patently malicious to banish the two sisters to the very islands on which their deported brother Nero Caesar and their mother had met hideous deaths only six years earlier,[121] islands Caligula himself had brought to prominence when retrieving his relatives' remains from them in 37.

Banishment on Pontia, 39–41

Agrippina the Younger went to Pontia (Ponza), which, like Julia Livilla's exile island Pandateria, could be closely watched by Rome's fleet at Misenum.[122] Modern scholars have stressed the inhospitable nature of these Pontine Islands.[123] The smaller island, Pandateria (1.75 sq. mi.), has no natural water, and modern Ponza has to import potable water from Naples. Yet both islands housed opulent Roman villas, and Pontia had received a Roman colony in the late fourth century BCE.[124] Recent archaeological work on Pandateria argues that its well-appointed "Villa a Punto Eolo" was used throughout the first century CE for the imperial exiles Julia the Elder (accompanied by her mother Scribonia, Augustus' first wife), Agrippina the Elder, Julia Livilla, Octavia (Claudius' daughter and Nero's first wife), and Flavia Domitilla (a member of the Flavian family). The villa, begun in the late Republic as a luxurious summer residence, was enhanced in the Augustan period and first century CE with cisterns and infrastructure to enable year-round residence. Among the amenities were ponds for fish breeding, irrigation for horticulture, and service quarters.[125] As for Agrippina the Younger on Pontia, her identification with any of the numerous Roman villas found there is less certain. Local lore holds that she was banished to a large Augustan/Julio-Claudian villa at Punta della Madonna, the southern end of Ponza's main harbor.[126] We may imagine that Agrippina's exile villa in Pontia had as many amenities as the better-known villa at Pandateria.

Whatever the conveniences of the villa to which she was banished, Pontia sharply contrasted with Agrippina the Younger's earlier life in Rome. She had just been ripped from her young son and from her husband of 11 years.[127] She later boasted of her natural maternal love;[128] if the claim is true, losing the toddler Nero was painful. Just as importantly, she was removed from the social and political circles in which she had been born and matured. Instead of imperial banquets at which she could recline on the couch of honor, as at Caligula's accession in March 37, now she dined alone under the surveillance of servants and jailers. Her isolation and presumable deprivation may have inspired her to begin her memoirs, which chronicled the misfortunes (*casus*) of her family as well as her own.[129] Pontia's clear and clean seas, accessible by tunnels from the Punta della Madonna villa, may have encouraged swimming, a skill that would save her in the initial stages of Nero's lethal plot in 59 (Chapter 5).[130] To pass the time on the tiny island, now an idyllic vacation spot for its uniformly temperate climate, sparse inhabitation, and seclusion, Agrippina may have domesticated or trained birds: Pliny the Elder later notes that as Claudius' wife, Agrippina owned a thrush that mimicked human speech and that she once received a white nightingale costing 600,000 sesterces.[131] But nothing definitively gives us any details about her banishment.

Other imperial women deported to the Pontine islands—Julia the Elder, Agrippina the Elder, and Octavia—retained popularity among Rome's *plebs* and even served as focal points for political resistance to the emperor.[132] In contrast, Agrippina and Julia Livilla drop from sight. Their property was confiscated and their influence cancelled.[133] They would regain their goods only when Claudius became emperor in 41 and, as a mark of magnanimity and distinction from Caligula, allowed those exiled by his assassinated predecessor to return and repossess their estates.[134] But Agrippina could not assume this rosy future: her grandmother Julia the Elder, great aunt Julia the Younger, and mother Agrippina the Elder had all died while banished.[135] It would be natural to imagine herself in this unfortunate series.

Her toddler Nero was also adrift, although we cannot know how much Agrippina could have picked up on this from Pontia. Ahenobarbus had assumed care of their son, whose standing as sole descendant of Augustus in the coming generation was weakened by the birth in 39 of Julia Drusilla, the daughter of Caligula and his fourth wife, Milonia Caesonia.[136] When sometime in 40 Ahenobarbus died of edema at Pyrgi (now S. Severa, Italy) before Nero's third birthday, Caligula seized all his assets, including the portion due Nero as legitimate heir.[137] Nero was then placed with one of Ahenobarbus' sisters, Lepida, to be raised. Often called Domitia Lepida, this seems to be the sister implicated in Ahenobarbus' incest indictment around 37, although there is no record of charges against her at that time.[138] Lepida, like her brother descended from Augustus' sister Octavia, had numerous grown children, including (Valeria) Messalina, who in 38 had married Claudius, Caligula's uncle.[139] With Nero, however, Lepida was notoriously lax, reportedly appointing a dancer and a barber as the child's pedagogues.[140] Tacitus stresses Agrippina's rancor against her former sister-in-law in his note that in 54 Agrippina's jealousy of Lepida, including of the bonds the indulgent aunt had earlier forged with Nero, caused the older woman's indictment and death.[141]

These were years of immense change. In 37 alone Agrippina had been transformed from the young wife of a precipitously fallen man charged with treason and incest to a celebrated part of the new imperial family with more privileges and visibility than living Roman women had hitherto enjoyed; by the year's end she had become the mother of a son. In the following year, however, she was eclipsed in Caligula's fancy by their sister Drusilla. Drusilla's death in early June did not restore Agrippina to Caligula's favor, however, and by 39 she had been charged with conspiracy against him. Banished to Pontia, she lived each day like the last, cut off from her family and former life. When Ahenobarbus died in 40, she could not have joined the mourning rites even had she wished.

Was Agrippina herself responsible for any of these changes? As we saw, Tacitus later credited her drive toward power (*dominatio*) to her involvement with Aemilius Lepidus and a conspiracy against Caligula. In any case, Agrippina's banishment kept her out of the capital city in 40 and early 41, ironically contributing to her survival during Caligula's progressively volatile and lethal rule. It also meant that she was free of suspicion for her brother's assassination on 24 January 41, where we start the next chapter.

Agrippina the Younger: A Dangerous Woman in Rome's Early Empire. Mary T. Boatwright, Oxford University Press.
 DOI: 10.1093/9780190945855.003.0003

3

Betwixt and Between (41–48)

Introduction

Though far from Rome on 24 January 41, Agrippina the Younger was in a terribly vulnerable position when Caligula was killed in the Palatine's imperial residence.[1] The violence in Rome threatened—and realized, for some—death to Caligula's imperial family, even to a few considered innocent. Even though Agrippina and Julia Livilla were among those Caligula had banished and Caligula had repeatedly vowed to kill all he had exiled,[2] they were the hated emperor's sisters. In the end Agrippina and Julia Livilla were returned safely to Rome through the unexpected events that brought their uncle Claudius to power on 25 January. This chapter explores Agrippina from this promising change of fortune in 41 through worsening conditions until 48, after which her luck drastically changed again. The pertinent information is scarce, in part because Tacitus' *Annals* are missing from Tiberius' death in 37 until sometime in the first half of 47.[3] But documentary evidence and other authors' remarks illuminate her general history within the increasingly capricious court of Claudius and his third wife Messalina. The very lack of testimony suggests that Agrippina survived and kept her son alive by keeping a low profile, often outside Rome. At the end of this chapter Agrippina comes more fully into historical view as she emerges flaunting her illustrious family and exploiting all her assets.

Caligula's Assassination in Late January 41

The plot or plots leading to Caligula's assassination on 24 January 41 are controversial.[4] The manuscript tradition of our longest and most detailed account of the assassination, Josephus in *Jewish Antiquities* (*Antiquitates Judaicae, AJ*), is flawed, notably about names, there are conflicting accounts even within single sources, and other sources differ on particulars.[5] The brief summary below does not aim to present a detailed narrative of the plot and its immediate aftermaths, but rather stresses information relevant to Agrippina the Younger. How could the plot and assassination have affected her?

Agrippina would surely have scorned the alleged hopes or plans of at least some conspirators: Cassius Chaerea, the senator Lucius Annius Vinicianus, and the two consuls Gnaeus Sentius Saturninus and Quintus Pomponius Secundus.[6] In various settings these men reportedly advocated restoring "Liberty" (*libertas*) and Republican government.[7] Such a step would totally undermine Agrippina's privileged life and eminence as a direct descendant of Augustus, the first princeps of Rome's empire. If Caligula's death allowed her to return safely from banishment in Pontia, as Tiberius' death had freed her former husband Ahenobarbus of charges, in a restored Republic Agrippina would be a mere *matrona*: prominent, to be sure, but no more so than other senatorial women like Lollia Paulina, Aelia Paetina, or her sisters-in-law Domitia Lepida and Domitia.[8] But she would have the burden of being a living reminder of the violently overthrown principate.[9] Agrippina may also have considered the Republic a total delusion. Augustus himself had apparently claimed to have restored it, and other prominent Julio-Claudians, Germanicus among them, also supposedly considered restoring it.[10] By 41, however, too much had changed: the "free" Republic had not functioned for almost a century.[11] After Caligula's death even the praetorians were said to think that a "republic was unworkable."[12]

More importantly, Agrippina probably realized the danger she would face as a member of the imperial family if Caligula were assassinated. In Rome the praetorians followed Caligula's murder by slaughtering his wife, Milonia Caesonia, and infant daughter, Julia Drusilla, the same day.[13] Josephus describes disagreement before they acted: some stressed the cruel rashness of venting their anger on a woman they held innocent of Caligula's misdeeds, and others blamed Caligula's wife for all the emperor's evils, charging that she had given him a maddening drug. But then Chaerea, the praetorian tribune spearheading Caligula's assassination and the murder of Caesonia and Julia Drusilla, convincingly proclaimed that it was "dangerous that [Caligula's] whole family had not perished with him; whatever was left of it would remain a deadly threat to the city and the rule of law."[14] Such views boded evil for Agrippina.

Others reportedly expressed similar opinions at the time. In their first session after Caligula's death the senate resolved to wipe out the entire family of the Caesars and all their relatives, including women; they would go so far also to destroy the temples of *divus* Iulius and *divus* Augustus.[15] Among the reactions of Agrippina's uncle Claudius to the "shock of a Caesar's death" was great fear, precisely because of "his noble birth."[16] (Once emperor, he executed some tribunes and praetorians who had been involved in Caligula's murder on the grounds that they had also demanded his own death.[17]) In 41 Claudius, Agrippina, and others of their family must also have recalled the murder of a family member after the death of Augustus in 14 CE. Immediately after Tiberius' accession Agrippa Postumus had been peremptorily cut down on the island of Planasia (modern Pianosa, near Elba), despite having been banished from Rome for eight years. Agrippa Postumus was Agrippina the Elder's youngest brother, and although his killing occurred the year before Agrippina the Younger's birth, it remained a source of speculation and suspicion.[18]

Claudius Becomes Princeps

In the end, "family" was responsible for Claudius' precipitate acclamation by praetorian guards moved by love for his brother Germanicus and other relatives,[19] despite Claudius' ambivalent relationship with the *domus Augusta.* Claudius, the grandson of Livia through his father Drusus the Elder and raised on the Palatine like Germanicus and others, had never been adopted into the Julian family. Under Augustus and Tiberius the notably sickly Claudius had been largely kept from public view, and after his choice as Caligula's co-consul in 37, he had gone back into obscurity.[20] Agrippina must have been as deeply shocked as all of Rome when the praetorians, after murdering Caligula as he departed the *ludi Palatini* staged in a small theater in the imperial Palatine 24 January 41,[21] found Claudius in the palace and set in motion the events that ended the next day with him as princeps.[22] Did she not have a more legitimate claim to the principate? Her direct lineage from Germanicus and Augustus himself, clearly central to her identity, had recently been promoted in Caligula's showy accession. But Agrippina could never have experienced Claudius' astonishing reversal of fortune. She was a mere woman.

Here, we focus on details in Claudius' acclamation that relate to Agrippina. Claudius famously quailed when identified by praetorian troops but was carried willy-nilly to the praetorian barracks on the edge of Rome.[23] Meanwhile, the senate met to restore order in the city and to debate next steps.

Some even espoused liberty and freedom—that is, the abolition of the principate.[24] When the senate heard that the praetorians had already taken Claudius to their barracks, they sent representatives to the camp to speak directly with Claudius, reportedly even ordering him threateningly to yield to the senate.[25] Although by 25 January Claudius clearly accepted the imperial position supported by the praetorians, the senate still dithered. Some individuals with "illustrious birth and marriage connections" had been named as candidates in Claudius' stead,[26] including Marcus Vinicius, Julia Livilla's husband before her conviction and banishment in 39, and Decimus Valerius Asiaticus. Such senators finally withdrew any claims they may have entertained.[27] In the meantime, Rome's urban cohorts, some 1,500 men strong, threw their support to Claudius and the praetorians. The senate had to capitulate and acclaim Claudius as well.[28] The People of Rome expressed their delight at Claudius' new position,[29] and Claudius became princeps. The events also catapulted Claudius' young wife Messalina and their growing family into the limelight and highest circle of power.

The whole process could not but emphasize to Agrippina, as well as to her uncle Claudius, some political realities of the time. The backing of the praetorian guard was essential for rule in Rome. Rome's populace was generally positive toward the imperial family. But senators were fickle: individually untrustworthy and diverted by their own ambitions and as a whole not easy to unite for a common cause, no matter how gloriously ideal.[30] In his 13-year rule Claudius would handsomely reward the praetorians and assiduously curry popular support, two endeavors that would ultimately benefit Agrippina. His interactions with the senate and senators, however, would not be as successful, despite his numerous and varied attempts to unify them behind him.

Such efforts began in Claudius' earliest days, when he made general promises that *his* principate would differ profoundly from that of Caligula. He offered amnesty toward those senators known or rumored to have opposed him.[31] The theme of "Liberty," so important to at least some of the conspirators, was appropriated as "Augustan Liberty" on coins struck in Rome.[32] Claudius exonerated Caligula's exiles, including Agrippina and Julia Livilla, and he reinstated their confiscated property and reputation.[33] The elite may have been less receptive to Claudius' obvious high regard of those who had brought him to power, the praetorian guard whom he rewarded with an enormous donation of some 15,000–20,000 sesterces.[34] He continued to give donatives to the praetorians on every anniversary of his imperial accession, when he also staged games at the praetorian camp,[35] and in 51 he celebrated the capture of the British king Caratacus in front of that camp.[36] This later event would feature Agrippina (Chapter 4), reinforcing her own ties with these dedicated protectors of the imperial family.

Agrippina and her Family in Early Claudian Rome

Among the first acts of Agrippina and Julia Livilla after they returned to Rome from the Pontine Islands in early 41 was to oversee Caligula's proper burial. After the murder his corpse had been secretly taken to the Horti Lamiani (in Rome's northeast), where it was partially cremated and lightly buried.[37] It is inconceivable that the sisters did not first discuss their plans for ritual burial with their uncle, Caligula's successor. The act helped re-establish the imperial family as a pious unit and manifested the magnanimity Claudius was otherwise displaying. It is less clear what Agrippina and her sister felt while performing this familial duty for the brother who had humiliated and banished them.

After the burial in early 41 Agrippina drops from most historical texts for some years. She is not noted among Claudius' new festivals and honors for his family.[38] As had Caligula, Claudius legitimized himself by reminding everybody of his venerable ancestors.[39] He gave games in the Circus in honor of his parents, Drusus (the Elder) and Antonia (the Younger), on their birthdays, even postponing long-established festivals customarily held on those days.[40] He sponsored the divinization of his paternal grandmother, Julia Augusta (Livia), installing a statue to her in the Temple of Augustus, charging the Vestals with the duty of offering proper sacrifices, and ordering women to use her name in taking oaths.[41] The divinization was finalized in 42 on January 17, the day Livia Drusilla had married Augustus over eighty years earlier. It may have superficially recalled the divinization of Drusilla only four years earlier (Chapter 2), but it was much more warranted than Caligula's innovation for his beloved Drusilla. Julia Augusta had commanded great respect during her own lifetime, when she had even received popular devotion in Italy and the provinces; at her death in 29 she had been voted unprecedented honors by the senate (Chapter 1). Claudius' own grandmother through her second son Drusus the Elder, this woman had been hailed unofficially as Mother of the Country.[42] She had advised her husband Augustus; raised many in the imperial family and her son Tiberius became

Augustus' successor; and been involved in politics, although more obviously in her later years after Tiberius' accession. For Agrippina and others of the day, Claudius' divinization of Julia Augusta was a permanent reminder of the political potential of women.

Claudius' planning for future generations of the imperial family, also undertaken in his first few months as princeps, may have involved Agrippina. On 12 February 41, within a few weeks of his accession, his wife Messalina bore him the son who would later be known as Britannicus.[43] Britannicus was the first son born to a ruling princeps, an event that gave great prestige and confidence to Claudius and Messalina.[44] The senate fell over itself offering honors such as the title of Augustus for the boy and that of Augusta for Messalina, both of which Claudius refused in a show of modesty.[45] That same year the new princeps arranged marriages for his two daughters: with Gnaeus Pompeius Magnus for (Claudia) Antonia, who had been born around 27 to Claudius and his second wife Aelia Paetina, and Lucius Junius Silanus for (Claudia) Octavia, his then-toddler daughter by his third wife Messalina.[46] Pompeius Magnus was descended from Pompey the Great on his mother's side,[47] and Junius Silanus was related to Augustus through his mother Aemilia Lepida, the daughter of Augustus' granddaughter Julia the Younger.[48] Claudius, scorned and ignored all his life, was concerned to surround himself with as many allies as possible.[49] Perhaps also at this time Claudius helped arrange the marriage of Agrippina to her second husband, Gaius Sallustius Crispus Passienus. Agrippina, now a widow, was only 26. Claudius was the *pater familias* of the imperial family. Both his predecessors had made sure to arrange marriages for younger female relatives, Tiberius for Agrippina the Younger, Drusilla, and Julia Livilla (see Chapter 1) and Caligula for Drusilla (Chapter 2).[50]

Agrippina's Second Marriage—Passienus

Agrippina's second marriage occurred long enough after her return to Rome for her to actively involve herself in seeking possible suitors. Suetonius' *Life of Galba* recounts that Agrippina so openly pursued Servius Sulpicius Galba, who was married at the time and would later become emperor, that Galba's mother-in-law quarreled with, and even slapped, her in a women's gathering.[51] Galba had been a protégé of Livia and boasted a social and political pedigree almost as high as that of the imperial family.[52] Suetonius' vignette, offered to stress Galba's sexual and marital propriety, incidentally reveals Agrippina's disrupting attempts at self-determination.[53]

In the end, however, and probably still in 41, Agrippina married Passienus.[54] Passienus knew Agrippina's relatives well, and he had surely spent time with her individually. His earlier marriage to one of Ahenobarbus' sisters, Domitia, connected him with the extended imperial family.[55] His own family included the renowned Republican historian Sallust.[56] Passienus was immensely wealthy, politically successful, an outstanding orator, highly cultured, and eccentric. His holdings included a house in Rome and an estate at Corne (near Tusculum, modern Tuscolo, Italy). Corne had a grove with a beautiful beech tree that so enamored him that he would lie under it, anoint it with costly wine, and kiss and embrace it.[57] Did the bucolic setting of this odd behavior attract Agrippina, later famous for her love of birds?[58]

Passienus was also notorious for sycophancy toward the emperors. His *Life* gives some memorable instances. His first speech in the senate cleverly accorded with Tiberius' professed deference to that group by commencing, "Conscript fathers and you, Caesar"; Tiberius praised it fulsomely.[59] Later, Passienus would run alongside Caligula's litter as the young emperor was carried through Rome. When Caligula once asked him whether he had sex with his own sister, as Caligula did with his, he replied "Not yet"—an answer the *Life* praises as fitting and cautious since it neither accused the emperor by denying the allegation nor dishonored Passienus with a lie by admitting it.[60] Less fawning is the verdict of Passienus that Tacitus quotes in an evaluation of Caligula and Tiberius: "The world had never known a better slave or a worse master."[61] Although Passienus was probably even older than Agrippina's first husband, Ahenobarbus (his first consulship had been in 27; Ahenobarbus' was in 32), Passienus' honors, refinement, wealth, and survival skills were appealing as Agrippina looked for stability in Rome in 41.

The Problem of Messalina and Other Troubles of Early Claudian Rome

Agrippina's sister Julia Livilla did not fare as well in the days after the sisters' return. Among the disreputable acts Cassius Dio attributes to Claudius' third wife is Messalina's destruction of "her niece" Julia Livilla in 41, because the "young woman" did not treat her with sufficient honor or adulation, was extremely beautiful, and was often alone with Claudius. Actual charges included adultery and obscurely involved the philosopher and writer Lucius Annaeus Seneca. Julia Livilla was exiled to Pandateria and killed within the year; Seneca was exiled to Corsica.[62] The terms Cassius Dio uses, "niece" and "young woman," veil that Julia Livilla actually was older than Messalina.[63] The note of her frequent presence with Claudius, however, accords with his renewed stress on the imperial family writ large.[64] The "conspiracy" of Julia Livilla and Seneca is obscure. This is the earliest known association of Julia Livilla and Agrippina with Seneca, whom Agrippina would later have recalled from exile in Corsica to be appointed as Nero's tutor (Chapter 4).[65] Despite the murkiness surrounding Julia Livilla's banishment and death in 41, the note underscores both the unpredictability of Claudian Rome and ancient historians' tendency to attribute misuse of power to women close to dominant men.

The many uncertainties of Julia Livilla's downfall, including its precise date in 41, should not distract us from its likely chilling effect on Agrippina. She was now the last of her once flourishing family, all of whom—other than Drusilla—had died violently or mysteriously. Sometime after her own marriage to Claudius in 49, Agrippina would commemorate Julia Livilla and other unfortunate siblings in a funerary monument near the Mausoleum of Augustus (Chapter 4).[66] In the meantime, Rome must have seemed ever more dangerous.

A story Suetonius recounts indicates Messalina's notoriously lethal jealousy and Agrippina's own audacious wiliness. About the time that Agrippina returned from banishment and reclaimed her influence, a snake in Nero's bedroom supposedly scared away men Messalina had sent to kill the napping boy. Agrippina put the snake's skin, sloughed off in the bed, into a gold bracelet Nero wore for much of his life.[67] Snakes were viewed as propitious, especially for great leaders. In the second century BCE Scipio Africanus had tacitly encouraged the rumor that his own conception was due to a serpent as had been that of Alexander the Great.[68] Closer to Agrippina is one omen of Augustus' greatness, that a snake had visited his mother, Atia, when she fell asleep during a midnight service at a Temple of Apollo. The serpent left on Atia a mark like a snake, unmistakably indicating that her baby born nine months later was the son of Apollo.[69] Agrippina's talismanic armband with a snakeskin, which Nero unluckily threw away in his last days in 68,[70] embodies her aspirations for her son.

Probably in spring or summer 42,[71] presumably only a short time after the alleged attempt on the young Nero, Messalina figures largely in the "Revolt of Scribonianus," a short-lived rebellion in 42 involving individuals in Rome and led by the imperial legate in Dalmatia (on the eastern shores of the Adriatic). The revolt is poorly documented, and its exact causes and extent may never be known.[72] Cassius Dio connects its beginnings to Messalina in a report attributing the princeps' worst excesses to his wives and freedmen.[73] One outrage was that in 42 Claudius had recalled Gaius Appius Junius Silanus from governing Hispania Citerior to make him marry Messalina's mother, Domitia Lepida. In a story recounted by both Cassius Dio and Suetonius, Messalina then demanded Junius Silanus have sex with her, the daughter of his intended. When he refused—somehow offending Claudius' imperial freedman Narcissus as well—she and Narcissus tag-teamed to invent and exaggerate an ominous dream in which Silanus killed Claudius. This persuaded the terrified princeps to condemn Silanus to death.[74] The anecdote, however far-fetched, is fundamental to the villainous image of Claudius' third wife.[75] Cassius Dio considers Messalina's intrigues for Silanus' death the catalyst for Scribonianus' revolt, since Silanus' fate convinced the elite in Rome that the new regime's promises were untrustworthy.[76]

Numerous influential individuals reportedly involved themselves in the conspiracy and revolt, although only a few are named.[77] Agrippina has possible links to one leader. The plot in Rome included the senators Annius Vinicianus and Pomponius Secundus, who had both been involved in Caligula's assassination and discussions of restoring the Republic, and Aulus Caecina Paetus, whose wife Arria heroically faced reckoning after the conspiracy was exposed.[78] But in Dalmatia the revolt was spearheaded by Lucius Arruntius Camillus Scribonianus, who commanded the VII and XI legions there. Agrippina must have known this man well:[79] in 32 Scribonianus had shared the eponymous consulship with her first husband, Ahenobarbus.[80]

The Revolt of Scribonianus reportedly lasted only five days. It panicked Claudius. Scribonianus' troops were reluctant to march against the new emperor, however, and when dire omens were seen, the unrest fizzled. Scribonianus fled to the island of Issa (now Vis, Croatia), where he died.[81] In Dalmatia the two legions and select individuals were honored for their loyalty to Claudius.[82] The repercussions of the conspiracy were severe: Vinicianus committed suicide, and consular and equestrian alleged accomplices also fell, reportedly because Messalina, Narcissus, and other imperial freedman exploited Claudius' innate terror.[83] Given Agrippina's connections to Julia Livilla, killed in 41 for some mysterious plot, and to Scribonianus, who actually led a revolt against the princeps, it was a good time for her to be away.

Agrippina in the East, 42/43

An interesting honorary inscription from the island of Kos (in the Aegean's Greek Dodecanese) shows that Agrippina accompanied her new husband, Passienus, to his proconsulship of Asia in 42/43. She thus followed the precedent of her ancestors: her grandparents Julia the Elder and Agrippa had travelled together to the East (16/15–14 BCE), as had her parents, Agrippina the Elder and Germanicus (17–19 CE). It is doubtful that Agrippina brought Nero with her, although her parents and grandparents had travelled with children.[84] Indeed, the inscription of 42/43 singularly focuses on her. Sometime after Agrippina married Claudius in 49 the white marble plaque from 42/43, with its primary honorary text for Agrippina, was turned over and its back reused for a second inscription. Both short Greek texts repay scrutiny.

The earlier inscription, once on the base of a (now lost) statue found in the Asclepios precinct on Kos, reads, "The People [of Kos] set up [this statue of] Agrippina the daughter of Germanicus Caesar, the wife of the proconsul Gaius Sallustius Crispus Passienus, ancestral patroness of the people" (42/43 CE).[85] This is our only evidence for Agrippina being with her husband as he performed his official duties in Rome's province of Asia, but by this time such travel was not rare. She is among a handful of women—all Roman proconsuls' wives—honored at the Asclepeion of Kos. More unusually, she is the only wife of a Roman administrator in the East who was herself acclaimed as a patroness of the people.[86] Perhaps Agrippina actually distributed some benefactions while on the island.

At the very least, the inscription reflects Agrippina's own high standing. She is identified by her father, the beloved Germanicus, and her status as patroness is termed "ancestral." The memory of Agrippina's own family was still alive in the Greek East.[87] Agrippa and later members of her family had been honored at Kos as benefactors, and dedications for Caligula and Drusilla from the island similarly qualify each as "ancestral benefactor."[88]

Augustus himself, with two known portraits now documented on Kos, was called its "founder and benefactor."[89] We can well imagine Agrippina's pride at the accolades to her, so congruent with those of her unique family.

Agrippina received further honors at Kos, although she is not known to have returned to the island. Her later tributes are tied to her marriage to Claudius in 49: for example, one inscription honored Agrippina *Sebastè* (Augusta) *Demeter Carpophora* (fruit-bearer) alongside Claudius *Zeus Sotèr* (Savior) in a familiar demonstration of provincial loyalty.[90] More significant is the repurposing of her honors of 42/43. Sometime between 50 and 54 the marble plaque was turned over and its formerly back side inscribed and displayed.[91] The second text, which lacks the decorative margin around the first, reads, "The People [of Kos] set up [this statue of] Julia Augusta Agrippina, the wife of Augustus Tiberius Claudius Caesar Germanicus Imperator, the savior and founder of the city."[92] Agrippina is here identified as Julia Augusta Agrippina,[93] the wife of Augustus Tiberius Claudius Caesar Germanicus. Her position subordinate to him is clear in the fact that now it is not she but he who is honored as "the city's savior and founder." Claudius is not documented as traveling with Agrippina as his wife to Kos or elsewhere in the Greek East.[94] This inscription of 50–54 reflects the tight connections of the emperor with this island where his trusted physician and aide, Gaius Stertinius Xenophon, was born and trained.[95]

The Kos inscription from 42/43 speaks both to Agrippina's own distinction and to the continuing importance of Germanicus and his family in the Greek East. It also suggests Agrippina's good luck: her presence there with Passienus, Rome's proconsul of Asia in 42/43, removed her from Rome during the Revolt of Scribonianus and its bloody aftermath. Although we might well imagine her delight in visiting Ephesus and other famed cities of Asia during her husband's year as governor there, nothing documents her in Rome's most prestigious province other than in Kos. She cannot be traced again until early 44, when she must have been in the capital when Passienus assumed his second consulship in January. But before then other momentous events took place in Claudius' Rome.

The War in Britain (43–44)—and Agrippina's Detachment

In 43 Rome entered a war in Britain, providing an external focus that might reunify Claudius with both the elite and the military after the Revolt of Scribonianus.[96] Claudius used the glorious military undertaking in Britain also as yet another way to promote his family and bolster his backers: for example, his sons-in-law accompanied him when he personally went to the scene of operations.[97] The war was declared accomplished in 44 after Claudius' own brief participation in the invasion, even though serious uprisings continued on the island for years (see Chapter 4). Most relevant to Agrippina is the prominence Claudius' wife Messalina gained in the celebrations of Claudius' victory.

In Claudius' triumph of 44, the first for a ruling emperor since that of Augustus in 19 BCE, Messalina appeared in an honorific *carpentum* behind Claudius' triumphal chariot.[98] Messalina is the first imperial woman unequivocally honored during her lifetime by use of the *carpentum*.[99] Just as significantly, she is unique in riding in a triumphal procession.[100] Messalina was also granted by the senate the right to sit in the front seats at games, a privilege she immediately used in Claudius' triumphal games.[101] Her son with Claudius was renamed "Britannicus," a permanent reminder of the victorious war.[102] Claudius' young wife was undeniably exalted. Her distinctions raised her almost to the heights Agrippina, Drusilla, and Julia Livilla had reached in the early days of Caligula's rule. Although Roman citizens were not enjoined to include Messalina in annual prayers and oaths, Claudius' wife now could sit in the front rows at spectacles as had Livia, Agrippina, her sisters, and Antonia the Younger. Further, Claudius' wife had an assigned part in the triumphal procession. Agrippina had ridden in her father Germanicus' triumphal chariot in 17 CE, in Rome's last triumph before that of Claudius in 44, but she had been one of five anonymous children. Messalina, the mother of the emperor's son, had ridden in her own *carpentum* behind Claudius' chariot.

No account of Claudius' triumph or related activities specifically notes Agrippina. Nonetheless, she must have witnessed the triumph of 44 in person: she was, after all, Claudius' niece and the wife of one of the highest-placed senators in Claudius' court. Other members of Claudius' family, his sons-in-law Pompeius and Silanus, personally attended Claudius at the culmination of the triumph on the steps of the Capitoline Temple of Jupiter Optimus Maximus. Claudius had also specially invited to the triumphal celebration exiles and individuals who were abroad administering provinces.[103] Further, Messalina was undoubtedly honored in the Claudian family monuments created or renovated to permanently commemorate the emperor's victory, the triumphal arch spanning the Via Lata in central Rome (the Arch of Claudius) and at least two nearby statuary installations.[104] One can well imagine Agrippina's jealousy as she watched Messalina preening in the spotlight.

Agrippina was surely in Rome in January 44, moreover, when her husband Passienus assumed a second consulship.[105] Second consulships were an imperial marker of prestige and trust that began only with Claudius.[106] Passienus' second consulship was all the more remarkable because he was a *consul ordinarius*, that is, one of the consular pair giving their names to the year. It indicates continued good relations between him—and presumably his wife Agrippina—and the court. But Passienus served only a few weeks. One of Rome's official calendars for January 44 lists Publius Pomponius Secundus as suffect consul (substitute consul) alongside Passienus' eponymous co-consul, Titus Statilius Taurus.[107] For some unknown reason Passienus was no longer serving.

The brevity of Passienus' second consulship suggests to some that he died in January 44; others more cautiously date his death merely before 47.[108] The *Life of Passienus* holds that he was "slain by the treachery of Agrippina, whom he had made his heir" and that he was honored with a public funeral. Although we have no idea of the cause of his death, it is hard to imagine that Agrippina deliberately killed the man who had brought her stability and wealth after her return from exile in 41. His public funeral, like his second consulship, indicates continuing official favor for him, and his tomb on the Via Appia was maintained into the 90s CE.[109] Another consideration is that the markedly negative accounts of Messalina suggest that single women were in particular danger from the young empress.[110] Agrippina, already suspect because of her "conspiracy" against Caligula in 39 and her sister Julia Livilla's "conspiracy" against Claudius' new regime in 41, would be a particularly obvious target once she inherited Passienus' vast wealth, which the *Life of Passienus* reports as two hundred million sesterces.[111]

Domestic Intrigue in the Mid-40s

After Passienus' consulship in January 44 there is even less trace of Agrippina until 47 and 48. Our deficient sources for the mid-40s are much more concerned with Messalina, if they attend to women at all. Agrippina barely appears in the lengthy treatments by Cassius Dio, Tacitus, and others of

Messalina's escalating transgressions, which they attribute to monstrous sexual lust and greed and which culminate in her fatal, bigamous marriage to Gaius Silius in 47.[112] Messalina reportedly worked closely with imperial freedmen (and select others) to accomplish her vicious aims, exemplifying the trope of Claudius' subservience to women and the formerly enslaved.[113] The most renowned of this latter group, who gained unusually great influence and high position in Claudius' court, were Narcissus, the supervisor of correspondence; Polybius, in charge perhaps of documentation; Pallas, supervisor of imperial finances; and Callistus, supervisor of appeals.[114] In pairs or small groups these traditionally scorned individuals—a woman and freedmen—allegedly exploited Claudius' fear and absentmindedness, as with the death of Gaius Appius Junius Silanus in 42. At times their motivation was said to be simple monetary greed—at other times, fear, rancor, jealousy, lust, and other base impulses.[115]

Messalina's actions are now often interpreted as political maneuvering to ensure the succession of her son Britannicus, rather than the "folly" or "nymphomania" Tacitus, Juvenal, and others ascribe to her.[116] Here, I am concerned not with judging Messalina but rather with sketching out the probable circumstances in these years when Agrippina, the niece of the emperor, lived as a wealthy widow with a young child. Although a precise timeline cannot be established, the survey of deaths and humiliations attributed to Claudius' third wife suggests a dangerously capricious imperial court in the 40s. Many of the victims were closely connected to Messalina and Claudius.

The list begins with Agrippina's sister Julia Livilla, banished and killed in 41, and with Messalina's intended stepfather, Junius Silanus, condemned in 42: two cases attributed to Messalina's lust and sexual insecurity. In 43 Messalina allegedly orchestrated the death of Julia, the daughter of Claudius' sister Livilla and Drusus the Younger, because of jealousy.[117] Julia Livilla's former husband Vinicius died in 46, purportedly poisoned by Messalina, who was angered about his refusal to have sex with her. (Cassius Dio also reports that this distinguished man, who had served as consul twice and received a state funeral, had survived "by keeping quiet and minding his own business"—behavior and honors reminiscent of Agrippina's second husband, Passienus, and indicating the perils of the Claudian court.[118]) The following year, 47, Valerius Asiaticus also fell: like Vinicius, Asiaticus had been involved in 41 in the senatorial debate about restoring the Republic. His death resulted not only from this history, recalled to Claudius by the imperial freedman Sosibius.[119] Messalina allegedly encouraged Claudius' paranoia about Asiaticus simply because she was keen to hurt Asiaticus' mistress Poppaea Sabina, her rival for the attentions of the actor Mnester. In this mess she managed also to force Poppaea Sabina to suicide.[120] Others reportedly cut down by Messalina's intrigues include a praetorian guard, Catonius Justus (in 43), the senators Asinius Gallus and Taurus Statilius Corvinus (in 46),[121] and Pompeius Magnus (in 47), who had married Claudius' daughter Antonia in 42.[122] Messalina even turned against her own agents of doom: for instance, by 48 she is said to have engineered the death of the imperial freedman Polybius, although he had helped her destroy others.[123]

By one account, Claudius brought about the deaths of 35 senators, 221 equestrians, and an uncountable number of others,[124] and the ancient authors' many notices of Messalina underline her instrumentality as she preyed on Claudius' credulous frights and collaborated with her venal minions.[125] Agrippina could not have been blind to what was happening, and she would have been stupid not to fear for her own life and that of her young son. Besides the women just named, others were cited as Messalina's targets: the innumerable individuals Messalina and the imperial freedmen brought down after the Revolt of Scribonianus in 42 included various women publicly punished in Rome whose bodies thrown down the Gemonian Steps.[126] Messalina is also said to have humiliated her ostensible peers by forcing them to have sex in the imperial residence in front of their husbands.[127] Even if some of these allegations are false—the last, for example, is a stock charge against tyrants—Rome in the mid-40s was a perilous and unstable place. Whether or not Messalina orchestrated the many deaths attributed to her, the imperial court abounded with individuals clawing for their own status by diminishing others around them.

Some insight into the court is provided by the sycophantic *Consolatio ad Polybium*, which Seneca, the later confidant of Agrippina, composed from his exile in Corsica in 43/44. Addressing one of Claudius' powerful freedmen, Polybius, on the occasion of the death of Polybius' brother, Seneca flatters the imperial secretary for his Stoic and historical pursuits and urges him to intercede with Claudius to rescind his exile (see esp. *Cons. Polyb.* section 6). Building from statements such as "You owe your entire self to Caesar" (*Cons. Polyb.* sect. 7) and "Caesar will possess your entire being" (sect. 8), Seneca fulsomely praises Claudius' clemency, "singularly retentive memory," and "practiced eloquence." He includes a long section detailing the many woeful deaths befalling the imperial family from the time of Augustus,[128] a passage that may strike modern readers as inopportune. Awash with abject fawning, Seneca's consolation piece now is a difficult read.[129] Its tone is particularly jarring when contrasted to the later *Apocolocyntosis*, a satire of Claudius' divinization credited to Seneca that we discuss in Chapter 5.[130] The *Consolatio ad Polybium* illuminates the inflated *personae* and vigilant self-policing of those in the emperor's entourage.

Perhaps Agrippina, Claudius' own niece later accused of exploiting familial ties to seduce her uncle,[131] could be more outspoken: it is hard now to imagine her suppressing herself for long. If she did speak up, it has left no trace. The lack of information about Agrippina in the mid-40s has led Barrett, for example, to assume that she was intentionally out of Rome in those years.[132] Perhaps: Rome's turbulence after the Revolt of Scribonianus in 42, when Agrippina was away in the East with Passienus, had undoubtedly convinced her of the virtues of lying low. But we should also note that the first mention of Agrippina in the late 40s comes from Tacitus' *Annals*, soon after the extant manuscript resumes coverage of Roman history sometime in the first half of 47.

Agrippina and the Downfall of Messalina

The opening chapters of Tacitus' extant *Annals* 11 include a report on Agrippina and Nero at Claudius' celebration of the *ludi saeculares* in early summer 47.[133] Claudius had called this city-wide festival to mark Rome's new beginning on what he reckoned as the 800th anniversary of Rome's foundation.[134] Among the ceremonies was the equestrian Game of Troy, in which rode noble boys including Britannicus and Agrippina's son. Tacitus notes that the latter, then known as Lucius Domitius but as Nero after adoption by Claudius,[135] received more popular acclaim than did Claudius' own son Britannicus. This was interpreted as portending Nero's coming ascendancy over his younger relative (Nero was about 9 and Britannicus, 6). Further, Tacitus holds, the memory of Germanicus swayed the people to Nero, Germanicus' last male descendant, who himself was rumored to have had good omens.[136] The historian's added comment, "Pity was rising for [Nero's] mother Agrippina because of the savagery of Messalina, a woman always dangerously agitated and at that time even more impetuous since she blazed with the fire of a new craving," incidentally documents Agrippina's presence in the city, as it leads directly into a description of Messalina's unusual sexual liaison—which he calls akin to madness—for Gaius Silius. This brought about Messalina's ruin.[137]

This notice has led some to infer that Messalina's ill-fated liaison with Silius in 48 was an attempt to strengthen her position in the face of Agrippina's "growing influence," to preclude Agrippina from making an imperial claim for Nero.[138] Perhaps—but no other evidence supports this.[139] Rather, Tacitus' remark is part of an overall contrast of Claudius' last two wives picked up elsewhere in the *Annals*.[140] Agrippina does not appear in his masterful and extensive depiction of Messalina's "marriage" to Silius that takes up about half of the extant Book 11.[141] His brilliant narrative and others' information have been investigated elsewhere and will not be recounted fully here, nor will I delve into Messalina's planned "marriage" with Silius, which would have been completely illegal in Rome were she not to have divorced Claudius.[142] My focus is on Agrippina's possible involvement. I can find none, a surprising absence especially in light of Agrippina's marriage to Claudius within a year of Messalina's death.[143]

Although inferring *ex silentio*, I believe that during the quick-paced events that led to Messalina's death in autumn 48, Agrippina had again left Rome.[144] Agrippina was neither among the invitees to the "wedding" and its accompanying Bacchanalian revel, nor among the many confidants informing and counseling Claudius in Ostia, where he happened to be sacrificing on the day of the "wedding."[145] She had no role in Messalina's pitiful journey on a rubbish cart to intercept Claudius on his return from Ostia, or in the attempts of Octavia, Britannicus, and the Vestal Virgin Vibidia to deflect Claudius' ire from his wife.[146] Further, Agrippina is not noted at the imperial feasts—a suitable venue for Claudius' niece—at which the emperor decided Messalina's fate and later impassively heard of her execution. In 48 Agrippina is not linked in any way to the elite imperial freedmen who orchestrated Messalina's death in the Lucullan Gardens in Rome, most obviously Narcissus, who extraordinarily assumed temporary supervision of the praetorians for the execution of the deed, and Pallas, who was later rumored as Agrippina's sexual partner (Chapter 4).[147] Agrippina's name does not appear when the narrative turns to Lucius Vitellius, Claudius' intimate who later became her fierce promoter (Chapter 4). We cannot link Agrippina with any of the eleven individuals Tacitus names as co-conspirators of Messalina and Silius[148] or with any of the eight Suetonius and Cassius Dio enumerate as executed.[149]

Admittedly, the historians' narrative focus on Messalina and Claudius might inhibit mention of others. But had Agrippina any influence or hand in these events, the hostile tradition about her would surely have ensured its record. Further, others involved in Messalina's folly are named.[150] Perhaps after the Secular Games of 47 Agrippina retired with Nero to one of her country villas, at Antium, Maevania, or Tusculum.[151] In any case, she is notably absent from reports about events that mattered in Rome until after Messalina's death in 48.

Agrippina's Luck Turns Again

Immediately thereafter, however, Agrippina emerges as savvy, commanding, and manipulative in another unforgettable Tacitean vignette, the deliberations about Claudius' fourth wife. This remarkably opens Tacitus' *Annals* 12 rather than being grouped with other events of 48 at the end of *Annals* 11.[152] The historian launches Book 12 of the *Annals* with the power struggle of three Claudian freedmen as each promoted a different marriage candidate for Claudius, "intolerant as he was of celibate life and submissive to his wives' commands."[153] The candidates were Lollia Paulina, married to Caligula briefly in 38 and granddaughter of Marcus Lollius, a trusted confidant of Augustus (see Chapter 2); Julia Agrippina, identified as "the offspring of Germanicus"; and Aelia Paetina, Claudius' second wife and from the noble family of the Tuberones.[154] All three had the assets of noble birth, attractive looks, and wealth. Lollia Paulina was supported by Callistus, Agrippina by Pallas, and Aelia Paetina by Narcissus. The three freedmen had been involved in Messalina's death, Narcissus most of all.

In a parody of serious imperial consultations and of the mythological beauty contest on Mt. Ida that led to the Trojan War, Tacitus' indecisive Claudius summoned his freedmen to a "council" (*concilium*) where they could openly argue their cases. Pallas pushed three advantages for Agrippina: she brought along Germanicus' grandson as her son; she belonged to both Julian and Claudian families; and she could still have children who would continue this brilliant lineage. Pallas' arguments outweighed those of his fellows. Agrippina, or so we are told, furthered her lead by seducing her uncle (see Chapter 4). At the beginning of a new book in his history of imperial Rome, Tacitus thus signals that Agrippina will be a major player not only for the lineage she paraded but also for the child she had borne and the wiles she practiced. Our own next chapter starts with the circumstances of this union, formerly forbidden because marriage between an uncle and niece was considered incest. It enabled the consolidation of Agrippina's "wifely power" over Claudius.[155]

Agrippina the Younger: A Dangerous Woman in Rome's Early Empire. Mary T. Boatwright, Oxford University Press.
 DOI: 10.1093/9780190945855.003.0004

4

At Last, at the Center (49–54 CE)

Introduction

In January 49 CE Agrippina married her uncle, the emperor Claudius, uniting herself and her preteen son with Claudius and the children Messalina had born to him, Octavia (then 9 or 10) and Britannicus (who would turn 8 on 12 February).[1] From this point on, Agrippina emerges much more clearly than before. Her five years at Claudius' side, arguably the most stable years of his rule,[2] are relatively fully documented, although ancient historians concentrate on the beginning and the end of the period while holding for Agrippina's "almost male dominance" of Rome.[3] Tacitus offers particularly memorable vignettes that represent her thoughts and utterances as well as those of others about her.[4] The historians' bias toward reporting Agrippina's transgressiveness and immorality obscures the lack of information about her choices and adjustments. Contemporary documentary evidence, however—inscriptions, coins and other visual sources, and incidental notes—adds information about Agrippina in settings and situations traditionally off-limits to women. She does not falter in her undertakings. Yet her august lineage, apparent aptitude, and political shrewdness could not outweigh her handicap as a woman. Agrippina could never be personally acknowledged as a ruler in the Roman world. The unyielding patriarchal system ensured that she could at most influence a man who had real power or *imperium*.[5] Her own capacities were necessarily limited by the abilities of the men closest to her. In this five-year period, it was Claudius, seemingly malleable until he was not, who held the power.

A Wider Perspective on the Marriage

Agrippina was neither foolish nor passive. As Pallas had noted when enumerating her potential advantages as Claudius' wife, she had birthed Germanicus' grandson, someone worthy of the imperial power.[6] But in fact she had a weak support system in 47 and 48. She was almost completely bereft of family other than Claudius himself. She had seen the suspicious deaths and murders of her parents and most of her siblings,[7] and her younger sister Drusilla had unexpectedly died in 38 at the height of her beauty and influence. Further, Agrippina had outlived two politically prominent and wealthy husbands, and she had alienated at least some of her peers over the years.[8] Withdrawal from Rome may have saved her in the unpredictable years of Messalina's influence, but it had also removed her from interaction with the politically powerful. She had witnessed Messalina, personally or through gossip, at the dizzying heights of her bold scheming and at her miserable downfall and death, which extended to memory sanctions against her.[9] Although she must have remained vivid in Agrippina's mind, the obliteration and destruction of Messalina's name and memorials throughout Rome and elsewhere were a powerful reminder of the fleeting, even dangerous nature of good fortune and high status in Rome.[10]

Agrippina knew Claudius personally from her childhood in the imperial residences and later familial gatherings, and she must have realized the potential dangers and benefits of marrying him. Yet the visibility and influence Messalina had obtained were amazing. Another consideration was Claudius himself. Perhaps he was not so personally loathsome as some sources imply by emphasizing his illnesses and quirks: the *Apocolocyntosis*, so full of barbed criticism, also notes his tall stature and full head of shining white hair.[11] Although we cannot date Agrippina's *Commentarii* that focused on her family's history, it shared interests with Claudius' many historical works, many dating to when he was growing up in the imperial residences. One of his planned works in Latin was a two-book Roman history beginning with the murder of Julius Caesar, which he had to discontinue because of family pressure from those descended from Antony.[12] He shared with Agrippina a fascination with his extended family and its impact on the history of Rome. Did she see him as an intellectual equal?

Other calculations are less speculative. Agrippina—really, any thinking woman of the time—could foresee an uncertain future for the fourth wife of this princeps. When advocating for the marriage, Lucius Vitellius boasted to the senate that Claudius had always "kept to his own wives," meaning that he did not engage in adultery with women of senatorial or equestrian standing.[13] His famed "uxoriousness" was sporadic, however, and always paired with promiscuity. He divorced his first wife, Plautia Urgulanilla, for "scandalous misbehavior, suspicion of murder," and presumed infidelity;

his second, Aelia Paetina, for "slighter offenses."[14] How trivial these latter were is suggested by Paetina as one of the three candidates proposed as Claudius' (fourth) wife after Messalina's death in 48.[15] Further, Claudius' conduct in 47 and 48, during and after the dangerous scandal of Messalina with Silius, had displayed weakness and indecision. He had been convinced of the affair only after validation from his two most trusted sexual partners, the freedwomen Calpurnia and Cleopatra, and Messalina had been executed without a public hearing and on the urging of freedmen.[16] Claudius had been unsteady as a husband and continued so as emperor.[17]

In 48/49 this fourth princeps of Rome was in the ninth year of a reign notable for highs and lows.[18] Agrippina, as we have seen, surprisingly had escaped the dangerous aftermaths of the Revolt of Scribonianus in 42, Messalina's lethal intrigues, and the plotting and downfall of Messalina's "marriage" to Silius in 47–48. Agrippina was similarly absent from Claudius' great achievements, the invasion of Britain in 43 and his triumph in 44. After 44 Claudius had continued to assert Rome's stability and growth in efforts that were often met with derision and resistance. When he was censor with Lucius Vitellius in 47/48, Claudius had advocated for select provincials' inclusion in the senate and celebrated a new beginning for Rome through holding its Secular Games; he received but mixed success.[19] When in 48 he extended the *pomerium*, Rome's sacred boundary, this too was questioned by Rome's *intelligentsia*.[20] Further, conflict spearheaded by the tribal king Caratacus continued troubling Rome in its new province of Britannia, putting the lie to Claudius' magnificent triumph. And, of course, Claudius' family and *familia* were shaken to the core when his wife, related distantly to Augustus, was killed at the order of imperial freedmen.[21] By the end of 48 Claudius' image as Rome's leader had been badly tarnished.[22]

At this moment Agrippina could be an asset for Claudius in Rome and the empire. Alongside her own steel resolve, a great boon for any counselor,[23] she could boost his general approval. His original backing had come from the praetorian guard, and in turn he had given them donatives, visibility, and unusual privileges (see Chapter 3). Agrippina, the last of Germanicus' family so revered by the praetorians, would reinforce this indispensable aid.[24] She had always maintained her ties to Germanicus and her natal family, to judge from monuments in Rome and elsewhere (later in this chapter and Chapter 5).[25] As Claudius' new wife she might help him redress his relations with senators and equestrians, who were appalled and terrified by the notorious cases attributed to Messalina and evidently condoned by

Claudius. At the start of his reign Claudius had carefully canvassed for wide support, on the one hand selecting relatively new military men for the British expedition and, on the other, choosing sons-in-law from outstandingly elite families. He had initiated the practice of second consulships for worthy individuals, granted triumphal ornaments to men outside the imperial family, and created new patrician families:[26] all gratifying marks of prestige for Rome's elite. But executions and simmering suspicions after the Revolt of Scribonius, an erratic court, and Claudius' perceived severity during his year as censor with Vitellius (47/48)[27] undermined much, if not all, of the goodwill Claudius had won. Agrippina's own lineage and her connections through her two former husbands could buttress her new husband's positive image among Rome's powerbrokers.

The most obvious benefit Agrippina could deliver to Claudius and the state, however, is the one we began with: her son, deemed suitable for the imperial position because he was Germanicus' grandson and directly related to Augustus himself.[28] By the end of 49 Agrippina's son with Ahenobarbus would be 12 years old. The three-year advantage Lucius Domitius Ahenobarbus (the later Nero) had on Britannicus may now seem trivial, but in Rome it placed Agrippina's son at an age when he could be distinguished as Claudius' successor, something for which Britannicus was still too young.[29] Marriage to her uncle offered Agrippina access to political influence and perhaps even action, as well as hope for a future in which her son would be more than just another senator subject to imperial whims.

Sex, Incest, and Power among the Julio-Claudians

Agrippina's marriage to her paternal uncle Claudius in 49, illegal when first proposed, may now seem the logical conclusion of imperial practices. From the beginning of the principate, the various families associated with Augustus and Livia had often conducted endogamous marriages and liaisons, even ones that strike modern sensibilities as incestuous or at least inappropriately intimate[30] (see Genealogy). As early as 25 BCE, just two years after Augustus consolidated autocratic power in the guise of the "first constitutional settlement," he had wed his daughter Julia (the Elder) to his nephew Marcus Claudius Marcellus (see Chapter 1).[31] Agrippina the Elder, the granddaughter of Augustus, and Germanicus, the grandson of Livia, had finally united the Julian and Claudian families, a great advantage that

Pallas made sure to cite when proposing their daughter Agrippina as Claudius' wife (see Chapter 3).[32] Agrippina herself, as well as her sisters Drusilla and Julia Livilla, allegedly engaged in incestuous sex with their brother Caligula; rumors held even that Caligula planned to bequeath the empire to Drusilla (Chapter 2). Messalina, Claudius' third wife, was a distant relation of Claudius. The ruin of Agrippina's youngest sister, Julia Livilla, in 41 is credited to intimacy with her uncle Claudius (Chapter 3). Similarly, the lead-up to Agrippina's choice as Claudius' fourth wife includes the detail that Agrippina often used her "niece's privilege of kissing and caressing Claudius" to ensnare her older uncle.[33] The connection between sex and Rome's imperial rule was widely assumed.[34]

Agrippina is the instigator in the latter note, and its point is to accuse her of female manipulation and illicit sex. It sets up the discussion of Agrippina's proposed marriage to Claudius as illegal and incestuous by Roman law,[35] which prohibited marriages of uncles to nieces and of aunts to nephews.[36] The case for a special exemption was brought to the senate by Lucius Vitellius, Claudius' close ally and co-censor in 47/48, who by 51 became known as Agrippina's fiercest defender.[37] In Tacitus' long report a large boisterous crowd of the *populus*, as well as some senators, vehemently promote the exemption for Agrippina and Claudius.[38] Thus encouraged, Claudius himself goes to the Forum to request senatorial approval of marriages between uncles and the daughters of their brothers (Tac. *Ann.* 12.7.1–2). Agrippina herself surely kept demurely out of sight during the proceedings. She did not yet have the clout she would gain as the emperor's wife—and later as an emperor's mother—that might embolden her to enter senatorial proceedings, long forbidden to her gender.[39] Emphasizing traditional disapproval of marriage between two such closely related individuals, both Tacitus and Suetonius report that the uncle-niece marriage of Claudius and Agrippina found almost no imitators.[40] Yet the cameo from Vienna that pairs Claudius and Agrippina the Younger with Germanicus and Agrippina the Elder (Ill. Intro.1) shows that at least some in the court celebrated the ties.

Agrippina's Wifely Power (*potentia uxoria*)

In Tacitus' *Annals* the marriage, and the radical means to achieve it, lead directly to Agrippina's dominance of Rome. After the proleptic note that the only other man who married his brother's daughter was the Roman knight

Alledius Severus, "who, most said, wanted to curry Agrippina's favor,"[41] the Tacitean report of the senatorial decree and its aftermath becomes a trenchant statement about the degradation of Rome under the principate. The historian scathingly summarizes the moment and Agrippina herself. I translate Tacitus' Latin, bolding words and phrases I then discuss:

> "From this point on the state was overturned, and all obeyed a woman who did not **deride** the Roman state through **carnality**, as had Messalina. Groveling **obeisance** was enforced, **almost like that to a man**; moral **rectitude** was on show, and arrogance even more; there was no **sexual deviance** at home unless it served to gain **power**. An **immeasurable desire for gold** had the excuse that it was being amassed as the foundation for **despotic rule**." (*Ann.* 12.7.3)[42]

The ringing condemnation is as unforgettable as it is vague. Loaded words and phrases, especially relating to slavishness and servitude, join others equally anathema to elite Roman men, such as despotic rule (viz., kingship) and dominating power.[43] At the same time the passage expresses stinging contempt for women—the new "master"—in vocabulary typical of beliefs in female flightiness, lack of purpose, and innate, uncontrollable emotionalism. Agrippina, although not named, is presented as even more despicable than Messalina.[44] Her legalized marriage to her uncle, which allied her with Rome's ruling man, is a pivotal moment in Tacitus' history.

Hereafter, Claudius' wife Agrippina gains great visibility and engages more openly in political areas claimed by men, but she brought no revolution to Roman politics. She began to greet in public any who desired, a fact noted in Rome's public records—which implies the act was something official, even though elite men had always been able to greet the public.[45] Agrippina stage-managed great shows of support for herself by arranging in advance to have "the senate, the populace, and the soldiers . . . join together to show their approval of her demands on every occasion."[46] She manipulated Claudius, transferred to herself the loyalty of the imperial freedmen, and dominated Claudius' other supporters and clients "partly by fear and partly by favors."[47] One such client was Lucius Vitellius, Claudius' loyal ally who had served as consul with the emperor in 43—Vitellius' second consulship—and supervised Rome during Claudius' expedition to Britain that year. In 47 Vitellius had been consul for an extraordinary third time, again serving with Claudius, and then served alongside Claudius in a different, but even more prestigious, position as co-censor when Claudius revived this traditional magistracy with its oversight of the entire Roman state.[48] Vitellius had spearheaded the senatorial decree allowing uncles to marry their nieces.[49] By 51, as noted above, he would be described as Agrippina's "foremost promoter" or "fiercest defender:"[50] in the zero-sum court described by the historians, this suggests that he had deserted Claudius.

We can see some of the means Agrippina employed to gain influence. She eagerly amassed wealth: although many other women in Rome's highest echelons did the same, Tacitus damns Agrippina's endeavors as aimed at monarchical rule.[51] In contrast to Messalina, who reportedly turned against her allies such as Polybius (see Chapter 3), Agrippina rewarded hers: Pliny the Elder says he personally witnessed the senatorial decree of praetorian insignia to Pallas in 52 "at the bidding" of Agrippina.[52] In 52, according to Josephus, Agrippina mediated with Claudius on behalf of the Hasmonean king Agrippa II and the Jews during a conflict with the Samaritans.[53] This last note, one of the few that does not obviously curry favor for her son, shows Agrippina as a go-between for provincials with Rome, a fairly well-attested role for imperial women.[54] Indeed, earlier and later Roman women, private and imperial, engaged in such political interactions and paybacks to a greater or lesser extent and taking their cue from their male relatives in positions of power. Agrippina differed, at least according to Tacitus, in working openly and not behind the scenes. But her endeavors resembled those of most other Roman women in their ultimate aim, the promotion of a close male relation. In Agrippina's case this was her one and only son.[55]

All for the Son

Even before marrying Claudius in 49, Agrippina set her plans for her son into motion, according to the historians who attribute numerous changes of 49 and 50 solely to her. First, she tied her 12-year-old boy more closely to the ruling princeps by arranging his betrothal to Claudius' daughter Octavia. Domitius Ahenobarbus (known as Nero after adoption by Claudius) was two or so years older than Octavia and the marriage could not take place immediately: 12 was considered the minimum age for a bride. A more serious obstacle was the 10-year old Octavia's engagement to Lucius Junius Silanus, which Claudius had set in 41. Agrippina—"not yet wife but enjoying wifely power"—made Claudius suspect Silanus of incest with his sister

Junia Calvina. The betrothal to Silanus was broken off, and Octavia was engaged to Domitius Ahenobarbus (the later Nero).[56] Tacitus discredits the whole business, a "crime" he uses to suggest Agrippina's power over the weak and uxorious Claudius,[57] by labeling the affection between Silanus and his sister as not incestuous but ill-advisedly too unguarded.[58] It resulted in Silanus' removal from the senate and his praetorship and then his suicide on the very wedding day of Agrippina and Claudius. Junia Calvina was exiled from Italy.[59]

Agrippina was soon credited with another significant change bolstering her son: the recall of the learned Seneca from banishment on Corsica and his appointment as tutor for Nero. Seneca had been banished in 41 on obscure charges that included adultery with Agrippina's sister Julia Livilla; Messalina and Claudius were both involved (see Chapter 3). Although Suetonius ascribes the tutoring position to Claudius,[60] Cassius Dio and Tacitus credit Seneca's recall and appointment to Agrippina.[61] Tacitus provides the longest and most memorable report. He imputes to Agrippina two reasons for the change, both deepening her portrayal in the *Annals* as nefarious, hungry for domination, and manipulative (cp. his previous chapter, discussed in the previous section). First, she wanted to contrast her mounting "evil deeds" (picking up the "crime" of the Silanus affair) by demonstrating popular clemency to someone "famous for brilliant studies." Second was so that "[Nero's] youth might develop under such a teacher, and they might take advantage of his advice for domination, since it was thought that Seneca would be loyal to Agrippina thanks to the memory of this benefaction and was filled with hate for Claudius because of anger at his punishment." (Who "they" are is unspecified.[62]) Seneca was one of Rome's most outstanding writers and would prove himself just as astute in politics.[63] He apparently worked at least initially with Agrippina on Nero's education.[64] As we see in Chapter 5, however, he would falter in his loyalty to Agrippina as soon as Nero became princeps in 54.

Agrippina was responsible in 49 for further entanglements of Claudius with her son, or so Tacitus intimates. A consul designate of that year, Lucius Mammius Pollio, was induced "by huge promises" (anonymous in Tacitus' text) to beg Claudius to betroth Octavia to Domitius Ahenobarbus (the later Nero): as Tacitus puts it, this was not unthinkable given the age of the two but would open the way to more serious consequences. Pollio's motion is said to have differed hardly at all from the recent one of Vitellius (advocating Agrippina as Claudius' wife). The historian comments that the engagement that equaled this boy to Britannicus came about "thanks to a mother's exertions and the cunning guile of those who feared vengeance from the son of Messalina, whom they had accused."[65] Agrippina, not directly named, is signaled with the phrase *studiis matris* ("mother's exertions"). Her self-expedient accomplices must be the imperial freedmen instrumental in Messalina's downfall (see Chapter 3). Agrippina manipulates Claudian powerbrokers and takes every opportunity to further her son's prospects. [66]

These included, according to the historians, Claudius' official adoption of her son as his own on 25 February 50.[67] Tacitus details the process: first, pressure on Claudius by Agrippina's adherent Pallas, who cited the precedents of Augustus' and Tiberius' adoptions of young men; then, Claudius' speech to the senate; and finally, passage of a comitial law replete with flattery of Claudius and especially of Domitius Ahenobarbus.[68] In Tacitus' account Claudius is belittled as parroting a freedman's words, historically incorrect, and garbled in his speaking.[69] Reporting that the law officially transferred the youth into the Claudian house with the name of Nero (Nero Claudius Caesar Drusus Germanicus), the historian then notes that Agrippina was enhanced by the cognomen "Augusta" (a title discussed below).[70] The stress on names and titles obscures the substantial changes afoot.

Tacitus' history switches to report growing pity for Britannicus himself, who, abandoned little by little by even his servants, became living proof of the falsity of his stepmother's attention to him. This is followed by the comment that Britannicus' rumored natural abilities would never be tested, an ominous foreshadowing of the boy's death in 55.[71] Agrippina's immoderate and immodest scheming is furthered heightened by the note that Pallas was her lover.[72] The emphasis in Tacitus' *Annals* is on Agrippina's seizure of ever more gains for her son, to the detriment of Claudius' boy Britannicus. Sharp-eyed members of Claudius' imperial court, attuned to small and large changes in prestige and ranking, must have inferred the same.

Left unexplored is the fact that after the adoption Octavia would be marrying her own brother had she not been adopted into another family.[73] The wedding itself, held when Nero had reached his 16th year in 53 CE, is inconsequential in the historians' narratives.[74] For instance, Cassius Dio reports that a grave illness of Claudius in 53 prompted Nero to enter the senate and vow a horse race should Claudius recover; when the emperor regained health Nero held the race and married Octavia. The third-century historian puts his focus on Agrippina, ceaselessly striving "to make Nero popular with the masses and to cause him to be regarded as the only successor to the imperial power": she is said to have actually arranged the popular horse race and to have "earnestly prayed" Claudius would not recover.[75]

Agrippina appears again as stockpiling public distinctions for Nero, which by the end of 51 seemed to designate him as Claudius' heir. Nero, now 13 years old, was honored by the senate with acceleration of his *toga virilis* ceremony marking, usually at age 16, a boy's maturity;[76] anticipation of a consulship for him at age 20, that is, at least 10 years before the usual minimum age; an immediate grant of proconsular power outside the city limits; designation as *Princeps Iuventutis* (Leader of the Youth); and a donative in his name for the soldiers and Rome's populace.[77] The accompanying equestrian event demonstrated his standing relative to Claudius' own son: Nero wore triumphal clothing, which people presumed denoted his future imperial rule, while the 10-year-old Britannicus rode in a *toga praetexta*, a young boy's purple-bordered white toga worn over a tunic.[78] Tacitus' report implies Agrippina's responsibility for her son's honors by placing this information directly before a vignette showcasing her intrusion in a dispute between Nero and Britannicus in which her stepson lost (see below).[79]

Agrippina's tight association with Nero's public honors is conveyed independently by coins celebrating her son as Rome's Leader of the Youth.[80] For example, silver *denarii* commemorating "Nero Claudius Caesar Drusus Germanicus, Leader of the Youth"—that is, Nero, with all his new names and epithet—portray her on the obverse encircled by the legend "For Agrippina Augusta"[81] (see Ill. 4.1). Two similar issues honoring "Nero

Ill. 4.1 Agrippina Augusta with Nero, *Princeps Iuventutis*, on a centrally struck *denarius* from 50–54. © The Trustees of the British Museum.

Claudius Caesar Drusus Germanicus, Leader of the Youth," back Nero's portrait to that of Claudius, who has the title "Tiberius Claudius Caesar Augustus Germanicus, Highest Pontiff, with Tribunician Power, Father of the Fatherland."[82] Agrippina's coins are remarkable. Not only is she the first living woman portrayed and identified on centrally struck Roman coins, but this issue, visually similar to ones of Claudius with the *Princeps Iuventutis*, hints at her responsibility for Nero's elevation. Many might not read the legends on Rome's *denarii*, silver coins about the size of our dimes, but they could quickly grasp the twinned honors to mother and son and the resemblance of Agrippina's issues to those of Claudius.

Behind the historians' emphasis on Agrippina's advancement of her son to ever more public positions is another thread that is especially prominent in Tacitus' *Annals*: her demotion and eclipse of Claudius' son Britannicus. We saw already that Claudius' betrothal of Agrippina's boy to his daughter Octavia in 49 "equaled him to Britannicus,"[83] that the adoption of Nero in 50 was juxtaposed to a proleptic note about Britannicus' desertion by servants and his eventual premature death,[84] and that the games of 51 celebrating Nero as "Leader of the Youth," in which Britannicus wore a boy's clothing in contrast to Nero's triumphal dress, were interpreted popularly as signaling Nero, not Britannicus, as Claudius' heir.[85] To the latter note Tacitus adds that Britannicus' guards and loyal freedmen were removed.[86] He illuminates the change in 51 in a vignette that could derive only from someone in the court. It displays Agrippina's dominance of Claudius as well as her political cunning.[87] In what now seems a petty slip, Britannicus had called his stepbrother "Domitius"—his born name—rather than "Nero," his proper name after adoption by Claudius. Agrippina complained bitterly to Claudius that within the imperial house such scorn for the adoption, and for other changes decreed by the senate and ordered by the populace, would lead to public disaster.[88] Spurred as if by formal charges, Claudius—not named but referred to as "husband"—removed each "best educator" of Britannicus by exile or death, substituting for them individuals chosen by "the stepmother." The Tacitean vignette indirectly quotes Agrippina's loaded language—she speaks of "the senate and the people"—and refers to her as a "stepmother," inviting the trope of an evil stepmother.[89]

Agrippina's cruel isolation of Britannicus for Nero's benefit is clear in Tacitus' *Annals* and is echoed in the fragments of Cassius Dio. The latter record that Agrippina kept Britannicus away from his father and the public, "in a kind of imprisonment," although without the story of Britannicus' misnomer of Nero.[90] The official view of the family, however, was not so stark: an inscribed vow dated 50–54 CE from the sacred grove at Nemi, Italy (some 30 km southeast of Rome) prays for the good health of the emperor Claudius, Agrippina Augusta, "Tiberius Claudius Britannicus," and Nero Claudius Caesar. Claudius' natural son is placed before his adoptive one, indicating their relative standing.[91] Also noteworthy is Suetonius' relevant report, which mentions neither Agrippina nor the removal of Britannicus' allies and protectors but focuses instead on Nero's reaction to not being called by his adoptive name. In the biographer's telling, the young Nero demonstrates his beastly character by attempting to persuade Claudius that Britannicus was illegitimate.[92] In Tacitus' *Annals*, however, the two boys are rivals, key to Agrippina's decision to murder Claudius in 54 (at the end of *Annals* 12). Britannicus' isolation later resurfaces to help explain the ease with which Nero accomplished his stepbrother's murder in 55.[93] We will explore these two significant events but turn now to Agrippina's activity outside the imperial residences.

Agrippina, Claudius' New Imperial Wife

Agrippina initially used her new position also in ways reminiscent of Messalina: spitefully getting rid of other women who might be rivals.[94] (See Chapter 3.) She allegedly harbored such deep and unrelenting hatred for Lollia Paulina, who, like herself and Aelia Paetina, had been proposed as Claudius' fourth wife,[95] that she found an accuser to charge Lollia with having consulted soothsayers, magicians, and even Apollo's oracle at Claros (now Ahmetbeyli, Turkey) about the wedding. The case made it to the senate, where Claudius bloviated about Lollia's stellar ancestry and marriage connections (withholding her marriage to Caligula in 38) but added vague references to plots against the state and her massive wealth. Agrippina may indeed have been spurred by Lollia's extraordinary wealth: while she was Caligula's wife, she flaunted tiered emerald and pearl jewelry in her hair and ears, in wreaths, and on her neck, arms, and fingers, worth 40 million sesterces in all.[96] Lollia was banished from Rome but allowed to keep five million sesterces.[97] She was soon killed by a tribune—that is, with official sanction.[98] Agrippina confirmed her rival's death by inspecting her peculiar teeth once the head was brought back to Rome.[99] Also in 49, Agrippina saw to the banishment of Calpurnia, who occasioned Agrippina's ire when the newly wed Claudius casually but approvingly mentioned the beauty of this woman of senatorial rank.[100] Designation of Claudius as princeps helps explain the lethal power of the new wife's jealousy.[101] These two banishments in Agrippina's first year of marriage to Claudius echo that of Julia Livilla in Messalina's first year alongside Claudius as princeps (see Chapter 3). But Agrippina would soon show that she was no Messalina.

Agrippina's Political Ascendency, 51–54

Agrippina had clearly moved beyond "catfights" by the next year, when she received the honorific title "Augusta" and a veteran colony was named after her. The conferral of the cognomen "Augusta," which Tacitus remarks "enhanced" Agrippina, came at her son's adoption by Claudius on 25 February 50. The honor conveyed no political rights or power but rather prestige and the hint of sacredness with its clear echoes of the first emperor's cognomen "Augustus."[102] Although Cassius Dio specifies that Claudius gave her the title, this honor was historically granted by the senate.[103] Livia had received the cognomen in 14 when she was adopted by testament into Augustus' *gens Iulia* and her name changed to Julia Augusta. Antonia the Younger had been granted it during her grandson Caligula's first year, although she refused; Claudius, her son, had it reinstated posthumously when he came to power four years later.[104] In the same year, however, Claudius expressly declined the title's offer to Messalina at the birth of their son (see Chapter 3).[105] Thus, Agrippina the Younger is the first imperial woman honored as Augusta during the rule of her husband. Coins and inscriptions hereafter call her Agrippina Augusta, often pairing her with Claudius Augustus.[106] The title may have suggested Agrippina's direct descendance from Augustus, a significant element of her self-fashioning.[107]

The year 50 saw another novel distinction for Agrippina. Attempting to "demonstrate her power [*vis*] even to allied peoples," Agrippina brought about the establishment of a veteran colony to be named after her and settled in Roman Germany's Oppidum Ubiorum, where she had been born. The name of the new city is not cited in the *Annals*' note, the unique literary reference to the foundation, but rather that her grandfather Agrippa had settled the Germanic group of Ubii there when they had crossed the Rhine.[108] The full name of the colony, Colonia Claudia Ara Agrippinensium, is documented by inscriptions and other evidence.[109] It evokes Agrippa as well as Agrippina and also refers to the community's altar for imperial cult. At a strategic location on the Rhine, the settlement developed into modern Köln (in English, Cologne), a name derived from "Colonia." Even now Cologne considers Agrippina its patron.[110]

This is the only instance of a Roman colony named for an imperial woman.[111] Soon after its foundation, Pliny the Elder lists "the Agrippinian colony among the Ubii."[112] By the late first century the colony is referred to simply as "Agrippina" on the Tropaeum Traiani in Moesia Inferior (now Adamklissi, Romania).[113] But other elements of the name should not be overlooked. The "Claudia" of Colonia Claudia Ara Agrippinensium honored Claudius, his father Drusus the Elder, and his brother Germanicus, both celebrated for military exploits in Germany. Bricks, honorary inscriptions, and other material from the city commonly use the acronym *CCAA*, preserving the Claudian element as well as referring to Agrippina.

Colonia Claudia Ara Agrippinensium is part of Claudius' larger imperial initiative of city foundations and encouragements, which was more extensive than that of Caligula or Tiberius. Evidence from Pliny the Elder and inscriptions have identified at least eight new veteran colonies founded by Claudius in the provinces other than Colonia Claudia Ara Agrippinensium. Further, the earlier colony of Narbo (now Narbonne, France) had the title Claudia added to its name. Lugdunum (now Lyon, France), the emperor's birthplace that was renamed Colonia Copia Claudia Augusta Lugudunum, was raised to tax exempt status and may have been reinforced by further veteran settlements. Dalmatian Salonae (now Solin, Croatia) received a veteran settlement.[114] The number and spread of Claudius' city foundations were part of his self-fashioning for the empire. As had Augustus, Claudius promoted himself and his family to provincials through municipal benefactions (see Chapter 1). Despite the Tacitean report, however, Agrippina herself did not establish the colony: this would be impossible for a woman.

Yet Agrippina undeniably assumed an ever-greater presence in Rome, the empire, and the court. Much of the evidence cannot be precisely dated. Most coins and sculptural installations can be assigned only to the years between 50, when Agrippina assumed the epithet Augusta, and 54, Claudius' death and deification. Reports in the histories are often undated.[115] Assembled together, however, the literary accounts and documentation show her frequently with Claudius in emergent settings for imperial women, like family sculptural galleries, as well as in untraditional situations, like meeting ambassadors. We can perhaps understand why Tacitus attributes the Colonia Claudia Ara Agrippiensium to Agrippina's desire "to show her strength also to allied groups": overall, Agrippina had more visibility and ostensible power than any woman before her.

Cassius Dio's now-fragmented history confirms Agrippina's dominance in this period.[116] For instance, Agrippina reportedly was often with her imperial husband in public as he transacted ordinary business or gave an audience to ambassadors: although she sat upon a separate tribunal, Cassius Dio calls this "one of the most remarkable sights of the time." She accompanied Claudius as he gave aid during a huge conflagration in Rome. Toward the end of his rule she instigated a riot over the sale of bread.[117] Only her appearance beside the emperor at the fire relief was anticipated by another imperial woman, and even this had been deemed irregular. Livia had helped Augustus during urban fires, and when she ventured such aid again during Tiberius' reign, he scolded her to keep away from important affairs having nothing to do with women.[118]

Some of Cassius Dio's notices fit the narrative of Agrippina masterminding the humiliation of Britannicus and elevation of Nero (remarked in an earlier section). For instance, Agrippina reportedly incited the bread riot so that she could persuade Claudius to calm People and Senate with the proclamation that, should he die, Nero was "already capable of administering the business of the state." Agrippina furthers hopes of Nero's competency by circulating rumors of Britannicus' insanity and epilepsy.[119] But other notes emphasize Agrippina's unprecedented power, said to be more than that of Claudius himself,[120] her possession of all the privileges Livia had enjoyed as well as additional honors,[121] and her exercise of power equal to that of Claudius—even her desire "to have his title outright."[122]

Actual feats attributed to Agrippina in this period are extraordinary, such as the administrative change in 51 of the command of the praetorian guard from two prefects to one: from Lusius Geta and Rufrius Crispinus to Sextus Afranius Burrus alone.[123] After Augustus had established this 9,000-man special guard in 27 BCE to accompany and protect the emperor and imperial family, he entrusted it to two equestrian prefects. By Tiberius' reign only one prefect was in command, first Sejanus and then Macro (Chapter 2); by the middle of Claudius' rule two prefects again were in control.[124] One, Rufrius Crispinus, served Claudius consistently well.[125] The other, Lusius Geta, is known mainly for being among those the befuddled emperor consulted during Messalina's last days in 48.[126] In 51, however, both were removed and Burrus was put in their place. The historians hold Agrippina responsible, Cassius Dio because Geta and Crispinus would not do her bidding and Tacitus for three reasons: she considered them partisans of Messalina and her children, she was building Nero's supremacy by diminishing support for Britannicus, and she needed someone obligated to her in the sensitive position.[127]

The actual argument Tacitus attributes to Agrippina, however, is just as likely for one experienced in Rome's ruthlessly competitive politics: she convinced Claudius by noting that the guard would be more disciplined under a single commander.[128] Other considerations likewise indicate a less self-serving reading of the change. The equestrian Sextus Afranius Burrus, an outstanding military commander, had served as the procurator of Livia's estates and then those of Tiberius and Claudius:[129] it is difficult to imagine anyone more loyal to the imperial family. Further, neither Geta and Crispinus suffered from being removed from their commands: in 54 Geta served as the prestigious and influential prefect of Egypt, and Crispinus, who received consular rank when dismissed as praetorian prefect in 51, lived until 66.[130] Had they truly run afoul of Agrippina, as the historians hold, would they have survived and prospered? Indeed, Agrippina seems to have brought about a constructive change by her "meddling" with the administration of the praetorian guard. Yet the involvement of an imperial woman in military matters was extremely rare,[131] confirming Agrippina's political sagacity and her boldness alike. Burrus would remain an important supporter until her death.

Agrippina features in other affairs that reflect an indisputable political presence. Tacitus reports a senatorial attempt in 51 to weaken Vitellius, Agrippina's "foremost promoter" (*praecipuus propugnator*), by accusations of treason. This failed when Agrippina badgered Claudius, and in the end it was Vitellius' senatorial accuser, Junius Lupus, who was banished.[132] The whole is somewhat murky: Vitellius had long been Claudius' right-hand man, serving with the emperor as co-consul twice and as co-censor in 47–48 (see also Chapter 3).[133] But the note fits the themes of Agrippina's manipulative aggression and her appropriation of Claudius' and others' allies.[134]

Her success in this latter endeavor is marked by the senatorial decree in 52 of praetorian insignia to Claudius' imperial freedman Pallas. Pallas had successfully advocated for Agrippina as Claudius' new wife in 48, and by 54 he was rumored to be Agrippina's lover. Pliny the Elder reports that Pallas' honors in 52 came "at the bidding" of Agrippina.[135] If so, Agrippina thus obligated to herself Claudius' powerful imperial administrator of finances.[136] In less Rome-centered affairs, Agrippina mediated with Claudius in 52 on behalf of Agrippa II and the Jews during a conflict with the Samaritans.[137] Here we may perhaps see an echo of her wish to show off her power even to foreign nations, allegedly behind settling Colonia Claudia Ara Agrippiensium in 50.

Finally, at the end of 53 Agrippina was involved in a case whose report stresses her malignant manipulation of Claudius, her greed, and her intrigues with senators and others.[138] Allegedly because she lusted after the opulent Roman gardens of Titus Statilius Taurus, she led Claudius "to the utmost savagery," hearing a case against Taurus.[139] Tarquitius Priscus, Taurus' aide when he governed Africa in 52–53, accused him of magic and embezzlement. When Taurus killed himself before the trial, the senate expelled Tarquitius Priscus. Tacitus called the expulsion of this hated informer a victory "against the ambition of Agrippina."[140] The event echoes earlier reports of Messalina's exploitation of Claudius for her own gain and whims (Chapter 3). If Tacitus' presentation here is correct, however, it reports one of the last times Claudius acted in concert with Agrippina. We will see their growing tension when we turn to Claudius' death in 54.

Agrippina in the Public Eye

Agrippina's growing confidence behind the scenes corresponds with exceptional public visibility. In 51 she was present at the submission of the Briton king Caratacus to Claudius in Rome.[141] Claudius' great triumph over the British kings, which he had celebrated in Rome in 44 with Messalina and others, belied the continuing defiance of much of the island. Caratacus and his family had resisted the Roman invasion in 43, and when the Romans withdrew most of their forces after Claudius' own appearance in the field that year Caratacus moved the fight to the island's southwest (around modern Wales). Only in 51 did resistance end, when Caratacus' wife, daughter, and brothers were captured and the king himself treacherously handed over to the Romans by Cartimandua, the Brigantes queen to whom he had fled.[142]

The ceremonial submission of Caratacus was staged in front of the people and armed praetorians in the broad plain (the *Campus Praetorianus*) adjoining the praetorians' barracks in northeast Rome.[143] Allegedly "everyone" was avid to see this insurgent, whose fame had spread through islands, provinces, even Italy and Rome itself. Agrippina figured extraordinarily as Claudius staged Caratacus' capitulation. After recounting a dramatic interchange between Caratacus and Claudius about imperial clemency, Tacitus—and those assembled—focused on Agrippina:[144]

> And [the pardoned], freed of their chains, also venerated Agrippina, conspicuous on another platform not at all distant, with the very same praises and thanks with which they had honored the princeps. It was indisputably novel, and indeed incompatible with our traditional customs, for a woman to preside over Roman standards. But she herself often said that she was a partner in the empire that had been gained by her ancestors.[145]

In the scene with its triumphal overtones,[146] Agrippina far surpassed Messalina's glory in Claudius' initial triumph of 44. Further, the historian's direct comment—"It was indisputably novel, and indeed incompatible with our traditional customs"—underlines the shocking innovation of Agrippina's public presence in a military setting.[147] Agrippina's reported words, moreover, emphasized the standing she claimed as due to her because of her ancestry.

She displayed her unique status also in the heart of Rome: the Forum Romanum and the Capitoline.[148] In 51 she entered the Capitol on the special carriage of the *carpentum*, availing herself of an extraordinarily prestigious honor:

> Agrippina raised her profile even higher by ascending the Capitolium Hill in a *carpentum*, an honor, conceded in the illustrious past to priests and sacred objects, that increased the veneration of this woman who—born from a great triumphing general [Germanicus], and the sister, wife, and mother of men who would control the world—is a unique example to this day.[149]

We have already seen this special carriage and its association with imperial women, first the individuals Julia Augusta and the deceased Agrippina the Elder, and then Messalina, who in 44 had followed Claudius' triumphal chariot in a *carpentum*. The triumphal procession traditionally ended at the Capitoline, although that detail is not made clear for 44. Now, however, Agrippina appeared alone in a *carpentum* while entering one of Rome's most sacred spaces. Her carriage would have been visible from the Forum and the northern Palatine Hill as it moved slowly up the steep Clivus Capitolinus. Agrippina's unprecedented prominence was inextricable from her family, as she herself made clear.

Agrippina was spectacularly in the public gaze again at the ceremonious culmination of the draining of the Fucine Lake in the early 50s. This engineering project, the drainage of a lake that had no surface outlets and lay some 50 miles (~110 km) east of Rome, was to render its lakebed arable. It was a long-standing challenge and was attempted repeatedly but unsuccessfully until 1876.[150] Caesar and Augustus had considered it,[151] and Claudius' attempt, though ultimately futile, is reckoned by Pliny the Elder as one of the emperor's most remarkable achievements.[152] Claudius' project, which he began in 42, long before marrying Agrippina, relied on local as well as imperial support.[153] Many laborers were needed—Suetonius cites 30,000 working continuously—to tunnel through a mountain from the lake to the River Liris (now the Garigliano).[154] Claudius' trusted freedman Narcissus oversaw the project.

Agrippina featured stunningly in the public events celebrating the project, which Pliny the Elder calls a spectacle (*spectaculum*). She sat alongside Claudius at its first "grand opening" in 51/51; Nero is also reported, but neither Octavia nor Britannicus.[155] The emperor wore distinguished military attire, as did Agrippina herself. Her golden cloak (a *chlamys* or *paludamentum*) is remarked by Pliny, Tacitus, and Cassius Dio probably as much for its prodigality as for her appropriation of this traditionally male mantle with military overtones.[156] Their specifics about her clothing contrast with the vague chronology of the proceedings.

A staged naval battle preceded the outlet's opening, but the water did not drain because the intake was not deep enough.[157] The project had to be renewed, and an unknown period passed while the channel was deepened. Once it was deemed ready and a crowd reassembled,[158] Agrippina and Claudius again presided over the lake's (second) planned discharge, again celebrated with military overtones. This time an infantry battle of gladiators on pontoons provided entertainment. But when the drainage began, the water rushed through the man-made outlet so violently that it terrified Claudius as it swept away people and equipment.

Tacitus reports an ensuing ugly scene. Agrippina, taking advantage of Claudius' alarm, accused his favorite, Narcissus, of embezzlement.[159] In turn, the freedman insulted her, calling out her frenzied, womanly rage and overweening presumptions.[160] The unseemly altercation ends the year in Tacitus' account. It stresses the worsening of Claudius' rule by emphasizing the political and public prominence of Agrippina and Narcissus, whose gender and status should traditionally relegate them to subordinate, almost invisible roles. The freedman Narcissus' reported affront was particularly pointed. If the account is true, however, Agrippina's rebukes suggest that she had gained an operational understanding of the state's finances since her marriage to Claudius a few years earlier.[161]

Agrippina's Public Image

A very different image of Agrippina comes from sculptural installations and coins, although her later murder and denunciation by Nero have suppressed material traces of her in Rome.[162] Agrippina's bullying of Narcissus at the Fucine Lake is typical of her presentation in Tacitus, and it is worth noting that Cassius Dio's report does not mention the altercation, although it criticizes Narcissus for the failed project.[163] A find from nearby Alba Fucens, the closest Roman city to the lake, offers another perspective (see Ill. 4.2). This small, gilded bronze bust was once on a pedestal. Its find spot in the ancient town's basilica suggests that it publicly displayed the town's allegiance to Claudius and his family.[164] The originally fine quality of the modeling evokes an urban workshop; if so, the piece must have been quite expensive. Alexandridis and others associate the piece with the presence of the imperial family in the town at the inauguration of the works to drain the Fucine Lake.[165] For the town involved in the years-long project instigated and partially funded by the emperor, his wife Agrippina could symbolize imperial benefaction.

The image of Agrippina's and Claudius' united concern for Rome is much more prominent on a full-size relief from the Sebasteion, or imperial cult sanctuary, at Aphrodisias (modern Geyre, Turkey), one of two reliefs from that large and multi-year building project that depict Agrippina. The fragmentary Claudian relief (see Ill. 4.3) once showed three frontal figures.[166] On our left Agrippina, wearing a diagonally arranged himation over a chiton, turns slightly to look toward Claudius while clasping his right hand with hers.[167] The portrait is identifiable, although R. R. R. Smith, who definitively published the Sebasteion reliefs, concedes that her head is slightly idiosyncratic in the treatment of the mouth and less finished than

Ill. 4.2 Bronze bust of Agrippina with traces of gilding, found in Alba Fucens (Italy). 12.7 cm H × 10 W × 6 D. Now in MUSE'Nuovo Museo Paludi di Celano (AQ). Image courtesy of the Ministero della Cultura, MAN Chieti—DRMN Abruzzo. (Reproduction and duplication forbidden.)

that of Claudius.[168] Claudius, originally in the middle of a tripartite relief, is heroically nude other than for a long cloak fashioned over his right shoulder with a round brooch. He wears a large oak-leaf crown apparently placed by the now headless figure to his left.[169] This male figure in a Roman toga was probably an ideal personification of the Roman People or the Roman Senate.[170] The relief seems not to be modeled on one in Rome. Nevertheless, it indicates the public view of Agrippina as Claudius' wife: she, together with the Roman People or Roman State, supports the emperor steadfastly. The *iunctio dextrarum* of their joined hands reflects the ideal concord of husband and wife and may even evoke the mutual respect of political leaders.[171] The idealized third figure once on the relief asserted to the provincial viewer the continued importance of S P Q R (the Senate and People of Rome) alongside the imperial family.

Ill. 4.3 Oversized marble relief of Agrippina clasping the right hand of Claudius. From the Sebasteion at Aphrodisias. © New York University Excavations at Aphrodisias (G. Petruccioli).

Agrippina's role in the imperial family is also stressed in her imaging in Rome from 49 to 54.[172] The familial context was presaged by her representation as one of five unnamed children on her father's sculpted triumphal chariot on the marble Arch of Germanicus in the Circus Flaminius (see Chapter 1). It was also key to her depiction on coins struck in the first year of Caligula's rule. On those base metal issues three female figures were identified by name as Agrippina, Drusilla, and Iulia [Livilla], a fitting reverse for their brother Caligula, the new princeps who realized the potential of coinage to advertise his lineage and family (see Chapter 3; Ill. 2.1). Agrippina became more distinct in 49 as imperial statuary groups proliferated.[173]

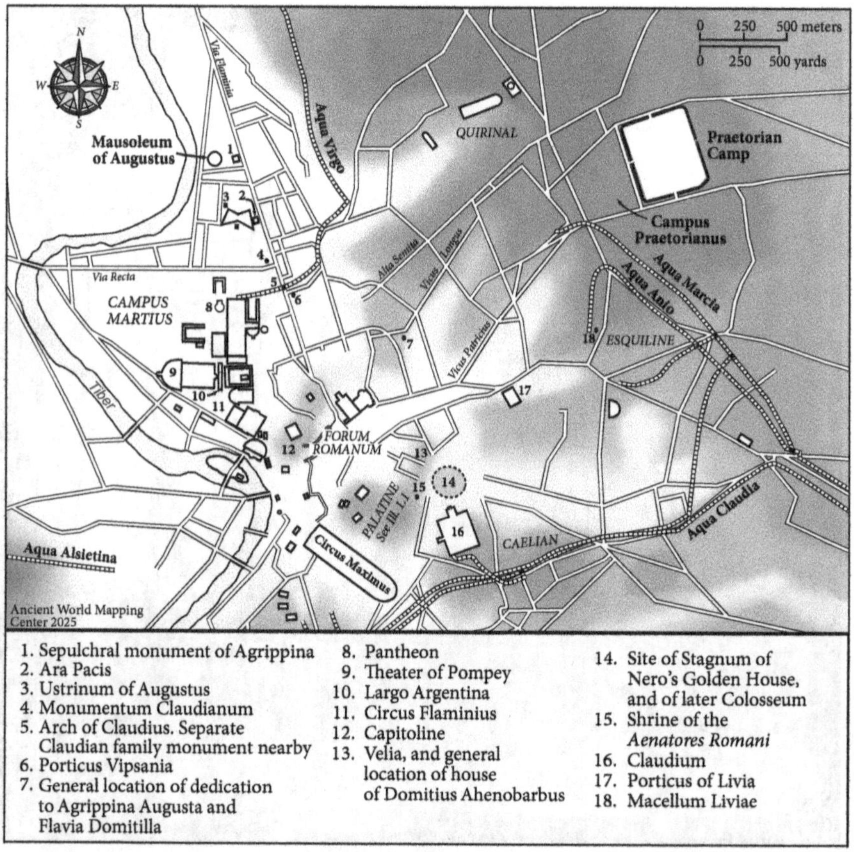

Ill. 4.4 Plan of Rome during Agrippina's lifetime, including monuments relating to her and discussed in the text. © Ancient World Mapping Center.

She featured on at least two monuments along the northern Via Flaminia celebrating Claudius' imperial family.[174]

Both are known only through fragmentary inscriptions. Remains of inscribed statue bases found in 1562 and 1641 near the Arch of Claudius (see Ill. 4.4) commemorate three generations of Claudius' family and can be dated to 50–54 CE. The fragments indicate that here once stood statue bases for Germanicus; Antonia Augusta "wife of Drusus, priest of *divus* Augustus, mother of Tiberius Claudius Caisar" [= Claudius]; Julia Agrippina Augusta "daughter of Germanicus Caisar, wife of Tiberius Claudius Caisar Augustus, Father of the Fatherland"; Nero; Britannicus; and Octavia "daughter of Tiberius Claudius Caisar Augustus, Father of the Fatherland."[175] Given the extant texts' emphasis on Claudius' family as it was configured in the latter part of his life, analogous ones—and corresponding statues—are presumed for Claudius himself and his father, Drusus the Elder.[176] The inscriptions display the archaic orthography advocated by Claudius "Caisar" as censor in 47/48.[177] The whole was once interpreted as the display of members of Claudius' family on the Arch of Claudius, but the archaeological evidence and context better fit a separate monument somewhere in the vicinity of the Arch.[178] The Arch itself focused on Claudius and his achievements in the war in Britain.[179] The family monument makes clear Agrippina's role as a link between the great general Germanicus and Claudius. H. I. Flower has persuasively proposed that the installation once honored Messalina but after Messalina's *damnatio memoriae* and Agrippina's marriage to Claudius was reconfigured to feature Agrippina instead.[180] Agrippina's centrality in Claudius' new imperial house and state is unmistakable.

Agrippina was honored by a statue in another installation also attested by fragmentary inscriptions naming her, Claudius, and other Claudian family members. These problematic pieces, some known only through antiquarian sketches, were unearthed at the corner of the Via dell'Impresa and the Vicolo dello Sdrucciolo (northwest of the later Column of Marcus Aurelius; #4 in Ill. 4.4), some 500 meters northwest of the Arch. The find spot of these fragments and the absence of Claudius' archaic orthography indicate that they belonged to a separate monument honoring the Claudian family.[181] The fragmentary texts include Agrippina (as Ju[lia Augusta]); Nero Caesar; Antonia Augusta; Tiberius; Tiberius' son Drusus the Younger; probably the emperor Claudius Augustus himself; and Claudius' brother Germanicus and two children, Britannicus and Octavia.[182] Scholars suggest a plausible albeit complicated history for this shrine, often referred to as the Monumentum Claudianum: Tiberius originally installed a monument here for the Claudian *gens* when his son Drusus the Younger was awarded tribunician power in 22; Claudius restored that Claudian monument at the beginning of his rule, perhaps to distinguish himself from the Julian Caligula; and after 50, now wed to Agrippina and having adopted Nero, Claudius enhanced the whole with statues of his fourth wife and adopted heir.[183] Again, Agrippina's position in the imperial family is key.

Agrippina herself seems to have been behind another familial monument along the upper Via Flaminia, this time a sepulchral one (see Ill. 4.4). In contrast to the two installations just discussed, this complex honored Agrippina's natal family rather than Claudius and his close relatives, which has suggested her responsibility for it. Travertine *cippi* ca. 66 cm high and an alabaster funerary urn were found near S. Carlo al Corso at the Via della Croce; a miniature bronze trophy may also come from this site. The whole commemorated the cremation or funerary site of Agrippina's three brothers who died as infants or children, her sister Julia Livilla, and Tiberius "Gemellus," one of the twins born in 19 to Drusus the Younger and Germanicus' sister Livilla (the aunt of Agrippina the Younger) and who had been forced to suicide by Caligula in 37 or early 38. None had received burial in the Mausoleum of Augustus, slightly west of the funerary installation. (A later, matching cippus honored Domitilla, wife of *divus* Vespasian, suggesting that Titus enhanced the whole.[184]) The monument, located alongside the vital northern route into Rome, alluded to Agrippina's ties to Augustus and the importance of her own kin. If the bronze trophy also belongs to it, Germanicus' military glory was also recalled. Its construction speaks to the active role of Agrippina in Rome in her prime.[185]

Agrippina's likeness surely graced the two Claudian monuments discussed above, and perhaps her name as patron appeared on the burial installation. Group installations to the imperial family, which had increased in number in Italy and elsewhere beginning in the Tiberian period, are especially noticeable under Claudius.[186] We should not conclude, however, that Agrippina herself was responsible for her images and her pronounced presence in sculptural remembrances. This lack of agency is reflected in her depiction on coins.

As discussed in the Introduction and elsewhere, Agrippina is the first woman portrayed and identified by name on coins centrally struck during her lifetime. During Claudius' reign she features on three issues dating after her elevation as Augusta in 50. On gold and silver coins (*aurei* and *denarii*), she appears on the reverse of portraits of Claudius: these high-value coins, perhaps aimed at Rome's elite and Rome's military (whose remuneration was in silver *denarii*), forefront the position of "Agrippina Augusta" (as she is identified) as the emperor's consort.[187] A second issue, discussed above, commemorated Nero's honor as "Leader of the Youth" in 51 by *denarii* with her on one side and the young Nero on the other, in an issue similar to that pairing Nero "Leader of the Youth" with Claudius.[188] Here, again, she is identified as "Agrippina Augusta," in hindsight suggesting her role in the later transmission of imperial power to her son. On a third issue, a lower-value *sestertius*, she appears on one side in profiled portrait. The *carpentum* on the reverse refers to the honorific carriage Agrippina so effectively used in 51. The design echoes that of a *sestertius* issued under Caligula displaying his (deceased) mother, Agrippina the Elder, on the obverse and, on the reverse, the *carpentum* used in her memorial games.[189] Like Tacitus' narrative for 51, the coin references her familial connections by labeling her "Agrippina Augusta, daughter of Germanicus, wife of Caesar Augustus Claudius,"[190] and—to those with long memories or coin hoards—its resemblance to the earlier issue featuring her mother. Since these lower-value coins circulated more widely than did Rome's precious coins in gold and silver (*aurei* and *denarii*), it is noteworthy that Agrippina the Younger appears on this issue without a male on the other side. Those using the coins may have inferred her independence.

Given the domineering personality the historians accord her, it is tempting to see Agrippina's own agency in being the first living woman portrayed individually and identified on coins. But nothing proves or even strongly suggests that any imperial woman of the Julio-Claudian period, even Agrippina the Younger, had decisive input in her numismatic likeness.[191] The scholarly consensus is that the emperor had nominal oversight in the choice of images his functionaries devised.[192] Moreover, coin issues with Agrippina's portrait are but three from more than a hundred different issues centrally struck in Claudius' Rome.[193] On the other hand, her very presence on such coins is remarkable and unprecedented. Those fortunate enough to handle the coins might easily surmise from them that she was an extraordinary woman.

Claudius' Death in 54

Ancient sources hold that Claudius died from ingesting a poisonous mushroom, and most blame Agrippina. Cassius Dio adds Nero as actively helping his mother, and Suetonius notes Nero being in on the plan.[194] But the facts are presented in various ways, allowing different views of Agrippina, and some scholars have even exonerated her completely.[195] The charge of poisoning is a classic trope for women, and Claudius's health was fragile at best.[196] We saw earlier in the chapter that Claudius suffered a dire illness but recovered in 53, after which Nero married Octavia.[197]

The consensus on Agrippina's responsibility never considers her emotions at the death of her father's brother, whom she had known all her life and lived with as spouse for some five years. The sensational stories of Claudius' murder also overshadow Rome's inability to remove peacefully a mad, inept, or gravely ill princeps: only death, whether natural or not, would allow a successor.[198] But such considerations are not as arresting or intriguing as stories of an emperor's poisoning.[199]

Reports of omens open the year's narrative in Tacitus, *Annals* 12, as often in annalistic Roman history and particularly noticeable in Tacitus' later books.[200] In this context it seems odd, especially in light of Agrippina's characterization as "almost man-like," that only Phlegon of Tralles reports the spontaneous sex-change in 53 of Philotis, a dependent on Agrippina's estate in Mevania (now Bevagna, Italy). Philotis had been betrothed to a man, but then she suddenly grew male genitals and became a man.[201] In Agrippina's Rome the transformation of a woman to a man, especially on Agrippina's own estate, would seem ominous indeed. This marvel, however, seems not even to have been officially reported.[202]

Nonetheless, Agrippina dominates Tacitus' *Annals* after his reported omens, and his stories could have no place in official documents. The first underlines Claudius' estrangement from her in 54: terrified by her husband's drunken remark that he was going to punish her shameful crimes, Agrippina got rid of Domitia Lepida, her former sister-in-law.[203] The two women are characterized by Tacitus as more or less equal in beauty, age, and wealth but real contenders in shamelessness, notoriety, violence, and other vices.[204] Domitia Lepida was, like Agrippina, a relative of Augustus and Antonia the Younger (Claudius' mother); she was also the mother of Messalina, Claudius' third wife. The real rivalry was over which woman would have more influence over Nero: Domitia Lepida beguiled the malleable young man through sweet words and presents, but Agrippina, truculent and menacing, browbeat him.[205] Domitia Lepida was charged and sentenced for magic and for letting her enslaved dependents in Calabria run wild. How the whole affair impacted Claudius' relationship with Agrippina is unclear, but it allows the historian to introduce Claudius' growing distance from his fourth wife.[206]

Narcissus then reappears, again as an opponent of Agrippina, and as at the Fucine Lake, damning criticism of Agrippina comes in the reported thoughts of this freedman. Tacitus' Narcissus weighs a future under Britannicus (whose mother he had overturned) or under Nero, concluding, "The whole house would be torn apart by a stepmother's plots [if Britannicus came to the throne], with more flagrant misdeeds than if he [Narcissus] had kept his mouth shut about the adultery of the former wife. Although now not even was adultery missing, with Pallas as [Agrippina's] lover: no one should question the fact that she considered her good name, her sense of shame, her body...everything cheaper than rule."[207] Narcissus' departure from Rome for Sinuessa (modern Mondragone, Italy) deprived Claudius of one of his most trusted advisors.

In Tacitus' *Annals* the way is thus cleared for Claudius' poisoning. The sources generally agree on the sequence of events, although stressing that there were alternative versions. Agrippina gets the noted poisoner Locusta to create a powerful venom to apply to Claudius' favorite mushrooms and then suborns Claudius' eunuch Halotus to administer it.[208] Suetonius' version introduces more ambiguity about where and by whom the poison was administered; his second, more memorable alternative has Agrippina herself give it to Claudius at a family feast.[209] Continuing to offer alternatives, Suetonius first notes that after eating the poisoned mushroom Claudius never regained consciousness but then reports that it took a second dose to kill the emperor.[210] The latter version concurs with Tacitus: when the initial dose of venom failed, Tacitus' Agrippina got Claudius' trusted doctor Xenophon to coat the emperor's throat with (a different) lethal poison while pretending to nurse him back to health.[211] In nasty mockery of the 64-year-old emperor, Tacitus, Suetonius, and the *Apocolocyntosis* note the dying Claudius' defecation,[212] with the court satire giving what seems to have been the official line: Claudius experienced an accidental and sordid death while gluttonously feasting.[213]

The death occurred in early October 54.[214] Both Tacitus and Suetonius note a delay in announcing Claudius' death publicly. In contrived sorrow Tacitus' Agrippina hugged and otherwise restrained her stepchildren Britannicus, Antonia, and Octavia from entering Claudius' bedchamber—all so she could prepare the accession of her son.[215] Finally (13 October 54), Claudius' death was announced from the imperial residences, and Nero, in military garb, went from the Palatine to the praetorian camp with the praetorian prefect Burrus. At the camp he was acclaimed *Imperator*. Senate and provinces echoed their allegiance.

Although Agrippina is not named in the *Annals*' rendition of these last decisive events, Tacitus' presentation overall stresses her as the instigator of Claudius' death and mastermind of a drawn-out scheme to smooth the imperial transition to her son Nero. That impression is strengthened by the final paragraph of Book 12, which returns to Agrippina:

> Heavenly honors were decreed to Claudius, and the obsequies of his funeral were celebrated in the manner of those for *divus* Augustus, with Agrippina rivaling the magnificence of her great-grandmother Livia. Yet

> Claudius' will still was not read out, lest the preference of stepson to son should, by resentment at its injustice, disturb the mood of the public.[216]

Later, when Tacitus recounts Agrippina's vindication of a treason charge in 55, she outrightly confesses that her counsels prepared Nero's adoption, proconsular power, designated consulship, and other steps to total power.[217] There can be no doubt that she is the mastermind of her son's rise. Most scholars similarly hold Agrippina responsible for Claudius' death after she tricked Claudius into preferring his stepson Nero to his own, but younger, son Britannicus as his designated successor, although some express doubts.[218] I agree with the majority: Agrippina acted not only to preserve herself, but also to advance her son and fulfill a long-standing Roman ideal.

In October 54, however, apparently no resistance to her son's accession was raised, whatever the suspicions of Agrippina's agency that now shadow the events. Indeed, a relief from Aphrodisias and a cameo now in Cologne, both discussed in Chapter 5, suggest that her support of Nero was recognized and applauded. Why oppose the transition? Claudius was old and had a history of grave mistakes (see Chapter 5); Domitia Lepida's disappearance and Narcissus' retirement showed the dangers of opposing Agrippina; and the dangerous chaos of Claudius' own accession, only 13 years earlier, must have still seemed quite present. Acceptance of the foibles and actions of the more powerful was also built into Rome's imperial court, as indicated by Nero's reported joking about Claudius' mushroom poisoning.[219] Our next chapter shows Agrippina triumphantly at work in the new court and the short-lived nature of her glory.

Agrippina the Younger: A Dangerous Woman in Rome's Early Empire. Mary T. Boatwright, Oxford University Press.
 DOI: 10.1093/9780190945855.003.0005

5
Best of Mothers—or Nero's Nemesis (54–59)

Introduction

Agrippina's 16-year-old son Nero was acclaimed as Rome's emperor in mid-October 54. As before, the installation of a new princeps in Rome brought Agrippina opportunities she quickly exploited. Her sudden good fortune, however, was as short-lived as it had been when Caligula came to power 17 years earlier. Her prominence and presumed influence with Nero and his court peaked in 54 and early 55, after which she faded from notice until her brutal murder at Nero's order in 59. In the first flush of her son's rule Agrippina enjoyed astonishing visibility on coins and monuments, providing support for ancient historians' reports that during this period she actually entered traditionally male political arenas including, most scandalously, senatorial hearings. In this brief period Agrippina focused her political maneuvering on working through her young son in an unusual relationship so close that it was rumored to involve incest. The charge of incest was not new for Agrippina: her prominence—and that of her sisters Drusilla and Julia Livilla—in Caligula's new court was first explained and then condemned as due to improper sexual relations, and her marriage to her uncle Claudius always seemed suspicious. But in 54 Agrippina was in her prime—39 years old—and her alleged consort was her own teen-aged son. The allegation of incest underscores both Nero's passivity and Agrippina's take-charge personality.

Like the previous chapter, this one is unavoidably shaped by Tacitus' *Annals* and its relatively long reports of Agrippina's political involvement, especially her fraught relationship with Nero.[1] The historian's treatment of her, however, abruptly ends sometime in 55 and resumes only in January 59. Moreover, Tacitus' compelling narrative can muddy chronology. The striking opening of *Annals* 13, examined in this chapter, repeats and revises some information about Claudius' consecration and funeral noted in the last chapter of *Annals* 12 (and treated in my preceding chapter), redundantly conflating events from early October to the end of December 54.[2] In *Ann.* 12.69.3, the impressive end of Tacitus' Book 12, Agrippina has Livia in mind while arranging that Claudius' obsequies would be celebrated like those of Augustus,[3] underscoring Agrippina's audacious confidence in her august familial history as well as her competitive nature. In contrast, Suetonius attributes to Nero Claudius' splendid funeral and divinization as a display of filial piety (*apparatissimum funus*, *Nero* 9.1). The opening of Tacitus' *Annals* 13 stresses again Agrippina's dominance of Rome by reporting anew the funeral (now specified as a censorial one), the emperor's consecration, and honors granted Agrippina, including the right of two lictors and a priesthood of *divus* Claudius.[4] Nero's general unsuitability and lack of agency are stressed in the note that Seneca, not Nero himself, wrote the new emperor's initial senatorial speech and that its praise of Claudius' wise foresight triggered incredulous laughter.[5] However emphatic it is about Agrippina's instrumentality in the events of October 54, Tacitus' presentation is selective. He omits in both books another signal honor for *divus* Claudius initiated by Agrippina: the great Temple on the Caelian Hill that she sponsored for the new cult. That information comes from Suetonius.[6] Tacitus focuses on power politics in Rome, especially in relation to Agrippina.[7]

Agrippina's distinction in late 54 is undeniable. Her exalted position as the priestess of *divus* Claudius recalled the earlier imperial cult priesthoods of *divus* Augustus held by Julia Augusta and Antonia the Younger. These novel responsibilities, which would not be replicated after Agrippina, granted official positions in state religion and unusual prestige to the three imperial women.[8] Their particular duties are now obscure, although we may assume that, marked out by special ritual garb, they partook in processions and rites in front of senators, equestrians, and the Roman populace on an emperor's birthday, the anniversary of his death, and other public observances.[9] Tacitus' detail that Agrippina was granted two lictors when performing her duties makes her prominence all the clearer. Julia Augusta (Livia) had been accompanied by only one lictor when she was priestess of *divus* Augustus,[10] and Antonia may never, or only rarely, have undertaken her priestly functions. Roman lictors were traditionally associated with political magistrates and Vestal Virgins,[11] and we can well imagine Agrippina reveling in her two attendants.

In late 54 Agrippina was on top of the world. Her splendid arrangements for Claudius' funeral displayed proper *pietas* toward her deceased husband, revealed her own superb flair, and reminded everyone of her descent from Augustus and Livia. Through her, the new princeps Nero, whom Claudius marked for succession by marriage to his daughter Octavia, was a direct heir of the principate's founding family. Rome's honors for Claudius included his consecration—still relatively rare in Rome—and helped ensure that his arrangements were honored.[12] Agrippina's future looked even brighter when, in Nero's first days, he chose as the praetorians' watchword "The Best of Mothers" (*optima mater*). This not only flattered her personally but reinforced the ties to the praetorians she enjoyed as Germanicus' sole remaining child.[13]

But the historians, writing at least a half century after the events, make sure at least to adumbrate Agrippina's malevolent agency even in these halcyon days. Tacitus' narrative, for example, opens *Annals* 13 dramatically with "the first death of the new principate," that of Marcus Junius Silanus attributed solely to Agrippina's deceit, "with Nero in the dark."[14] This man was the brother of Lucius Junius Silanus, Octavia's first fiancé, who had killed himself after being renounced by Claudius in 48 so Octavia could betroth Agrippina's son (the later Nero; see Chapter 4). Tacitus' chapter goes into great detail about the blamelessness of Marcus, whose innocent, apolitical life—underscored by Caligula's reported nickname of "the golden sheep" for him—belies Agrippina's alleged fear of Marcus' revenge for his brother Lucius.[15] The real reasons for this "first death of the new principate," it seems, are that Marcus was potentially more popular than Nero: besides his blameless life, he was mature, noble, and descended from Augustus.[16] Immediately after follows the death of her inveterate enemy, Claudius' trusted freedman Narcissus, attributed to Agrippina in spite of Nero's reluctance.[17] Then we hear that Agrippina, now burning for evil domination, has as her supporter Nero's disliked imperial freedman Pallas, who had convinced Claudius to sabotage himself by his incestuous marriage and lethal adoption.[18] Such intrigue and wiles juxtapose the following list of public honors for her, including the watchword "Best of Mothers."[19] The whole clearly suggests that Nero's initial days were overshadowed by his mother, who was still wickedly scheming.

Agrippina's Unquenchable Thirst for Power and Eminence? Alternative Voices

Was it enough to have her son be Rome's emperor? Perhaps not. Agrippina's competitiveness was keen. Like Livia, she was both wife and mother of a ruling princeps. For the last five years she had been prominent at Claudius' side, and in the flush of her son's first days as Rome's new ruler, she might anticipate continued influence with his young successor. She lived in the same imperial residence as did her son.[20] Could Agrippina not rightly be called a *princeps femina*, a leading woman (even "prince among women") as Julia Augusta had been?[21] Could she be still more? Her initial appearances with Nero, if we believe Cassius Dio, broadcast her eminence: in public the two were seen often reclining in the same litter, or even with her in the litter and him walking alongside.[22] (Did she here recall the stories of her second husband, Passienus, obsequiously trotting alongside Caligula's litter?) Further, in this period she enjoyed much more public visibility than was documented even for Julia Augusta in either Augustus' or Tiberius' reign.[23]

But Agrippina is absent from the *Apocolocyntosis*, an extraordinary piece written and presumably performed precisely at this juncture. This satire, transmitted anonymously but now attributed to Seneca, entertained the new emperor Nero and his court in late 54 CE.[24] Prefaced by a panegyrical passage auguring that Nero, the new, Apollo-like emperor, will initiate a new Golden Age,[25] the *Apocolocyntosis* focuses on Claudius' regime. In 15 chapters of prose and verse it lampoons Claudius' apotheosis, his physical infirmities and ignominious death, his erudition that is ridiculed as literary pretension, his all-too-zealous participation in judicial matters, his subservience to his freedmen and to Messalina, and his savagery in killing "35 senators, 221 equestrians, and innumerable others," many of whom are named in the short work.[26] But Agrippina is not named even once, despite her activities as Claudius' wife since 49.

Among the satire's many victims appear only two otherwise ascribed to Agrippina's maleficence.[27] Lucius Silanus, to whom the toddler Octavia had been betrothed in 41 but who was "removed" in 48 so Nero could be affianced in his stead (see Chapter 4), surfaces in three passages. None refers to Agrippina.[28] The death of Domitia Lepida in 54 CE is alluded to when Claudius' unnamed mothers-in-law are cited among the relatives he massacred. Agrippina is not named in the satire, contrasting Tacitus' later unmistakable indictment of her for her sister-in-law's death.[29] Yet Agrippina does not have a positive role in the satire: the effusive praise of Nero depicts the Apollo-like youth alone, making no nod to advisors, much less to his mother as the mastermind of his accession.[30]

Seneca set himself a dicey task with the *Apocolocyntosis*. The catalogue of Claudius' disgraces and crimes made a mockery of the state-sanctioned apotheosis,[31] yet the official honors for *divus* Claudius conveyed special prestige to Nero and Agrippina.[32] How did the piece actually play out at an imperial banquet? Did Agrippina laugh heartily throughout the malicious take-down of her husband, even when it turned to Lucius Silanus, incest, or other potentially incriminating topics? Did other diners look to her as well as to Nero before reacting to the jibes?[33] Where were Antonia, Britannicus, and Octavia—the latter now wife of the new princeps—during the mortifying spoofs of their father's life and death?[34] They too have no roles in the biting skit. Agrippina's absence in the *Apocolocyntosis* suggests her problematic position in Nero's principate. No matter her influence, power structures had not changed: especially in these early days, the court had to focus on the new male princeps.

Non-literary Evidence

Yet Agrippina's exceptional prominence is signaled in a contemporary depiction of her harmonious, almost equal relationship with Nero: earlier imperial women had no such public visibility in their lifetimes. In 54–55 CE Agrippina extraordinarily appears face to face—really, nose to nose—with Nero on the obverse of gold and silver coins (see Ill. 5.1).[35] This is Rome's first instance of a centrally struck coin's obverse depicting an emperor together with a woman; just as remarkable is that Agrippina, not Nero, is

Ill. 5.1 Agrippina face-to-face with the new emperor Nero on an *aureus* from Rome struck 54–55. © The Trustees of the British Museum.

Ill. 5.2 Agrippina and Nero, jugate, on an *aureus* from Rome struck 54–55. © The Trustees of the British Museum.

identified on the obverse.[36] Only on the reverse is Nero identified, by a legend surrounding an oak-wreath, "To Nero Caesar Augustus Germanicus Imperator, son of *divus* Claudius, in his first tribunician power."[37] The issue is also noteworthy as a rare face-to-face double portrait. The whole is astonishing in its apparent acknowledgement of Agrippina's power.

Agrippina is less visually dominant on another type centrally struck in gold and silver that same year (Ill. 5.2), although it still is rare to have a woman honored by such public exposure. On the obverse Agrippina is shown posed behind Nero and facing the same way, and Nero's foregrounded head overlaps and partially obscures hers.[38] The reverse image, adorned with Agrippina's name, titles, and EX S C (in accordance with a senatorial decree), depicts a quadriga of elephants bearing two thrones on which sit radiate figures of *divus* Claudius and *divus* Augustus. The quadriga references the games associated with Claudius' deification, and the juxtaposition of Agrippina's name with the image suggests her responsibility for Claudius' funeral ceremonies as well as her pivotal role in the imperial transmission.[39] The precious gold and silver issues presumably targeted the audience of Rome's elite and military, those whose support of the principate was indispensable. After these splendid issues of 55, however, Agrippina does not appear again on central coinage of any denomination.

Agrippina's role in Nero's new principate is commemorated outside Rome as well, although with less secure dating. A full-sized relief from the Sebasteion in Aphrodisias depicts Nero being crowned by a woman who must be Agrippina[40] (see Ill. 5.3). The hairstyle and face accord with

Ill. 5.3 Oversized marble relief of Agrippina crowning Nero, from the Sebasteion at Aphrodisias. © New York University Excavations at Aphrodisias (G. Petruccioli).

Agrippina's depiction on the two coin issues of 54–55 just discussed.[41] On the relief Agrippina stands next to Nero facing forward. The two figures are roughly the same size, although Nero's visage is slightly larger than hers.[42] Her thick himation (Greek mantle) is slung low over her hips and reveals a thin chiton belted under her breasts. Above her characteristic curls rises a *stephane*, an upright, pediment-shaped diadem.[43] Looking toward her son with a slightly inclined head, she crowns him with a laurel wreath in her right hand. In her left hand and arm she cradles a full cornucopia, an attribute of Tyche/Good Fortune that here symbolizes the prosperity of the new age under the new princeps. Nero, whose stance somewhat mirrors her pose, tilts his upper body slightly away from her.[44] His military outfit once included a spear in his right hand and perhaps an orb in his left. His helmet, presumably removed for the crowning illustrated in the scene, is depicted behind his right foot.[45] Overall, Agrippina is as visually dominant as Nero.[46]

The relief apparently echoes the ancient historians' depiction of Agrippina as the engineer of her young son's accession. This Agrippina is more explicitly active than in her depiction with Claudius in the Sebasteion discussed in Chapter 4 (see Ill. 4.3). The Neronian relief presents two roughly equivalent and symmetrical figures. The Claudian scene, in contrast, originally centered on the emperor, frontally posed between Agrippina and a personification of the Roman People or Roman Senate. In that scene Agrippina clasps the hand of Claudius in a gesture associated with marital harmony, creating a strong horizontal in the tableau.[47] Her broad face, thin and somewhat downturned lips, and wide-set eyes resemble those of Claudius, further suggesting concord. No diadem or other hair adornment suggests special status for her.[48] Not Agrippina, but the now-headless Roman People or Senate on the viewer's right places the imperial oak-leaf crown on Claudius. In sum, in the Claudian relief Agrippina was balanced by a male figure personifying the Roman state. In contrast, the Neronian relief displays Agrippina and Nero alone. On it Agrippina's face, so unlike her earlier depiction in the sanctuary, is long and triangular like that of Nero, making their relationship the more obvious.[49] But her crowning of Nero suggests that she is of equal, perhaps even greater, status than he.[50]

If R. R. R. Smith is correct in inferring from the finish, detail, and design of the Agrippina and Nero relief that this creation in Aphrodisias is "a likely candidate for having been based on a Roman composition,"[51] Agrippina's authority in Nero's accession was well known and openly acknowledged. Corroboration may be the 8-cm (3.14 in) cameo now in the shrine of the Three Kings in Cologne's Cathedral (see Ill. 5.4).[52] On it Agrippina crowns Nero, although in this case the wreath she holds is redundant given the laurel crown Nero already wears.[53] On the cameo, as in Aphrodisias, Agrippina carries a cornucopia and the young Nero wears a cuirass as the new *imperator.* The cameo was almost certainly made for someone in the imperial court.[54]

Ill. 5.4 Agrippina crowning Nero on a cameo, 8.04 × 6.41 cm. Cathedral of Cologne, Shrine of the Three Kings (Dreikönigsschrein), front Epiphany side, trapezoid plate, right side (cameo Catalogue 1, position number 55). © The High Cathedral of Cologne, Cathedral Office (Photo: Matz and Schenk).

That court's attitude toward Nero's mother is also reflected in a poem presented as a birthday present to her. Preserved in the *Anthologia Palatina*, this is an *isopsephia*, or epigram in which the sum of letters taken as numerical signs is identical in each pair of lines. The clever piece by Leonidas of Alexandria reads, "One will send crystal, another silver, a third topazes, rich birthday gifts. I, look, having merely made two 'isopsephon' couplets for Agrippina, am content with this my gift, which envy will not damage." Leonidas is known to have been in Nero's court.[55] Given the historical circumstances of 55 and following, this birthday of Agrippina must be 6 November 54, that is, within Nero's first month as emperor. Leonidas' epigram underscores alike the high standing of Nero's mother in Nero's first days and the opulence of Rome's imperial family.

Neither material from Nero's new court nor the more public relief in Aphrodisias, however, hints at the scandalized horror Tacitus and others evince about Agrippina at Nero's accession. But how many details about Nero's accession and initial months could Aphrodisias' citizens and visitors know?[56] They were surely ignorant about Agrippina's intrigues at the court and among Rome's elite that get such play from the historians, even if the death of Marcus Junius Silanus—"the first death of the new principate" that Agrippina contrived in Tacitus' account—may have impacted them. The "mild and noble" Silanus had been killed while proconsul of Asia, poisoned by minions of Nero's estates in that province that also included Aphrodisias.[57]

Nonetheless, almost everyone outside the capital city would have been unaware of the horrified fear the historians depict in Rome. After noting the death of Marcus Silanus at the opening of *Annals* 13, for example, Tacitus hyperbolically adds, "Full-scale slaughter would have ensued if Burrus and Seneca had not moved to prevent it... they strove in tandem against the brutality of Agrippina who, blazing with every desire for evil domination, had (the imperial freedman) Pallas on her side."[58] In the *Life of Vespasian* Suetonius explains an early lull in the political career of Vespasian, Rome's emperor from 69 to 79, by adducing his dread of "Agrippina, who was still powerful with her son and additionally bursting with lethal hate for the friends of Narcissus—even though that man was now dead."[59] If this is true, Vespasian's pointed fear of Agrippina would date to 54 and early 55, since Narcissus died almost immediately after Claudius.[60] Suetonius' note, obviously written with hindsight, suggests how ephemeral Agrippina's power over Nero would be even as it pointedly conveys the fear she caused.

Some Realities of Power in 54–55

The new emperor, Nero, who turned 17 by the end of 54, had need of advisors, experienced generals, financial experts, and many others. His "training" for his position was weak indeed: mainly rhetoric and an avoidance of philosophy.[61] Claudius' imperial functionaries Pallas and other imperial freedmen passed into the new emperor's control and service.[62] Others offering Nero more prestige, as well as continuity and experience, were Seneca, Burrus, and Agrippina. Seneca and Burrus, men some 15 years older than Agrippina,[63] were both deeply obligated to her. She had arranged Seneca's recall from exile in 49 to tutor Nero, and it was she who brought Burrus to eminence two years later as sole praetorian prefect (see Chapter 4). The historians portray the two men united in opposition to Agrippina even in Nero's first days:[64] "the first death of the new principate" (that of Marcus Junius Silanus) reportedly led to Seneca and Burrus working together to restrain Agrippina's "brutality" (Tac. *Ann.* 13.1–2). Similarly, after Cassius Dio sweepingly states that initially Agrippina managed all the business of the empire, received various embassies, and corresponded with peoples, governors, and kings, he then notes that Seneca and Burrus, "the most sensible and most influential of the men at Nero's court, put a stop to her meddling."[65] Such constructs set up the well-worn Roman trope: an experienced, self-controlled man—or even more than one—against an unstable and lethally impulsive woman, in this case Agrippina.

But the ties of obligation, what Romans called *gratia*, undoubtedly made the situation less obviously antagonistic, especially in Nero's early days as princeps.[66] More importantly, all the advisers were dealing with an immature, unproven boy suddenly handed unlimited power. Seneca's and Burrus' deep obligations to Agrippina and investment in imperial continuity surely allied them with her in a joint attempt to guide the young Nero on his first steps. The three must have seen each other often as they attended Nero daily during the regular round of feasting, entertainments, and festivities. Burrus, as praetorian prefect, presumably attended daily debriefings in the imperial residence. Seneca's close relationship with Nero is particularly stressed: authors make a point of his ghost-writing Nero's speeches, including the eulogy of Claudius.[67] Its praise of Claudius' ancestors, his erudition, the foreign successes of his rule, and his intelligence and foresight must have pleased Agrippina, the lynchpin of the succession, even if the senators had laughed at Claudius' cited wisdom.

Agrippina, too, surely had a lot of advice for her son Nero, the new princeps. Financial matters, which she was said to have keenly pursued (see Chapter 4), were a natural topic: she and Nero jointly used the procurator Gaius Julius Spartiaticus to oversee shared imperial estates (probably in Achaea),[68] and they undoubtedly had other resources in common. (We discuss shortly some later bitter arguments over money between mother and son.) Agrippina's long experience and intelligence prepared her for other undertakings. She had been active in the court for over five years, meeting embassies, receiving the submission of foreign leaders, and attending weighty discussions. Her entire life, other than the years in exile and those under Messalina, had been devoted to socializing and networking with Rome's elite, even if she is presented as increasingly isolated from her peers by competitiveness and overweening self-confidence. She interacted so closely with the imperial freedmen administrators that she was rumored to be lovers with Pallas, the supervisor of finances.[69] Her father's name endeared her to the praetorians and the wider military. Finally, her public appearances alongside Claudius assisting Rome's populace during conflagrations and bread shortages gave her popular cachet and knowledge of the city that more conservatively retiring women lacked, and of which even Nero was as yet naïve.[70]

At this point Agrippina apparently considered that her ancestry, background, and interests entitled her not only to transmit imperial power, but also to wield it. She pushed ever harder to enter traditionally male politics in Nero's first days, according to the historians. She caused the senate to meet on the "Palatium" rather than in the Curia or another usual meeting spot.[71] This "Palatium" may be the Library of Apollo, part of Augustus' house on the Palatine that had served senatorial meetings in the emperor's failing later years,[72] or the term may more generally indicate all the imperial residences that by 54 covered most of the Palatine[73] (see Ill. 1.1). Agrippina reportedly listened to the debating senators while she hid behind a curtain at an entry into their meeting room. To corroborate the unusual story of Agrippina surreptitiously partaking in senatorial meetings, Tacitus adds a detail of senatorial business. Despite Agrippina's opposition to this undermining of her former husband's authority, in 54 the senate removed the obligation that quaestors designate give gladiatorial shows, a change Claudius had enacted in 47.[74] Although this tense moment between Agrippina and the senate cannot be verified,[75] Cassius Dio also reports her being at the edge of senatorial meetings. An excerpt usually placed in 54 holds that "Agrippina used to attend the meetings of the senate, receive the embassies, and other like actions."[76] This report echoes the third-century historian's summary of Livia's political prominence: "except that she [Livia] never ventured to enter the senate-chamber or the camps or the public assemblies, she undertook to manage everything as if she were sole ruler" (57.12.3). Agrippina went a step farther, at least in Nero's early days.

Subtle signs suggest that even in these first months, however, Nero was already distancing himself from his mother. At the end of 54 he requested that the senate install an honorific statue to his natal father, Gnaeus Domitius Ahenobarbus, and grant consular insignia to his former tutor Asconius Labeo.[77] Nero's honor for Ahenobarbus—who had openly disparaged his own marriage with Agrippina (see Chapter 2)—contrasts with Agrippina's stress on her connections to Augustus, Germanicus, Caligula, Claudius, and Livia. Although "Augustan" connections helped legitimize Nero, his memorial for his biological father pushed against his mother and her touted benefits to him. The statue is long gone, but perhaps its original placement was on the Via Sacra near Ahenobarbus' house. The Arval Brethren are known to have offered sacrifices there in Ahenobarbus' memory on his birthday, 11 December, in 55, 58, and 59.[78] As for Asconius Labeo: he is a cipher now. All we can say is that he is not connected to Agrippina. The statue and consular insignia seem timid, but perceptible, pushbacks to Agrippina's apparent strength at the end of 54.

An even more notorious incident that year was Agrippina's actual attempt to meet foreign ambassadors in a formal setting. Nero, enthroned, was being approached by an embassy from the Armenians when Agrippina also began to advance to his tribunal. This would have been an unparalleled scene: a Roman woman receiving dignitaries from a foreign state.[79] Seneca (as Tacitus holds), or Seneca and Burrus together (according to Cassius Dio), averted the scandal by suggesting to Nero that he descend from the tribunal to greet his approaching mother.[80] The scene depicts Agrippina at her most transgressive: only the concerted attempt of Nero's other advisors maintained the façade of a strong, male-dominated empire.[81]

In the historians' narratives this marks the end of Agrippina's effective interference. Subsequent incidents disclose her weakened influence. According to Cassius Dio, after the incident with the Armenian embassy Nero entrusted all business to Seneca and Burrus.[82] Although Nero "had previously yielded the upper hand to his mother," now, whenever she admonished him, he simply persisted in whatever he was planning or doing—but feigned being abashed.[83] In an undated vignette, Agrippina piled up tangible coins worth 10 million sesterces in front of Nero as she tried to stop him from giving that amount to his freedman Doryphoros. Upon seeing the mound Nero exclaimed, "I did not realize I had given him so little!" and then doubled the sum.[84] The story, aimed at emphasizing Nero's profligacy and base affections, reveals Agrippina's weakening sway with her headstrong son.

Agrippina in 55—Tacitus' Portrayal

Agrippina's increasing frustration, wrath, and desperation are projected at length by Tacitus, who devotes much of his history of 55 to the breakdown of her influence (*Ann.* 13.12–22). He makes the catalyst, however, not her setback with the Armenian ambassadors—as does Cassius Dio—but rather Nero's infatuation with a freedwoman, Acte.[85] Historical causation is thus reduced to sexual lust. Ten long chapters contain a dizzying run of private and public events that highlight Agrippina raging, scheming, and even dumbfounded; not once is she presented sympathetically. The section begins when her discovery of Nero's affair with Acte—whom Agrippina scorns as a "freedwoman rival" and "serving-maid daughter-in-law"—leads to her promoting Britannicus to remind her son of her role as kingmaker.[86] This triggers the Claudian boy's murder at a family banquet.[87] Nero's isolation of Agrippina then unfolds: he removes her trusted helpmeet and imperial freedman, Pallas, and maliciously demeans her socially and politically with changes Tacitus accentuates with the gnomic, "There is nothing among human affairs so unstable and fleeting as the reputation of power not rooted in its own strength."[88] The quick-moving and vivid chapters end with Agrippina's angry rebuke of a treason charge against her. Tacitus corroborates all this detail, which includes accounts of intimate banquets and long speeches even by Agrippina herself, by referring to Fabius Rusticus, Pliny the Elder, and Cluvius Rufus as his sources and by pointedly stating his own authorial impartiality.[89] In short, the ten chapters brilliantly and convincingly depict Agrippina's precipitous loss of political power. Nonetheless, this is Tacitus' construct.

At each step Agrippina is depicted distinctly, sometimes as she acts or speaks, at times in others' words. The Acte section paints Agrippina interacting with her son arrogantly and threateningly,[90] then seductively,[91] and then tamely and indulgently showering him with her resources. She also acts impulsively, self-righteously, and indignantly, so that friends warn Nero not to be trapped by a "woman always fierce (*atrox*) and now also false."[92] She imprudently rejects Nero's conciliatory offer of some prized jewels and clothes owned by earlier imperial women, haughtily asserting that by rights they all belonged to her: it was *she* who had given them to him.[93] When she is further isolated by Pallas' dismissal, she recklessly blurts out in Nero's presence that Britannicus was the rightful heir to Claudius, not he who, adopted and brought to imperial power through his mother's wrongdoings, was ruling. She additionally threatens to widely publicize the "evils of the unhappy house" she caused while masterminding ungrateful Nero's accession, particularly her marriage that led to Claudius' poisoning. Finally, she vows to go with Britannicus to the praetorian camp, where her descent from Germanicus will ensure welcome.[94]

Her escalating desperation reached an unbearable peak in February 55. In Agrippina's attempts to control her son she had begun to advance Britannicus, reminding Nero of her role in his accession as she vainly grasped at her former power. Her scheme backfired when Nero arranged the poisoning death of his stepbrother.[95] At Britannicus' death during a feast with family and friends, on 11 February 55, Agrippina's total panic and shock revealed—or so "one could conclude from her face"—that she was as unaware of her son's plot as was Octavia, Nero's wife and Britannicus' own sister.[96] The sorry incident demonstrates both her sidelining in the new imperial court, and the collateral damage her plots could cause.

Despite the horrors of that February evening, in Tacitus' presentation Agrippina remains unbowed, at least initially. Her two-faced treatment of Britannicus—whom she had initially sequestered and diminished so that her own son could shine—is brought into relief as she embraces the bereft Octavia and scrambles to create a powerful group of "friends" to counter Nero. Agrippina's emotion is anger (*ira*), not fear, remorse at her neglected stepson's death, or anything of the ilk. She honors nobles and welcomes military tribunes and centurions "as though she were seeking a leader and a faction."[97] But her canvassing comes to nothing. Could it ever have succeeded? Nero soon leaves her residence, moves her into Antonia the Younger's house, and visits her rarely, perfunctorily, and always surrounded by centurions.[98]

A spurious treason accusation of Agrippina anchors the end of Tacitus' section on her in *Annals* 13, and its denouement shows her at her most arrogant and assured. The details of the charge were farfetched though perhaps plausible in her obvious attempts to control her son. In the setup Agrippina is depicted as mean-spirited and deceitful, belittling, and exploiting other women.[99] The gossipy indictment centered not on "the clichéd and often-heard charge that Agrippina was mourning the death of Britannicus or publicizing the wrongs to Octavia," but rather that she was supporting Rubellius Plautus, the great-grandson of Tiberius who was thus connected to Rome's first imperial family.[100] But in this telling the duplicitous web had little to do with Plautus; rather, it involved high-placed women, their clients, and their freedmen. The named accusers, Junia Silana, Domitia, Iturius, Calvisius, Atimetus, and the actor Paris, who was a favorite of Nero's,[101] are said to be moved not by concern for state or emperor but rather to settle old scores with Agrippina.[102] The denunciation before Nero widens even to implicate Burrus, although no reason is adduced. When the praetorian prefect appears before Nero, he not only exculpates himself but convinces Nero to give Agrippina a chance to defend herself. (It is here that Tacitus cites various authors, as mentioned above.[103]) Nero's fickle spinelessness emerges the more when we realize he does not dare face Agrippina in person.

In the long and brilliant speech Tacitus' Agrippina delivers to Burrus, Seneca, and imperial freedmen witnesses (*Ann.* 13.21, in direct speech), she vilifies Junia Silana and Domitia for decadent frivolity and contrasts the care with which she prepared Nero to rule Rome. She scoffs at the charge that she might have suborned troops in Rome, loyal provinces, or imperial slaves and freedmen. She finishes with the ironic admission that should Britannicus, Plautus, or some other gain the throne, *then* she would face real criminal charges—from which only Nero could absolve her (viz., charges of murdering Claudius to ensure Nero's accession). As she concludes, she peremptorily obtains a meeting with her son. Saying nothing to Nero about her innocence (Tacitus adds, "as if she seem not to trust in it") or her benefits to him ("as if she might seem to fault him for not acknowledging them"), she gains revenge on her accusers and rewards for her supporters.[104] The exile of Junia Silana, relegation of Calvisius and Iturius, and death of Atimetus are noted in the following short chapter (Tac. *Ann.* 13.22). After her starring role in these crowded but illogical chapters, Agrippina herself disappears from Tacitus' text until the beginning of the next book.[105]

The New Neronian Court

Other individuals and details in these ten intricate chapters provide unparalleled glimpses into Nero's imperial court. Tacitus names Nero's friends—nobles and imperial freedmen alike—who aided the teenager's encounters with the freedwoman Acte.[106] He notes the customary inclusion of "noble youths" at imperial banquets[107] and observes Nero's lavish benefactions to Rome's elite, especially when the young emperor wished to deflect criticism.[108] In the procurement and strengthening of Britannicus' lethal poison, Nero deployed the praetorian tribune who was the guard of the poisoner Locusta, suggesting there were meticulous files on anyone who came through the imperial residence. When initial attempts at the boy's poisoning failed, Nero impatiently lashed out at the tribune and Locusta, a small detail that underscores the emperor's impetuosity.[109] While charting Nero's swelling *animus* against the hapless Britannicus, Tacitus details the celebration of the palace's Saturnalian festival in 54,[110] adding to our understanding of court ritual. The list of actions Nero takes to humiliate and isolate Agrippina discloses that by this date wives and mothers of emperors were routinely assigned military guards, and that Agrippina earlier had a special honor of a German contingent.[111] We incidentally see that the imperial family's possessions on the Palatine included a storehouse of imperial women's clothes and jewels.[112]

Most importantly for this biography, Tacitus' ten packed chapters depict Agrippina doubling down on her inimitable arrogance, tenacity, and guile even as Nero shows himself ever more vile, unstable, and destructive. His murder of Britannicus is especially condemned: the historian cites public fear of the omens attending the youth's cheap and hurried burial as well as the rumor that Nero had earlier raped his stepbrother, the "last of the Claudian bloodline."[113] Later Nero, drunk and mistrustful at a late-night feast, is goaded by the actor Paris—although popular, scorned as low-born—to decide to kill his mother and Rubellius Plautus and to remove Burrus as a creature of Agrippina.[114] This belies Tacitus' description, five chapters earlier, of Nero's realization that he could not openly order the death of the stepbrother his mother was threatening to elevate.[115] Has Nero's impunity for Britannicus' murder encouraged him to ever more open criminality? In 55, even as the false treason charge against Agrippina falls apart, Nero is "fearful yet impatient to kill his mother."[116]

The final section on Agrippina's false accusation in 55 ends portentously, "For the moment Plautus was passed over in silence."[117] Together with the preceding chapters, this leaves no doubt that not only is Plautus doomed but so is Agrippina, despite her apparent victory in this skirmish. This was a court whose only norm was volatility, shifting alliances, and suspicion, much centered around Nero's and Agrippina's tense struggle for power.

Agrippina from 55 to 59

Curiously, however, Agrippina does not appear again in Tacitus until 59 CE and the opening of *Annals* 14, 35 chapters and four years later. There, schemes for her murder begin in earnest. What happened in the intervening four years? Indeed, what really happened in Nero's first year? Suetonius gives more detail about Agrippina's segregation from Nero's court, specifying that Nero forced her off the Palatine, enlisted people to harass her with lawsuits while she remained in Rome, and even after she left the city had them constantly badger her with insults and ridicule, from land and sea.[118] This suggests that her fall from Nero's favor was not so precipitous: Agrippina probably moved first from her home with Nero to the house of Antonia, then from the Palatine to elsewhere in Rome, and thereafter to other houses, such as the seaside villa at Antium or her country estates in Tusculum and Maevania in the Alban and Umbrian hills.[119] Further, Tacitus himself later remarks that, after killing his mother and returning to Rome in 59, the princeps threw himself into all the pleasures that some residual reverence for his mother had delayed.[120] This suggests that even after 55 Agrippina exerted some influence over her son.[121]

Documentary evidence provides more information about her presence and popularity between 55 and 59. In 56 in the important port city Puteoli (modern Pozzuoli, Italy), the wealthy Augustales—a largely freedman group devoted to Rome's imperial cult—dedicated games to Nero Claudius Caesar Augustus, "Agrippina Augusta," Jupiter Optimus Maximus, and the Genius of the Colony.[122] In Rome the Arval Brethren celebrated her birthday on 6 November in 57 and again in 58 (this time on the Capitoline Hill) and honored her in 58 during the celebration of Nero's birthday on 15 December.[123] In 55/56 the Brethren also made vows for the health and safety of Nero, Agrippina Augusta, and Octavia, Nero's wife.[124] Agrippina was still a significant member of the imperial house.

Further light on Agrippina in this hazy period comes from a fascinating find on the lower slopes of the Palatine near the later Colosseum and from a reworked magnificent image of Agrippina from the nearby Caelian Hill. Agrippina was exalted in 55/56 in an imperial cult installation raised by the group of the Aenatores Romani, Rome's Brass-Wind Instrument Players, on the northeast foot of the Palatine Hill along the valley used in Rome's triumphal processions[125] (see Ill. 4.4). Agrippina is the only woman known to have been honored in this shrine,[126] although her memory there underwent important vicissitudes. The Aenatores, to use their collective name, were minor functionaries who supplied music for Rome's official celebrations.[127] Their sacred precinct dates originally to the Augustan period, and it was repeatedly renovated. Together with other archaeological

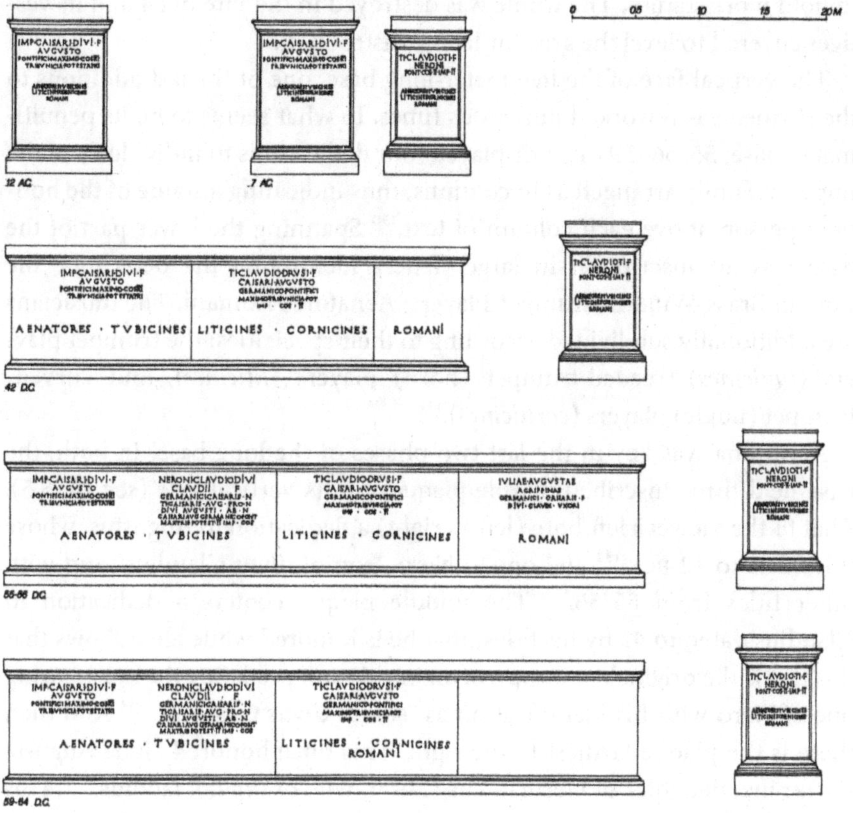

Ill. 5.5 Reconstruction of the phases of the dedications to the imperial family in the Shrine of the Aenatores Romani. The final two phases indicate honor for Agrippina and its subsequent obliteration. Material now in the Museo Nazionale Romano delle Terme di Diocleziano. Image from Morizio in Panella 1996, Fig. 180; courtesy of C. Panella and the Archivio Fotografico Scavo Meta Sudans, Dipartimento di Scienze dell'Antichità, Sapienza Università di Roma.

material, inscriptions for statues within its remains, including what was ultimately a five-meter-long statue base faced with three inscribed marble plaques, allow the following interpretation [128] (see Ill. 5.5). In the Augustan period, perhaps in 12 BCE, the Brass-Wind Instrument Players raised a statue to Augustus. In 7 BCE they added an honorific statue to Tiberius.[129] In January 42 (CE), soon after Claudius' accession, the group had an enclosure built that would house the freestanding statues and an additional long base to hold more statues. The whole was destroyed in the Fire of 64 and its vestiges covered to level the area for later construction.

The vertical face of the five-meter-long base, one of the last additions to the shrine, was reworked numerous times. In what seems to be its penultimate phase, 55/56–59 CE, it displayed four dedications to individuals of the imperial family arranged as in columns, thus indicating a statue of the honored person above each column of text.[130] Spanning the lower part of the base was an inscription in larger letters identifying the dedicants, the Roman Brass-Wind Instrument Players: Aenatores Romani. The musicians are additionally subdivided according to their specialties: the trumpet players (*tubicines*), reeded-trumpet (horn) players (*liticines*), and curved-trumpet (bugle) players (*cornicines*).[131]

Agrippina was key in the last two phases of the long base. In both, the base held three inscribed marble plaques on its vertical face (see Ill. 5.5). That to the viewer's left bore (left to right) a dedication to Augustus, whose titles date to 12 BCE,[132] and one to Nero, "son of *divus* Claudius" and with other titles from 55/56.[133] The middle plaque centers a dedication to Claudius dated to 42 by his titles; that he is honored while alive shows that this text is the original, or a copy, of an inscription predating the neighboring one of Nero with his identification as "son of *divus* Claudius."[134] And then there is the plaque farthest to the right. This once honored "Julia Augusta Agrippina, daughter of Germanicus Caisar, wife of *divus* Claudius."[135] This seems part of the shrine's redecoration in 55/56, the date of Nero's honorific text.[136] If so, even after her reported fallout with Nero by mid-55 the Aenatores' shrine in Rome's heart witnesses continuing public approbation of Agrippina as part of the imperial house. In particular, her acclamation as "wife of *divus* Claudius," and Nero's as "son of *divus* Claudius," hint at her pivotal role in the transfer of imperial power.[137]

The archaic spelling "Caisar" found in all the base's dedicatory texts, including that to Nero, nods to Claudius' additions to the Roman alphabet, of which he was quite proud (see Chapter 4). It is particularly apt for the Aenatores' shrine. The Claudium, or Temple of *divus* Claudius, whose construction was sponsored by Agrippina, began probably in 55 and loomed over the little aedicula from its dominating position on the western slope of the Caelian Hill (see Ill. 4.4). Additionally, the *Apocolocyntosis*' note, that *tubicines*, *cornicines*, and other brass-wind players played so loudly at Claudius' funeral that even that addled, semi-deaf emperor could hear them, suggests Claudius' fondness for these musicians.[138]

Yet the honors for Agrippina were rescinded before the shrine was destroyed in the Great Fire of 64. Sometime after 55/56, the marble plaque inscribed for Agrippina was reworked and its inscription effaced. This caused the word *Romani*, the last element of the long inscription identifying the dedicants of 55/56 CE, to be (re)inscribed on the second slab, under *liticines* and *cornicines*[139] (see Ill. 5.5). To judge from the final placement of *Romani*, low on the base's second slab, about a third of the long base was then left blank. Only the honors to Augustus, Nero, and Claudius remained trumpeted by the Aenatores Romani. The removal of Agrippina's inscription and presumable statue left a conspicuous void.[140] This surely occurred after her murder and denunciation by Nero in 59, the conclusion of this chapter.

The erasure of Agrippina from the Shrine of the Aenatores is echoed by a presumably more official eradication of her in the Claudium, or Temple of *divus* Claudius on the Caelian, although this history is even more uncertain. In 54 Agrippina had become the *flaminica* of *divus* Claudius. She began construction of a temple honoring the new *divus* that was later "almost totally destroyed" by Nero before being renewed and finished by Vespasian.[141] Martial, writing at the end of the first century when the shrine again had a religious use, remarks that Nero had repurposed the edifice as a nymphaeum.[142] The nymphaeum is often associated with Nero's development of his Golden House after the Great Fire of 64,[143] but it could just as easily date earlier, to his mother's death and disgrace in 59. The Claudium, on its platform measuring 200 × 180 m, is the largest imperial cult sanctuary in Rome[144] (see Ill. 4.4). Its size and splendor—it was adorned with statuary, fountains, niches, and ordered rows of trees or shrubs with a large west-facing hexastyle prostyle *aedes* (what we might call a temple structure)—reflect Agrippina's aspirations and resources in 54. Particulars of the Claudium remain obscure in the absence of new excavations,[145] but the scant information we have suggests that Nero's modifications of the grandiose structure partly erased Agrippina from the city.

A fine portrait statue of Agrippina found nearby ties into the history we conjecture here. Remains of an over-life-size female standing statue in graywacke, fragmented into 41 pieces, were discovered by R. Lanciani on the Caelian in 1885 in a semicircular late-antique wall northeast of the Claudium, after which the find passed into Rome's Conservatori Museums.[146] More than a century later, R. Belli Pasqua recognized that the restored statue fit a graywacke head of Agrippina the Younger purchased in Rome in

Ill. 5.6 Head of Agrippina from the Caelian statue. Graywacke, 30 cm H. Ny Carlsberg Glyptotek, Copenhagen (inv. no. 753). © Ny Carlsberg Glyptotek, Copenhagen/Ole Haupt.

the late 19th century and now in the collection of the Ny Carlsberg Glyptotek of Copenhagen (see Ill. 5.6). That head, slightly reworked but originally with diadem and a veil, is from the fourth (Stuttgart) portrait type for Agrippina[147] (see Ill. 5.7). In 2007 its cast was added to the reconstructed statue in the latter's permanent display in Rome's Centrale Montemartini Museum[148] (see Ill. 5.8). The whole measures over 2 m tall.[149] It is commanding for its large size, open gesture, and voluminous robes.

This portrait statue of Agrippina underwent changes over the years, with its head recut twice (see Ill. 5.7). The first modification assimilated her face more closely to that of the young princeps Nero, in particular by refashioning her mouth to have more cupid's-bow lips.[150] The greater similitude of Agrippina's portrait to images of her son apparently emphasized her harmony with Nero. A later modification of the portrait, in which the diadem was scalloped on top and otherwise cut to accommodate the insertion of large gems, can be dated to the fourth century CE.[151] One

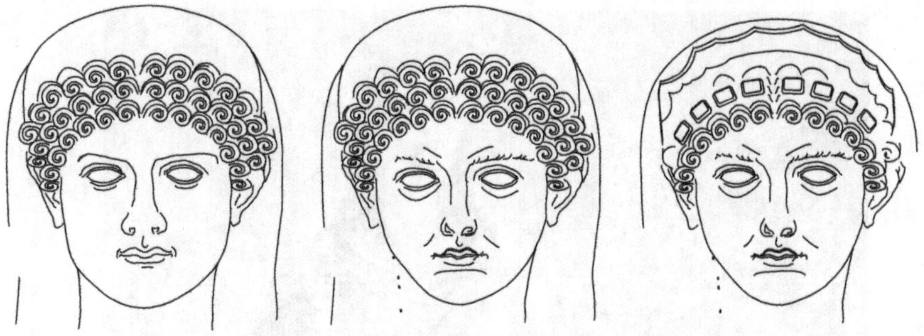

Ill. 5.7 Reconstructed phases of graywacke head of Agrippina from the Caelian. The second phase includes recutting of lips to more closely resemble those of the young Nero. The final phase includes recutting of the diadem to accommodate inset gems. Drawings of Ny Carlsberg Glyptotek inv. no. 753 by Thora Fisker (kindness of M. Moltesen).

wonders whether at that late date the handsome female visage was still identifiable as Agrippina.

The statue's body type remains uncertain. Early reconstructions of the fragments suggested the *orans* type, in which the female subject's hands lifted in a praying gesture also raise a thick swath of her mantle above her front midsection. This is a conventional type.[152] But more recent restorations better fit the fragments and liken the statue to the "hip-swath" type, in which the sculpted woman's lowered arms allow a thick fold of the mantle to fall around the hip section[153] (see Ill. 5.8). Both types are common for priestess commemorations[154] and appropriate for Agrippina as *flaminica* of *divus* Claudius. It may be, in fact, that this image of Agrippina does not follow any single type but is exceptional, albeit incorporating religious elements:[155] Tacitus' Agrippina, "a unique example up to this day" (*Ann.* 12.42), would have appreciated a distinctive statue like no other. Sometime after the head was recut to accommodate jewels, probably in the fourth century (Ill. 5.7), the statue was deliberately damaged in the neck, back of the head, mid-thoracic region, and forward left hip areas. Remarkably, the face remained mostly intact[156] (see Ill. 5.8).

The statue's find spot near the precinct and Agrippina's praying stance strongly suggest that it was originally installed someplace in the large shrine to *divus* Claudius.[157] If so, since it represented a living person and not the deity to which the whole shrine was consecrated, it was surely outside the temple building proper.[158] As we see shortly when turning to Agrippina's

Ill. 5.8 Statue of Agrippina (graywacke; body 180 cm H) from the Caelian Hill, as reassembled in the Musei Capitolini, Centrale Montemartini, Rome (inv. no. MC1882), with a cast of the portrait head now in the Ny Glyptotek, Copenhagen (inv. no. 753). © Sovrintendenza di Roma Capitale—Foto in Comune.

death, the more obvious assimilation of her mouth to that of Nero did not draw the two together. What happened to the statue after Agrippina's murder in 59, when Nero repudiated his mother, imputed her death to treacherous guilt, and irresolutely urged suppression of her memory? (See Chapter 6.) Surely, Agrippina's striking graywacke statue could not have remained visible in the Claudium after 59, especially since Nero's return to Rome from Campania late that year passed by the shrine while celebrating his escape from Agrippina's alleged conspiracy.[159]

We may conjecture the following. After her death in Campania in 59 Agrippina's glorious graywacke statue in Rome was carefully removed and stored by a follower or sympathizer,[160] akin to the effacement of the Aenatores' honorific dedication to Agrippina. In some form, however, both survived the city's devastation in the Fire of 64 and Nero's subsequent transformation of at least part of Claudium into a *nymphaeum* for his Golden House.[161] When Vespasian completed the Temple of *divus* Claudius (Suet. *Vesp.* 9), markedly respecting his former commander and the principate overall while conspicuously rejecting Nero's wastefulness, he may have reinstalled Agrippina's statue in the precinct.[162] Alternatively, it may have been exhibited in another spot on the Caelian, such as in a shrine to Isis or in the great Antonine palace now identified as the home of Commodus.[163] In any case, its recutting to accommodate inset gems in its diadem indicates it was on display around the fourth century, although we have no way of knowing if it had been exhibited continuously since the Flavian restoration of the Claudium.

Together, material evidence indirectly suggests that—despite reports of open acrimony between Agrippina and Nero and concerted efforts of Seneca and Burrus to limit her influence—Agrippina hopefully enjoyed some détente with her son.[164] She had acted ever more impetuously and imperiously during her marriage to Claudius and at the beginning of Nero's rule. But in menacing and troubled times she knew how to lie low and wait for a break. Her retreat in 55 had precedents: she left no trace while her first husband Ahenobarbus navigated Tiberius' precarious Rome, and she vanished while Messalina acted ever more unpredictably and lethally during Claudius' early principate. Agrippina had experienced enough vicissitudes to hope that in time Nero might want her again—perhaps even need her again—to strengthen the *domus divina*. It may have been with no real surprise that she responded positively to Nero's feigned reconciliation four years after Britannicus' death and her triumphantly rebutted treason charge.

The *Annus Horribilis* 59

By 59 Nero, now 21, and the court were functioning effectively enough: no calamity had struck the Roman world for five years.[165] True, starting at the latest in 56 Nero disreputably engaged in wandering drunken and disguised through Rome's streets while attacking others, but this stage of public brawling ended fairly soon.[166] The mainly uneventful quinquennium (five-year period) after his accession did include a number of sexual liaisons for Nero, but nothing extraordinary for a Roman emperor.[167] Nero generally ignored his young wife, Octavia, whom he had married in 53 and would kill in 62.[168] His initial infatuation with the freedwoman Acte, which supposedly triggered Agrippina's disastrous attempt to tighten control over him, gave way to other sexual affairs,[169] including with a mistress who strikingly resembled Agrippina.[170] His steadiest sexual partner since 58, however, was Poppaea Sabina (hereafter called Poppaea), previously married twice and reputedly the most beautiful woman in Rome.[171] Although she is depicted as having extraordinary influence over Nero—both Tacitus and Cassius Dio depict her nagging as activating Agrippina's death[172]—at this point her aspirations focused on securing marriage with Nero.[173] She would be a worthy consort for the princeps. Her family was long connected to the imperial court—indeed, her mother had been forced to suicide by a jealous Messalina in 47—and she had demonstrated her fecundity in the young boy, Rufrius Crispinus, she bore to her first husband.[174]

Agrippina's general absence from historical notice after 55 must correspond with her abandonment of obvious political maneuvering. Yet she was still a political force. In 58 a sensational senatorial trial defamed her as sexually involved with Seneca. Publius Suillius Rufus, a hated informer, was arraigned in the senate for infractions of the Cincian law restricting payment to advocates. Instead of refuting the charge openly, Suillius deflected the hostility against him by faulting the powerful Seneca on various grounds. Among his other criticisms were that Seneca had been "an adulterer in Germanicus' household" and had "defiled the women of imperial men." Suillius was found guilty.[175] A fragment of Cassius Dio, which must refer to this trial although it now lacks Suillius' name, reports that Seneca himself was accused, including for a sexual liaison with Agrippina.[176] Although the details of this report fit Cassius Dio's patent antipathy toward Seneca,[177] the note suggests that Agrippina's retirement from Rome had not ended her contact with Nero's advisor. This must have been true as well for Burrus, who perilously had been implicated in Agrippina's fictitious treason charge but who was equally indebted to her. The report also stresses Agrippina's continuing identification with the popular Germanicus.

Thus, although Tacitus does not name Agrippina from *Annals* 13.22 until the opening of *Annals* 14,[178] she certainly was not absent from the minds of those in Nero's court. Indeed, in 59 Agrippina reportedly dominated the thoughts of Poppaea and Nero alike. Tacitus' Poppaea claims that Agrippina was preventing her marriage with Nero; Cassius Dio's Poppaea fears that Nero's fixation on his Agrippina-double lover proved a continuing dependence on his mother.[179] Indeed, Agrippina was still actively resented, not forgotten at all: "*Everyone* wanted the power of Nero's mother to be broken, and no one believed that the loathing of the son would go so far as to her murder"—or so Tacitus says.[180] But with that, we come to Agrippina's death in 59.

Death, Sex, and Agrippina

Agrippina certainly did not prompt the events leading to her brutal murder. But was there a specific trigger? With hindsight the ancient historians agree that once Nero gained power, his mother's killing was inevitable.[181] If we believe her fabled retort to Chaldaeans at Nero's birth, "Let him kill me, only let him rule!" (see Chapter 2),[182] with Nero's accession she had achieved her life goal. What more could there be, other than her son heeding her advice and needing her? As Tacitus' Agrippina pointed out in self-defense in 55, what really mattered in Rome was the loyalty of the praetorians and other troops in Rome, the devotion of the provinces (viz., their inhabitants and occupying armies), and the allegiance of the enslaved and freed members of the imperial administration.[183] But since 55 Agrippina had few ways to interact with these important players. Once Nero seized Rome's resources, her own were meaningless, as she had bitterly learned in their arguments over imperial gifts in 55. Her threats to expose the dirty secrets of Nero's accession—her speciously legal marriage with her uncle Claudius and his poisoning at a feast—similarly had no effect: Claudius' marriages, banquets, and weakness for mushrooms were open jokes, mocked in the *Apocolocyntosis* and otherwise freely by Nero.[184] Various scholars have made much of Agrippina's ties with the praetorians, still loyal to her as Germanicus' daughter:[185] for instance, Burrus advised Nero in 59 that the praetorians would not harm Germanicus' offspring, since they were sworn to the family of the Caesars and remembered Germanicus.[186] But it is inconceivable that Agrippina could have raised the praetorians against Nero. Women did not command troops. Rome's ingrained patriarchy afforded Agrippina few, if any, means to gain or exert power.

Did Agrippina herself push for power at this moment? Every ancient account has her son, not she, initiate the measures leading to her death. In the cramped paragraph Suetonius devotes to her murder, Nero's resentment of Agrippina simply built up over time until, "terrified by her threats and violence," he finally decided to do away with his mother.[187] Tacitus and Cassius Dio also have Nero scheme for murder, although Poppaea—and perhaps Seneca as well—pushes the indecisive Nero to action through sexual intrigue and jealousy.[188]

Agrippina is reported to have engaged in incest with her son to retain her influence. This is unsurprising given Julio-Claudians' recurrent charges for this anathema (see Chapter 4). Further, at least dreams of sex with one's mother were reckoned as good for rulers. Artemidorus' *Oneirocritica* (*On Dreams*; ca. 200 CE) holds that a dream of having face-to-face sex with one's mother "is auspicious... for every politician and statesman, because a mother symbolizes one's homeland. So just as anyone [male] having sex, in accordance with the law of Aphrodite, with a compliant and willing partner is given authority over every part of her body, so a politician or statesman having this dream will preside over all the affairs of his city."[189] For Nero, however, even fantasy sex with his mother is confounded by the insistence that Agrippina desired Rome's rule for herself. The same tension holds for the historians' stories of her incest with her son.

Tacitus' chapter (*Ann.* 14.2) cites various authorities to corroborate rumors of incest, naming two. Cluvius (Rufus) blamed Agrippina for the shameful act, gave juicy particulars about her illicit seduction, and was seconded by unnamed authors. Added details make Cluvius' story the more plausible: Seneca worked actively against the indignity and sent in Nero's former lover Acte, who dissuaded Nero by emphasizing both Agrippina's gloating over the incest and the soldiers' intolerance of such a sacrilegious leader (*Ann.* 14.2.1). In contrast, Fabius Rusticus held Nero responsible, not Agrippina. This is only the second time in the extant later *Annals* that Tacitus identifies variant sources to enhance his credibility (and his earlier reference also refers to Agrippina).[190] Here Cluvius' blame of Agrippina is validated not only by "other authors'" claimed endorsement, but Tacitus also cites additional instances of Agrippina's "reprehensible" use of sex in the hope of domination: adultery with Lepidus (see Chapter 2), her long affair with (the imperial freedman) Pallas, and her transgressive marriage to her uncle.[191]

Cassius Dio's slightly different account (61.11.3–4) is more ambiguous yet just as damning. He first asserts that Agrippina promoted incest to prevent Nero from marrying Poppaea, even writing that the seductive Agrippina "enslaved" Nero much as she had earlier captivated her uncle Claudius.[192] The historian then backtracks, however, to wonder if she actually engaged in such activity or if its plausibility inspired the tale. Concluding that "it was agreed upon by all" that Nero conspicuously enjoyed a woman who closely resembled Agrippina, Cassius Dio insinuates Nero's culpability without completely exonerating Agrippina. Again, Agrippina is condemned for incest.

Suetonius, too, reports the incest, although not with Agrippina's death but in his section five chapters earlier on Nero's sexual behavior.[193] After asserting that "Nero's lust for his mother was notorious," he then wavers about whether Nero ever indulged in that passion. When "her enemies" would not let Nero consummate his lust for Agrippina, in fear that her awful power would increase still further, Nero sublimated by finding a mistress who strongly resembled his mother. Like the other historians, however, Suetonius substantiates the charge of incest with details, citing (anonymous) reports that bear out incestuous acts by the stains seen on Nero's clothes each time he shared a litter with his mother.[194]

Can we conclude that Agrippina engaged in incest with Nero in 59? The damning trope should not be unthinkingly dismissed given Nero's transgressive pansexuality and Agrippina's relative youth, physical fitness, and sex positivity.[195] Furthermore, by now she had been unmistakably relegated to the sidelines, displaced not by some lower-born woman she could scorn as a "freedwoman rival" but by the elite and beautiful Poppaea, who was keen to marry Nero and had already proved her fertility. Perhaps Agrippina also suspected Nero's increasing impetuosity and vileness would end in her own elimination, and incest was a last-ditch effort to save herself. But death at her son's orders was something even the redoubtable Agrippina could not prevent.

Denouement, March 59

Whether or not Agrippina engaged in incest with Nero, by 59 CE she had run out of time. Our authors present various versions of what led to her murder, with Tacitus including the most alternative stories and diverse explanations.[196] Nonetheless, and indicating that they drew on a common source, they generally agree on the following.[197] Nero began actively plotting in 59 to do away with his mother; after months of canvassing various options for her death, he settled on a contrived shipwreck of a trick boat in the Bay of Naples, so that she would drown; when she survived the wreck, he had her cut down by sailors.[198] He then panicked at the enormity of his crime and had her hurriedly cremated and buried, putting out the story that she had been justly killed after trying to assassinate him. Only after some more months in the Bay of Naples did Nero return to Rome, after he had sent to the senate the account of the alleged conspiracy we discuss at the end of this chapter. To his relief he found widespread acceptance of her death.[199]

We can never know all the details leading to her killing on 23 March 59, and more than one scholar has pointed out the contradictions and absurdities of what has been transmitted: the shipwreck, for instance, has seemed implausible since antiquity.[200] Nonetheless, at least some specifics sound likely, like the admission that poison would be futile against Agrippina because she had long taken antidotes.[201] That no one could be trusted to attack her incidentally denotes her continuing high esteem, something we have seen in the documentary evidence.[202] Likewise, it makes sense that the act did not take place in Rome, where Agrippina and her family were so prominent, and that it took some months for all the parts to fall into place.[203] But the historians' particulars are what make the story unforgettable, especially those of Tacitus.[204] He devotes the first thirteen chapters of *Annals* 14 to Agrippina's fall in 59 and its immediate aftermath. A fifth of the 65-chapter book, his memorable and elaborate narrative includes alternative versions, vivid quotations and indirect speech, complicated chains of events and double deceptions, poeticisms tinged with mordant cynicism, paradoxes and unexpected turns, and unusual minutiae. One example is that Anicetus, Nero's freedman who was long opposed to Agrippina, tricks out the boat with a lead ceiling for Agrippina's stateroom that should fall on her couch and crush her.[205] The historians' details and underwater archaeology have allowed L. Keppie to convincingly reconstruct the topography of the events[206] (see Ill. 5.9).

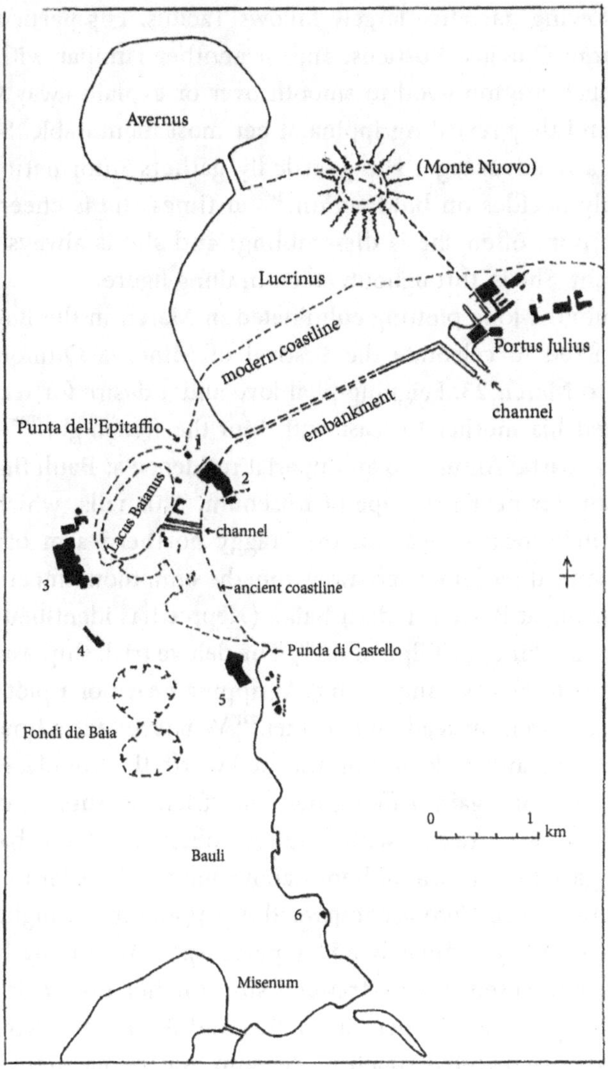

Ill. 5.9 The topography of Agrippina's murder in 59 in Baiae in the Bay of Naples. Key: 1 = Claudian nymphaeum; 2 = Villa of the Pisones; 3 = bath complexes; 4 = modern monumental park; 5 = Castello di Baia; 6 = Cento Camerelle. (Keppie 2011, 38; drawn by L. Keppie and used with his permission.) © The Classical Association 2011.

The following narrative largely follows Tacitus. His particulars, surely deriving from Cluvius, Rusticus, and/or another familiar with Agrippina and the court, are too good to smooth over or explain away with source criticism, and they reveal Agrippina at her most memorable. She schemes to exploit any advantage; she guardedly gathers information but then conclusively decides on bold action;[207] at times she is cheerily sincere, but much more often she is dissembling; and she is always strong and self-sufficient. She is, throughout, an enthralling figure.

Nero's months-long plotting culminated in March in the Bay of Naples, where he liked to celebrate the Festival of Minerva Quinquatrus from March 19 to March 23. Feigning filial love and a desire for reconciliation, Nero invited his mother to feast with him the first night.[208] She boated down from coastal Antium to an imperial residence at Bauli that Nero had arranged for her near the Cape of Misenum. This villa, which has never been definitely located, was on the craggy northern arm of the Bay of Naples,[209] some three kilometers away from the sumptuous imperial residence Nero was using at Baiae (modern Baia). (Keppie has identified Nero's villa as one at Baia's Punta dell'Epitaffio.[210]) The deluxe trick ship was offered for her transport to Nero's banquet, but Agrippina heard of a plot through an informant and went instead on her litter.[211] Whatever extra time this might take on the steep and rocky terrain was well worth the trouble, now that she would see her son again. Among her son's friends—surely not including Poppaea!—she was treated with carefree solicitude at the banquet, and Nero even gave her the seat of honor above himself.[212] After the protracted feast drew to a close Nero accompanied Agrippina out, clinging closely to her and kissing her intimately and repeatedly.[213] At last she boarded the specially ornamented, booby-trapped ship for her boat ride home. She was with two friends, Crepereius Gallus and Acerronia. Reclining on a sumptuously ornamented couch in the ship, Agrippina shared with them her delight at the reconciliation.[214]

Under a tranquil and star-filled sky the ship began to move smoothly from the shore when at a signal the ceiling above Agrippina's couch crashed down.[215] Gallus, standing next to the couch, was instantly killed, but the couch's high posts protected the reclining Agrippina and Acerronia. Around them swirled debris and confusion. Complicit sailors rushed to one side of the ship to capsize it and drown Agrippina, while those not in the evil plan struggled to keep the ship afloat. In the confusion Agrippina and Acerronia both slipped into the sea.[216] Ignorant of the plot and hoping to save herself,

Acerronia called out that *she* was the mother of the emperor and should be rescued! At which she was immediately bludgeoned to death with oars, pikes, and other sailors' tools. Agrippina, wounded in the shoulder during the mêlée but still physically strong, silently swam away in the dark.[217] She was serendipitously picked up by some light skiffs, perhaps fishing or oystering boats, and taken to the Lucrine Lake. From there she was carried to her villa at Bauli. By then her rescuers had recognized her and spread the word that Agrippina had been in a shipwreck.

Once back in her own villa at Bauli, Agrippina reflected on the evening: her gratifying invitation and welcome by Nero at such odds with the inexplicable damage to the ship "that had collapsed from the top like something on land," Acerronia's violent end, her own wound.[218] She decided to studiously ignore the plot. Instead, she would send her freedman Agermus to Nero with the news that, "due to the benevolence of the gods and his own good fortune," she had escaped a grievous accident.[219] Nero should postpone visiting her, the message continued, despite his apprehension at his mother's peril: she needed rest. In Agermus' absence she applied a poultice to her wound and lotions to her body, characteristically self-sufficient and keenly aware of her high station: she must appear above it all. Yet, greedy even in these dire straits, she made sure to call for Acerronia's testament and have the woman's goods consigned to her.[220]

Nero, meanwhile, was on pins for news. When told that his mother had escaped with her life, he was shocked and aghast: her light wound was just enough to identify him as the author of the plot. The young princeps feared she would soon be after him for vengeance, whether she armed her slaves, incited the army, or stirred up the Senate and People of Rome.[221] He consulted Burrus and Seneca, only to have Burrus confirm that the praetorians would never take up arms against Germanicus' offspring.[222] Nero then turned to his freedman Anicetus, Agrippina's inveterate foe who had masterminded the collapsable boat: as fleet commander at Misenum, he should finish the job and rid Nero of his mother. During the deliberations, Agrippina's messenger Agermus arrived, provoking Nero to further playacting: while the freedman Agermus was delivering Agrippina's message, the emperor had a sword dropped at his feet. The chance weapon would allow her death to be framed as a suicide provoked by guilt when her perverse schemes against her own son—the princeps!—were discovered.

While such devious plans were afoot in the court, the people of Campania were distressed at the news of Agrippina's danger—yet another demonstration of her general popularity. They ran to the quays, boarded skiffs, and even waded into the water extending their hands and filling the shoreline with queries and lamentation.[223] Upon hearing that she had survived the shipwreck, a crowd went with torches to congratulate her. But her supporters were soon scattered: marching, armed marines, led by Anicetus, surrounded her villa, broke down its gates and doors, and burst in. Anicetus finally reached the innermost bedchamber, where Agrippina, troubled by Agermus' continued absence and by the utter silence that then was replaced by a strange commotion outside the villa, was all alone other than one of her enslaved women. As this *ancilla*, too, slipped away, Agrippina, who once inspected British chieftains, praetorian troops, and massed gladiators, said only, "Are you, too, deserting me?" She then espied Anicetus and his officers Herculeius and Obaritus.[224]

To the end Agrippina was supremely aware of her position and never lost her courage. Treating Anicetus as a mere messenger and reminding him of her vastly superior position as the emperor's mother, she told him that had he come to see her, he could report to Nero that she was recovered; but if he were aiming to commit a crime, she would believe no such thing about her son: no parricide had been ordered. Her words did not cow the freedman and his companions, who surrounded her couch ready to kill her. The trierarch Herculeius was first as he savagely clubbed her head. But Agrippina did not succumb. When Herculeius' companion Obaritus unsheathed his sword, she protruded her abdomen towards him exclaiming, "Strike here! For *this* bore Nero."[225] Cassius Dio sums it up: "Thus it was that Agrippina, daughter of Germanicus, granddaughter of Agrippa, and a descendant of Augustus, was murdered by her own son, on whom she had conferred the supreme power and for whom she had murdered others, in particular her uncle."[226] Even in her final moments the extraordinary Agrippina exulted in her body and owned her actions; even in her own bloody death she had the last word.

Reactions in Campania and Rome

Agrippina's body remains the focus of most accounts of the murder's aftermath. Tacitus, Suetonius, and Cassius Dio each report Nero's personal inspection of her corpse. Perhaps Nero simply needed assurance that Agrippina was actually dead: an earlier mistress of his strongly resembled

Agrippina, and Agrippina's companion Acerronia had been killed while claiming to be Nero's mother.[227] In keeping with general condemnations of Nero, however, the inspection is sexualized. Tacitus reports authors' disagreement over whether Nero appraised his dead mother to commend her beautiful body. Suetonius reports that "not untrustworthy authors" held that Nero actually fondled the dead woman's limbs, criticizing some and praising others, while insouciantly taking a drink as he became thirsty. Cassius Dio recounts that in disbelief of the actual murder and wanting to see himself what she had suffered, Nero stripped Agrippina's body naked and examined the wounds, finally uttering the comment "more abominable than the murder itself: 'I did not know I had such a beautiful mother.'"[228] (Nero's inspection of his mother's corpse is discussed further in Chapter 6.)

The treatment of Agrippina's mortal remains was rushed and disrespectful. She was cremated that same day, not even on a proper funeral couch. Her freedman Mnester killed himself at the pyre, but Tacitus (our sole witness for this) doubts Mnester's loyalty (and Agrippina's worthiness) by adding, "maybe from affection for his patroness, or from fear of execution."[229] No tumulus or enclosure marked her burial spot, although some of her dependents later raised a small tomb for her alongside the road to Misenum near the "villa of Caesar."[230] As with Britannicus' earlier murder and cheap, hurried funeral in 55, the depraved Nero's need for concealment rushed suppression of any potential evidence.

Nero then suffered nightmares and horrible visions of pursuit by his mother's ghost and the avenging Furies; he moved from house to house, and more than once he wished to expiate his terrible crime ritually.[231] But even more important was to convince the praetorians, court, senate, and all of Rome that the death of Agrippina was justified and not some malevolent whim.[232] Long letters went to the senate, asserting that Agrippina had committed suicide after her plot unraveled when her freedman was caught with a sword in Nero's presence. To this were added numerous charges: she had hoped for joint rule (*consortium imperii*) and to have the praetorians, the Senate, and the People of Rome swear allegiance to her, a mere woman; when thwarted in that plan she plotted against eminent men and opposed cash distributions to the soldiers and Rome's populace; finally, Nero had only barely stopped her from bursting into the senate house and even receiving foreign embassies. The letters also detailed disgraces from the Claudian period and provided information on the shipwreck.[233]

Nero's matricide amazingly found more acceptance than he had dared to hope for. The senate—with the notable absence of Thrasea Paetus, who wordlessly left the proceedings—passed numerous resolutions hailing the propitious end of Agrippina's alleged plot: her birthday, 6 November, would thereafter be among the *dies nefasti* (days on which public business could not be transacted), and the festival Quinquatrus, on which the plots (*insidae*) were revealed, was to be celebrated with annual games.[234] Soldiers, praetorians, and the people of Campania joined the Senate and People of Rome in felicitous vows for the emperor's safety.[235]

Widespread sycophancy finally convinced Nero to leave Campania for Rome later in 59. When he arrived in the city, the Roman *populus* met him in their traditional divisions, with the senators, their wives, and their children on spectator seats splendidly arranged by sex and age—all as though he were returning in triumph.[236] The procession must have passed between the Claudium and the shrine of the Aenatores, both now undoubtedly stripped of any honors for Agrippina.[237] Suetonius remarks some public postings criticizing Nero's matricide: does this suggest continuing support for the last daughter of Germanicus, descendant of Augustus, and participant in Rome's court and administration for over forty years? But such popular reproaches of Nero's murder of his mother sparked no official reaction (Suet. *Nero* 39.1). Now that she was dead, Agrippina was no longer any concern for the indolent young ruler. The next and final chapter, however, reveals her continuing significance in later Rome and up to the modern era.

Agrippina the Younger: A Dangerous Woman in Rome's Early Empire. Mary T. Boatwright, Oxford University Press.
 DOI: 10.1093/9780190945855.003.0006

6
Agrippina's Afterlife and Legacy: Conclusions

Introduction

> "The memory of my impious killing lies always heavy on me among the shades, my hands still unavenged.... The tyrant [Nero] raged savagely against his mother's very name. He wished my worth completely effaced. With fear of death he destroyed my images and inscriptions throughout the whole world, a world which my ill-fated love gave him, a mere boy!, to rule—just so he could punish me."
>
> (Spoken by the Shade of Agrippina, *Octavia* 598–600, 609–13)[1]

In 59 Nero hurried to minimize Agrippina's memory: he allowed only a cheap and inconspicuous burial outside Rome, and he slandered and belittled her in letters to the senate. The lines of the epigraph above, quoted from the historical play *Octavia* that was written soon after Nero's death in 68, have suggested that Nero also called for memory sanctions against his mother. That action would erase her name and image from public monuments but leave enough traces to preserve the effacement.[2] But even within Rome such obliteration was undertaken only half-heartedly, and no such sanctions were undertaken systematically outside the capital city.[3] Although Cassius Dio notes that Nero's entrance into Rome occasioned public ruin of her statues, he also specifies one image that escaped destruction and was later marked with criticism of Nero (62.16.2[a]). That statue is not extant. The number of identifiable images of Agrippina with more or less secure provenances, however, is second most in A. Alexandridis' catalogue of extant identifiable portraits of imperial women: 20 likenesses, compared to 36 for Livia.[4] Inscriptions and visual material, including perhaps Agrippina's reinstalled Caelian statue, indicate her presence in the city in the latter part of the first century.[5] But it is the authors of the second century and later, Tacitus, Suetonius, and Cassius Dio, who ensured Agrippina's legacy.

Review of some salient moments after Agrippina's death and some artistic renditions of her through the centuries emphasizes the divergent, sometimes contradictory, ways in which she was remembered. I focus here on pre-20th-century material.[6] In most instances her image has been that of a viciously ambitious political woman, the ruthless and transgressive individual intermittently dominating the previous chapters. Less often Agrippina the Younger appears as a victim of the men around her. These types of reception, and the surprising scarcity of visual images of Agrippina after antiquity, reinforce the vital importance of Tacitus' and other ancient histories for her biography.

Those texts, as crucial as they are for my attempt to understand Agrippina, had different vicissitudes over the years. Tacitus' *Annals*, for example, seems virtually unknown from after its appearance in the early 2nd century until the 14th; in contrast, European scholars demonstrated knowledge of Suetonius, especially beginning in the 9th century. Cassius Dio's history of most of the Claudian period (from 46 CE on) and the Neronian period does not survive as originally written. Further, until the mid-16th century the excerpts made by Byzantine scholars, Xiphilinus in the 11th century and Zonaras in the 12th, were accessible only to those who could read Greek.[7] The varied transmission of the ancient texts describing Agrippina the Younger has helped shape her reception since her death, but the authors' captivation with her has undeniably ensured that she lived long after her murder in 59.

Agrippina in Flavian Rome

Nero's push to justify Agrippina's death by accusing her of treason and improper political meddling met with mixed results. On the one hand, no ancient author impugns her with conspiracy against her son. After Britannicus' murder in 55 there was no viable Julio-Claudian alternative to Nero, certainly not anyone Agrippina could conceivably influence.[8] Later in 55 she had successfully evaded charges of supporting a potential rival to Nero, the Rubellius Plautus who was Tiberius' great-grandson. Her vindication included her bitter admission that should Britannicus, Plautus, or some other gain the throne she would face real criminal charges from which only her son could absolve her: since *she* had removed Claudius and enthroned Nero, it was in her own interests that he stay in power.[9] The various details of the events leading to her death were frankly artificial, something noted even when Nero's letters were read to the senate in 59: senators laughed incredulously at both the reported shipwreck and the idea that a shipwrecked woman would send one armed man alone against the emperor and his many guards.[10] The unveiling of her "plot" brought down no co-conspirators other than her freedman Agermus.[11] In sum, Agrippina never conspired against her son Nero.

Despite the magnitude of Agrippina's alleged filicidal plot and the effusive state celebration of its suppression, Agrippina falls from notice for the rest of Nero's reign. She surfaces only three times later in the extant *Annals* in events of 65 and 66, after growing dissatisfaction with Nero resulted in the unsuccessful Pisonian conspiracy of 65.[12] Even so, after her death she was only marginally historical. No one was accused of advocating any cause in her name or memory, although connection to her was an added mark against anyone already suspect to Nero or one of his cronies.[13]

On the other hand, the accelerating pace of spectacles and danger in Neronian Rome left little time for attention to Agrippina.[14] Nero staged city-wide festivals glorifying himself, including the Juvenalia that marked the official shaving of his facial hair in later 59 and his crowning of Tiridates as king of Armenia in 66. Besides being so extraordinarily costly that they necessitated requisitions, confiscations, and even the debasement of Rome's currency, such shows often deliberately humiliated senatorial and equestrian men and women.[15] Nero's own exhibitionism, including public appearances as an actor and charioteer, was shockingly at odds with Rome's conservative traditions, and his profligacy surpassed belief. His public abuse of Christians and others after the Great Fire of Rome in 64 marred his efforts to rebuild the city and contributed to his infamy as the first Christian persecutor.[16] At last, Nero's unpredictability and lack of interest in Rome's military, infrastructure, and systemic problems sparked revolts in Gaul and Germany, leading to Nero's own suicide on 9 June 68. After more than a year of civil war, order was reestablished in 69 under Vespasian.

Nero's excesses and ignominious downfall deeply scarred Rome's elite and contribute to Agrippina's reception. I argue that her cautionary image as a politically intrusive, innately duplicitous woman came to life in the early second century. In the latter part of the first century Agrippina appears mostly as a member of the imperial family caught up in political maneuvering, paradoxically birthing a child whose imperial ascent she lethally engineered, only to be repaid by him killing her. This fate is expressed poignantly in what seems to be the earliest literary reference to her after her death, the *Octavia*. Contemporary with Vespasian's consolidation of power in Rome in late 69 and 70, the historical drama focuses on women prominent in Nero's court, especially his first wife Octavia, whose death Nero forced in 62. In the play Agrippina is repeatedly linked with the murder of Octavia's father, Claudius. But the drama just as often treats her sympathetically as a key victim of Nero. As L. Ginsberg points out, Agrippina figures in the play as a kind of doublet to Octavia as the young, pitiful protagonist struggles to challenge her husband, Nero, and his all-consuming self-image.[17] The historical drama, which was fundamental in the development of opera in 17th-century Italy and Germany,[18] circulated among Nero's survivors a decade or so after he murdered his mother.

Agrippina otherwise had an infrequent but perceptible presence in Flavian Rome. Pliny the Elder, whose encyclopedic *Historia Naturalis* was published in the late 70s, lists her as one of his sources and refers to her by name nine other times.[19] Five of his references are relatively benign and have been mentioned in previous chapters, such as his mention of her lucky canine tooth and two notices of her pet birds.[20] A sixth reference, to Agrippina "wife of Claudius Caesar" ordering praetorian insignia for a freedman (Pallas), comes in a passage censuring formerly enslaved individuals whose rise to power damaged Rome overall.[21] Although here Pliny clearly acknowledges Agrippina's influence in Claudian Rome, his focus is on social disruption. In a section on mushrooms he notes that Agrippina used them to poison Claudius: she thus brought upon the world, and herself, yet another poison—her own son Nero.[22] The final two references also name her in connection with Nero, whom Pliny vehemently condemns.[23] Overall, Pliny does not dwell on Agrippina: her worst reported action was poisoning Claudius, which resulted in great damage to the empire but also her own death.

Other writers of the era are even less attentive to Agrippina. Josephus names Agrippina three times in his historical works. She was a successful interlocutor with Claudius for King Agrippa II in 52; she reportedly poisoned Claudius, only to be "openly" killed by Nero, which Josephus judges fair retribution for birthing Nero and achieving his accession; and she facilitated Claudius' adoption of Nero over his own son Britannicus.[24] In the late Flavian period Martial casts aspersions on Nero but not his mother, referring to Agrippina (not by name) only by the attempted shipwreck (4.63). In sum, in comparison to Tacitus, Suetonius, and Cassius Dio, authors of the Flavian period deal lightly with Agrippina. Even in the next generation, Juvenal treats Agrippina comparatively evenly. The satirist refers to her briefly and only in connection with Claudius' mushroom poisoning.[25] In contrast, he offers a long and shocking portrait of Messalina as "'harlot' empress" (*meretrix Augusta*), expatiates on Messalina's "marriage" to Silius (naming Messalina as the instigator), and refers to that imperial woman's death at the decree of the freedman Narcissus.[26]

Agrippina appeared occasionally in the cityscape of Flavian Rome. One of Vespasian's many demonstrations of dissimilarity with Nero was his restoration of the Claudium after its repurposing as a nymphaeum for Nero's private estate.[27] Vespasian may even have reinstalled Agrippina's graywacke statue in the precinct (see Chapter 5). Even if not, the renovation of the sacred temenos may have revived in the public's mind its original sponsor, Agrippina, the *flaminica* of *divus* Claudius. Vespasian was demonstrating the respect this new, non-Julio-Claudian emperor held for the institution of the principate. Other traces of Agrippina in late-first-century Rome reflect her prominence as imperial wife and member of the imperial family. A fragmentary honorific inscription, discovered on the modern Via Nazionale on Rome's Quirinal Hill, records that the imperial freedman Apollonius commemorated Agrippina Augusta, wife of *divus* Claudius and daughter of Germanicus Caesar, together with Flavia Domitilla Augusta, wife of Imperator Caesar Vespasian Augustus.[28] Dating between 69 and 79, the now-lost text makes no mention of Nero.[29] In the northern Campus Martius, Titus—who had attended the imperial banquet at which Britannicus was poisoned—apparently added a commemoration of Domitilla, wife of *divus* Vespasian, to those for Agrippina's natal family in the funerary installation opening from the Via Flaminia toward the Mausoleum of Augustus. (See Chapter 4.) The Domitilla inscription indicates that the funerary precinct, for which Agrippina the Younger seems to have been responsible, was still respected, even as it subtly connected the Flavian *gens* to Augustus' own.[30] In this Flavian and early-second-century background, the judgmental, detailed information about Agrippina the Younger offered by Suetonius and Tacitus in the early second century is all the more striking.

W. Eck was perhaps the first to argue that Agrippina's legacy is a negative one: she was a fearsome exemplar of behavior for imperial and other women to avoid.[31] As we have seen, this perspective is traceable to the

Trajanic and early Hadrianic period, when it coincides with greatly reduced visibility and public roles for imperial women.[32] And yet, if the historiographic modeling of Agrippina the Younger as a deterrent model was deliberate, it is more than ironic that the nuanced brilliance of her depiction by the historians—particularly Tacitus—ensured later ages' fascination with her.

Images of Agrippina

As mentioned earlier, identifying Agrippina the Younger's portraits and likenesses is beset with difficulties. This might seem startling to modern eyes trained to distinguish Agrippina by her apparently unmistakable hairstyle, which features a central part leading to "snail curls" or deep waves framing the face and often accompanied by ringlets down the neck. Yet in addition to the 20 sculptural portraits of Agrippina the Younger in Alexandridis' definitive work on portraits of imperial Roman women,[33] a number of other sculptural images display this hairstyle. Most have been tentatively identified as Agrippina at some point or another,[34] often controversially. Modern identification of a bust or statue as Agrippina the Younger unquestionably increases its historical, cultural, and financial value: for example, the Getty Villa head now identified as Agrippina the Younger (Ill. Intro.2) reportedly was once considered for Hitler's projected Führermuseum in Linz, Austria.[35] From a more scholarly perspective, however, a clearer understanding of the visual representation of Agrippina the Younger and Agrippina "look-alikes" sheds light on her reception, the subject of this chapter.

Identification difficulties are tied to the methodology of classifying Roman portraits and to the history of Agrippina. Agrippina's position as the first woman portrayed and identified on Roman coinage while alive confounds the standard method of categorizing imperial portraits. Imperial portrait typologies are established by discerning similarities of sculptural portraits to images on coins that include an identifying legend and can be dated at least to a decade or so, if not to a precise year.[36] But imperial women appear much less frequently on coins than imperial men. Their images reveal greater variety, especially in their faces.[37] Scholars thus attend primarily to the delineation of the portrayed women's hair.[38] Establishing the portrait types of Agrippina the Younger is additionally complicated by Nero's senatorial denunciation of her in 59 and fitful memory sanctions against her images.[39]

Despite such hurdles, scholars have identified four basic portrait types for Agrippina.[40] All are classified by variations in the treatment of the hair: for instance, the Milan-Florence type is recognized by a line of small, relatively flat snail curls on the hairline at the top of the forehead and by corkscrew curls descending behind visible earlobes.[41] The most frequent type is the Ancona type (see Ill. Intro.3), dated to the late Claudian and early Neronian years by the similarity of its sculptural replicas both to portraits of "Agrippina Augusta" on coins and to the Aphrodisias relief showing Agrippina crowning Nero (Chapters 4 and 5; Ill. 5.3).[42] The Milan-Florence type (see Ill. 6.1), is identified not from coins but rather by its relationship to the Ancona type. Its floruit has been dated between Agrippina's marriage to Claudius and the grant of her honorific title, Augusta (49–50 CE).[43] The third, the Parma-Naples type (see Ill. 6.2), is now known in four accepted replicas but on no coins. In the Parma-Naples type Agrippina's hair, seen from the front, is in waves rather than snail curls.[44] W. Trillmich tenders that it was created around the time of Agrippina's wedding to Claudius but was then eclipsed by the Ancona and the Milan-Florence types.[45] In the fourth, the Stuttgart type (see Ill. 6.3), the hair on Agrippina's head springs

Ill. 6.1 Standing portrait of Agrippina the Younger, Milan-Florence type. From the Metroon at Olympia, Greece, probably 54–59. Marble, 203 cm H, (head) 26.5 cm. Olympia, Archaeological Museum A 143. Carine Vaissiere/Alamy Stock Photo.

Ill. 6.2 Detail of head of marble standing portrait of Agrippina the Younger (203 cm H), Parma-Naples type, from imperial family installation at Velleia. From the Museo Nazionale di Antichità, Parma, inv. no. 830. With the permission of the Ministero della Cultura—Soprintendenza Archeologia, Belle Arti e Paesaggio per la città metropolitana di Bologna e le province di Modena, Reggio Emilia e Ferrara. Reproduction prohibited for profit, even indirect.

Ill. 6.3 Head of Agrippina the Younger, Stuttgart type, 54–59 CE, marble, 40.5 cm H. Stuttgart, Landesmuseum Württemberg, Arch. 68/2. Landesmuseum Württemberg, Hendrik Zwietasch CC BY 4.0 https://creativecommons.org/licenses/by/4.0/deed.de.

directly from her part into three rows of short snail curls; relatively long ringlets descend symmetrically down her neck from behind her ears.[46] The Stuttgart type, seen also on coins and reflected in Agrippina's statue from the Caelian, dates to the early years of Nero's reign. Its "softer and fleshier" treatment has been said to emphasize Agrippina's resemblance to her young son.[47]

A few scholars have distinguished additional types that are poorly represented, such as the Cameo Paris 277 type with a row of small curls along the hairline[48] and a Munich-Antioch type claimed on the basis of coins of Antioch on the Orontes and one sculptural replica.[49] But all concur that precisely identifying sculptural images of Agrippina is extremely hard. For instance, the Getty head has some characteristics of Agrippina's Stuttgart type—four tiers of snail curls and waves—but lacks others, such as the neck curls.[50] Agrippina's physiognomy is inconsistent, as is clear when contrasting the two reliefs of her in Aphrodisias' Sebasteion that demonstrate the tendency to depict imperial women visually like the ruling emperor (Ill. 4.3, Ill. 5.3).[51]

Differences in sculptural images sometimes identified as Agrippina are associated with the *Zeitgesicht*, or "period face," concept. This art-historical theory holds that the official depiction of the emperor was so dominant and charismatic that private individuals in the Roman empire chose to have themselves represented in ways reminiscent of imperial portraits.[52] The concept extends to *privatae*, non-imperial women, even though representations of imperial women, even of any one such woman, are less distinct than those of imperial men.[53] Nonetheless, images of imperial women reflected and set expectations concerning the imperial house, and they reproduced and contributed to gender norms in Rome.[54]

A good example of *Zeitgesicht* is a standing female statue now in the Minneapolis Institute of Art (see Ill. 6.4). Its panel reads (in part) "Portrait of an Older Woman, 60-70 A.D.... Once identified as Agrippina the younger,... this statue is now thought to represent an unidentified Roman matron."[55] The meticulously depicted hair, which rises from the face in four tiers of snail curls that are balanced by corkscrew curls down the neck, contrasts with the woman's thin, aged face.[56] No face among Agrippina's accepted portraits is like that of the statue now in Minneapolis:[57] a seller probably once hyped this piece as Agrippina the Younger as a way to inflate its value. Nonetheless, the current identification of the portrait as that of a

Ill. 6.4 Standing female statue now in the Minneapolis Institute of Art. Once identified as Agrippina the Younger, this is now titled "Roman Matron, 50–60 CE." Marble, 128.27 × 33.02 × 26.67 cm. Accession number 32.16. Photo: Minneapolis Institute of Art.

privata intimates Agrippina's popularity.[58] If individuals chose to have their permanent likenesses modeled after Agrippina's, or someone else made that decision, was Agrippina really the notoriously fearsome shrew depicted by Tacitus, Suetonius, and Cassius Dio?

Ill. 6.5 Colossal marble head from the Forum of Trajan (106–112 CE), 80 cm H (head 62 cm from chin to vertex). Rome, Museo dei Fori Imperiali, Mercati di Traiano (inv. FT 6116)—Archivio Fotografico del Museo dei Fori Imperiali. © Roma, Sovrintendenza Capitolina ai Beni Culturali.

Perhaps the most controversial sculpture identified as Agrippina the Younger is a colossal female head found in the Forum of Trajan, part of the original Trajanic program and thus dating between 106 and 112 (see Ill. 6.5).[59] Elements of the representation recall Agrippina the Younger, particularly the treatment of the hair with its central part, tiered snail curls, thick rows of curls in front of the ear, and corkscrew curls down the neck.[60] But historical considerations and oddities of the portrait have led some to identify this as Agrippina only tentatively, and D. Boschung and W. Eck reject the identification completely.[61] These two scholars have argued that the portrait could not possibly represent Agrippina the Younger.[62] Boschung emphasized a number of small variations from the generally accepted portrait types of Agrippina, and Eck stressed that at the beginning of the second century all political considerations militated against installing Agrippina the Younger's image in Trajan's Forum.[63] They proposed instead that the colossal image is of Trajan's now unknown mother. Stressing that Trajan was born in 53 (that is, at Agrippina's zenith), Eck posited that the sculpture represented the mother of Trajan himself—from Baetica, far from Rome—as Trajan remembered her, wearing her hair in the fashion current in his youth.[64] Trajan's mother's portrait would have joined images of others of his family, like his father Marcus Ulpius Traianus, in the glorious celebration of this emperor's dominant role in Roman history.[65]

Their argument has not been universally accepted.[66] Although historical considerations also have me question why Trajan's Forum might have highlighted Agrippina the Younger in a colossal image, it is striking that such an Agrippina "look-alike" would be included at all in this official space created between 106 and 112. The likeness suggests that Agrippina was not yet the definitively negative example of overweening ambition and meddlesomeness she is made to be in Tacitus and Suetonius, whose relevant works appeared between 115 and 130 CE.

Notwithstanding her vividness in those two historians' accounts, Agrippina Augusta slips from notice until the late medieval and Renaissance periods after Cassius Dio's *Roman History*, a century later, largely echoed Tacitus and Suetonius on her. Her obscurity partly coincides with that of Tacitus' *Annals*, which were "surprisingly unpopular" even in antiquity and into the later Middle Ages. The *Annals* survived in only two manuscripts, a 9th-century one at Fulda (Germany) with *Annals* 1–6, and an 11th-century one at Montecassino (Italy) with much of the later *Annals*, including the books covering the years of Agrippina as Claudius' wife and Nero's mother.[67] When Agrippina re-emerges in literature and the arts, she appears in two very different ways: either as abject victim or as an active, noteworthy woman. The two opposing constructs overlap almost from when she comes back into notice, the late 13th century, because her active depiction begins with Giovanni Boccaccio's use of Tacitus in the middle of the 14th century. Despite Boccaccio and others, however, "Agrippina as victim" has remarkable persistence.

Agrippina the Younger in the Late Middle Ages and Early Renaissance: Abject Victim

One source of her passive imaging is her victimization by Nero as it was elaborated in the immensely popular *Golden Legend*. In the late thirteenth century a northern Italian monk, Jacobus de Voragine, put together the *Golden Legend* to provide liturgical and doctrinal instruction along with lives of saints notable for miracles and dramatic events. Jacobus started gathering materials in the 1260s, and his work was influential even by the 1280s, a decade or so before his death in 1298. The *Golden Legend* circulated widely in Europe in Latin and vernacular languages, and parts of it were freely adopted and transformed by other hagiographers and writers.[68] Nero, guilty of killing numerous Christians in the first Christian persecution (64 CE), figures prominently in the "Life of Saint Peter, Apostle."[69]

The *Golden Legend* digresses on Nero's other crimes and evil madness after discussing the life of St. Peter up to his martyrdom in Rome. One instance is Nero's desire to have his mother killed and cut open so that he could see "how it had been for him in her womb." He then went a step farther, demanding that his physicians make him pregnant so he could give birth "'so that I may know how much pain it cost my mother!'"[70] They cleverly have him swallow a potion with a frog that they nurture in his belly with a special diet. When Nero can stand the swelling pain no longer, the doctors make him vomit and "deliver" the repulsive frog. "Life of Saint Peter, Apostle" recounts more of Nero's crimes and his gruesome death before returning to the martyrdom of St. Peter, that of St. Paul, and various miracles.[71]

Agrippina is not even named in this brief reference to her death at her son's orders, and she certainly is not the meddlesome, domineering woman so often described by Tacitus and other historians.[72] The abhorrent story of Nero killing his mother and slicing her open apparently derives mostly from Suetonius and a few lines in the sixth-century Boethius' *On the Consolation of Philosophy*.[73] As we saw in Chapter 5, Suetonius noted that "credible authors" reported that at news of Agrippina's murder Nero ran to inspect his mother's corpse, handled her limbs while praising some and condemning others, and called for drink when he got thirsty.[74] The Christian Boethius more modestly recounted how Nero, his savage hand wet with his mother's blood, gazed on her cold corpse not with tears but rather cool appraisal of her dead beauty.[75]

Despite the *Golden Legend*'s omission of Agrippina's name, its lurid story of Nero and Agrippina circulated widely in Europe until the 16th century. The episode of Nero and the frog was popular: parts of it surface, for example, in editions of Jean de Meun's *Roman de la Rose*.[76] Few illustrations, however, focus on Nero's preposterous desire to experience pregnancy and labor himself and his comeuppance with the frog.[77] Much more common is representation of Agrippina as a cadaver being dissected in front of her son, Nero.[78]

The image fits the period's growing interest in dissection and anatomy, which culminated in the 1543 publication of Andreas Vesalius' masterpiece *Seven Books on the Makeup of the Human Body*.[79] By examining this and other anatomy books' title pages, A. Carlino has traced the development of the anatomy lesson into a spectacle that reasserted academic authority, classical learning, and empirical anatomy.[80] While almost every title page Carlino reproduces puts male cadavers on view, a female corpse undergoing dissection centers the title page of Vesalius' masterpiece. The prevalence of males reflects the reality that convictions for capital crime, the source of most cadavers for public dissections, were rare for women.[81] Agrippina's purported dissection in front of Nero permitted the public depiction of a woman's dead body.

But the gory depiction seems to have been titillating in its own right. For example, an early 15th-century French manuscript illustrating an edition of *Fates of Noble Men and Women*, a compendium work elaborating on Boccaccio's *Famous Women* and his *On the Fates of Famous Men*, foregrounds the naked and bound Agrippina on a dissecting table with men behind her (Ill. 6.6; dated 1413–1415).[82] At the table's head stands a barber surgeon in work clothes holding a bloody knife. A gesticulating man in academic robes flanks him. At the corpse's foot is a bearded Nero, denoted by his crown, sword, and sheltering canopy. A servant kneels before the emperor and offers a cup of wine, an apparent reference to Suetonius' Nero, who grew thirsty while critiquing his dead mother. Other illustrations more graphically present Agrippina's torn body as if in an anatomy lesson or public staging of a dissection. Ill. 6.7, from a late-15th-century manuscript of the *Roman de la Rose* (ca. 1490–1500), fronts an adult bearded Nero, crowned, holding a scepter, and with a sword at his side; he watches the autopsy of Agrippina that takes place in the middle register.[83] With staring eyes and open mouth, the female corpse, more youthful than would have been the 44-year-old Agrippina at her death, lies with her ankles tied together and her hands bound below the table.[84] Her startled, pitiful face contrasts the intent, brutal one of the assistant who handles her entrails.[85] Two other attendants wear academic robes.[86]

In these and similar depictions the naked cadaver is young, with no features identifiable as Agrippina's. The dead body is humiliated: its bound wrists and ankles are gratuitous, especially in Ill. 6.6 where the wrists are

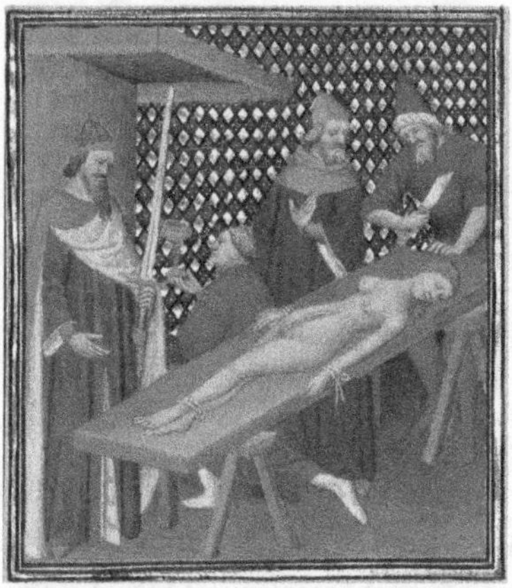

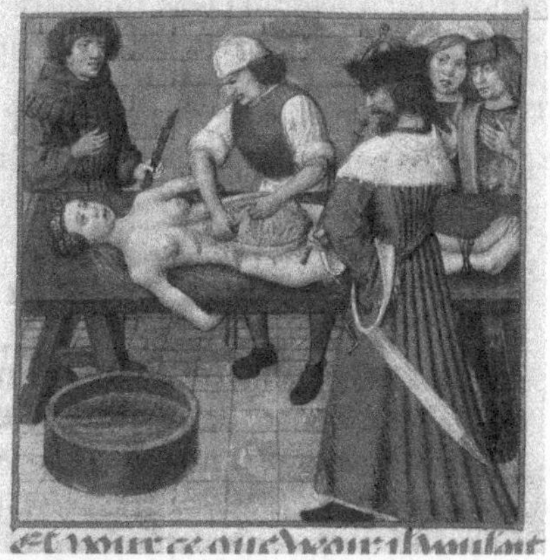

Ill. 6.6 "Nero Pauses for a Drink during the Mutilation of His Mother's Body," French manuscript illumination in *Des cas des nobles hommes et femmes*. Getty Ms. 63 (96.MR.17), fol. 224v, Boucicaut Master, ca. 1413–1415, Paris. Open Content image courtesy of the Getty Museum.

Ill. 6.7 "Nero and Agrippina," illumination from the late 15th-century manuscript *Roman de la Rose* by Jean de Meun and Guillaume de Lorris. © British Library Board, Harley 4425, f. 59r, Bruges, ca. 1490 to ca. 1500.

tied to nothing at all. Moreover, no male corpse depicted on Carlino's collected title pages is fettered. No ties are shown even on the female corpse centered on Vesalius' title page, a woman known to have been a convicted criminal.[87] The pictured dissection of Nero's mother reduces to a wordless, exposed female body the exceptional Agrippina, whose extraordinary lineage, astute scheming, and vast resources were acknowledged by all ancient writers. She is reduced to a small element in an episode highlighting the emperor Nero's hubris.

K. Park has further analyzed the image of Agrippina's dissection in the context of Renaissance ideas about women's bodies, anatomies, and contributions to reproduction and society. She concludes that as theories and practices of absolutist control were increasingly elaborated for men in the 15th and 16th centuries, the lurid story represented men's violent control of female reproductive bodies.[88] M. Beard holds that the gruesome depiction connects with "issues of women's role in imperial succession and the transmission of power."[89] A little after 1470 the *editio princeps*, or first printed edition, of Tacitus' *Annals* 11–16 was published,[90] detailing the dynamic Agrippina on which much of my biography is based. But even after that publication, Agrippina was sometimes illustrated as a cadaver dissected in a more or less public autopsy, as in Ill. 6.7 from 1490–1500. That depiction strips her of autonomy and individuality, reducing her to a wordless, exposed female body and highlighting female helplessness in the face of male imperial power.

Agrippina in History Paintings

Agrippina is the subject of some history paintings from the mid-17th through the 19th century.[91] The representations I have found seem surprisingly few in comparison to, for example, images of Messalina. Messalina's death was the subject posed for the 1870 Prix de Rome painting competition, for example, and Aubrey Beardsley's two prints depicting reported activities of Claudius' third wife are infamous.[92] The history paintings of Agrippina the Younger victimize and sexualize her, although less appallingly than the autopsy depictions.

Most center on Nero's inspection of his mother's corpse, inviting the viewers to focus voyeuristically on Agrippina's body just as he does. She is beautiful and not perceptibly older than Nero. Her torso is exposed but her wounds are minimized, with that to her womb at most suggested by a small sword puncture; her head is usually unsullied. The type apparently began in northern Italy, probably encouraged by the rise of operas about the Neronian court we turn to later in this chapter. One of the earliest such paintings I have found, *Nero before the Corpse of his Mother Agrippina* by the Venetian artist Antonio Molinari, dated to 1680, shows Nero bending over a woman's foregrounded naked body as he confers with an assassin and two secondary figures. The woman's wounds are barely visible on her chest and lower abdomen.[93] In *The Death of Agrippina* by Antonio Zanchi, who also worked in Venice before his death in 1722, a ruler in armor gazes down on a dead woman whose uninjured body is held up by a soldier. Another crouching man puts his hand on her slightly swollen abdomen while three male figures talk to each another at the lower right.[94] In neither painting do any attributes or labels allow us to definitively identify the naked dead woman as Agrippina or the ruler as Nero. Representing the genre of "history painting," these two works could depict any number of historical or legendary scenes in which a beautiful dead woman is appraised by a Roman leader. One such painting, created by Luca Ferrari (1644–1649) and recently used for the dust jacket of Carandini's *Io, Agrippina*, for example, has actually been identified as the *Death of Cleopatra* as well as the *Death of Agrippina*.[95]

The voyeuristic composition endured in the infrequent paintings of Agrippina the Younger. In 1887 Arturo Montero y Calvo painted a large canvas showing Nero handling Agrippina's hand and knee, peering at the unblemished body with four counsellors.[96] One of the most elaborate and identifiable of these paintings is by Antonio Rizzi, composed in 1894 (see Ill. 6.8). More graphic about her death than earlier paintings, Rizzi's work also lavishes attention on the presumed setting's sumptuousness. In its foreground a timid Nero crouches over the dead Agrippina; he gingerly lifts the diaphanous wraps draped around her hips, presumably to see if she is actually dead. Copious blood pools under her body and around her head, and a trail of blood drips from her couch in the upper left. Servants and an older togate man, presumably Seneca, look on from a slight distance. Rizzi fills the painting with rugs, beautiful marble décor, and other signs of opulence.[97] Despite the rich surroundings, the painting sensually objectifies the woman at its center. The historic Agrippina is reduced to an alluring, nonthreatening prop.

Ill. 6.8 Antonio Rizzi, "Nero and Agrippina" (1894; now in the Museo Civico "Ala Ponzone" in Cremona, Italy). Courtesy of the Musei Civici di Cremona.

The shipwreck on the Bay of Naples is the subject of another few paintings relating to Agrippina; they, too, show her as weak and passive. One by Antonio Zanchi, the northern Italian artist mentioned above, shows a disheveled woman being lifted by a burly man and a barebacked woman, flanked by an oarsman or boat pilot. The calm sea in the background and hints of a ship have led to the painting's identification as *Agrippina Saved from the Shipwreck* (1680),[98] even though Tacitus' version stresses that Agrippina saved herself. In Gustav Wertheimer's 1874 canvas Agrippina comforts another woman, presumably her companion Acerronia, as the ship breaks apart in turbulent seas around them (an anachronistic element).[99] The artist collapses time to include on the right the impalement of a naked woman by mariners: although those familiar with Tacitus know this victim is Acerronia, the composition presages Agrippina's own murder a few hours later.[100] The ancient historians, who focused on Agrippina's vigorous and often successful political scheming, would not have recognized the weak victim depicted in post-Classical visual art.

An Active Agrippina the Younger

Yet there is another Agrippina in these years, a remarkable, take-charge woman who often gets the better of those around her, including men. She is one of the 106 women described in Giovanni Boccaccio's *Famous Women* (*De Mulieribus Claris*; 1361, revised 1366), the first collection of biographies in Western literature devoted to women.[101] Boccaccio, who like others had written a compendium of the lives of famous men (*De Casibus Virorum Illustrium*),[102] defends the novelty of his *Famous Women*: the book will memorialize for posterity women renowned for acts of vigor and courage; women notable for their boldness, intellectual powers, perseverance, natural endowments, or fortune's favor or enmity; and even a few women instrumental for the performance of mighty deeds.[103] If some non-virtuous women are included, says Boccaccio, the volume's praise of good deeds and forthright reproach of evildoing and crimes will edify the readers even more. He specifies his addition to *Famous Women* of "some pleasant exhortations to virtue and incentives for avoiding wickedness."[104]

The relatively full "Agrippina, Mother of Nero," #92 in the collection, depends heavily on Tacitus and on Suetonius as Boccaccio details her marriage to Claudius, schemes for Nero's accession to power, and ultimate murder at the orders of her no-good, disgruntled son.[105] Suetonius' *Lives of the Caesars* had long been known in European literary circles, and in the early ninth century Einhard used it as a model for his biography of Charlemagne.[106] But Boccaccio is the first scholar since the sixth century to demonstrate knowledge of Tacitus' writings, and the first humanist to do so.[107]

Boccaccio's "Agrippina, Mother of Nero" suggests a deep knowledge of Tacitus' Agrippina. Numerous particulars apparently derive from Tacitus almost verbatim, such as Agrippina's death scene with the final desertion of her sole remaining maidservant (Chapters 15–23, here *ancillula* rather than Tacitus' *ancilla*). This *Life* (#92) is more than twice the length of most other Greco-Roman women's *Lives* in Brown's translation. Only "Sabina Poppaea, Wife of Nero" (#95 in the collection) is similarly long, and it, too, echoes Tacitus' treatment of its subject. The details and length of "Agrippina, Mother of Nero" reveal Boccaccio's indebtedness to the second-century historian. Tacitean echoes in Boccaccio's other works confirm that the humanist personally consulted the lone medieval manuscript containing Tacitus' *Annals* 11–16 and *Histories* 1–5, the "Second Medicean." This was held at the monastery of Montecassino, which Boccaccio is recorded as visiting in 1362 and where he probably often stopped while traveling between Rome and Naples.[108]

Boccaccio's "Agrippina, Mother of Nero" does not condemn its subject outright. Agrippina is introduced as one who "attracted attention for her noble birth, lineage, power, and the monstrous character of her son—and herself—as well as for famous actions."[109] At times she is the victim of men around her, especially when Boccaccio erroneously transfers to her Suetonius' note that Caligula raped Drusilla as a girl.[110] Boccaccio stresses her beauty,[111] something no ancient writer notes. But he also depicts her repeatedly as a transgressor: sleeping with Lepidus in the hope of power (*Life* 92.3) and later with Pallas (*Life* 92.7, *Life* 92.14);[112] keen for control of the empire for herself and her son after Messalina's death (*Life* 92.4); inflicting cruel punishments on her opponents as Claudius' wife (*Life* 92.6); poisoning Claudius with mushrooms with the help of Halotus and Xenophon (*Life* 92.8–11); and allegedly incestuous with Nero (*Life* 92.14). The kernels of these and other vignettes are in Tacitus and Suetonius. A good example of Boccaccio's mixed presentation comes after Agrippina succeeded in placing Nero on the throne, for which, Boccaccio writes, Nero was so pleased that he honored her publicly and privately: "Thus Agrippina, atop the pinnacle of Roman domination, shone radiant throughout the world. But this great splendor was marred by an ugly stain: she had long fits of rage in which she killed and exiled many people."[113]

Unlike "Agrippina [the Elder], Wife of Germanicus" and most other *Lives* in his innovative compendium, Boccaccio's biography of Agrippina the Younger contains no moralizing passages. Nor does it conclude with an edifying lesson. The vivid events of the younger Agrippina's life, her use of intelligence and sex to gain her way,[114] and her dramatic death apparently were more than enough to merit her inclusion in Boccaccio's *Famous Women*. Agrippina the Younger has been a part of collections of lives of active and noteworthy women ever since this pioneering work in the 14th century.[115]

Agrippina in Opera

An active Agrippina the Younger was prominent also in opera, or *dramma per musica*, when it developed in 17th- and 18th-century Venice and spread through most of western Europe.[116] The Latin historical drama *Octavia*, to which we have referred repeatedly, seems to have been influential for the creation of musical operas about Roman themes. The first of many popular operas centered on Nero and his court was *L'incoronazione di Poppea* (1642/1643), with music attributed to Claudio Monteverdi and libretto by Giovanni Francesco Busenello.[117] G. Manuwald has noted, however, that this and later operas about Nero and those around him include events not in the *Octavia* and often combine various incidents of Nero's reign into one play.[118] The many details provided by the ancient sources on Agrippina, Poppaea, and others provided a rich assortment from which librettists and composers could choose while elaborating on their subjects and interests. At first sight, Nero might seem a poor candidate for either of the two main themes of this period, which R. Ketterer has identified as "the myth of the clement prince" and "the myth of liberty."[119] But opera's generally uninhibited manipulation of historical information to please sponsors and audiences, and to conclude in happy endings, allowed for great latitude.[120]

Georg Friedrich Handel's *Agrippina*, first produced in Venice in 1709–1710 with a libretto by Vincenzo Grimani, follows some six earlier Nero operas for the Venetian stage.[121] As in Monteverdi's seminal *L'incoronazione di Poppea*, its titular character is not Nero but a woman close to him. Agrippina dominates the Handel piece, although Poppea (Poppaea) also has a big role.[122] The opera, which opens in Agrippina's rooms, centers around Agrippina's persistent scheming to have her son Nero ascend to the throne, plots she repeatedly tailors and re-elaborates according to differing reports, individuals, and circumstances.[123] Startling upsets and romantic intrigue color almost every interaction among the protagonists: Agrippina, Claudio (Claudius), Poppea, Ottone (Otho), Nerone (Nero), and Pallante and Narciso (Pallas and Narcissus, Claudius' minions).[124] The opera begins with the shocking news of Claudius' drowning while returning from the invasion of Britain. After numerous surprises and reversals (for example, in order to obtain their support for her son's accession, Agrippina promises her love separately to Pallante and to Narciso, and over the three acts Poppea expresses longing and love for Ottone, Claudio, and Nerone alike), the opera ends triumphantly with Claudio uniting Poppea and Ottone and naming Nerone as his successor. Albeit with numerous historical discrepancies, such as a dramatic date of 43 furnished by Claudius' alleged drowning,[125] *Agrippina* has been immensely popular. Contemporary sources hold that it was performed 27 times when first staged.[126] It enjoyed a stunning revival in the New York Metropolitan Opera's 2019–2020 season, with the title role hilariously sung by an impressive Joyce DiDonato.[127]

Exploiting Handel's music and Grimani's libretto, DiDonato's Agrippina was central to the 2020 show's acclaim. She totally controlled the action—busy, sometimes fussy, and always shameless and opportunistic. She was also funny, not a common characteristic of Nero's mother. The role is in fact written for a prima donna: the libretto and music ensure that *Agrippina*'s titular character has the main role as "a political operator in a satire on the lust for power." Moreover, the happy ending of the opera softens criticism of Agrippina, allowing her resilience and wits to shine.[128] This comparatively sympathetic view may hint at some real roots of Agrippina's relatively long success in Rome's cut-throat imperial court as it evolved during her lifetime under emperors from Tiberius through Nero.

Conclusion

At this remove from Agrippina's lifetime and given the limited sources for women in the Roman world, we cannot pretend to know the inner self of this woman. Nonetheless, the documentary traces of her life and her unique portrayals by various authors make clear that the astute, resilient, even ruthless Agrippina the Younger crafted so memorably by Tacitus, Suetonius, and Cassius Dio is no mere construct. Agrippina was both an active force and a casualty in the power struggles of Rome's early empire, which remained staunchly patriarchal even as it evolved. Her paradox is neatly expressed by the irony stressed by so many who wrote about her: she was a mother who did everything and stopped at nothing to put her son in power, only to have the worthless creature kill her. But beyond this oxymoronic truism of politics—how many people repay their obligations and remain trustworthy once they gain power?—stands Agrippina herself. She remains fascinating as a woman who dared to enter arenas that men hitherto claimed as theirs alone, who fully engaged in the fight with gusto and aplomb, and who boldly survived for many years.

Did Agrippina the Younger change the course of history? Did she contribute to culture? The first question must be answered with a qualified no. Over time she utilized her resources and political influence ever more openly, bristling against conventions such as the ban of women from senatorial deliberations (Chapter 5). In so doing, she contrasts with Livia and other imperial women, who used their authority primarily to serve men. Yet Agrippina's grasp at political power was not repeated, at least not until Julia Domna and other Severan women of the early third century.[129] It is true that Agrippina is universally acknowledged as masterminding the accession of Nero.[130] Whatever his failings or achievements, however, her son—and thus also the mother responsible for his imperial power—did not fundamentally alter Roman history. When Nero, the last of the Julio-Claudians, took his own life in 68 without a successor, the ensuing civil war ultimately re-established and advanced the disguised monarchical system Augustus and his successors had forged. Even at her most transgressive, the self-reliant Agrippina the Younger never aimed to replace the political and patriarchal structures of Rome in which she grew up, which had privileged her above other Roman women, and which she frequently outwitted. She played the same game as the men around her, often better than them but in ignorance or denial that the game was irreversibly rigged against her. She could never win. She was, after all, a woman.

Agrippina's contribution to culture is more uncertain. Her image has persisted in various forms despite her death and ignominy in 59, as we saw when assessing her reception. Buttressing my claims about her ambiguous historical significance, some of her later depictions emphasize her as the wretched victim of the men around her but others show her as their cunning manipulator. Her shifting position between provocateur and prey renders her an undeniably fascinating figure, but one who can scarcely be an uncomplicated exemplar for good or evil.[131] That so much of her reception victimizes her, at times in the most inhumane ways, is due to a persistent fear, even hatred, of women in power.

It has been stimulating to spend time with Agrippina. My research has not clarified some details of her life, for instance the year of her birth or the charges resulting in her exile in 39, but such problems will never be resolved without new information. More important for Agrippina's biography has been to see that Rome's general indifference to women extended even to female births in the imperial family and to underline the perils of Rome's mistrustful court, especially for the autocrat's relatives. I have tried to evaluate all the pertinent evidence dispassionately while centering on Agrippina sympathetically. This woman, born into the highest echelons of Rome, seized the opportunities afforded her by her birth, pushed against the restrictions of her patriarchal society and family, and unapologetically owned her actions and destiny. My Agrippina should not be a cautionary tale, the *exemplum* for fear, hatred, and avoidance the male ancient historians made her. Instead, may she be an example of a clear-eyed woman who faced her life boldly, adapted to exigencies, and left her own mark.

Agrippina the Younger: A Dangerous Woman in Rome's Early Empire. Mary T. Boatwright, Oxford University Press.
 DOI: 10.1093/9780190945855.003.0007

Notes

Introduction

1. Tac. *Ann.* 12.42.2. The triumphing general is Germanicus (see Ch. 1).
2. Unless otherwise noted, all dates are in the Common Era (CE), although CE is added to potentially confusing dates.
3. From Livia through Julia Mamaea (38 BCE to 235 CE): Boatwright 2021. Livia married Octavian, the later emperor Augustus, in 38 BCE; Julia Mamaea was the mother of Alexander Severus, who ruled from 222 to 235 CE until he was assassinated with his mother (in 235).
4. For the year 57, *CFA* 25b records a sacrifice *natale Agrippinae Augustae* (on the birthday of Agrippina Augusta); for 58, *CFA* 27 records a sacrifice *ob natalem Agrippinae Aug(usti) matris* (for the birthday of Agrippina, the mother of Augustus [Nero]). We return to the date of her birth in Ch. 1, n.78.
5. The memoirs, to which we often return, are cited by Tac. *Ann.* 4.53; Plin. *HN* 7.46 and 7, praef. They are of uncertain date. Wilkes 1972, 181, suggests between 54 and 59; Carandini 2018, 3, has her start in Nov. 55, and Wood 1999, 257, in 39–41 while she was on Pontia. Tac. *Ann.* 4.53.3 references an incident noted in the memoirs that concerned Agrippina the Elder in 26.
6. Hemelrijk 1999, 186–88. Ancient historians' generally hostile presentation suggests her memoirs did not much influence those who accessed them.
7. Pliny the Elder lived ca. 24–79; Josephus' *Jewish War* (*BJ*) appeared in 75–79 and his *Jewish Antiquities* (*AJ*) ca. 93/94. Kragelund 2018 (144–46, 298–360) discusses the different claims and evidence for the date of the *Octavia*, slightly favoring a Galban date; most simply place it early in Vespasian's rule, i.e., 69–70 (e.g., Ginsberg 2017, 1). See also Ch. 6.
8. Tacitus is the most overt in this judgment, albeit attributing such views to others: e.g., *Ann.* 12.7.3: *versa ex eo civitas et cuncta feminae oboediebant, non per lasciviam, ut Messalina, rebus Romanis inludenti. adductum et quasi virile servitium: palam severitas ac saepius superbia; nihil domi impudicum, nisi dominationi expediret. cupido auri immensa obtentum habebat, quasi subsidium regno pararetur* (cf. 12.65.2 and 14.2). For the misogyny expressed in such statements, see, e.g., Ginsburg 2006; Santoro L'Hoir 1994 and 2006; Kaplan 1979.
9. Part of the criticism of Agrippina stems from her failings as a mother who did not educate Nero the right way (cf. Gill 1983, 475–76).
10. *Haud multo post flagitia uxoris noscere ac punire adactus est ut deinde ardesceret in nuptias incestas*: *Ann.* 11.25.5. We return (e.g., Ch. 5) to Tacitus' bias and occasional chronological problems.
11. For example, despite her five-year marriage to Claudius she appears just five times in Suetonius' *Claudius*: in the chapter on his wives (*Claud.* 26); to give the exact date of Lucius Silanus' forced suicide (*Claud.* 29, "the very day of Claudius' and Agrippina's wedding"); to emphasize Claudius' obliviousness (*Claud.* 39, where he is cited as repeatedly stressing her filial relationship to him despite their incestuous projected marriage); and at his death, when she poisons him (*Claud.* 44) after he regrets their marriage and threatens to punish her (*Claud.* 43).
12. The *Life* is preserved in the *scholia Pithoeana* on Juvenal 4.81, where Crispus Passienus is confused with Vibius Crispus (Gibson 2014, 222). The *Life* is conveniently translated in Suetonius, Volume II of the Loeb Classical Library.
13. Cassius Dio's history of most of the Claudian period (from 46 CE on) and of all the Neronian one does not survive as originally written. The main summarizers are the 11th-century Xiphilinus, from 69 BCE to the end of Cassius Dio's work in the third century CE, and the 12th-century Zonaras, who covered 44 BCE to 96 CE: Millar 1964, 1–4.
14. In a still pervasive trope, most powerful Roman women were said to have exploited their sexual attractiveness.
15. Tac. *Ann.* 12.57.2: *impotentia muliebris nimiaeque spes*, a condemnation voiced in 52 by the imperial freedman Narcissus (see Ch. 4). Elsewhere, Tacitus reports the senatorial speech of

Caecina Severus (21 CE) holding that "the female sex is not only weak and unequal to hard work but also, if given license, brutal, ruthless, and greedy for power" (*saevum, ambitiosum, potestatis avidum*, *Ann.* 3.33).

16. Power 2014 shows that Suetonius does not turn to his older contemporary Tacitus as a source. Hurley 2001, 14, n.48: Fabius Rufus does not seem to have written about Claudius.
17. Syme 1958, 287–303; Wilkes 1972; Hurley 2001, 14–17; Ch. 5. Josephus also turned to Cluvius Rufus (Wiseman 2013) but seems more independent: for instance, he reports that some historians actually praised Nero (*AJ* 20.154–57; Champlin 2003, 24–25).
18. See, e.g., Treggiari 2019, 22; Riess 2012; Strong 2016, 18–41 (comparing the construct of the virtuous Roman matron to that of the prostitute); Carlon 2009, 139–45. The ideal extended to Rome's imperial women: Boatwright 2021.
19. Livia's friends include Plautia Urgulania (Tac. *Ann.* 2.34, 4.21.1; PIR[2] V 1010) and Munatia Plancina (Tac. *Ann.* 2.43.4; SCPP lines 109–20; FOS #562); Agrippina the Elder's, Sosia and Claudia Pulchra (Tac. *Ann.* 4.19.1, 4.52, 4.66). Purcell 1986 and Welch 2011 discuss Livia's ties with Rome's matrons.
20. Erstwhile friends are Junia Silana (FOS #474) and Domitia, identified in this passage as Nero's aunt. Domitia had been wed to Crispus Passienus before he married Agrippina, perhaps explaining her nasty rivalry with Agrippina (Tac. *Ann.* 13.19.4; FOS #319). For Acerronia (Polla), Agrippina's *familiaris* (Tac. *Ann.* 14.5.1), see FOS #2 and Ch. 5.
21. Mommsen described her as "a mass of riddles," though damning her for political meddling: Keegan 2018, 147. Agrippina's treatment contrasts modern discussions of the emperors, as (e.g.) Barrett (2017, 64), who ventures that throughout his principate Nero "seems to have craved female domination and yet to have simultaneously resented it."
22. Plin. *HN* 7.71.6; see Ch. 1.
23. Alexandridis 2004, Table 1 and 156–66, cat. nos. 99–123, plates 22–27 and 61.3. The next highest numbers are 17 for Sabina, and 16 for Julia Domna. Ginsburg 2006, 79, identifies 15 statue groups with Agrippina. J. Dähner (see this chapter, n.32) suggested, in personal communication 4/4/22, the reason for the Getty head's absence from Alexandridis 2004. The white marble Getty head, 32 × 27 × 28 cm (12 5/8 × 10 5/8 × 11 in.), is object no. 70.AA.101 now displayed in the Getty Villa.
24. Buonocore 2007, 76, 81–82, 86–87, 89–90; Rose 1997; Cogitore 1992, 2002, 163–64 (dating the dynastic conception to Claudius); Hurlet 2015, 188–89.
25. See Ch. 6, n.53 for comparative numbers of extant and presumed large-scale images of Livia, Augustus, and others. Ch. 4 and 5 of this volume discuss examples of sculptural installations in Rome epigraphically attested to have included images of Agrippina that are now lost.
26. Trillmich 1994 and Pangerl 2019–1920 provide overviews of the vexed identification of her portrait types.
27. See, e.g., the sketches in Boschung 1993a.
28. See Ginsburg 2006, 57; Rowan 2011, 244; Boatwright 2021, 125–27.
29. See Bartman 2001.
30. Trillmich 1994, 115; Wood 1995, e.g. 466–71; cf. D'Ambra 2013.
31. Copenhagen 636 inv. no. 755; Alexandridis 2004, 159 cat. no. 107; Wood 1999, 296–97.
32. For Agrippina the Younger's hair, see, e.g., Boschung 1993a, 73–74 Xb-d. The Getty head, apparently from an oversized statue, has not yet been fully published. My observations include kind communications with Jens Dähner, associate curator of the Department of Antiquities of the J. Paul Getty Museum (4/4/22).
33. See, e.g., Smith 1987, 129–31; Trillmich 2007, 46. Indeed, the marble head of Agrippina the Younger now in the Getty was first identified as Livia when it surfaced in Rome in the 1930s, undoubtedly because its broad forehead and wide-set eyes echo the physiognomy of Augustus.
34. Weaver 1972.
35. Boatwright 2022.
36. See especially Edmondson 2022.
37. See recently Carandini 2018 and Carandini and Carafa 2017.
38. Trier and Naumann-Steckner 2015, including two new contributions by Werner Eck.
39. Barrett 1996, e.g., 98, 101–13, noting (e.g.) that her years as Claudius' wife coincide with fewer murders and less unpredictability. A. A. Barrett's Batsford, London publication earlier in 1996 was titled simply *Agrippina: Mother of Nero*.
40. Ginsburg's publication is posthumous. See also Santoro L'Hoir 2006, 111–57, and Ambühl 2022.

41. The disjointed pieces are owned by Copenhagen's Ny Carlsberg Glyptotek and Rome's Conservatori Museums.
42. Carandini 2018 adds a fictitious epilogue by Caenis, Antonia the Younger's freedwoman and later mistress of emperor Vespasian (r. 69–79), who was supposed to have hidden Agrippina's writings in the imperial palace.
43. For example, Southon (2019, 180) writes, "But when we actually look at Agrippina's role in the running of the empire [in the early 50s] and try to dodge the repulsed misogyny that fuelled our sources, we mostly see a competent woman getting shit done. Sometimes she won, sometimes she lost but she kept going." See also (e.g.) https://www.moaninc.co.uk/ancient-women/agrippina-the-younger, and I. Barceló, "Roman Empress Agrippina: Her Rise and Fall," in *National Geographic*, March 18, 2021.
44. See, e.g., the bibliographical discussion with which Kolb 2010, 12–14, introduces the topic of *Augustae* before turning to Agrippina the Younger (discussed on her pages 17–22) to exemplify the limitations of an Augusta's power.
45. See especially Späth 2000, 274–75, rejecting censorious judgments found in previous scholarship on her.
46. For Nero's continuing fascination and re-evaluation, see (e.g.) the recent museum shows "L'Amato di Iside. Nerone, la Domus Aurea e l'Egitto" (Rome: Golden House Exhibit, 2023) and "Nero: The Man behind the Myth" (London: British Museum, 2021); the recent publications of Drinkwater 2019, Barrett et al. 2016, Champlin 2003, Bartsch et al. 2017; and other "Companion" volumes. Nevertheless, generally, in these even Agrippina receives short shrift: e.g., the *Cambridge Companion to the Age of Nero* (Bartsch et al. 2017) has just one relevant chapter, "Nero's Women." I thank M. Baroff for this point in her 2024 Duke University dissertation, "Rereading Octavia and Poppaea: Unraveling the Literary Afterlives of Nero's Wives."
47. To the point that early in my research I intended to use the lens of "the King's two bodies," the concept elaborated by Kantorowicz (1957) of a leader's physical body and simultaneous embodiment of the state (often captured by "The king is dead. Long live the king!").

Chapter 1

1. See, in brief, Boatwright 2021, 85–93.
2. This is often called "the Julio-Claudian family," but see Simpson 2008.
3. Millar 1993, 3, cf. 6 and 15–16, and Moreau 2009, 39, lean toward the court and various elite families as responsible for developing the idea of the imperial house; Moreau notes that the gradual development was evidenced diversely (e.g., the Narbo altar and Corinth inscription mentioned below), showing the lack of central planning. Hurlet 2015, 186, suggests Augustus' agency.
4. Winterling 2009, 79–81. For the following section, see also Boatwright 2021, 93–99.
5. Found on an altar documenting a dedication by the people of Narbo (now Narbonne, France) to Augustus, his (unnamed) wife and children, and his *gens*, as well as to the Senate and People of Rome and others in the Narbonese community, in accordance with a vow made in 11 CE: *CIL* XII 4333 = EDCS-12100286, esp. lines 6–8. Rome also had an "Altar of the Gens Julia in the Area Capitolina" in the first century: see *LTUR* 2.269–70, s.v. "Gens Iulia, ara" (E. La Rocca).
6. The Carthage inscription (*AE* 1914, 87 = EDCS-16201132) seems Tiberian or late Augustan/Tiberian; the fragmentary Corinthian inscription, *AE* 1922, 1 = EDCS-10300681 may date to 37 CE.
7. Hurlet 2015, 186; von Hesberg and Panciera 1994, 91, cf. *Consol. ad Liviam* 65–74. Buried there were (in 23 BCE) Marcellus, who married Julia the Elder in 25, and Agrippa (in 12 BCE), who married her in 21.
8. Tac. *Hist.* 1.16 and *Ann.* 6.8.
9. See Saller 1994, 80–88: *domus* can legally include relatives through women.
10. Corbier 1994 and Dettenhofer 2000 see the *domus Augusta* as an innovation.
11. Ov. *Pont.* 2.2.67–74; *Fast.* 1.532, 1.721, 6.810; *Tr.* 3.1.41, 4.2.10; Flory 1996, 292–93, 301; Corbier 1995.
12. The Tabula Siarensis (*AE* 1984, 508 = EDCS-45500034; Lott 2012, 90, lines 18–21).
13. Flory 1996. Germanicus' arch (Lott 2012, 90, lines 18–21) was to display Germanicus in triumph; his "natural father Drusus [the Elder], the brother of Tiberius Caesar Augustus"; and his mother Antonia (the Younger), his wife Agrippina (the Elder), his sister Livia (Livilla), his brother Claudius (the future emperor), and Germanicus' (unnamed) sons and daughters. The lacunose text now lacks *Agrippinae uxoris*, but the sense is clear: see Lott 2012, 221.

14. She would have been about four years old in 19.
15. *AE* 1984, 508 b, II.22–23.
16. SCPP, line 16; lines 143–44 with Lott 2012, 304 ad loc. for Livilla.
17. Suet. *Claud.* 3.2, 4.2, reporting what now seem particularly cruel judgments about him as a youth.
18. Dusmia Numisilla rebuilt an aqueduct in Teate Marrucinorum (modern Chieti, Italy) in honor of the Augustan house (*In honorum domus Augustae CIL* IX 3018 [p. 677] = EDCS-14804019, dated 31–70 CE).
19. Grant 1950, 96–98, 104, and Morizio 1996, 211, see this as indicating growing acceptance of the principate as a more or less hereditary monarchy already by Tiberius' rule; Cogitore 1992, 833, and Flory 1995, 134, date the change to the time of Claudius.
20. A dedication from a *sevir Augustalis* that begins, "In honor of the Divine House" (*In honorem domus divinae*): *AE* 1988, 553 = EDCS-09200248.
21. The *flaminica* Iulia C. f. Laeta, *CIL* II 1678 = EDCS-08700099, dated between Tiberius and the Flavians: Hemelrijk 2015, 425. See also *CIL* II 1978 = EDCS-05501676.
22. *AE* 1927, 2 = EDCS-08200293, 54–59 CE. See Ch. 4, n.129 and Ch. 5, n.68.
23. *Ludi Palatini* were at the end of January: Plin. *HN* 12.94; Cass. Dio 56.46, 59.16; Tac. *Ann.* 1.73. Caligula was assassinated at the end of the *ludi Palatini* in 41: see Ch. 2. The palace's Saturnalia in December 54 may have seen a performance of Seneca's *Apocolocyntosis* and certainly witnessed Nero's altercation with Britannicus: Ch. 4.
24. Tac. *Ann.* 4.52.1–6: *Agrippina semper atrox, tum et periculo propinquae accensa, . . . non eiusdem ait mactare divo Augusto victimas et posteros eius insectari. Non in effigies mutas divinum spiritum transfusum: se imaginem veram, caelesti sanguine ortam, intellegere discrimen, suscipere sortes.* Claudia Pulchra was Agrippina the Elder's *sobrina* (cousin on the mother's side; *Ann.* 4.50.1–3) and was sentenced for *maiestas* and *impudicitia* (*Ann.* 4.66.1).
25. Suet. *Aug.* 72.
26. See, most recently, Pflug and Wulf-Rheidt 2022, 207.
27. See, e.g., summary remarks and literary evidence in George and Kelly 2022, 45–50, noting "the reconstruction of coherent building plans [from Tiberius to Claudius] is impossible" (p. 49).
28. See, e.g., Winterling 1999, 209–17.
29. Suet. *Aug.* 72.
30. Joseph. *AJ* 19.117; Vell. Pat. 2.81.3; Suet. *Gram. et Rhet.* 17.1–2. Wiseman 2019 is a splendid contextualized investigation of the "House of Augustus."
31. Antonia the Younger is also the widow of Drusus the Elder, Augustus' younger stepson who died in 9 BCE.
32. Joseph. *AJ* 19.117. Kokkinos 2002, 67, 152, tentatively endorsed by Barrett 1996, xix, holds that Germanicus' house can be identified as that of Antonia and ultimately that of Livia.
33. The exhibition that opened in the Domus Tiberiana in 2023 focused on Julio-Claudian finds. Others from that era are in an apparently permanent exhibit in the Palatine Antiquarium. Gasparri 2014, who emphasizes the difficulties of identifying that material chronologically, also stresses (88–90) the excellent quality of works displayed by Augustus and his successors.
34. Though Augustus ostentatiously performed austerity with his granddaughter Julia the Younger, having her house torn down as too extravagant: Suet. *Aug.* 72; Boatwright 2021, 30.
35. Plin. *HN* 9.81.172. George 2022 assesses representative imperial villas through the Severans.
36. Edmondson 2022 focuses on freed and enslaved imperial dependents attendant to the imperial residences; see, in general, Weaver 1972.
37. During the early empire, *columbaria* were owned by elite families as well as by imperial family members. See Hasegawa 2005; Bodel 2008; Treggiari 1975 on the *Monumentum Liviae.*
38. E.g., Foubert 2016, 129–31, on the development from the Republic.
39. See Davenport 2022, 292–304, on the ceremonial, noting (e.g.) the accumulation of public honors in Augustus' *vestibulum* (entrance hall).
40. Cass. Dio 54.30.1; Suet. *Aug.* 53.2–3.
41. Cass. Dio 57.12.1–2. Tiberius worked hard to remove his mother from public affairs, though allowing her to do whatever she wanted at home: Cass. Dio 57.12.4.
42. Cass. Dio 60.33.1, cf. Tac. *Ann.* 13.18.2–19.1; Foubert 2016, 138–45. Foubert points out (ibid., 142, with Tac. *Ann.* 4.68) that Agrippina the Elder may also have received *salutationes*, albeit not as formally.
43. See, e.g., Roller 2022, 319–32.

44. Roller 2022, 332. E.g., Livia helped host banquets in 36 BCE at the Capitoline temple of Jupiter Optimus Maximus (with Octavian: Cass. Dio 49.15.1), in 9 BCE for the women of Rome to celebrate Tiberius' military successes (with Julia the Elder, then Tiberius' wife: Cass. Dio 55.2.4–5), in 7 BCE to celebrate Tiberius' triumph that year (apparently alone, and with no venue noted: Cass. Dio 55.8.2), and in 14 CE for elite women at the dedication of a statue to *divus* Augustus in her house on the Palatine (alone: Cass. Dio 57.12.5)
45. Tac. *Ann.* 13.16.1; Suet. *Claud.* 32.
46. Suet. *Aug.* 64; *CIL* VI 8730. L. Caesar died in 2 CE. Edmondson 2022, 176, suggests that each member of the imperial family had an individual slave designated to look after his or her dining and drinking service.
47. Kienast et al. 2017, 73: June 26 (perhaps 27), 4 CE.
48. See Corbier 1995; Dixon 1985.
49. Tac. *Ann.* 1.8.1, cf. Cass. Dio 56.46.1–2; Tac. *Ann.* 1.14.3.
50. See, e.g., Boatwright 2021, 167–210; Purcell 1986.
51. Tac. *Ann.* 12.69: ***aemulante Agrippina proaviae Liviae magnificentiam.*** See Ch. 5.
52. This assumes that she, like Drusilla and presumably Julia Livilla, lived with the better-attested Caligula, who moved to Julia Augusta's house after his mother was relegated in 27 CE (to Herculaneum: Deline 2015, 770), and then to Antonia's house after Livia's death in 29 (Suet. *Calig.* 10.1, 24.1). Agrippina the Younger would move back into Antonia's house after her fall from Nero's favor in 55: Suet. *Nero* 34.1; Tac. *Ann.* 13.18.
53. Joseph. *AJ* 18.6.4: Antonia lent Herod Agrippa 300,000 drachmae so he could repay a debt and return to Tiberius' friendship. Nicols 1975 argues that Antonia's role in Sejanus' downfall (see next note) was magnified by Josephus.
54. Rumor held that in aiming to succeed Tiberius, Sejanus had seduced Livilla and had her aid him in poisoning her husband, Drusus the Younger (Tiberius' son) in 23: Tac. *Ann.* 4.3.2–4; Cass. Dio 57.22.2. Joseph. *AJ* 18.6.6: Antonia sent to Tiberius a secret letter about Sejanus' plans through her enslaved man, Pallas (who later was influential with Claudius and Agrippina: see Ch. 4). Cass. Dio 65.14.1 has Antonia's freedwoman Caenis carrying the memorized information.
55. Cass. Dio 58.11.6–7: Tiberius put to death Livilla and others implicated in the plot, although an alternative version has that the emperor spared Livilla thanks to her mother, who in turn starved her. We discuss Sejanus further below (e.g., Ch. 1, n.93).
56. Tacitus calls it a *pulcherrimum matrimonium* (a most beautiful marriage) in the thoughts of unnamed observers in 19 (*Ann.* 2.75.1).
57. Tac. *Ann.* 2.73.3: among the praises of Germanicus at his death is that he had lived in one marriage alone, and with children definitely his own (*uno matrimonio, certis liberis egisse*).
58. Agrippina would later commemorate in a funerary installation near the Mausoleum of Augustus the three siblings who died before their time: a Tiberius, another male, and a Gaius who was born about a year before Caligula (Ch. 4, n.184).
59. The five children of Julia the Elder and Agrippa were Gaius (20 BCE to 4 CE), Julia the Younger (~19 BCE to 28 CE), Lucius (17 BCE to 2 CE), Agrippina the Elder (~14 BCE to 33 CE), and Agrippa Postumus (12 BCE to 14 CE). For the uncertainty of the birthdates of Julia the Younger and Agrippina the Elder, see Fantham 2006, 108–109. Tiberius and his brother Drusus the Elder were raised by their father Ti. Claudius Nero after divorce from Livia; when the father died in 33 BCE, Tiberius was adopted by M. Gallius, a former opponent of Octavian (later Augustus): Suet. *Tib.* 6.3; Cic. *Phil.* 13.26.
60. Sen. *Ben.* 6.32.1; cf. Plin. *HN* 21.9; Cass. Dio 55.10.12; Fantham 2006, 85–91, 139–46; Boatwright 2021, 65–69.
61. Suet. *Aug.* 65; Cass. Dio 55.10.14; Vell. Pat. 2.100.5. Barbera 2021, 32–34, unpersuasively argues that Scribonia also was relegated; see Fantham 2006, 89–91.
62. Shotter 2000, 343, less plausibly dates Julia the Younger's exile to 7 BCE (see Boatwright 2021, 65–69). Tiberius abandoned both stepdaughters when he left for Rhodes in 6 BCE.
63. Adoption: Cass. Dio 54.18.1
64. Inexplicably cut down on his exile island Planasia (now Pianosa, Italy): Suet. *Aug.* 65; Cass. Dio 55.32; Vell. Pat. 2.112.7.
65. This date is controversial: Shotter 2000, 343; Valentini 2018, 66 (referring to Mommsen). Lindsay 1995, 3, opts for 4 CE for the wedding.
66. Valentini 2018, 65, citing Tac. *Ann.* 2.73.1, has Germanicus' birth in 15–14 BCE. For Germanicus, see PIR^2 I 221, and Benoist 2013.

67. See Kokkinos 2002. Antonia the Younger's model was her mother Octavia, for whom see (e.g.) Plut. *Ant.* 54.1–2.
68. Antonia never remarried.
69. See, e.g., Valentini 2018, 65; Cass. Dio 55.31.1, 56.26.1. Augustus simultaneously adopted his grandson Agrippa Postumus, thus ensuring two possible successors (a motif of Augustus' maneuvering after the death of Agrippa in 12 BCE), but Postumus was banished in 6 CE for uncontrollable behavior. Tac. *Ann.* 5.1 notes in Livia's obituary, after recounting her marriage to Augustus while pregnant, "she bore no offspring after this; connected to the blood of Augustus through the marriage of Agrippina and Germanicus, however, she had greatgrandchildren in common with him" (*nullam posthac subolem edidit sed sanguini Augusti per coniunctionem Agrippinae et Germanici adnexa communis pronepotes habuit*).
70. Shotter 2000, 347, even calls Germanicus and Agrippina the Elder the "dream couple."
71. The Pannonian revolt, 7 CE; German campaigns in 12: Suet. *Calig.* 1.1; Barrett 1996, 23–24.
72. Tac. *Ann.* 2.75.1, recounting a popular view of Agrippina the Elder after Germanicus' death in 19, notes her outstanding lineage, superb marriage, life in the limelight, and fecundity that now rendered her many times liable to misfortune (*femina nobilitate princeps, pulcherrimo modo matrimonio inter venerantis gratantisque aspici solita... anxia sui et infelici fecunditate fortunae totiens obnoxia*).
73. Suet. *Calig.* 7.1; Plin. *HN* 7.57; SCPP line 139; Tac. *Ann.* 1.41.2 (also praising her *pudicitia* or chastity); Tac. *Ann.* 2.71.4. Suggesting a ferociously competitive court, Tacitus (*Ann.* 2.43.6) notes fecundity as a point of rivalry between Agrippina and her sister-in-law Livilla: *et coniunx Germanici Agrippina fecunditate ac fama Liviam uxorem Drusi praecellebat.*
74. Birthdates are uncertain other than that of Caligula, born 31 Aug. 12 at Antium (Suet. *Calig.* 8; Barrett 1996, 23: in Augustus' villa there). Favoring 5 CE for the wedding, I assume 6 CE for Nero Caesar (PIR^2 I 223, though see Lindsay 1995, 5–6 for 5 CE); 8 CE for Drusus Caesar (PIR^2 I 220); between 5 and 8 or between 8 and 10 for Tiberius/*ignotus* and *ignotus*, the two who died as *infantes* (Suet. *Calig.* 7); and the first half of 11 for "Gaius" (PIR^2 I 218), born at Tibur about a year before Caligula. I refer to the two eldest as Nero Caesar and Drusus Caesar, to distinguish them clearly from others in the Julio-Claudian family called Nero or Drusus.
75. See, e.g., Corbier 1995.
76. Suet. *Aug.* 34. Augustus died in 14, before any girls were born. For the official encouragement of procreation in the Augustan period, see Dixon 1988, 71–78.
77. Suet. *Calig.* 7–8.
78. Barrett 1996, 230-32, contra Lindsay 1995, 8–10. For convenience's sake my text does not question Agrippina's birthdate. All three girls were born outside Rome (Julia Livilla on Lesbos).
79. For the ideal, see Suet, *Aug.* 89; Livy, *Per.* 59; Cic. *Leg.* 3.3.7, *pro Marc.* 23; Boatwright 2021, 85–88. It is true that some moralists decried wet nursing, but not for considerations of mother-child bonding.
80. Given the insalubrious nature of Rome itself, women might choose to give birth outside the capital city if they could travel to a country villa in Italy: Agrippina the Younger later gave birth to Nero in Antium.
81. The day of her birth is known from its later celebration by the Arval Brethren: see Intro., n.4.
82. As we see below, Augustus sent a physician to her when she was along the Rhine (Suet. *Calig.* 8.4). She also employed wet nurses: *CIL* VI 5201; see *CIL* VI 9901b.
83. See, in brief, Boatwright 2021, 258–64; Horster 2013. Weisser 2017 discusses Germanicus' 14 provincial coinage types (found in Spain and the Greek East; 10 date from Tiberius' reign). For imperial journeys in general, see Halfmann 1986, 2022.
84. Suet. *Claud.* 2.1; Sen. *Apocol.* 6; Suet. *Tib.* 7.3; Boatwright 2021, 260.
85. Lindsay 1995, 12. Treggiari 1975, 56, notes the presence of midwives in imperial retinues.
86. Shotter 2000, 343, assumes that she was in Germany in 11 but notes she was in Antium, Italy, for the birth of Caligula on 31 August 12 CE (Suet. *Calig.* 8; Shotter deems Tac. *Ann.* 1.41.3 incorrect). Barrett 1996, 24, suggests she went to Germany late in 13, leaving Caligula in Italy.
87. Augustus' letter: Suet. *Calig.* 8.4. Barrett 1996, 24, suggests she was then pregnant.
88. *Ann.* 1.40.3: *cum se divo Augusto ortam neque degenerem ad pericula testaretur.* Tacitus could not have known the words of this surely private exchange. Barrett 1996, 26, suggests it was "she who thought up the scheme to end the mutiny."
89. Tac. *Ann.* 1.40.4. Agrippina the Younger's womb (*uterus*) figures prominently in Tacitus' depiction of her death: see Ch. 5.

90. The pregnancy (see also Tac. *Ann.* 1.44.2, Cass. Dio 57.5.7) is too early to be that of Agrippina the Younger and may be of one of the lost infant children: Lindsay 1995, 7.
91. Cass. Dio 57.5.5–7; see Suet. *Calig.* 48.1 (not noting Agrippina); Barrett 1996, 258, n.15.
92. Tac. *Ann.* 1.69.1–3: *Femina ingens animi munia ducis per eos dies induit.*
93. Tac. *Ann.* 1.69.4–6: *nihil relictum imperatoribus, ubi femina manipulos intervisat, signa adeat, largitionem temptet, tamquam parum ambitiose filium ducis gregali habitu circumferat Caesaremque Caligulam appellari velit.... conpressam a muliere seditionem, cui nomen principis obsistere non qui verit.* In Tacitus' brief report of the chance meeting of Piso's and Agrippina's ships in 19 as she returned to Rome with her husband's ashes, he seems to attribute military decision to her: *Igitur oram Lyciae ac Pamphyliae praelegentes, obviis navibus quae Agrippinam vehebant, utrimque infensi arma primo expediere: dein mutua formidine non ultra iurgium processum est* (Tac. *Ann.* 2.79.1). For Sejanus (L. Aelius Seianus), who began serving as praetorian prefect in 14 CE, see PIR^2 A 255 and Birley 2007.
94. We see this again in Tacitus' report of Germanicus' dying words to his wife, that she should strip off her ferocity and, when back in Rome, should not annoy the more established by a competition for power: *exueret ferociam,... neu regressa in urbem aemulatione potentiae validiores inritaret, Ann.* 2.72.1.
95. Barrett 1996, 24, stresses the indirect nature of Tacitus' criticism that is attributed to Tiberius and Sejanus, in contrast to Tacitus' own judgments about Agrippina the Younger. Beard 2021, 31–32, 259–64, links postclassical confusion of mother and daughter to persistent unease about women's role in imperial succession.
96. Tac. *Ann.* 12.27.1. We return to the site in Ch. 4. For the year of her birth, see Ch. 1, n.78.
97. Lindsay 1995, 14, points out Agrippina's use of wet nurses (see Ch. 1, n.82), which would enable her to become pregnant again more quickly than if she was lactating.
98. Tac. *Ann.* 2.26, 2.73.3.
99. Tac. *Ann.* 1.40 gives Germanicus worries for his son and pregnant wife.
100. Tac. *Ann.* 1.41.3, 1.69.5; Suet. *Calig.* 9.
101. See, e.g., Tac. *Ann.* 4.67.3–4.
102. Tac. *Ann.* 2.41.4; *I. I.* 13.2, p. 462 for the date. The children must have been Nero Caesar, Drusus Caesar, Caligula, Agrippina the Younger, and Drusilla. Julia Livilla was born later, in 17 or early 18 (Ch. 3, n.63), and the three boys who died young died during Augustus' lifetime.
103. Webb and Brännstedt 2023, 65–71, discuss some (controversial) Republican precedents. Children of captured or slain enemy leaders traditionally were paraded among the spoils, as the three-year-old boy Thumelicus in Germanicus' (see following note).
104. Strabo 7.1.4: "Segimuntus, son of Segestes and chieftain of the Cherusci; his sister Thusnelda, the wife of Arminius (the man who at the time of the violation of the treaty against Quintilius Varus was commander-in-chief of the Cheruscan army and even to this day is keeping up the war); and Thusnelda's three-year-old son Thumelicus; also Sesithacus, the son of Segimerus and chieftain of the Cherusci; Rhamis, his wife and a daughter of Ucromirus chieftain of the Chatti; and Deudorix, a Sugambrian, the son of Baetorix the brother of Melo.... Libes too, a priest of the Chatti... also other captives from the plundered tribes—the Caülci, Campsani, Bructeri, Usipi, Cherusci, Chatti, Chattuarii, Landi, Tubattii" (Loeb translation, 1924). Segestes, the pro-Roman father-in-law of Arminius, was present at the triumph as Rome's guest of honor.
105. Tac. *Ann.* 2.41.4.
106. Kienast et al. 2017, 81; Tac. *Ann.* 2.54.2.
107. Carandini 2018, 46; Barrett 1996, xix. By this time Claudius lived in his own house, probably on the Caelian: Suet. *Claud.* 6.2, with Hurley 2001, 85 ad loc.
108. Joseph. *AJ* 19.117.
109. See, e.g., Cassius Dio's assessment of Tiberius at ascent to the throne aged 56 (57.1). He was almost 60 in 17 CE.
110. He replaced the opening hymn to Zeus with honors to the Roman emperor Augustus: Possanza 2004, 111.
111. Suet. *Aug.* 86: he remarked on her cleverness (*ingenium*) and warned her against writing affectedly (*moleste*). Cassius Dio (59.19.1–2) recounts her later paraphrase of a line from Homer as she spoke with a senator. Tiberius spoke to her in Greek, sure she would understand (Tac. *Ann.* 4.52).
112. Although the females also had to exemplify traditional domestic duties such as wool working: Suet. *Aug.* 64. See Hemelrijk 1999, 22–23; Valentini 2019. Agrippina the Younger later would

be concerned with the quality of her own son's education, entrusted to the tutelage of Domitia Lepida's barber and a dancer during Agrippina's exile: Cass. Dio 61.32.2; Suet. *Nero* 6.2, 52.

113. For the letters, see Suet. *Calig.* 24.5; for the memoirs, of uncertain date, see Intro., n.5.
114. This was an *imperium proconsulare* (Tac. *Ann.* 2.43), granting him power superior to that of all but the emperor. The eastern trip consumes most of Tac. *Ann.* 2.52–61, 68–73 (for the date, see Kienast et al. 2017, 74). The province of Asia had suffered a devastating earthquake in 17 (Tac. *Ann.* 2.47–48).
115. Halfmann 1986, 168–70.
116. See, e.g., Tac. *Ann.* 2.43, 2.55–57, 2.71.1; Cass. Dio 57.18.6–10; SCPP lines 109–20 in Potter and Damon 1999, 30. In 55 Agrippina the Younger reportedly tried to enter an encounter of Nero with an embassy from Armenia, Rome's buffer with Parthia (Ch. 5).
117. Tac. *Ann.* 2.69; Cass. Dio 57.18.6–10.
118. Tac. *Ann.* 3.1.4, cf. 2.70.2.
119. Tacitus (*Ann.* 2.79) makes the voyage more exciting and deepens the portrayal of Agrippina the Elder as volatile by reporting that en route her fleet encountered that of Piso and Plancina off Lycia and Pamphylia (southwestern modern Turkey) and almost came into armed conflict.
120. Tac. *Ann.* 3.1–3.
121. Tac. *Ann.* 2.82–83; see Lott 2012, 79–115, for remains, transcription, and translation of the Tabula Siarensis (*TS*) and the Tabula Hebana, two records of such honors.
122. Lott 2012, 90–91 (*TS* 115–18 = EDCS 45500034, lines 18–21, cf. EDCS 56900016).
123. See, e.g., *CIL* IX 6362 = EDCS-18200346 = EDR168902 from Trebula Mutuesca in 49; *CIL* IX 2633; *CIL* XI 1167 = *ILS* 179; *CIL* 3379; *CIL* XI 3600 = *ILS* 223 from Cerveteri, 50–54 CE, where she is first identified as daughter of Germanicus and then as wife of Claudius; *CIL* X 1417 = EDCS 11500352 (49–50); *CIL* X 933 (p. 967), 49–50 CE; and *CIL* VI 921.
124. Tac. *Ann.* 2.73.
125. Funeral at Antioch: Tac. *Ann.* 2.72 (the Epidaphna mentioned here seems to have been a section of Antioch); burial in Augustus' Mausoleum: Tac. *Ann.* 3.4.
126. Tac. *Ann.* 3.4–6.
127. Tac. *Ann.* 3.3. Tacitus seems remarkably interested in their absence, which he corroborates by referring to "authors" (historians) and "daily accounts" (some sort of official gazette, cf. *Ann.* 13.31.1, 16.22.3; see Woodman 2004, 84, n.7). Cassius Dio (57.18) describes Tiberius and Julia Augusta as greatly pleased at Germanicus' death.
128. Tac. *Ann.* 3.11–18; for the SCPP and its relationship to Tacitus' account, see esp. Eck, Caballos, and Fernández 1996 and Potter and Damon 1999.
129. The SCPP (lines 109–20 in Potter and Damon 1999, 30) clearly shows that Julia Augusta was instrumental in Plancina's pardon. Piso's son Marcus, who went with his parents to Syria but advised his father against using force (Tac. *Ann.* 2.76.2–4), was exonerated with Tiberius' input.
130. Agrippina the Elder appears only twice in Tacitus' account of the trial, in anonymous grumblings that Julia Augusta saved Plancina so that she might later poison Agrippina and her children (*Ann.* 3.17) and in a senator's proposal that Agrippina, along with Tiberius, Augusta, Antonia, and Drusus, should be publicly thanked for having avenged Germanicus (*Ann.* 3.18).
131. Although the masculine plural for children, "*filii*," does not specifically include the girls.
132. Tac. *Ann.* 4.8.4; Barrett 1996, 32, suggests Tiberius thus singled them out for the imperial succession. Location surmised from Tac. *Ann.* 4.68: Foubert 2016, 142.
133. Joseph. *AJ* 19.117. Kokkinos 2002, 67, 152, tentatively endorsed by Barrett 1996, xix, holds that Germanicus' house can be identified as that of Antonia and ultimately that of Livia.
134. More detail appears in Carandini 2018, Tav. 4, and Carandini and Carafa 2017, Tab. 70; cf. ibid. Tab. 76, from which our more schematic plan is derived.
135. Tacitus notes Tiberius as being inherently hostile to the house of Germanicus (*Ann.* 4.17.2: *haud umquam domui Germanici mitis*), although he also blames Tiberius' ambitious confidant Sejanus (e.g., *Ann.* 3.12, 4.17.3) and points to destructive rivalry between Livia/Julia Augusta and Agrippina the Elder (*Ann.* 3.12.5; 1.33.6, 2.43.5, and elsewhere).
136. Claudia Pulchra's son Quinctilius Varus was once betrothed to Agrippina the Elder's daughter Julia Livilla. Varus was charged in 27, but the trial was postponed (Barrett 1996, 36).
137. Tac. *Ann.* 4.52, which also includes her accusation that it was not proper for one and the same person to sacrifice for *divus* Augustus and persecute his relatives: see Ch. 1, n.24.
138. Tac. *Ann.* 4.53, a story he attributes to the *commentarii* of Agrippina the Younger.
139. Tac. *Ann.* 4.54.1–4.

140. We will see these banqueting behaviors in action at Britannicus' murder in 55 (Ch. 5).
141. See, e.g., Tac. *Ann.* 4.70.7, 71.7. Barrett 1996, 36, notes that Tacitus has Agrippina's downfall occur with that of her son Nero Caesar, both after Livia's death in 29 (something Velleius seems to corroborate, 2.1.130.4–5); Pliny the Elder (*HN* 8.145) implies that Nero Caesar was charged by 28 at latest. See below for Tacitus' reports of other charges in 29 (*Ann.* 5.3.2). Bellemore 1995 focuses on authors' chronological inconsistencies regarding Sejanus and Livilla; Deline 2015, esp. 770–72, resolves the inconsistencies by proposing that Tacitus erroneously transposed events of 27 and 29.
142. Despite Tiberius' absence from Rome, family interactions continued: e.g., he gathered the family in Campania to celebrate Agrippina the Younger's marriage in 28 (Tac. *Ann.* 4.75).
143. Tac. *Ann.* 3.56–57. The death was later attributed to his wife Livilla, allegedly Sejanus' lover, and to Sejanus: Tac. *Ann.* 4.3, Suet. *Tib.* 62; cf. Cass. Dio 57.22.2.
144. In 23 Caligula was 11. For Gemellus, b. 20 Dec. 19 (less plausibly in 20 CE) and officially known as Tiberius Julius Caesar Nero, see PIR[2] I 226 and Kienast et al. 2017, 76–77. Gemellus' twin died in 23.
145. Tac. *Ann.* 4.39–41. From a reconstruction of the Fasti Ostienses and re-examination of the evidence for Sejanus and Livilla, Bellemore 1995 proposes that Sejanus actually married Livilla shortly before his downfall and execution on 26 October 31, which led to her forced suicide slightly later.
146. Barrett 1996, xix, 36, and 40; Suet. *Calig.* 10.1; see Ch. 1, n.132; Suet. *Tib.* 53.1; Tac. *Ann.* 4.67.3–4. Julia Augusta was now in her early 80s.
147. Agrippina the Elder herself reportedly stressed her connection to Augustus, according to Tacitus (*Ann.* 1.40.3, 4.52.4). See Ch. 1, nn.24, 137. For Sejanus' responsibility, see Tac. *Ann.* 4.12.
148. Sen. *De Ira* 3.21.5 (undated) for Herculaneum; Deline 2015, 770.
149. Suet. *Calig.* 7; Tac. *Ann.* 5.3.2–3.
150. For Drusus Caesar, see Tac. *Ann.* 6.23; Suet. *Tib.* 54.
151. Suet. *Calig.* 24 specifies that the rape occurred before Caligula was 16. Among others, Winterling 2009, 108–109, questions the veracity of this and other reports of Caligula's incest that are standard for the image of a tyrant.
152. For instance, Suetonius remarks that the deaths of Drusus Caesar and Agrippina the Elder were at first attributed to Sejanus but later discovered as the work of Tiberius (*Tib.* 58.22.4–5). It is true as well that the imperial family judged their own family members at home, so there are no good records: Boatwright 2021, 65–77.
153. Julia Livilla was betrothed to Quintilius Varus before 33 (Sen. *Controv.* 1.3.10); the marriage did not take place.
154. As noted above, Tacitus credits those memoirs for the account that in 26 Agrippina the Elder begged Tiberius for permission to marry: Tac. *Ann.* 4.53.
155. See Intro., n.5.
156. Tac. *Ann.* 4.71.6, a note in which Tacitus notes compassion on Livia's part for her stepchildren, although typically critically: "Julia had tolerated twenty years of exile in the Trimeri islands with the help of Augusta, who—although she had secretly cut down her stepchildren in their prime—openly showed them pity once they were ruined."
157. For the date: Suet. *Calig.* 10.1; Birley 2007, 145–46. Kienast et al. 2017, 78, specify after 31 August.
158. Tac. *Ann.* 4.75, significantly ending the fourth book of the *Annals.* For Domitius Ahenobarbus, see PIR[2] D 127. His date of birth, 2 or 1 BCE, is calculated from his later consulship; if true, in 28 CE he would have been 30, more than twice his bride's age.
159. Agrippina the Elder and Nero Caesar surely were not part of the ceremonies, despite living in Herculaneum.
160. Suet. *Nero* 1–5 (his ch. 5 for negatives); Sen. *Controv.* 9.4.18; Vell. Pat. 2.72.3, Joseph. *AJ* 20.148.
161. Tac. *Ann.* 4.75. Tacitus does not note here that Antonia the Elder was also the sister-in-law of Tiberius. Her sister Antonia the Younger was the widow of Drusus the Elder, Tiberius' younger brother, and she would raise in her own home the family of Germanicus, one of her three children. See Genealogy.
162. Suet. *Nero* 1–5, but we should reject his story (*Nero* 5) that Domitius Ahenobarbus had accompanied Gaius Caesar East: see Barrett 1996, 44, with earlier discussion.

163. In 55 the Arval Brethren performed sacrifice there on the order of the new princeps, Nero, his natural son (*CIL* VI 32352 = EDCS-21300003 = *CFA* 24); see Ch. 5.
164. Presumably, she was often with Ahenobarbus, although she probably also spent time in suburban villas.
165. The oblivion of her two sisters in the historical record suggests that girls were simply ignored as a threat.
166. For Sejanus' fall, see Birley 2007, who discusses (141–46) the gruesome consequences detailed by the ancient historians and documentary evidence (e.g., Tac. *Ann.* 5.9.1–2, 6.19–20; Cass. Dio 59.11.5; *ILS* 157; *Fasti Ostienses*).
167. In 33 CE: *CIL* VI 32342 = *CFA* 7; in 37, *CIL* VI 32343 = *CFA* 8; in 38, *CIL* VI 32344 = *CFA* 12; in 27 (restored): *CIL* VI 32341 = *CFA* 5.
168. Tac. *Ann.* 6.1.1. In this period most held the consulship for only six months (Cass. Dio 59.6.5), a practice opening up the prestigious annual and collegial magistracy to more among the elite.
169. His year-long tenure may also have been a way for Tiberius to manifest the interest of the Julio-Claudians for Rome despite his own absence on Capri.
170. Tac. *Ann.* 6.45.1–2; Cass. Dio 58.26.5; for Rubellius Blandus, see PIR² R 111. P. Petronius (PIR² P 269) was added to the group by nomination of the consuls. Tiberius contributed one hundred million sesterces (Tacitus discredits the five supervisors by noting they proffered various honors for Tiberius). For the weddings of the imperial women in 33, see Cass. Dio 58.21.1 and Ch. 1, n.173.
171. Agrippina the Younger survived her own later exile there (see Ch. 3).
172. Suet. *Tib.* 53–54.
173. Tac. *Ann.* 6.15. For L. Cassius Longinus, *cos. ord.* 30, and member of the *XVviri sacris faciundis* (*AE* 1930, 70), see PIR² C 503. The family was so eminent that Lucius' brother, C. Cassius Longinus (PIR² C 501), also served as *cos. suff.* that year. M. Vinicius was also *cos. ord.* in 30, when Velleius dedicated his historical work to him (Vell Pat. 1.8.1, 13.5), but he seems to be of more recent nobility: PIR² V 661; Syme 1986, 173, 278. Later, Julia Livilla may have accompanied him to Asia: *IGRR* IV 464.
174. Cass. Dio 58.3.8.
175. As Caligula and Claudius famously did.
176. By "birthday celebrations" I mean private ones undertaken within family and friend circles (see Argetsinger 1992), not the more public rites undertaken by, e.g., the Arval Brethren. Imperial (and presumably other elite) engagements were perhaps also celebrated; cf. *CIL* X 6561 from Velletri.
177. Caligula's assumption of his *toga virilis* unusually was celebrated in Antium: Suet. *Calig.* 10, cf. Cass. Dio 57.18.11, 59.2.1–2; Kienast et al. 2017, 78.
178. FOS #470; Ch. 2, n.55. Her father was M. Iunius Silanus (PIR² I 832). Birley 2007, 146–47: Suet. *Calig.* 12.1 appears to put the marriage before Sejanus' fall in 31. Junia Claudilla was sister to Junia Silana, with whom Agrippina came into conflict in 55 (Ch. 5).
179. Suet. *Claud.* 26–27. For Aelia Paetina, see FOS #18. She will resurface as a contender for Claudius' hand in 48.
180. They occurred soon after Sejanus' murder: Tac. *Ann.* 5.9.1–2; Cass. Dio 58.11.5; Birley 2007, 141–42.
181. Cass. Dio 58.27.2; Suet. *Nero* 5; Tac. *Ann.* 6.47.2, who mentions adultery with Albucilla (PIR² A 487) but not Domitia Lepida. Q. Naevius Cordus Sutorius Macro (PIR² N 12) had become praetorian prefect in 31 after Sejanus' downfall, in which he had a role.
182. Suet. *Nero* 5; Cass. Dio 58.27.2. Tiberius died at Misenum: Suet. *Tib.* 75.3; Kienast et al. 2017, 72.

Chapter 2

1. Despite Tiberius' attempt to disguise his illness, according to Tacitus (*Ann.* 6.50); cf. Cass. Dio 58.28.3. Rumors: Philo, *Leg.* 6.38–40; Tac. *Ann.* 6.45; Suet. *Calig.* 12.2, 26.1; Cass. Dio 58.28.4, 59.10.6; Sheldon 2018, 89–91.
2. Joseph. *AJ* 18.224–25, 234, vividly describes the spread of the news in Rome over two days. News must have reached Tiberius' relatives and the elite more quickly. There is no explicit evidence of the praetorians' acclamation, which seems acknowledged in the unprecedented *sestertii* coined in 37/38 depicting (rev.) the emperor addressing soldiers: *RIC*² I, Gaius no. 32.
3. March 18 became his *dies imperii*, the acknowledged day of his assumption of imperial power (*CFA* 12c).

4. Others, like Julia the Elder, Julia the Younger, Livilla, and Agrippina the Elder, had notoriously gone amiss: Ch. 1.
5. For the muddled information for Junia Claudilla (e.g., Tac. *Ann.* 6.20 calls her Junia Claudia), see FOS #470. Cass. Dio 58.25.2 notes the wedding at Antium (over 150 km distant from Capri). For Caligula's *toga virilis* see Ch. 1, n.177.
6. Cass. Dio 58.23.1. Kienast et al. 2017, 78, suggests that he was also pontifex since 33 and augur from before 37.
7. For the uncertainty of the succession in 37 see Tac. *Ann.* 6.46; Suet. *Calig.* 19.3.
8. Suet. *Tib.* 76, *Calig.* 14.2; Philo, *Leg.* 23, 87, cf. *In Flacc.* 10; Cass. Dio 58.23.1–4, 59.1.1.
9. For the poorly documented Gemellus, see Ch. 1, n.144. He was made augur sometime before 37. He must have moved to Capri after his mother's death in 31. Cramer 1954, 107, however, places him in Capri after 29.
10. Tac. *Ann.* 1.12.
11. Gemellus, Tiberius' own grandson, was under a cloud: Tiberius suspected that Gemellus' father was not Drusus the Younger, and his mother Livilla underwent a *damnatio memoriae* in 31 after her disgrace and death (Cass. Dio 58.23.2).
12. For recent collection and discussion of the ancient evidence, see Barrett and Yardley 2023.
13. Suet. *Tib.* 47, *Calig.* 13; see also Cass. Dio 59.6.1; *CFA* 12c.
14. Suet. *Calig.* 14.1, 15. Hurley 1993, 49–50, makes the case that Gemellus' adoption by Caligula, noted in Suet. *Calig.* 15.2, was not a legal one. For the will, see Cass. Dio 59.1.1.
15. Suet. *Calig.* 13, which ends by describing Caligula's ecstatic greeting in Rome by a dense crowd with altars, sacrifices, torches, and endearments after he made his way north from Misenum with Tiberius' funeral procession.
16. Suet. *Calig.* 15.
17. Echoed also in centrally struck coins depicting *divus* Augustus (rev.) and Caligula (obv.): *RIC*² I, Gaius no. 1–4, 6, 9–10, 15–16.
18. Fasti Ostienses (Smallwood 31.16); Cass. Dio 59.3.7; Philo, *Leg.* 12; Joseph. *AJ* 18.236.
19. Suet. *Tib.* 76.1, *Calig.* 16.3; Cass. Dio 59.2.1–4 (noting that such generosity contrasted with Caligula's later greed); Fasti Ostienses (Smallwood 31.21). Donatives to the praetorians and military were key.
20. Barrett and Yardley 2023, ch. 3, n.13.
21. A *bireme.* Pace Cass. Dio 59.3.5, the ashes of Drusus Caesar could not be located.
22. Their epitaphs were erected there: *CIL* VI 40372 ("The bones of Agrippina, daughter of Marcus Agrippa, granddaughter of *divus* Augustus, wife of Germanicus Caesar, mother of C. Caesar Augustus Germanicus, princeps") and 40374 ("The bones of Nero Caesar, son of Germanicus Caesar, grandson of *divus* Augustus, flamen of Augustus, quaestor").
23. Centrally-struck *sestertii* dated 37–41 CE: (obv.) portrait and legend AGRIPPINA M(arci) F(ilia) MAT(er) C(aii) CAESARIS AVGVSTI; (rev.) ornamented *carpentum* drawn by two mules, sometimes with S P Q R MEMORIAE AGRIPPINAE: *RIC*² I, Gaius no. 55; Wood 1999, 208, n.14.
24. Latham 2016, 113–28; Boatwright 2021, 135–37, 178–79.
25. Suet. *Calig.* 15.
26. In 37–38: Agrippina the Elder, *RIC*² I, Gaius no. 7–8, 13–14, 21–22; Germanicus, *RIC*² I, Gaius no. 15–18, 35, 43 (obv. portrait often with "Germanicus Caesar, son of Tiberius Augustus, grandson of *divus* Augustus," but no. 11–12 and some others have the legend "Germanicus Caesar, father of C. Caesar Augustus Germanicus").
27. Wood 1995, 458–60.
28. NERO ET DRVSVS CAESARES: *RIC*² I, Gaius no. 34 (37 CE), no. 49 (41 CE); Wood 1995, 460; Rose 1997, 33. Provincial coins honored Caligula's maternal grandfather M. Agrippa as well: Rose 1997, 34.
29. Suet. *Claud.* 7.1, 9.1–2, adding that the work with statues went so slowly that Caligula almost removed him from office. We hear also that Claudius' appointment to an imperial priesthood by Caligula almost beggared him and that when Claudius presided over games in Caligula's place, the crowd acclaimed him "Uncle of the Emperor" and "Brother of Germanicus" (indicating who was important). For honors to Drusus Caesar, see *CIL* V 4953.
30. See Rose 1997, 32.
31. Cass. Dio 59.3.3: "Towards his mother, his sisters, and his grandmother Antonia, he conducted himself at first in the most dutiful manner possible."

32. Suet. *Calig.* 15.2.
33. Cass. Dio 57.12.1–3; cf. Suet. *Tib.* 50.2. The extraordinary rights granted Octavia and Livia during the triumviral period—security and protection against verbal insult similar to that provided for tribunes, the right to be honored by public statues, and administration of their own affairs without a guardian (Cass. Dio 49.38.1; 35 BCE)—were never explicitly repeated for later imperial women, and the first right is hard to trace: Boatwright 2021, 20–31.
34. Purcell 1986; Barrett 2002, passim; Boatwright 2021, 40.
35. E.g., Sen. *Clem.* 1.9; Cass. Dio 55.14–22. She publicly helped Augustus bring aid during fires, but Tiberius suppressed such activity: Suet. *Tib.* 50.2.
36. Adoption, "Augusta," position as priest in the new cult of *divus* Augustus, accompaniment by a lictor: Tac. *Ann.* 1.8.1; cf. Cass. Dio 56.46.1–2. Tiberius refused many other honors such as her title of *Mater patriae* (Mother of the Fatherland) and an altar commemorating her adoption: Tac. *Ann.* 1.14.3; cf. Suet. *Tib.* 50.3.
37. Cass. Dio 56.46.2 is more trustworthy than Tac. *Ann.* 1.14.3 for Julia Augusta's lictor: Boatwright 2021, 32; Barrett 2002, 144 and 160; above. For the right of the *carpentum* granted in 22, see Ch. 2, n.24; for special seating, granted in 23, see Tac. *Ann.* 4.16.6.
38. Suet. *Calig.* 15.2; Cass. Dio 59.3.4 (holding that Caligula harassed her into suicide; cf. Suet. *Calig.* 23). She would receive the title posthumously in Claudius' first days: Suet. *Claud.* 11.2; Kienast et al. 2017, 62. Despite her refusal of the title in 37, Antonia is called Augusta in the Arval *acta* of 31 January 38: *CFA* 12c. Antonia possessed naturally the right of three children, which was granted Livia extraordinarily in 9 BCE as consolation for Drusus the Elder's death (Cass. Dio 55.2.5–6).
39. Cass. Dio 59.3.4.
40. Cass. Dio 59.3.4.
41. Suet. *Calig.* 15.3.
42. Tac. *Ann.* 4.17.1; Suet. *Tib.* 54.1 (*praemia*).
43. Suet. *Tib.* 53, 50.
44. Cp. *ILS* 190 from 11 May 37, Aritium Vetus (now Alvega, Portugal); *IGRR* 4.251, from 37, Assos (now Behramkale, Turkey).
45. E.g., Barrett and Yardley 2023, ch. 3, n.29, explain the sisters' absence from the Aritium oath "presumably because [it was sworn] before the formal accession and the formal inclusion of the sisters in the vows." In any case, few oaths are recorded from the Roman world.
46. *RIC*[2] I, Gaius no. 33 (*sestertius*, our Ill. 2.1); *RIC*[2] I, Gaius no. 41 (*dupondius*). S(enatus) C(onsulto) appears in the exergue of the reverse. The low denomination of the issue probably correlates with greater circulation.
47. Cass. Dio 59.7.4. Di Brino 2016, 263, explores the prolonged festivities at the temple's completion.
48. Wood 1995, 459. Of the 12 such groups catalogued by Rose (1997, 35 and n.52), from the areas of modern Italy, France, Switzerland, Greece, and Turkey, four included at least one of Caligula's sisters. The frequent reconfiguration of such groups makes precision difficult. Wood 1995 is especially insightful in dealing with the three sisters' imaging.
49. See Houston 1985.
50. Cass. Dio 59.23.5.
51. He was charged with treason, adultery, and incest: Suet. *Nero* 5.2; see also Cass. Dio 58.27.2; Ch. 1.
52. Suet. *Calig.* 7, reporting that the charges against the two had been brought by Tiberius.
53. Suet. *Calig.* 15.4; Cass. Dio 59.6.2, 59.10-7-8, 59.16.3, 60.4.5.
54. Cass. Dio 59.9.5; see also Philo, *Leg.* 285; Talbert 1984, 14–15.
55. Suet. *Calig.* 12.2. For this poorly known woman, see Wardle 1998, 109–10; FOS #470; PIR[2] I 857. Houston 1985, 183–84, plausibly assumes that Julia Claudilla moved to Capri to live with Caligula. Later, Cassius Dio's Livia advised Augustus that the only truly dependable and sincere confidant for a princeps was his wife (55.16.1–2).
56. Suet. *Calig.* 24: Caligula habitually committed incest with each of his three sisters in turn (cf. Cass. Dio 59.3.6, 22.6, 26.5; Aur. Vict. *Caes.* 3.10; Orosius 7.5.9), raped Drusilla in Antonia's house in Rome before he was 16 (she would have been 11 or so; see Ch. 1), and later "took her" from Cassius Longinus and treated her as his wife; cf. Cass. Dio 59.11.1–6. Among others, Barrett 1990, 85, and Winterling 2009, 108–109, question the veracity of the reports, which are standard for the image of a tyrant (cf. Vinson 1989; Meister 2014), noting that contemporary witnesses Philo and Seneca do not mention incest with Agrippina and Julia Livilla. Tacitus' account of Caligula's reign is not extant.

57. For Caligula's wives, see Wardle 1998, 117–26, and below. For Milonia Caesonia, whom he wed perhaps at the end of 39 and who was the only wife who bore him a child, see FOS #550; PIR^2 M 590. For Drusilla, see the preceding note.
58. Suet. *Calig.* 25.1; Cass. Dio 59.8.7. She may have been exiled, perhaps on charges of adultery, to prevent remarriage. For Cornelia (Livia) Orestina or Orestilla, see FOS #285 (doubts the legitimacy of union with Caligula); PIR^2 C 1292.
59. For Lollia Paulina, see FOS #504; PIR^2 L 328; Cass. Dio 59.12.1; Suet. *Calig.* 25.2. The marriage, entered into after Drusilla's death on 10 June 38, ended in September/early October that year (*CIL* VI 2028e; pace Wardle 1998, 111–22). Agrippina is not mentioned in these reports, although a later anecdote reveals that she knew Lollia Paulina so intimately as to recognize peculiarities of her teeth (Cass. Dio 61.32.4).
60. Suet. *Calig.* 24.1. Chronology means that this habit affected only Cornelia Orestina.
61. Suet. *Calig.* 24: *mox Lucio Cassio Longino consulari conlocatam abduxit et in modum iustae uxoris propalam habuit.* The chapter overall contrasts Caligula's "extreme love and respect" for Drusilla to his disrespect for Agrippina and Julia Livilla, "whom he often handed over to his depraved cronies" (*ut quas saepe exoletis suis prostraverit*). Given other reports of incest with all three, we may date this reported series of events to late 37 and 38.
62. Views of the illness as causing or at least marking a deterioration in Caligula's reign began in antiquity: see, e.g., Joseph. *AJ* 18.256, 19.210; Philo, *Leg.* 67; cf. Cass. Dio 59.6.7; Winterling 2009, 113–14; Wardle 1998, 113–15.
63. Philo, *Leg.* 14; Wardle 1998, 113–14.
64. Cass. Dio 59.8.1; Philo, *Leg.* 23; cf. Suet. *Calig.* 23; Philo states that the charge of conspiracy was false (*Leg.* 30–31). Sheldon 2018, 89. Gemellus' death is usually dated to 37, but Herz 1981 argues from the Acts of the Arval Brethren (*CIL* VI 2028e = *CFA* 12), recording P. Memmius Regulus in his place on 24 May 38, that Gemellus died sometime between February and May that year.
65. Sheldon 2018, 89–91.
66. See PIR^2 A 371; FOS #437 (date).
67. Father: M. Aemilius Lepidus, *cos.* 6 CE, *capax imperii*, a worthy contender for the throne: Tac. *Ann.* 1.13.2, with Syme 1955 and 1958, 751–52. Another relative was Aemilius Lepidus Paullus (*cos. suff.* 34 BCE), Augustus' friend and the husband of Cornelia (daughter of Octavian's first wife Scribonia): Barrett 1996, 58–67, 235. Less appealing were alleged calumnies launched by Aemilius' sister Aemilia Lepida (PIR^2 A 421; FOS #30) against her husband Drusus Caesar (the brother who starved to death in the imperial palace in 33 CE), although later Aemilia Lepida was accused of adultery with a slave and committed suicide in 36 (Tac. *Ann.* 6.40.3). Lepidus' youth is suggested by Caligula's privilege to him to stand for office five years before the lawful time (Cass. Dio 59.22.6–7).
68. Suet. *Calig.* 24.1; Joseph. *AJ* 19.204; Aur. Vict. *Caes.* 3; Suda 1.503 (Adler).
69. Cass. Dio 59.11.1–6, 59.22.6; cf. Suet. *Calig.* 36.1 and Tac. *Ann.* 14.2.2.
70. Suet. *Calig.* 24.
71. Cass. Dio 59.22.7: Wardle 1998, 114–15; Wood 1995, 458–61. Cogitore 2014, 172–73 notes that Cassius Dio's narrative places this information after Drusilla's death, confusing chronology.
72. Cass. Dio 59.11.1. Such public respect for eminent women began in the late 2nd century BCE but became more linked to the imperial family: Flower 1996, 122–27; Boatwright 2021, 114–15, 171–77; Benoist 2005, 103–46.
73. Cass. Dio 59.11.
74. Cass. Dio 59.11; cf. Suet. *Calig.* 24.2. Herz 1981 points out that her consecration was not immediate; Di Brino 2016, 264, remarks its coincidence with Augustus' birthday. The cult did not long survive (Boatwright 2021, 148, 303–304), though some testimony comes from inscriptions from which Caligula's name is erased (*CIL* XI 3598). Most imperial consecrations after Augustus were prompted by the following emperor: see Boatwright 2021, 145–47.
75. Cass. Dio 59.11.4; see Sen. *Apocol.* 1.3. He was rewarded with a million sesterces. For this person, whose name Cassius Dio transmits as Geminius, see PIR^2 L 296.
76. The day and year of Drusilla's birth are controversial (e.g., Lindsay 1995, 8–11), but the Acts of the Arval Brethren in 40 suggest it was early in June (2–5): *CFA* 14. At the first celebration Caligula brought her statue into the circus on a cart drawn by elephants, and the senators and their wives received presents (Cass. Dio 59.13.7). Cassius Dio also describes Caligula's misuse of his sister's honors to exploit others through specious lawsuits for lèse-majesté, noting a man who was put to death for selling hot water during the mourning period (59.11.6).

77. See Boatwright 2021, 303–304: e.g., *CIL* V 7345 = EDCS-05400594, Forum Vibii Caburrum (Cavorre, Italy); *IG* IV^2 1, 600, Epidaurus, Greece; dedications, e.g., *CIL* XIV 3576, Tibur (Tivoli, Italy).
78. *CIL* XIV 3576. In 33 Rubellius had wed Julia, the daughter of Livilla (Germanicus' sister) and Drusus the Younger; he served with the sisters' husbands on the special fire commission of 36 (Ch. 1).
79. *CIL* XII 1026, to Iulia Drusilla, not *diva* but *parens*, from Tiberius (Claudius), *num(inis)/ honore delato*: Gascou 1998.
80. Hahn 1994, 171, 359. E.g., from Pergamum (near modern Bergama, Turkey) three inscriptions associate Julia Livilla with Athena and title her *Nikephoros* ("Victory Bearer"); one also calls her *synthronos*, or "throne-sharing": *IGRR* IV 328, 464, and 476 (37–39). Hahn has no evidence for worship or deific assimilation of Agrippina the Younger in this period. See also Boatwright 2021, 144, 148.
81. Suet. *Calig.* 24.1.
82. The sources give no hint of her advising Caligula, in contrast to references to (e.g.) Livia advising Augustus and Tiberius (Cass. Dio 54.7.2; Sen. *Clem.* 1.9 and Cass. Dio 55.14–22): Boatwright 2021, 40; Wood 1995, 458.
83. E.g., Purcell 1986, 79, 82, 85, and passim.
84. Suet. *Nero* 5; Cass. Dio 58.27.2.
85. For Antium, see Tac. *Ann.* 15.23.1. The year of Nero's birth is somewhat uncertain, due to inconsistencies in the sources: see Barrett 1996, 234, and Barrett et al. 2016, 18–21, settling on 37 (cf. Suet. *Nero* 6.1). We cannot know if she had conceived earlier but not brought a child to term in the interim after her wedding in 28 CE, when she was some 13 years old.
86. To be sure, there was no such "role," since the only precedent was Octavia, who was decidedly retiring and maternal while her brother Augustus consolidated power: Boatwright 2021, 186–87, 258–59.
87. See, e.g., Tac. *Ann.* 12.52.1; Sen. *Apocol.* 3.2. Among others, Cramer 1954, 82, 108, explores the importance of astrology and omens for the imperial house.
88. Plin. *HN* 7.46. Here, he may also be trying to make genealogical and etymological points, since he starts with the similar birth of Marcus Agrippa and glosses his name as "born with difficulty." Boccaccio's *Life of Agrippina the Younger* (see Ch. 6) notes that Nero, famous the world over as a beast, was born feet first from her womb.
89. The situation is among those classified by Soranus as difficult labor (*Gyn.* 4.1; 8). Pliny's note, not repeated among other authors' clutch of omens, is intimate history.
90. Suet. *Nero* 6.1. Cassius Dio (61.2.1–3) gives slightly different versions: that the father "foresaw clearly enough his son's future depravity and licentiousness, ... [and] declared, 'It is impossible for any good man to be sprung from me and this woman,'" and that at the birth, just before dawn, rays not cast by any visible beam of the sun enveloped the baby.
91. Cass. Dio 61.2.1–2, commenting that her exclamation was thoughtless, and she later bitterly regretted it.
92. He thus decisively concludes her presence in the extant *Annals* (*Ann.* 14.9.5); see Ch. 5. In *Ann.* 6.22.6 Tacitus notes briefly that he will later record an astrologer's prediction of Nero's rule, but his narrative is missing from after Tiberius' death in March 37 through some time in 47.
93. Caligula was fond of Antium, his birthplace (Suet. *Calig.* 8), and Nero later favored it by founding a veteran colony and building a harbor there (Suet. *Nero* 9.1).
94. Wardle 1998, 115, suggests that "Agrippina may have been requesting ... adoption for Nero."
95. Suet. *Nero* 6.2: *inter ludibria aulae.*
96. In 51, Britannicus called him Domitius, causing Agrippina to complain to Claudius that the adoption was being disregarded: Tac. *Ann.* 12.41 (something suggested also by *Octavia*, 248, a now anonymous Flavian tragedy: Intro., n.7 and Ch. 6). Pliny the Elder often calls him "Domitius Nero" (*HN* 2.92, 4.10, 7.45, 11.238).
97. For rumors of the three's sexual liaison, see Suet. *Calig.* 24.1; Joseph. *AJ* 19.204; Aur. Vict. *Caes.* 3; Suda 1.503 (Adler).
98. For the history of this interim time, see, e.g., Barrett 1990; Barrett and Yardley 2023, ch. 4.
99. Plin. *HN* 9.117–19; the moralist laments that the dripping jewels were not even the gift of the profligate princeps but rather came from provincial plunder amassed by her grandfather M. Lollius. For Lollius, see PIR^2 L 311.
100. E.g., Barzano 2011. See also Sheldon 2018, 256, n.47, for doubters (e.g., Simpson 1980, esp. 347), advocates (e.g., Rutledge 2001, 162–63), and the undecided (e.g., Barrett 1996, 62–70). Rather than argue for or against the authenticity of the conspiracy, I focus here on Agrippina.

101. Cass. Dio 59.23.8.
102. Cass. Dio 59.22.5–9 lumps together Gaetulicus (noted first), Lepidus, Agrippina, and Julia Livilla in a paragraph on Caligula's victims; Suet. *Claud.* 9.1 sketchily notes the "conspiracy of Lepidus and Gaeticulus" (*Lepidi et Gaetulici coniuratio*): Sheldon 2018, 92, stresses the weakness of this evidence. For the Arval Brethren's thanks, see *CIL* VI 2029 = *CFA* 13.
103. Although Julia Livilla's husband Vinicius also is not mentioned, this "company man" (Cass. Dio 60.27.4) was later seated with Caligula, Claudius, and Valerius Asiaticus at the Palatine games before Caligula's assassination (Joseph. *AJ* 19.102) and was deemed a contender for the principate. He apparently accompanied Claudius in the invasion of Britain (Syme 1933) and became proconsul of Asia, to fall to Messalina's wiles in 45. See Ch. 3.
104. As some have argued: see Sheldon 2018, 256–57, n.54.
105. Cass. Dio 59.22.5–9.
106. Suet. *Calig.* 24: *quo facilius eas in causa Aemili Lepidi condemnavit quasi adulteras et insidiarum adversus se conscias ei.*
107. Suet. *Calig.* 24: *chirographa omnium requisita fraude ac stupro divulgavit.* Sheldon 2018, 258, n.65, notes doubts that the letters were real. Suetonius distances himself also from the other "proofs," the three swords Caligula dedicated to Mars Ultor, by noting that they needed identification through a placard.
108. Tac. *Ann.* 14.2.2: *credibilior novae libidinis meditatio in ea visa est quae puellaribus annis stuprum cum Lepido spe dominationis admiserat.* This brief reference may have been explained in the missing books of the *Annals.* See Ch. 5.
109. Furneaux 2.234 *ad Ann.* 14.2.2 notes Tacitus' use of *puella* elsewhere when referring to Octavia (*Ann.* 14.64.1). But in this later occurrence Tacitus is stressing Octavia's innocence.
110. The scenario, bruited by (e.g.) Barrett 1996, 64, is similar to the later one sometimes proposed for Messalina and Silius: see Ch. 3.
111. Cass. Dio 59.23.1.
112. Sen. *Ep.* 4.7.
113. Banishment to islands is more appropriate for those condemned for adultery than for conspiracy: Cogitore 2014, 173. Sheldon 2018, 94, remarks on the "comparatively mild treatment" that the sisters received, however, particularly in light of the legal proceedings taken against ever more individuals alleged as conspirators. She suggests that the mildness may "perhaps point to the close relationship they once shared."
114. Suet. *Calig.* 39.1: "...finery, furnishings, slaves, and even freedmen"; cf. Cass. Dio 59.21.4–6, 59.22.8, 60.4.1. Kleijwegt 1996 attempts to reconstruct the muddled sequence of events (see also Barrett 1990, 103–105, 236). Kleijwegt (1996, 56) argues that the two sisters were with Caligula and only the personal items they carried with them were sold at the first of two auctions.
115. For Lepidus' condemnation, see Syme 1986, 180.
116. It seems implausible that Caligula would have allowed discussion of his incest with his two sisters at Lepidus' trial. For divorce in the case of adultery trials, see, e.g., Harries 2007, 98–99; Treggiari 1991, 286–87.
117. Cass. Dio 59.23.9. After his later return to Rome, Tigellinus (PIR^2 O 91) gained baleful influence with Nero, and he was instrumental in Octavia's death in 62. Julia Livilla here has no named adulterer other than Lepidus. See Ch. 3 for her charge of adultery with Seneca the Younger in 41.
118. Cass. Dio 59.22.6–8. Barrett 1996, 62–63, 66, 236, suggests she began that journey in Maevania (now Bevagna, Italy), where she and her sister had accompanied Caligula on his trip north. Phlegon confirms that Agrippina owned property there: *Mir.* (FGH 2.1179.VII; see Ch. 4). That would have been a ca. 150-km trip to Rome.
119. See Sheldon 2018, 94. Yet Caligula would now be belittling his mother while accruing pity for his sister.
120. Cass. Dio 59.22.7, not naming the conspirators and implying that Caligula was outside Rome when he sent the daggers.
121. Suet. *Tib.* 53–54. Drogula 2011, 235, in his App. 2, remarks that members of the imperial family were banished only to small islands near the coast of Italy. He argues overall (e.g., 230) that relegation to islands was the principate's way to "limit the aristocracy's ability to organize and mobilize resistance."
122. Pontia is 37.4 km south of S. Felice in Circeo; Pandateria is 48 km south of Gaeta. The two islands are about 40 km apart, with Pontia about 100 km from Misenum, and Pandateria about 50. Pandateria is documented for Julia Livilla (Tac. *Ann.* 14.63.2; cf. Cass. Dio 59.3.6, 59.22.6–8). Nothing definitively attests to where Agrippina went, but it is most unlikely that the two would have been on the same island.

123. E.g., Drogula 2011, 236–37. Mussolini was imprisoned on Ponza for 10 days in July 1943.
124. Livy 9.28.7; Diod. Sic. 19.101.3.
125. See Barbera 2021, esp. 27–31; De Rossi 1986. When banished, Julia the Elder was not allowed wine, male visitors, or other indulgences (Suet. *Aug.* 65; Cass. Dio 55.10), but if she lived in this villa on Pandateria she had some comforts. If the villa was used for Agrippina the Elder and Julia Livilla, both of whom starved to death while on Pandateria (Suet. *Tib.* 53; Sen. *Apocol.* 10.4), the surrounding comforts may have offered more malicious pain.
126. This villa is now under the Punta della Madonna that houses the modern town's cemetery. Bruno and Will 1985, 46, note a pool, fishponds, and an odeion.
127. Scribonia's presence with her daughter Julia the Elder on Pandateria provided some familial comfort: Barbera 2021, 32–34.
128. Tac. *Ann.* 13.21.2, comparing herself favorably to the childless Junia Silana.
129. Tac. *Ann.* 4.53 (*repperi in commentariis Agrippinae filiae quae Neronis principis mater vitam suam et casus suorum posteris memoravit*); Plin. *HN* 7.46 and 7, praef. Wood 1999, 257, suggests that Agrippina at least started her memoirs on the island. Agrippina's banishment is not associated with the rancor, dissimulation, and descent into deviancy that Tiberius' semi-exile in Rhodes from 6 BCE to 4 CE supposedly caused (Tac. *Ann.* 1.4.4; cf. 2.42, 4.57.2, 6.51.1–2).
130. Passageways are cut through the rock from the villa to the seafront at Pontia.
131. *HN* 10.59, 7.43; Maxwell-Stuart 1997.
132. Suet. *Aug.* 19.2, 65.3; cf. Suet. *Tib.* 53.2 and Tac. *Ann.* 14.60.1–63.3.
133. Drogula 2011, 233, notes that permanent banishment to an island also involved loss of citizenship and interdiction (being killed with impunity if found on Roman territory). Even if Caligula's auction in Gaul concerned only the personal possessions his sisters carried (although Suetonius' note that he also "sold" their freedmen suggests otherwise: Ch. 2, n.114), by the time of their arrival on their islands they had been stripped of their goods.
134. Suet. *Nero* 6.3–4; Cass. Dio 60.4.1–2, 6.3; Levick 2015, 51.
135. Julia Livilla's good fortune at her return in 41 was short-lived (see Ch. 3). There was, to be sure, the counter-example of Ahenobarbus, saved from Tiberius' charges by Caligula's accession.
136. Cass. Dio 59.23.7, 28.7; Suet. *Calig.* 25.3–4. Barrett 1990, 94–96, suggests that the birth occurred in the early summer of 39. For Milonia Caesonia, see FOS #550.
137. Suetonius' (Nero) *trimulus patrem amisit* (*Nero* 6.2) is not very precise. We cannot know whether Nero was with his father. Suet. *Nero* 6.3 notes Caligula's appropriation of the estate.
138. Suet. *Nero* 5. For Domitia Lepida, see PIR[2] D 180, FOS #326 (mother of Messalina). Barrett 1996, 45–46, discusses the difficulty of distinguishing the two sisters. To preclude confusion I refer below to this sister generally as Lepida (sometimes Domitia Lepida) and the other simply as Domitia.
139. Messalina (FOS #774), b. ~17/18 CE, was the daughter of Lepida and her first husband, M. Valerius Messalla Barbatus. The date of Messalina's birth allows prosopographers to date Lepida's birth to ca. 5 BCE, although this presents problems for Tacitus' note (*Ann.* 12.64.4) that her age was comparable to Agrippina's (b. 15 CE). Lepida's son, Faustus Cornelius Sulla Felix, was born around 22 CE to Lepida' second husband, Faustus Cornelius Sulla (*cos. suff.* 31; a descendant of the dictator L. Cornelius Sulla). In 47 Faustus Cornelius Sulla Felix would marry Antonia, the daughter of Claudius' second wife Aelia Paetina, further cementing the ties between these two branches of the Julio-Claudian family that would be broken at Messalina's disgrace and downfall in 48. Tacitus praises Lepida's behavior in 48: *Ann.* 11.37.3.
140. Suet. *Nero* 5–6, prefiguring Suetonius' later depiction of the emperor's frivolity and passion for performance. This also contrasts with the care for Nero's education evinced by Agrippina, who in 49 appointed the brilliant philosopher and rhetor Seneca as his tutor (see Ch. 4) and who also steered the youth away from philosophy as unsuitable for one who would rule (Suet. *Nero* 52).
141. See Ch. 5. Tacitus contrasts Lepida's enticement of Nero by flattery and gifts to Agrippina's harsh and menacing behavior and cites Agrippina's jealousy of Lepida's fame, beauty, age, and wealth (a standard criticism of women): Tac. *Ann.* 13.19.4 (*infensa aemulatio*), 13.21.3. Agrippina supposedly arranged charges against Lepida for sorcery against her, the wife of the emperor, and for endangering southern Italy by not restraining her slaves there. Lepida's death was one of the last Agrippina supposedly masterminded before Claudius' own (Tac. *Ann.* 12.64.4–65.2).

Chapter 3

1. Most scholars concur on 24 January 41, although Wiseman 2013, 56–57 *ad* Joseph. *AJ* 19.77, 85, prefers 22 January (dismissing Suet. *Calig.* 58.1, whose manuscripts vary between 24, 25, and 26 January). This was the first open murder of a Roman leader since Julius Caesar's in 44 BCE.
2. Suet. *Calig.* 28; Cass. Dio 59.18.3; Oros. 7.5.9; cf. Joseph. *AJ* 19.125.
3. Malloch 2013, 1–2: Tacitus' extant manuscript of the later books of the *Annals* (and early books of the *Histories*) resumes in Book 11, apparently in late spring 47, but we cannot know what was contained in the earlier part of that manuscript. See Ch. 6.
4. Wiseman 2013 is particularly valuable on Joseph. *AJ* 19.1–273, the most detailed account of the plot and its aftermath. Josephus completed this work in Rome in the 90s, turning to at least Caligula's contemporaries Cluvius Rufus and Fabius Rusticus (Wiseman 2013, xiv–xvii). See also Joseph. *BJ* 2.205, 209; Suet. *Calig.* 56–60, *Claud.* 10.3; Cass. Dio 59.29–30.3, 60.1.1.
5. See Swan 1970, focusing on *AJ* 21.251–252. Wiseman 2013, 47–48 *ad* Joseph. *AJ* 19.18 notes that Josephus calls one of the main conspirators, Vinicianus (see following note), "Minucianus" each of the 12 times he names him; Wiseman also points out (60–63) that the two variant accounts of Suet. *Calig.* 58 both differ from Joseph. *AJ* 19.17–273.
6. I follow Wiseman 2013, 52, on Joseph. *AJ* 19.49–63: Chaerea and Sabinus enlisted Vinicianus as their senatorial leader. For Vinicianus, see PIR² A 701; Pomponius, PIR² P 757; Sentius, PIR² S 396. Joseph. *AJ* 19.17–19 names as another conspirator Aemilius Regulus from Corduba, Spain, but never returns to this individual, who is otherwise unknown (Wiseman 2013, 47 ad loc.).
7. Suet. *Calig.* 60; Joseph. *AJ* 19.54, 19.167–84; cf. 186.
8. Rome's women related to those of senatorial rank did compose a rarefied group: Raepsaet-Charlier's (1987) catalogue of all known and presumed senatorial women from 10 BCE to 200 CE (FOS) names only some 900 individuals.
9. A difficult position for an imperial woman, although later, Domitia Longina survived the assassination of her hated husband Domitian (r. 81–96): Boatwright 2021, 47–50.
10. For Augustus, see Aug. *RGDA* 34.2; Drusus the Elder: Tac. *Ann.* 1.33.2 and Suet. *Tib.* 50.1, Suet. *Claud.* 1.4; Germanicus: Tac. *Ann.* 2.82.2. See also Tiberius' reluctance to assume sole power in 14: Tac. *Ann.* 1.13.4.
11. Tacitus maintains that even at Augustus' death in 14 there were very few who remembered the Republic: *Ann.* 1.3.7.
12. Joseph. *AJ* 19.225, 228, on their motives for supporting Claudius.
13. Josephus' narrative (19.190–200) separates these secondary murders. For the killings, see also Suet. *Calig.* 59.
14. Joseph. *AJ* 19.190–94; tr. Wiseman 2013, 298. Joseph. *AJ* 19.190 adds that Chaerea was also eager to finish the job and gratify his deep hatred of Caligula
15. Aur. Vict. *Caes.* 3.16; Oros. 7.6.3; Suet. *Calig.* 60; Wiseman 2013, 72.
16. Joseph. *AJ* 19.212; cf. 218. Some have argued that Claudius was aware of (if not complicit in) the plot against Caligula (Levick 2015, 39–43; Osgood 2011, 29–32).
17. Suet. *Claud.* 11.1.
18. Tac. *Ann.* 1.5–6. He was exiled in 6 CE to Surrentum (modern Sorrento, Italy) and then moved to Planasia: Suet. *Aug.* 65.1; Cass. Dio 55.32; Vell. Pat. 2.112.7.
19. Joseph. *AJ* 19.217, 219, 223, 225, 228.
20. Suet. *Claud.* 3.2, 4.2; Osgood 2011, 9–11; Ch. 2. On Claudius' non-Julian heritage, see, e.g., Simpson 2008, 362 (who warns in general against the modern conception of a "Julio-Claudian dynasty").
21. Chaerea and accomplices Clemens (praetorian prefect) and Pomponius (military tribune) (Joseph. *AJ* 19.37); Cornelius Sabinus (praetorian tribune, *AJ* 19.48; cf. Cass. Dio 59.29.1); and Aquila (Joseph. *AJ* 19.110). In Suetonius' two versions (in *Calig.* 58; both slightly differing from Josephus), 30 individuals are involved.
22. Josephus presents the events twice (*AJ* 19.162–65 and 19.212–28); the second version is more hostile to the senate and "assumes a popular enthusiasm for the Principate, and for Claudius in particular, which is inconsistent with the attitude expressed in the [first]" (Wiseman 2013, 84). Josephus' doublet version of the choice of Claudius (*AJ* 19.164–65) has the praetorians decide on Claudius before physically seizing him (Wiseman 2013, 73 ad loc.). For full overviews of Claudius' accession, see Levick 2015, 33–46; Osgood 2011, 29–46.
23. Joseph. *AJ* 19.162–65, 216–29; Suet. *Claud.* 10.1; Cass. Dio 60.1.2–3.

24. The consul Sentius Saturninus spoke eloquently (Joseph. *AJ* 19.167–84). For the meeting (the exact location in Rome's city center is debatable), see Joseph. *AJ* 19.158 and *BJ* 2.205; Suet. *Calig.* 60; Cass. Dio 60.1.1.
25. Joseph. *AJ* 19.229, 232. Wiseman 2013, 89–91, *ad* Joseph. *AJ* 19.229–36 notes discrepancies. Suet. *Claud.* 10.3: the senate summoned Claudius, and he replied that he was forcibly detained.
26. This too is disputed in the sources: Suet. *Calig.* 60 holds that the senate did not want any one successor; one passage of Josephus has a first meeting of the senate devoted to returning to Republican government and liberty (Ch. 3, n.7); elsewhere (*BJ* 2.205), Josephus holds that the senate wanted to choose a successor to Caligula.
27. Joseph. *AJ* 19.251. A third potential successor may have been Vinicianus (perhaps the son of M. Vinicius' sister: Barrett 1990, 108, cf. 33), who committed suicide after the revolt of Scribonianus in 42 (Cass. Dio 60.15.5). Asiaticus had been publicly humiliated by Caligula's boast of sex with his wife Saturnina: Sen. *Constant.* 18.2. Vinicius' and Asiaticus' newfound loyalty to Claudius would later be rewarded by second consulships for both (45 and 46 respectively), although their short time as imperial contenders is thought to have contributed to their downfalls later in Claudius' reign (see below).
28. Joseph. *AJ* 19.259–60. Joseph. *AJ* 19.263–66 describes mistreatment of targeted senators until Claudius rescued them.
29. Joseph. *AJ* 19.228; Suet. *Claud.* 10.4.
30. Joseph. *AJ* 19.250–53; Cass. Dio 60.1.1–2.
31. Claudius proclaimed transparency and clemency, including toward individuals allegedly involved in the assassination (other than Chaerea and other select praetorians): Suet. *Claud.* 11.1; Cass. Dio 60.3.5; *RIC*² I, Claudius no. 5, 6, 15, 16, and 96 (*aurei*, *denarii*, and *sestertii* with reverses EX SC OB CIVES SERVATOS, 41–42 CE). Claudius also got the right to use the names Caesar and Augustus.
32. *RIC*² I, Claudius no. 97 and 113 (small denomination *as*, struck 41–50 and 50–54): (obv.) Claudius' portrait and titles; (rev.) personification of Liberty, with LIBERTAS AUGUSTA S C ("Augustan Liberty, by Decree of the Senate").
33. Cass. Dio 60.4.1. This was part of Claudius' annulment of Caligula's acts and decisions: Suet. *Claud.* 11. Barrett 1996, 85, notes that Claudius must also have revoked the sisters' convictions as adulterers, allowing Agrippina to remarry.
34. Joseph. *AJ* 19.247 (20,000 sesterces); Suet. *Claud.* 10.4 (15,000). Caligula had given the praetorians only 1,000 sesterces at his accession (Cass. Dio 59.2.1).
35. Cass. Dio 60.12.4; Suet. *Claud.* 21.4. The camp was featured on high-value *aurei* and *denarii* struck during the first eight years of his reign (Levick 2015, 43–44): *RIC*² I, Claudius no. 7, 8, 11, and 12.
36. Tac. *Ann.* 12.36–37.
37. Suet. *Calig.* 59; Noy 2000, 189. The location of the tomb the two sisters erected is unknown, but it was probably not at Lake Nemi (as hopefully announced by Italian police early in 2011).
38. See Osgood 2011, 55–65.
39. At least initially such acts raised the Claudian *gens* (family) above the Julian one, which Caligula had extolled equally and to which Agrippina and her sister more obviously belonged.
40. Cass. Dio 60.5.1.
41. Suet. *Claud.* 11.2; Sen. *Apocol.* 9.5; Cass. Dio 60.5.2; Osgood 2011, 56–60. For a posthumous dedication (45/46 CE) to the new *diva* from Rhamnous, which unusually names her Livia rather than Julia Augusta, see Stafford 2013.
42. Cass. Dio 58.2.3; Tac. *Ann.* 1.14.1; cf. Cass. Dio 57.12.4 and Suet. *Tib.* 50.3.
43. PIR² C 820. His original name, Ti. Claudius Caesar Germanicus, was changed to Ti. Claudius Caesar Britannicus after Claudius' triumph in Britain in 43 (Suet. *Claud.* 27.1).
44. Gues 2019, 510 and passim.
45. Cass. Dio 60.12.5. This complicates a linear development of the honorific Augusta, which, e.g., Flory (1988, 113) has argued developed to designate the mother of the emperor or heir. Further for "Augusta," see Ch. 4.
46. Suet. *Claud.* 27.2; Cass. Dio 60.5.7, Tac. *Ann.* 12.3.2. Silanus' fiancée is identified by Swan 1970, 160, n.46; Syme 1958, 385. For Aelia Paetina, see Ch. 1, n.179; for (Claudia) Antonia, FOS #217 (Barrett 1996, 78: d.o.b. "no later than 29"). After Pompeius' death in 47 Antonia married Faustus Cornelius Sulla Felix (son of Messalina's mother Domitia Lepida and her second husband, Faustus Sulla, thus half-brother of Messalina) and bore him a son. After 65 (and the deaths of Sulla and Poppaea) she was killed by Nero because she refused to marry him. For Octavia, born in 39 or 49, see FOS #246.
47. PIR² P 630; he also held several priestly offices.

48. FOS #29. For Junius Silanus, see PIR[2] J 829. He became a designated companion (*comes*) in the Britain campaign of 43, was awarded triumphal insignia, and was privileged to hold political office five years before the legally stipulated time. See Ch. 4 for his later alleged incest with his sister Junia Calvina.
49. Levick 2015, 65. Swan 1970, 160: Claudius also detached himself from Caligula's "preferment of ignoble men."
50. As *pater familias*, Tiberius also had refused to allow either Livilla, the widow of his son Drusus the Younger (in 25: Tac. *Ann.* 4.39–40), or Agrippina the Elder, Agrippina's mother and the widow of Germanicus (in 26: Tac. *Ann.* 4.53), to remarry.
51. *Galba* 5.1. For Galba's wife Aemilia Lepida, see PIR[2] A 422; FOS #31 (inexplicably dating her death to 40).
52. Ser. Sulpicius Galba: PIR[2] S 1003.
53. Perhaps Agrippina had heard of the ailing Tiberius' remark to Galba that someday this younger man would rule (Tac. *Ann.* 6.20.2). Barrett 1996, 83–84, discusses chronological problems of Suetonius' story and doubts its veracity.
54. Crispus Passienus, *cos.* II in 44: PIR[2] P 146; Eck 1993, 24; Plin. *HN* 7.91; further references below. A member of three of the most prestigious priestly colleges (the *VIIviri epulonum, sodales Augustales,* and *sodales Titii*), Passienus was honored with a statue in the Basilica Julia. His estate was worth two hundred million sesterces. For date of marriage, see Barrett 1996, xviii; Eck 1993, 23–24.
55. Domitia: FOS #319, PIR[2] D 171; Barrett 1996, 45–46. Like her brother Ahenobarbus and sister Domitia Lepida, she was the child of L. Domitius Ahenobarbus, *cos.* 16 BCE, and of Antonia the Elder, daughter of Augustus' sister Octavia. FOS #319 holds that she was divorced so Crispus Passienus could marry Agrippina; Heil 2013, 186, thinks the divorce was earlier; Eck 1993, 24, leaves the question undecided. For Domitia's later history, see Ch. 5.
56. Passienus was the adoptive son of C. Sallustius Crispus (PIR[2] S 87; Tac. *Ann.* 3.30.2), himself the adoptive son of the historian Sallust: Heil 2013, 186.
57. A lead pipe, *CIL* XV 7508, attests his property in Rome. For Corne, see Plin. *HN* 16.242.
58. Plin. *HN* 7.43, 59, noting her nightingale and thrush, in both cases identifying her as Claudius' wife.
59. Suet. *Pass.* "Conscript fathers" was a traditionally honorific address to the senate.
60. Suet. *Pass.*
61. Tac. *Ann.* 6.20.1; Barrett 1996, 84–85.
62. Cass. Dio 60.8.4–5; 60.18.4; Osgood 2011, 42–43; Levick 2015, 63–64. For Seneca, see PIR[2] A 617. For his involvement and punishment (Sen. *Cons. Polyb.* 13.3; Tac. *Ann.* 13.42.3; Schol. *ad* Juv. *Sat.* 5.109), see Furneaux 2, Introduction p.50, n.9; Wilson 2014, 78–82 (suggesting Seneca was not sent to Corsica until 42).
63. Julia Livilla was born in 18 CE (FOS #443); Messalina was born perhaps before 20 CE and at the latest in 24 (Syme 1958, 437; FOS #774). Panoussi 2018, 212: Messalina's implied superiority in age reflects her higher rank and power.
64. Agrippina supposedly seduced Claudius in 48 by visiting him frequently as "family" (Tac. *Ann.* 12.3.1).
65. Wilson 2014, 79, holds that in 41 Seneca was close with Passienus, "the then-husband of Agrippina."
66. See Ch. 4, n.184. The lacunose text of the relevant inscription, *CIL* VI 891, has been restored as *Lìvilla, [M(arci) Vinici(:uxor)], Germanicì C[aesaris f(ilia)], hìç sita e[st].*
67. Suet. *Nero* 6.4, casting some doubt on the tale by calling it a *fabula* (Bradley 1978, 51–52 ad loc.). Tac. *Ann.* 11.11 and Cass. Dio 61.2.4 also mention snake skins in association with Nero and Agrippina, but without Messalina.
68. Livy 26.19.8.
69. Suet. *Aug.* 94.4; cf. Nocchi 2016.
70. Suet. *Nero* 6.4.
71. See Parat 2016, 201, for date.
72. Tacitus' *Annals* is missing for this period. Parat 2016 reviews all the evidence; see also Osgood 2011, 43–46.
73. Cass. Dio 60.14–15.
74. Cass. Dio 60.14.3–15.1; Suet. *Claud.* 37.2; cf. Sen. *Apocol.* 11.5. For C. Appius Junius Silanus, see PIR[2] I 822.
75. Other key texts include Suet. *Claud.* 29; Juv. 6.115–35; Cass. Dio 60.2.4–7, 60.8.4–6, 60.18.1–4. 60.27.4. For Tacitus' presentation of Messalina in 47 and 48, see Joshel 1995; Fagan 2002; Cenerini 2010; and discussion at the end of this chapter.

76. Cass. Dio 60.15.2; Wiseman 1982, 63.
77. Cassius Dio (e.g., 60.15.4–16), our main literary source, hyperbolically says all ranks and sexes were tortured and executed.
78. For Vinicianus and Pomponius, see Ch. 3, n.6; A. Caecina Paetus, PIR^2 C 103; Arria the Elder, PIR^2 A 1113; FOS #96; Plin. *Ep.* 3.16; Tac. *Ann.* 16.34.2.
79. See PIR^2 A 1130 for this great-grandson of Pompey (*CIL* III 7043). Descended from the fourth-century (BCE) hero Camillus, Scribonianus' natural father received triumphal ornaments for defeating Tacfarinas (Tac. *Ann.* 2.52). His adoptive father, L. Arruntius (PIR^2 A 1130), was famously identified by Augustus as *capax imperii* (Tac. *Ann.* 1.13, cf. 6.48).
80. For Scribonianus' co-consulship with Domitius Ahenobarbus, see, e.g., *CIL* X 899 (Pompeii).
81. Suet. *Claud.* 13.2; Tac. *Hist.* 1.89. The sources hold that he either committed suicide or was killed by a soldier named Volaginius, dying in the arms of his wife Vibia, who was later exiled by Claudius (Tac. *Hist.* 2.75, cf. Cass. Dio 60.15.3; Plin. *Ep.* 3.16.9; Tac. *Ann.* 12.52). Parat 2016 holds that Scribonianus did not want the rule himself.
82. The legions were renamed Claudia Pia Fidelis.
83. Ehrhardt 1978, 63–64, notes this is often seen as a turning point in Claudius' reign. For the "bloody purge," see Cass. Dio 60.15.5–16; Suet. *Otho* 1.2; Plin. *Ep.* 3.16; Tac. *Ann.* 13.43; Sen. *Apocol.* 13.5, cf. 11.5, 14.1.
84. Had Nero visited Asia with his mother and her new husband, surely some remembrance would have surfaced in his later recorded speeches, such as that for Ilium in 53: Tac. *Ann.* 12.58.1 (cf. *Ann.* 11.11.6).
85. *IG* XII 4.2, 890, side A. See Barrett 1996, 222; Eck 1993, 24; Heil 2013, 184–85.
86. Hahn 1994, 196.
87. Belli Pasqua 2018, 341, notes three other Roman women honored there: in 46–44 BCE, 27/26 BCE, and 94/93 BCE. The text of 42/43 does not identify Agrippina in relation to the ruling emperor Claudius, Germanicus' brother. Germanicus is not known to have stopped in Kos: Halfmann 1986, 168–69.
88. For the tight connection of Agrippina's maternal family with Kos (particularly Agrippa, Julia the Elder, Drusilla, and Caligula), see Heil 2013, 185; Belli Pasqua 2018, 343.
89. Belli Pasqua 2018, 343, citing *IG* XII 4.2, 1157; on pp. 349–51 she identifies a colossal head of Agrippina found on the island as from its theater. In Ch. 6 I discuss Agrippina the Younger's portraiture.
90. The inscription is repeated twice: *IG* XII 4.2, n.643. For Demeter Carpophora, see Hahn 1994, 190–94. Belli Pasqua 2018, 343–44, also references two fragmentary inscriptions, a dedication from Kos's Isthmus deme to Agrippina Dea Demeter Carpophoros and an honorary inscription to her as Sebastè Rhea. Agrippina received the honorific Augusta in 50 (Ch. 4).
91. The display is corroborated by the holes for brackets, noted by *IG*.
92. *IG* XII 4.2, 890, side B, 50–54 CE.
93. This is her identification in the Monumentum Claudianum (Ch. 4).
94. Halfmann 1986, 172–73.
95. In 53 Xenophon cured Claudius of a serious illness, for which the emperor restored to Kos freedom from tribute. In 54 Agrippina reportedly involved him in the poisoning of Claudius (Tac. *Ann.* 12.61, 67; see Ch. 4). If a fragmentary text really attests Xenophon's later dedication of a statue to Nero at Kos's Asklepieion (*IG* XII 4.2, 644), the poisoning story may be true: Belli Pasqua 2018, 347.
96. For Claudius' war in Britain, see Osgood 2011, 84–106; Levick 2015, 162–77.
97. Cass. Dio 60.21.5: they also personally brought back to the senate the news of Claudius' victory. Levick 2015, 142: Claudius and his entourage probably sailed to Britain from Gesoriacum (now Boulogne-sur-Mer, France) at the end of July or in early August but spent very little time in Britain (only 16 days, according to Cass. Dio 60.23).
98. Suet. *Claud.* 17.2.
99. For the *carpentum*, see Ch. 2, n.24; Boatwright 2021, 135–37, 178–79.
100. Webb and Brännstedt 2023, 62, hold that even in the Republic Roman women were not kept apart from triumphal processions and were part of "Roman imperialism," but they provide few examples. Contra, Flory, 1998; Boatwright 2021, 178–79.
101. Cass. Dio 60.22.2–3; Suet. *Claud.* 17.2. See also Flory 1998, 492; Brännstedt 2015, 40.
102. Britannicus: Suet. *Claud.* 27.1.
103. Suet. *Claud.* 17.2–3; Cass. Dio 60.22–23.

104. Cass. Dio 60.22; *CIL* VI 40416 = EDCS-00900120, the inscription of the Arch, with Osgood 2011, 101. Memory sanctions against Messalina after her death (Tac. *Ann.* 11.38) bedevil the documentary and material evidence for her: see, e.g., Wood 1992; Flower 2006, 182–89.
105. *Life of Passienus*; Plin. *HN* 16.242; Cass. Dio 60.23.1; *ILS* 7061 (before 25 Jan. 44).
106. Syme 1933, 142–43; Gallivan 1978, 408.
107. The *Fasti Antiates*: Gallivan 1978, 408 (cf. 412 and 424): under Claudius eponymous consuls (other than the emperor) usually served for six months, sometimes four, and occasionally only two. This Statilius Taurus, whose enormous gardens reportedly triggered his death in Claudius' reign (see Ch. 4, n.139), was the father of Nero's (third) wife Statilia Messalina.
108. Barrett 1996, 85–86 (following Syme 1958, 328, n.12), suggests he died before 47, for Tacitus' *Annals* resumes then and we would expect an obituary notice. Agrippina's (second) widowhood is cited in L. Vitellius' advocacy for her before the senate in 48, Tac. *Ann.* 12.6.2.
109. Martial 10.2.10.
110. Such as Julia Livilla in 41: Cass. Dio 60.8.4–5; see below for the deaths in 43 of Julia (the daughter of Drusus the Younger and Livilla) and others.
111. For the inheritance, two hundred times more than the property qualification for senatorial rank, see also Suet. *Nero* 6.1.
112. For this woman, generally reviled in ancient and modern writing, see, e.g., Strong 2016, 97–98, 107–109; Fagan 2002 (focusing on the stories of her bigamous wedding and death); Levick 2015, 61–75 (Messalina was politically manipulative). Juvenal termed her a *meretrix Augusta* (6.118; "'harlot' empress"), a memorable term echoing what Propertius had called Cleopatra, *meretrix regina* (3.11.39; "'harlot' queen"). For her perceived authority, see also Tac. *Ann.* 13.43.3–4.
113. See, e.g., Suet. *Claud.* 29; Cass. Dio 60.28.2; Philostr. *VA* 5.32; Hurley 2001, 10.
114. Furneaux 2.1 *ad Ann.* 11.1.2 presumes Britannicus' freedman tutor Sosibius was also influential in the court (see Suet. *Tit.* 2). For Narcissus, *ab epistulis*, see PIR[2] N 23; C. Julius Polybius, perhaps *a studiis* but whose exact mandate is uncertain, PIR[2] I 475; M. Antonius Pallas, originally enslaved by Antonia the Younger, then Claudius' *a rationibus* and later reportedly Agrippina's lover, PIR[2] A 858; C. Julius Callistus, *a libellis*, PIR[2] I 229. Messalina also worked with various informers (*delatores*) such as P. Suillius: Tac. *Ann.* 13.43.
115. E.g., Cass. Dio 60.14.1.
116. Levick 2015, 63 ("Messalina should not be seen as an adolescent nymphomaniac; in the main she used sex as a means of compromising and controlling politicians"); Ehrhardt 1978. "Folly" is the word Fagan (2002) aptly uses to categorize the disparate and senseless acts attributed to Messalina as he disputes any political plot on her side. Despite arguing for Messalina's political aims rather than moral failures, many modern scholars persist in damning her (e.g., Syme 1958, 184; Syme 1986, 182).
117. Tac. *Ann.* 13.32; Cass. Dio 60.18.4; Suet. *Claud.* 19; FOS #422, PIR[2] I 636. Julia, born probably in 3 CE, was married to Agrippina's brother Nero Caesar before his condemnation; in 33 she married C. Rubellius Blandus and bore to him Rubellius Plautus, Rubellius Blandus, Rubellius Drusus, and Rubellia Bassa (Ch. 5, n.100).
118. Cass. Dio 60.27.4, cf. 60.8.5.
119. Tac. *Ann.* 11.1.2; Wiseman 2013, 71. Asiaticus, too, had been consul twice.
120. Tac. *Ann.* 11.1.1–2; Cass. Dio 60.27.1–3, 61.29.4-6[a]. This Poppaea Sabina (FOS #645) is the mother of Poppaea Sabina, the second wife of Nero (Ch. 5).
121. Suet. *Claud.* 13.2; Cass. Dio 60.27.5. For Asinius, see PIR[2] A 1228; for Statilius Corvinus, PIR[1] S 595.
122. Cass. Dio 60.29.6[a].
123. Cass. Dio 61.31.2.
124. Sen. *Apocol.* 14.
125. Suet. *Claud.* 25.5, 29.1; Cass. Dio 60.2.4. Tac. *Ann.* 11.28.2 reports the imperial freedmen's accusation that she was solely responsible.
126. Cass. Dio 60.16.1.
127. Cass. Dio 60.18.1–2.
128. Drusilla and Caligula, but not Julia Livilla or Agrippina, are mentioned. Plin. *HN* 7.45–46.147–51 presents a similarly dour list of Augustus' misfortunes.
129. Cassius Dio holds that Seneca later suppressed the work "out of shame" (61.10.2). Gloyn 2014, however, interprets the whole as an erudite manipulation of Stoic language to appeal to Polybius and Claudius.

130. Cass. Dio 61.35.
131. Suet. *Claud.* 26; Tac. *Ann.* 12.3: see Ch. 4.
132. Barrett 1996, 88, positing in Asia; at Crispus Passienus' Tusculan estate; or in Padua, the home of Asconius Labeo, Nero's tutor (Furneaux 2.165 *ad Ann.* 13.10.1; Barrett et al. 2016, 32, n.20).
133. Tac. *Ann.* 11.11; Suet. *Claud.* 21.2, noting mockery of his calculations for the games. The Claudian *ludi* are poorly known.
134. Malloch 2013, 176, 181–85, suggests they were held in June. The Augustan *ludi saeculares* had been held in late May and early June, and the Severan ones at the beginning of June.
135. Tac. *Ann.* 11.11.5–6. Furneaux 2.16 ad loc. remarks that this is the first time either boy is mentioned in the extant *Annals* and that the description of Nero (*L. Domitius adoptione mox in imperium et cognomentum Neronis adscitus*) suggests he had not been featured previously. Malloch 2013, 175, agrees.
136. The good omens included snakes in his boyhood bedroom (typically a sign of future success). See Ch. 3, n.67, for other reports about snakes and Nero.
137. Tac. *Ann.* 11.12.1: *Verum inclinatio populi supererat ex memoria Germanici, cuius illa reliqua suboles virilis; et matri Agrippinae miseratio augebatur ob saevitiam Messalinae, quae semper infesta et tunc commotior quo minus strueret crimina et accusatores novo et furori proximo amore distinebatur.*
138. See, e.g., Barrett 1996, 91–94, and Cenerini 2010.
139. Fagan 2002, 573, n.32, supplies other references for political interpretations of Messalina's marriage to Silius, all of which he refutes.
140. See Tac. *Ann.* 12.7.3, discussed in Ch. 4.
141. Tac. *Ann.* 11.12, 26–38 for the marriage.
142. In addition to other references mentioned here, see the treatment of Tacitus' account as a "narrative of court crises" by Hug and Kelly 2022, 228–33. Some have argued that she had repudiated him "by implication": Levick 2015, 72. This would have been unique: no woman is known to have instigated divorce from an imperial husband (Boatwright 2021, 61–64).
143. As we see in the next two chapters, Tacitus is otherwise keen to chronicle Agrippina's doings (especially transgressive ones) and influence.
144. The grape harvest scene sets this in autumn. Furneaux 2.45 *ad Ann.* 11.31.4 suggests October.
145. Tac. *Ann.* 11.27, 31.2–3; Tac. *Ann.* 11.26.3, 29.3–31.1, respectively. Antonia the Younger reportedly played a key role in denouncing Sejanus (Syme 1958, 752); the freedwomen Calpurnia and Cleopatra consulted with Claudius (Tac. *Ann.* 11.30.1). Cassius Dio has Claudius in Ostia for the purpose of inspecting the grain supply: 61.31.4.
146. *Ann.* 11.34.2–3. For Vibidia, see FOS #805.
147. Tac. *Ann.* 11.37–38. Nor is anything said about Agrippina when Tacitus notes Domitia Lepida, former sister-in-law of Agrippina and guardian of Nero, present at her daughter's death. Cassius Dio (61.31.2–5) emphasizes the roles of the freedmen, particularly Narcissus. No imperial woman had yet perished so ignominiously, without even the semblance of a trial or the emperor's input: Boatwright 2021, 65–78.
148. Tac. *Ann.* 11.35–36: four senators (C. Silius, Iuncus Vergilianus, Suillius Caesoninus, Plautius Lateranus) and seven equestrians (Titius Proculus, Vettius Valens, Pompeius Urbicus, Saufeius Trogus, Decrius Calpurnianus, Sulpicius Rufus, Traulus Montanus).
149. Suet. *Claud.* 39.1; Cass. Dio 60.31.5.
150. Tacitus often anticipates a major character by a seemingly incidental aside, as with Nero at the Secular Games.
151. For Maevania (now Bevagna, in Italian Umbria), see Ch. 2, n.118.
152. Tac. *Ann.* 12.1–3. See Syme 1958, 259; Malloch 2013, 467.
153. This last strikes an ironic note given Claudius' reported pledge to the praetorians after Messalina's death that they could kill him should he marry again (Suet. *Claud.* 26.2).
154. See above Ch. 2, n.59 (Lollia Paulina) and Ch. 1, n. 179 (Aelia Paetina).
155. Tac. *Ann.* 12.3.1: *potentia uxoria.*

Chapter 4

1. Antonia, his daughter by Aelia Paetina, had been married since 41 to Pompeius but seems to have remained close to Claudius.
2. See Barrett 1996; Levick 2015; Eck 1993.

3. *quasi virile servitium* (Tac. *Ann.* 12.7.3), discussed below.
4. Some of the most striking come from narrators whom senators like Tacitus considered disreputable, such as the imperial freedmen (e.g., at Ch. 4, n.160). Agrippina's swelling importance dominates much of Tacitus' *Annals* 12 (Malloch 2009, 117–20, 123), a book that opens and closes with her, from her candidacy as Claudius' fourth wife (*Ann.* 12.1–9), to her connections to Claudius' death and Nero's accession (*Ann.* 12.64–69).
5. Boatwright 2021, most recently; as in Tac. *Ann.* 12.2 (see following note), Nero is considered worthy of imperial power, not she.
6. Tac. *Ann.* 12.2: *quod Germanici nepotem secum traheret, dignum prorsus imperatoria fortuna.*
7. She later commemorated a number of her siblings near the Via Flaminia in Rome: see Ch. 4.
8. Such as Galba's mother-in-law in 41: see Ch. 3.
9. Tac. *Ann.* 11.38.3: the senate voted that her name and images be removed from public and private places.
10. Messalina's *damnatio memoriae*: Tac. *Ann.* 11.38.3. Agrippina would later relearn this lesson painfully: Tac. *Ann.* 13.19.1, set in 55.
11. Sen. *Apocol.* 5.1–2, while emphasizing Claudius' infirmities (see also Suet. *Claud.* 4.6, 30; Cass. Dio 60.2.1–2).
12. As, for example, his mother Antonia the Younger, Antony's youngest daughter with Octavia. For Claudius' literary interests, see Suet. *Claud.* 41–42, cf. Suet. *Claud.* 33.2; Cass. Dio 60.2.1; Sen. *Apocol.* 5.4. We do not know Agrippina's reaction to his addition of three letters to the Latin alphabet during his censorship of 47/48.
13. Tac. *Ann.* 12.6.3, with Furneaux 2.69 ad loc.: "That Claudius had led a moral life would be notoriously untrue."
14. Suet. *Claud.* 26. Plautia Urgulanilla: FOS #619 (related to Urgulania, the powerful friend of Julia Augusta; Intro., n.19); Aelia Paetina: FOS #18.
15. E.g., Barrett 1996, 78.
16. Tac. *Ann.* 11.30, 33–34, 37.
17. One might compare Livia's enviable security at Augustus' side.
18. Suet. *Claud.* 13.
19. For Claudius' speech advocating expansion of the senate to include some of the elite of "further Gaul," preserved both in Tacitus and on bronze tablets from Lugdunum (Lyon, France), see Tac. *Ann.* 11.23–25.1; *CIL* XIII 1668; Malloch 2020. The censorship, a venerable Republican practice, had not been held for nearly seven decades: Suet. *Claud.* 16.1; F. X. Ryan 1993, 617; Levick 2015, 114–17; O'Neill 2020, 216.
20. Sen. *Brev. Vit.* 13.8; Boatwright 1984.
21. No imperial woman had yet perished so ignominiously, without even the semblance of a trial or the emperor's input: Boatwright 2021, 65–78.
22. A Roman man, much less this emperor who had served as censor, should ensure his wife and *familia* behave properly at all times (e.g., Osgood 2011, 212–13). Augustus had exemplarily denounced and punished his daughter, granddaughter, and Agrippa Postumus.
23. For her personal resolve, see, e.g., Tac. *Ann.* 12.7.3.
24. See, e.g., nn.185 and 186, this chapter.
25. Despite the reused dedication from Kos discussed in Ch. 3, many other inscriptions continued to label her as the daughter of Germanicus even after her marriage to Claudius. One can also see this emphasis on her natal family in the funerary compound along the Via Flaminia (Ch. 4, n.184).
26. E.g., Tac. *Ann.* 11.25; Cass. Dio 60.23; Gallivan 1978; Dudley 1959.
27. He removed many from the list of equestrian jurors (Suet. *Claud.* 16.2) and from the senate, although he invited senators "notorious for their bad conduct" to resign voluntarily (Tac. *Ann.* 11.25). Tacitus, however, contrasts the "modern" leniency of Claudius with the old-fashioned severity of former censors (see F. X. Ryan 1993, 616–17). After Claudius' death the *Apocolocyntosis* reveals the resentment and fear Seneca and others felt for him (Ch. 5).
28. Both Suet. *Claud.* 26.3 and Cass. Dio 61.31.8 report the senatorial speech stressing that the marriage was good also for the state.
29. See, e.g., Horster 2011. Osgood 2011, 215, also suggests Britannicus was tarnished by Messalina's downfall.
30. Corbier 1995 discusses the tendency of Julio-Claudian women to marry within their extended imperial family to avoid bearing children to potentially rival families; see also Dixon 1985.

31. M. Claudius Marcellus was the son of Augustus' sister Octavia and her first husband Marcellus.
32. Tac. *Ann.* 12.2.3, cf. Tac. *Ann.* 5.1. For *Iuliae* supplied to Tac. *Ann.* 12.2.3, see Furneaux 2.64–65 *ad Ann.* 12.2.3; Koestermann 3.111 *ad Ann.* 12.2.3.
33. Suet. *Claud.* 26.3; Cass. Dio 61.31.6 notes familiarity with him greater than became a niece. Agrippina was now 33 or 34; Claudius was 59. Tacitus twice stresses her seduction, *amor inlicitus* (*Ann.* 12.3.1 and 12.5.1). Her advantages are also stated twice in Tacitus (first by her supporter Pallas, 12.2.3 and then parroted by Vitellius to the senate, 12.6.1). In Ch. 5 Agrippina again appears in an overly familiar embrace, as Nero clings to her eyes and breasts while bidding her goodbye on the beach at Baiae: Tac. *Ann.* 14.4.8.
34. Boatwright 2021, 58–78 discusses the treasonable aspects of imperial women's charges of adultery.
35. Cass. Dio 60.31.8; Tac. *Ann.* 12.5–7 (emphasizing Claudius' fastidiousness regarding the law).
36. Moreau 2002, 198–204, noting that the restricted exception to this general rule enacted by the senatorial decree in 49—that uncles could marry the daughters of their brothers—lasted until 342. Cf. Gai. *Inst.* 1.62.3.
37. *praecipuus propugnator*, Tac. *Ann.* 12.42.3. Presumably, Vitellius acted as censor: cf. Tac. *Ann.* 12.4.1. Special marriage arrangements for Augustus' family were not unprecedented: a senatorial decree allowed Octavia to marry Antony in October 40, earlier than the 10 months required after the death of her first husband, C. Claudius Marcellus (Plut. *Ant.* 31.3); Octavian (later Augustus) consulted the pontifices, Rome's highest religious college, for sanction to marry Livia (on 17 January 38 BCE), newly divorced from her first husband and some six months pregnant (with Drusus the Elder). But the earlier exceptions were individual; now the legal system itself was changed.
38. Cass. Dio 61.31.8 does not mention popular support. How did the people learn of the proposition?
39. Among the accusations later leveled against her was her intrusion into the senate (Cass. Dio 62.14.3; Tac. *Ann.* 14.10.3–11.3; see Ch. 5). Women were barred from the senate unless on trial (Marshall 1990), and one praise of Julia Augusta (= Livia) is that she never entered the senate chamber, camps, or public assemblies (Cass. Dio 57.12.3).
40. Suet. *Claud.* 26.3; for Tacitus, see below; *Oct.* 141–42; Eck 1993, 38. The later involvement of Domitian with his niece Julia Titi was similarly unpopular: Juv. 2.29–33; Plin. *Pan.* 52.3, 63.7; Plin. *Ep.* 4.11.6; Suet. *Dom.* 22.2; Cass. Dio 67.3; Boatwright 2021, 63–64; Moreau 2002, 202.
41. *Quem plerique Agrippinae gratia impulsum ferebant* (*Ann.* 12.7.4; Furneaux 2.70 ad loc.). Severus is otherwise unknown.
42. *versa ex eo civitas et cuncta feminae oboediebant, non per lasciviam, ut Messalina, rebus Romanis inludenti. adductum et quasi virile servitium: palam severitas ac saepius superbia; nihil domi impudicum, nisi dominationi expediret. cupido auri immensa obtentum habebat, quasi subsidium regno pararetur.* Woodman 2004, 217–18, translates: "It was as a result of this that the community was overturned, and there was universal obedience to a female who did not, like Messalina, sport with Roman affairs through recklessness: it was a tightly controlled and (so to speak) manlike servitude. Openly there was severity, and more often haughtiness; there was no domestic immorality unless it availed domination. An inordinate desire for gold had as its screen that a bulwark was being prepared for the kingdom." Tacitus later returns to Agrippina's greed for money for political support (*subsidium*): *Ann.* 13.18.2.
43. For Tacitus' use of *potentia*, *dominatio*, and other such terms with women, see Santoro L'Hoir 1994. Here, Tacitus echoes earlier scorn for the imperial house and Tiberius, "raised from infancy in a despotic house" (*hunc et prima infantia eductum in domo regnatrice*; Tac. *Ann.* 1.4.4).
44. Her hubris and abject downfall had just been recounted at length in Tacitus' previous book (*Ann.* 11). The reconstituted text of Cassius Dio less damningly notes that Agrippina became a "second Messalina, the more so as she obtained from the senate the right to use the *carpentum* at festivals, as well as other honors" (60.33.2[1]).
45. Cass. Dio 61.33.1. Rome's public records also recorded that Livia earlier had the right to greet whomever she wanted in her home: Cass. Dio 57.12.1–2.
46. Cass. Dio 60.32.2.
47. Cass. Dio 61.32.1–2.
48. Suet. *Vit.* 2.4; Tac. *Ann.* 14.56.1; PIR[2] V 741. See Suet. *Claud.* 16.1 with Hurley 2001, 128 ad loc.; F. X. Ryan 1993; and Osgood 2011, 158–59, for Claudius' revival of the censorship, in which he served as censor alongside Vitellius apparently for the regular 18 months. No one had actually

served as censor for nearly 70 years. Vitellius received a *funus censorium* and memorial statue after dying late in Claudius' reign (Suet. *Vit.* 3.1); his son A. Vitellius would be a short-lived emperor in 69.

49. Agrippina's backing enabled him to survive a challenge in the senate in 51 (Tac. *Ann.* 12.42; see below). Vitellius seems to have been close to both imperial women: he had helped bring down Asiaticus for Messalina.
50. *praecipuus propugnator*: Tac. 12.42.3.
51. Tac. *Ann.* 12.7.3 (set in 49). See also Cass. Dio 60.32.2 and 62.6.4 (in an excerpt placed in 54). The charge of imperial women's misuse of their influence to raise money, by "selling offices" or the like, is common (Boatwright 2021, 25–27).
52. Plin. *HN* 35.201.4: *praetoria quoque ornamenta decerni a senatu iubente Agrippina Claudius Caesaris.* Oost 1958, 132, downplays Agrippina's influence for this award.
53. Joseph. *AJ* 20.6.3. Poppaea similarly interceded with Nero around 62 and 64 regarding Jewish affairs: Joseph. *AJ* 20.189–96, *Vit.* 16; cf. Boatwright 2021, 163.
54. Boatwright 2021, 17–18, 163–64.
55. See especially the story that at Nero's birth Agrippina cried out, "Let him kill me, only let him rule!" when the Chaldaeans said that the child would rule and would murder his mother (Cass. Dio 61.2.1–3; Tac. *Ann.* 14.1; cf. Suet. *Nero* 28.2). It is modern readers who see her desiring power of her own and for herself.
56. Tac. *Ann.* 12.3.1–2 uses *scelus* and qualifies Agrippina as *nondum uxor potentia uxoria*; cf. *Ann.* 12.4, 12.8. In 55 Tacitus' Agrippina admits her hand in the deaths of L. Junius Silanus and his brother (see Ch. 5): Tac. *Ann.* 13.14.3. Syme 1986, 174, 185–96, highlights the role of L. Vitellius (the former father-in-law of Junia Calvina), as Silanus' accuser and also the senatorial proposer of the changed law on incest.
57. It is reminiscent of Messalina prompting another Junius Silanus' death by exaggerating an ominous dream (Cass. Dio 60.14.3–15.1; Suet. *Claud.* 37.2; cf. Sen. *Apocol.* 11.5; Ch. 3 above). For "crime," see previous note.
58. Tac. *Ann.* 12.4.2; cf. Sen. *Apocol.* 8.2, 10.4, 11.5. Moreau 2002, 46–47, also stresses Tac. *Ann.* 12.8: Silanus' suicide on the day Claudius and Agrippina wed, Calvina's exile from Italy, and Claudius' command that sacrifices for atoning incest be undertaken at the grove of Diana (at Nemi), which raised universal mockery. For a vow made for the health and safety of the new imperial family at Nemi in 50 or so, see Ch. 4, n.91.
59. Tac. *Ann.* 12.4, 8. In 59 Nero recalled the exile Junia Calvina (and another woman) as a way to discredit Agrippina further. Junia Calvina lived until the end of Vespasian's rule (Tac. *Ann.* 14.12; Suet. *Vesp.* 23.4). See FOS #469 for Junia Calvina, the great-great-granddaughter of Augustus and once married to Lucius Vitellius (the son of Claudius' ally Lucius Vitellius).
60. Suet. *Nero* 7.1, to adumbrate Nero's future by recounting that the night after his appointment Seneca dreamed that his pupil was Caligula in a portent soon proved true by Nero's rapid descent into depravity.
61. "Agrippina was training her son for the throne and was entrusting his education to Seneca" (Cass. Dio 60.32.3).
62. Tac. *Ann.* 12.8: *at Agrippina ne malis tantum facinoribus notesceret veniam exilii pro Annaeo Seneca, simul praeturam impetrat, laetum in publicum rata ob claritudinem studiorum eius, utque Domitii pueritia tali magistro adolesceret et consiliis eiusdem ad spem dominationis uterentur, quia Seneca fidus in Agrippinam memoria beneficii et infensus Claudio dolore iniuriae credebatur.* The plural *uterentur* implicates others, but no one is named.
63. Griffin 1976.
64. Suet. *Nero* 52: she forbad Nero to study philosophy, a subject she deemed unfit for one who would rule.
65. *Ann.* 12.9: *Placitum dehinc non ultra cunctari, sed designatum consulem Mammium Pollionem ingentibus promissis inducunt sententiam expromere, qua oraretur Claudius despondere Octaviam Domitio, quod aetati utriusque non absurdum et maiora patefacturum erat. Pollio haud disparibus verbis ac nuper Vitellius censet; despondeturque Octavia, ac super priorem necessitudinem sponsus iam et gener Domitius aequari Britannico studiis matris, arte eorum quis ob accusatam Messalinam ultio ex filio timebatur.* For Mammius, see PIR^2 M 126.
66. See Cassius Dio's note about Agrippina appropriating Claudius' freedmen: 61.32.1–2.
67. Date furnished by the Acts of the Arval Brethren (*CIL* VI 32356 = *CFA* 34) and by Tac. *Ann.* 12.25.1. Besides Tacitus (below), see Joseph. *BJ* 2.12.8 and Cass. Dio 60.32.1 (who nods also to Claudius' freedmen and the senate, populace of Rome, and military).
68. Tac. *Ann.* 12.25–26.2.

69. Tac. *Ann.* 12.25.1: Claudius upheld the adoption to place "a protective cordon of maturity around the boyhood of Britannicus" (*Britannici pueritiam robore circumdaret*: tr. Woodman 2004, 224, noting the odd Latin; cf. Syme 1958, 295–96). Tac. *Ann.* 12.25.2: *adnotabant periti nullam antehac adoptionem inter patricios Claudios reperiri* ("experts noted that no previous adoptions could be discovered among the patrician Claudii"). In contrast, Suet. *Claud.* 39 makes Claudius' remark an ill-judged utterance he himself devised, something Hurley 2001, 223–24 ad loc., accepts despite noting other mistakes in Suetonius' passage, such as labelling Britannicus *adultus*.
70. Tac. *Ann.* 12.26.1: *rogataque lex qua in familiam Claudiam et nomen Neronis transiret. augetur et Agrippina cognomento Augustae*. Cass. Dio 61.33.2[a] records that Claudius gave her the title.
71. Tac. *Ann.* 12.26.2: *quibus patratis nemo adeo expers misericordiae fuit quem non Britannici fortuna maerore adficeret. desolatus paulatim etiam servilibus ministeriis perintempestiva novercae officia in ludibrium vertebat, intellegens falsi. neque enim segnem ei fuisse indolem ferunt, sive verum, seu periculis commendatus retinuit famam sine experimento*. The Second Medicean's description of Agrippina's *officia* (duties, dutifulness, ministrations) as *perintempestiva* is very unusual: for *Ann.*12.26, see both Furneaux 2.92 and Koestermann 3.152.
72. "Pallas, tied to Agrippina as the facilitator of her wedding and then secured by sex with her" (*qui obstrictus Agrippinae ut conciliator nuptiarum et mox stupro eius inligatus*, Tac. *Ann.* 12.25.1).
73. Cass. Dio 60.33.2[2]; see Moreau 2002, 261–62. Cassius Dio makes no mention of Agrippina here.
74. Tac. *Ann.* 12.58.1, placed at the opening of a year. The rest of the chapter details Nero's public speeches advocating relief for Ilium (Troy, the origin of the Julian *gens*), Bononia (now Bologna, Italy), Rhodes, and Apamea (Syria), to enhance his reputation for good pursuits and eloquence. Suet. *Nero* 7 presents the speeches before Claudius as consul, i.e., two years earlier. Woodman 2004, 240, n.79, suggests that Tacitus' Latin in the following chapter on Statilius Taurus' gardens (*At Claudius saevissima quaeque promere adigebatur eiusdem Agrippinae artibus*: *Ann.* 12.59.1; see below) seems "to imply that it was Agrippina who had pushed the young Nero into delivering the speeches mentioned in the previous chapter."
75. Cass. Dio 60.33.9.
76. Horster 2011 investigates the ceremony as signifying an emperor's successor.
77. Tac. *Ann.* 12.41.1. Tacitus emphasizes the senate's sycophancy (*adulationes*). In 37 Caligula had designated Gemellus as *Princeps Iuventutis* to display his ties to the imperial power: see Ch. 2.
78. Tac. *Ann.* 12.41.2: *et ludicro circensium, quod adquirendis vulgi studiis edebatur, Britannicus in praetexta, Nero triumphali veste travecti sunt: spectaret populus hunc decore imperatorio, illum puerili habitu, ac perinde fortunam utriusque praesumeret*. Tacitus characteristically attributes the inference generally to the *populus*.
79. Tac. *Ann.* 12.41, which ends with a reference to her as *noverca*, or stepmother. Rome's *novercae* are often conceived of as "evil stepmothers": Noy 1991.
80. *Aurei* and *denarii*: *RIC*[2] I, Claudius no. 75–77, 81–83; *dupondius*, *RIC*[2] I, Claudius no. 107. Some issues (76, 77, 107), with Nero PRINC(eps) IVVENT(utis) on the obverse, celebrate on the reverse his co-option as a supernumerary into all colleges of the priests and show the symbols of the four most important religious colleges of the Roman state.
81. *RIC*[2] I, Claudius no. 75: Silver *denarius*. Obv: AGRIPPINAE AVGVSTAE (To Agrippina Augusta). Rev: NERO CLAVD(ius) CAES(ar) DRVSVS GERM(anicus) PRINC(eps) IVVENT(utis) (Nero Claudius Caesar Drusus Germanicus, Leader of the Youth), in the nominative. The coin shown in Ill. 4.1 is probably an ancient forgery of a real issue: *RIC*[2] I, Claudius no. 75, p. 125.
82. *RIC*[2] I, Claudius no. 82–83, *aurei* and *denarii*: obv: TI CLAVD CAESAR AVG GERM P M TRIB POT P P; rev: NERO CLAVD(ius) CAES(ar) DRVSVS GERM(anicus) PRINC(eps) IVVENT(utis). Both Claudius and Nero are named in the nominative.
83. Tac. *Ann.* 12.9, quoted above in Ch. 4, n.65.
84. Tac. *Ann.* 12.26.2.
85. Tac. *Ann.* 12.41.2.
86. *simul qui centurionum tribunorumque sortem Britannici miserabantur, remoti fictis causis et alii per speciem honoris; etiam libertorum si quis incorrupta fide depellitur tali occasione* (at the same time those of the centurions and military tribunes who pitied the lot of Britannicus were removed, some on trumped-up grounds and some through the guise of promotions; if anyone even among the freedmen was still loyal, he was removed at this time, Tac. *Ann.* 12.41.3).

87. Tac. *Ann.* 12.41.4, with words stressing Agrippina's political cunning (my emphasis below): *sperni quippe adoptionem, quaeque censuerint* ***patres****, iusserit* ***populus****, intra penatis abrogari; ac nisi pravitas tam infensa docentium arceatur, eruptura* ***in publicam*** *perniciem.*
88. That is, by discrediting the adoption of the presumptive heir.
89. Rome's *novercae* are often conceived of as "evil stepmothers": Noy 1991.
90. Cass. Dio 61.32.5, naming Britannicus' tutor Sosibius as one who was removed. The editors place this fragment in 49, as they do the removal of the praetorian prefects Crispinus and Lusius Geta (60.32.6[a]), which Tacitus places in 51. Sosibius was also the tutor of Titus, Vespasian's son who was Rome's emperor from 79 to 81 (Suet. *Titus* 2).
91. *ILS* 220 (50–54 CE). The *ILS* editors suggest that since Britannicus still has first place, the (now-lost) inscription dates to 50 or so.
92. Suet. *Nero* 7.1 (*immanitas naturae*), on Seneca's dream (Ch. 4, n.60) and noting that Britannicus' slip, in which he called Nero "Ahenobarbus" (not "Domitius"), was due to habit.
93. Tac. *Ann.* 13.15.3.
94. Tacitus' reports of Agrippina, as in Tac. *Ann.* 12.22, are often juxtaposed to more traditional narratives, such as the eleven chapters discussing Rome's affairs in the East and ending with the deliverance to Claudius of Mithridates, King of Bosphorus (*Ann.* 12.10–21). Agrippina is not noted at the semi-public submission of Mithridates to Claudius at Rome's Rostra.
95. *Ann.* 12.22.1: *atrox odii Agrippina ac Lolliae infensa, quod secum de matrimonio principis certavisset, molitur crimina et accusatorem qui obiceret Chaldaeos.* Lollia Paulina was wed briefly to Caligula in 38 (above, esp. Ch. 2 at n.59). Aelia Paetina, who had been Claudius' second wife (Ch. 1, n.179), disappears from the historical record after her "bid" in 48.
96. Plin. *HN* 9.117–19.
97. Tac. *Ann.* 12.22.1–3; cf. Sen. *ad Helv.* 12.4. She was probably relegated, a less severe punishment that did not strip her of citizenship and all property.
98. Tac. *Ann.* 12.22.4.
99. Cass. Dio 60.32.4. The gruesome report echoes ones about Fulvia with the head of Cicero in 42 BCE (Cass. Dio 47.8.4) and Poppaea with that of Claudia Octavia in 62 (Tac. *Ann.* 14.23).
100. Tac. *Ann.* 12.22.3, *illustris femina pervertitur*; Cass. Dio 60.33.2[b]. Tacitus qualifies that Claudius' remark was "without real lust," *nulla libidine*, as explanation of why she was merely exiled. In 59 Nero returned Calpurnia (FOS #174) and other victims of Agrippina to Rome to increase ill-will toward his deceased mother (*Ann.* 14.12.5).
101. Tac. *Ann.* 12.22: *Agrippina ac Lolliae infensa, quod secum de matrimonio* ***principis*** *certavisset,... Calpurnia inlustris femina pervertitur, quia formam eius laudaverat* ***princeps.***
102. See, Kolb 2010, 23–35, with numerous references; Boatwright 2021, 32–36.
103. Tac. *Ann.* 12.26.1: *rogataque lex qua in familiam Claudiam et nomen Neronis transiret. augetur et Agrippina cognomento Augustae*; Cass. Dio 61.33.2[a]. Tacitus' presentation suggests the senate (not Claudius) conferred the title: Eck 1993, 40.
104. Suet. *Calig.* 15.2; Cass. Dio 59.3.4; Suet. *Claud.* 11.2; Kienast et al. 2017, 62; Ch. 2.
105. Cass. Dio 60.12.5, cf. Levick 2015, 34.
106. At times her name appears as Julia Augusta Agrippina: *CIL* XI 3600 (50–54 CE; from Caere/Cerveteri, Italy); *ILS* 220 (50–54, Nemi, Italy); *CIL* VI 31204 (51–54 CE, Rome; discussed below); *CIL* VI 40307 (55–56 CE, Rome; discussed in Ch. 5).
107. See Tac. *Ann.* 12.37.4, discussed below; Kuhoff 1993, 247.
108. *Ann.* 12.27.1: *Sed Agrippina quo vim suam sociis quoque nationibus ostentaret in oppidum Vbiorum, in quo genita erat, veteranos coloniamque deduci impetrat, cui nomen inditum e vocabulo ipsius. ac forte acciderat ut eam gentem Rhenum transgressam avus Agrippa in fidem acciperet.* This follows Tacitus' note of her new cognomen, Augusta.
109. See Galsterer 1990, 125–26.
110. See, e.g., Trier and Naumann-Steckner 2015.
111. Galsterer 1990, 125; Eck 2015, 38–39. The inclusion of an imperial woman's name in a city's name later becomes a mark of prestige, especially in the East as in Faustinopolis (now Halala, Turkey): Angelova 2015, 93.
112. *HN* 4.106.11: *in Ubis colonia Agrippinensis.*
113. See, e.g., *CIL* III 14214 (87–90 or 87–107 CE).
114. *Claudio imperatore* 2019, 228. Keppie 1984, 78, n.13, lists Aequum, Aprum, Camulodunum, Cologne (Colonia Agrippiensis), Lixus, Oppidum Novum, Ptolemais, and Savaria. Eck 2015, 39, holds that the "Agrippienses" reflects Agrippina's desire to equal Claudius, whose birthplace, Lugdunum, was newly honored as a colony with his name.

115. Especially true for Suetonius and Cassius Dio, but Tacitus' general chronological framework can be suspect.
116. Collected in the Loeb edition in 60.32–33.
117. Cass. Dio 60.33.7, 60.33.3, 60.33.10, respectively. The last is particularly suspicious.
118. Suet. *Tib.* 50.3; Cass. Dio 57.16.2 (16 CE). Barrett 2005, 306–307, notes the "quasi-military" nature of firefighting in Rome.
119. Cass. Dio 60.33.10, a report ending with Nero's magnificent staging of a horse race vowed for Claudius' recovery and his marriage to Octavia. In the reconstructed book of Cassius Dio these notices about Agrippina are introduced by the report of Agrippina's isolating Britannicus (including her slaying of Sosibius, Britannicus' tutor, on the pretext that he was plotting against Nero) and keeping him in a kind of imprisonment (60.32.5–6).
120. Cass. Dio 60.33.1.
121. Cass. Dio 60.33.12.
122. Cass. Dio 60.33.12.
123. Cass. Dio 61.32.6[a]; Tac. *Ann.* 12.42.1, discussed further below.
124. Details cannot be pinned down.
125. See Tac. *Ann.* 11.1.3, 11.4.3, P. Rufrius Crispinus (PIR[2] R 169), who at his accession as praetorian prefect in 47 was granted the rank of praetor and 1.5 million sesterces by the senate, received the rank of a consul at his dismissal in 51. He was married to Poppaea Sabina, who would become Nero's second wife, but he ultimately fell under Nero's suspicion and killed himself in 66: Tac. *Ann.* 13.45.4, 15.71.4, 16.17.
126. Tac. *Ann.* 11.31.1. Lusius Geta (PIR[2] L 435) would serve as prefect of Egypt in 54.
127. Cass. Dio 61.32.6[a]; Tac. *Ann.* 12.42.1. The second explanation is clear in the *Annals*' presentation: the opening of the report, *Nondum tamen summa moliri Agrippina audebat* (which Woodman 2004, 231, translates as "Nevertheless Agrippina did not yet dare her supreme feat of engineering"), picks up Tac. *Ann.* 12.3.2. The third explanation, to indebt Burrus to Agrippina (*transfertur regimen cohortium ad Burrum Afranium, egregiae militaris famae, gnarum tamen cuius sponte praeficeretur*), reappears later in Tacitus' text at *Ann.* 13.20.1.
128. Tac. *Ann.* 12.42.1: *distrahi cohortis ambitu duorum et, si ab uno regerentur, intentiorem fore disciplinam adseverante uxore.*
129. *CIL* XII 5842 = *ILS* 1321. For Burrus, see PIR[2] A 441. Later, C. Julius Spartiaticus served as procurator of "Caesar and Augusta Agrippina" (*Corinth* 8.2, 68 = *AE* 1927, 2): see Ch. 5.
130. See this chapter, nn.125, 126.
131. The last example was Octavia during the war between her brother Octavius (later Augustus) and her husband Mark Antony: Boatwright 2021, 258–59.
132. Tac. *Ann.* 12.42.3: *is crimina maiestatis et cupidinem imperii obiectabat; praebuissetque auris Caesar, nisi Agrippinae minis magis quam precibus mutatus esset, ut accusatori aqua atque igni interdiceret. hactenus Vitellius voluerat.*
133. Further, Tacitus casts doubt on the matter by using conditional verbs indicating "contrary to fact": ***praebuissetque*** ***auris Caesar, nisi Agrippinae minis magis quam precibus*** ***mutatus esset.*** In the end, Vitellius settles the affair, not Agrippina: Tac. *Ann.* 12.42.3.
134. Agrippina similarly uses threats and entreaties when dealing with Nero (Tac. *Ann.* 13.13–14). See also her characterization as *atrox odii*, "horrendous in her hatred" (Tac. *Ann.* 12.22.1).
135. *HN* 35.201.4: *praetoria quoque ornamenta decerni a senatu iubente Agrippina Claudius Caesaris*; see Plin. *Ep.* 7.29, 8.6; Tac. *Ann.* 12.53.2–3. Pallas was praised as a man "who subordinated to the public good his nobility as the offspring of Arcadia's kings" and exemplified old-fashioned frugality, despite possessing three hundred million sesterces. The senate's decree to him of 15 million sesterces more was rejected by Claudius. For Pallas, see Oost 1958, 114, 121, n.20 (doubting the sexual liaison, asserted also in Schol. *ad Iuven.* 1.109), and Ch. 3, n.114.
136. This would be is especially apt for her alleged greed for wealth to build and maintain power (Tac. *Ann.* 12.7.3, discussed above)
137. Joseph. *AJ* 20.6.3. Poppaea similarly interceded with Nero around 62 and 64 regarding Jewish affairs: Joseph. *AJ* 20.189–96, *Vit.* 16; cf. Boatwright 2021, 163. Salome (the sister of Herod the Great) had bequeathed much property to Livia in 8 CE: Joseph. *AJ* 18.2.2 and *BJ* 2.167.
138. Tac. *Ann.* 12.59, whose beginning stresses Claudius' "savagery" and Agrippina's wiles: *At Claudius saevissima quaeque promere adigebatur eiusdem Agrippinae artibus, quae Statilium Taurum opibus inlustrem hortis eius inhians pervertit accusante Tarquitio Prisco.*

139. As Statilius (PIR² S 856) had served in early 44 as co-consul with Agrippina's second husband Passienus, Agrippina may have known his gardens personally.
140. For M. Tarquitius Priscus, see PIR² T 25; for the gardens, see *LTUR* 3.85 s.v. "Horti Tauriani" (E. Papi); Boatwright 2022, 112.
141. The date is not certain in Tacitus' text. This section of the *Annals* (12.36–38) dates to 50, although citing Caratacus' capture as *nono post anno* after the war's inception in Britain, i.e., in 51. Osgood 2011, 91–92 provides only the *terminus post quem* of 51; Levick 2015, 83, 172, 174, holds for 51.
142. Tac. *Ann.* 12.36, *Hist.* 3.45. The Brigantes were north of Rome's new province. For the war, see Osgood 2011, 87–106; Levick 2015, 162–74.
143. Tac. *Ann.* 12.36–37. The Campus Praetorianus was outside Rome's *pomerium* on the Viminal Hill.
144. Tac. *Ann.* 12.37.1. In Tacitus' extant Claudian books the scene with Caratacus is her first depiction in public.
145. Tac. *Ann.* 12.37.4: *novum sane et moribus veterum insolitum, feminam signis Romanis praesidere: ipsa semet parti a maioribus suis imperii sociam ferebat.* Among others on this scene, see Ginsburg 2006, 26, 28–29, 114–16.
146. Tac. *Hist.* 3.45 hyperbolically refers to it as a "triumph" won for Claudius by Caratacus' capture.
147. *Novum sane et moribus veterum insolitum.* See Boatwright 2021, 167–71.
148. In Tacitus' narrative this report immediately follows that of Burrus' elevation in 51.
149. Tac. *Ann.* 12.42.2: *suum quoque fastigium Agrippina extollere altius: carpento Capitolium ingredi, qui honos sacerdotibus et sacris antiquitus concessus venerationem augebat feminae, quam imperatore genitam, sororem eius qui rerum potitus sit et coniugem et matrem fuisse, unicum ad hunc diem exemplum est.* Woodman 2004, 232, translates: "Agrippina elevated still higher her own exaltedness too: she entered the Capitol by carriage, a custom whose concession in ancient times to priests and sacred objects increased veneration of the lady, whose example of being begotten by a commander and of having been sister, spouse, and mother of one who was in charge of affairs is unique to this day." The *augebat* picks up on Tacitus' report that Agrippina had been enhanced (*augetur*) by the honorific "Augusta" in 50: *augere* (to increase, extend, enlarge; honor, exalt) is connected with "Augustus."
150. The surface area of the lake, 655 m above sea level, was 155 km²: Hurley 2001, 146. Other than those discussed in this section, Trajan and Hadrian tried to drain the lake (*ILS* 302, *CIL* IX 3915; HA, *Hadr.* 22.12). Count Alessandro di Torlonia finally accomplished the feat.
151. Suet. *Iul.* 44, *Claud.* 20.
152. Plin. *HN* 36.124–25.
153. See Cass. Dio 60.11.5 for the inception date; Suet. *Claud.* 20.2 for the funding.
154. Plin. *HN* 36.124–25 gives an almost breathless description of Claudius' project and scolds Nero ("his malicious successor") for abandoning it. For the remains of Claudius' attempts, see *CIL* IX 3888–3890; Thorton and Thorton 1985.
155. Tac. *Ann.* 12.56.2; Cass. Dio 60.33.3 (uniquely noting Nero, and that Claudius erected stands to assemble a multitude); Plin. *HN* 33.63. Did Agrippina personally exclude Britannicus and Octavia? According to Tacitus, so many from neighboring towns and Rome itself attended that the site "resembled a theater."
156. Plin. *HN* 33.63; Tac. *Ann.* 12.56.3; Cass. Dio 60.33.3; Ginsburg 2006, 29.
157. Tacitus reports that the convicted criminals on the boats fought fiercely (*Ann.* 12.56); Cassius Dio, deepening his depiction of an ineffectual Claudius, that they sailed through their opponents' lines with as little injury as possible until forced to destroy one another (60.33.4). Barrett 1996, 129, notes an ancient graffito, found on a temple wall at nearby Alba Fucens, that depicts a quadrireme (a ship with four banks of oars) and documents the event.
158. Tacitus' chronology is vague and compressed; Cassius Dio does not indicate two stages.
159. Tacitus' report of the two's enmity is at odds with Cassius Dio's statement (60.33.1.3ª, placed by editors in 50) that "Agrippina possessed all power, since she dominated Claudius and had won over Narcissus and Pallas."
160. *Impotentiam muliebrem nimiasque spes*; Tac. *Ann.* 12.57.2. Ginsburg 2006, 29–30, notes "*impotentia* connotes lack of self-control and immoderate behavior."
161. See also Tac. *Ann.* 12.7.3, 13.18.2. In Ch. 5 we discuss her rage at Nero's profligacy (Cass. Dio 61.5.4).

162. See Ch. 6 and Boatwright 2022.
163. Cass. Dio 60.33.3–5.
164. Dimensions: 12.7 × 10 × 6, now in Chieti Museo Nazionale Archeologico dell'Abruzzo, inv. no. 8605. See Alexandridis 2004, 156 cat. no.100, and *Claudio imperatore*, 179 cat. no. 101. Alexandridis ibid., n.100 remarks that the small dimensions might suit it also for private display; if so, it would be the expression of a local grandee's loyalty to the imperial house.
165. Alexandridis 2004, 156; *Claudio imperatore* 2019, 179 cat. no. 101.
166. Smith 1987, 106–110; 160 × 170 (top); 164 × 43 (bottom).
167. In her left hand, raised to shoulder height, she carries a small bunch of ears of wheat. See Smith 1987, 109.
168. Smith 1987, 109, noting the mouth's likeness to that of the Copenhagen bust (inv. no. 755; see Ill. Intro.3). Alexandridis 2004, 158 cat. no. 104, classifies the Sebasteion relief portrait as a variant of the Ancona type.
169. Smith 1987, 108, noting that Claudius' figure is slightly stocky and his head "perhaps a little too large" (as is Nero's in another relief from the Sebasteion; see Ch. 5). Smith, ibid. and 109, discusses the careful detail of Claudius' portrait and notes that the emperor already has the wreath firmly on his head.
170. Smith 1987, 107–108, noting that the figure could not be historical "because to bestow a wreath implies higher rank than the recipient—here an emperor."
171. The *iunctio dextrarum* also signifies *fides* or *concordia* between political leaders (Smith 1987, 107) and armies.
172. We do not discuss here the *Lavacrum Agrippinae* (Bath of Agrippina), attested by two inscribed (Hadrianic) lead pipes from near the church of S. Lorenzo in Panisperna on the Viminal Hill: Richardson 1992, 234, s.v. Lavacrum Agrippinae (belonging to either our Agrippina or her homonymous mother). I also omit the private Horti Agrippinae on Tiber's right bank (Sen. *De ira* 3.18.4, Philo, *Leg.* 2.572). Perhaps near S. Pietro, these are usually attributed to Agrippina the Elder, perhaps because of *CIL* VI 4346= EDCS-19100542, *Cydnus / Ti(beri) Germanici <servus>, supra / hortos. Narcissus / fratri merenti f(ecit)*).
173. Buonocore 2007, 76, 81–82, 86–87, 89–90; Rose 1997; Cogitore 1992, 2002, 163–64; Hurlet 2015, 188–89.
174. Rose 1997, 113–15 cat. 42; Flower 2006, 192; Barrett 1991.
175. Nero's name, as "Nero Claudius Caisar Drusus Germanicus, Son of Augustus [Claudius], Pontifex, Augur, *XVvir sacris faciundis*, *VIIvir epulonum*, Consul Designate, Leader of the Youth," provides a *terminus post quem* of 50. The honorific dative case is used for all honorees.
176. *CIL* VI 921 and 922 = EDCS-17301042; EDR103896, EDR103898, EDR103900.
177. Tac. *Ann.* 11.13; Suet. *Claud.* 41.3; F. X. Ryan 1993, 611–13.
178. Rose 1997, 113–15 cat. 42; Flower 2006, 331, n.70.
179. See *CIL* VI 40416 = EDCS-00900120, the inscription of the Arch, with Osgood 2011, 101.
180. Flower 2006, 186–87. For the memory sanctions against Messalina, see Tac. *Ann.* 11.38.3, and Ch. 3, n.104.
181. *CIL* VI 40420–40430; Alföldy, Kolb, et al. 1996, 4416–19; De Caprariis 1993, 93–114; Boatwright 2021, 237–28. Further, those honored by statues in this installation are named in the nominative, not the dative used for the monument near the Arch of Claudius.
182. See *CIL* VI 40420 = EDCS-00900124; *CIL* VI 40424 = EDCS-00900128; *CIL* VI 40425 = EDCS-00900129; *CIL* VI 40426 = EDCS-00900130; *CIL* VI 40423 = EDCS-00900127; *CIL* VI 40427–28 = EDCS-00900131–32. Rose 1997, 114, refers also to an inscription naming Agrippina as the mother of Nero but cites no evidence.
183. Alföldy, Kolb, et al. 1996, 4416; De Caprariis 1993, 105; apparently accepted by Flower 2006, 186, and Osgood 2011, 61–62.
184. See von Hesberg and Panciera 1994, 148–61: *CIL* VI 888–893 = EDCS-17301016–17301021, cf. Suet. *Calig.* 7. The monument must date between 49 and 55 (less plausibly, 59). Julia Livilla: *CIL* VI 891 = EDCS-17301019; Domitilla: *CIL* VI 893 = EDCS-17301021; *LTUR* 3.239, s.v. "Mausoleum Augusti" (M. Macciocca). For the trophy, see *Claudio Imperatore* 2019, 261 cat. no. 134. We return to the Flavian history of this monument in Ch. 6.
185. Panciera in von Hesberg and Panciera 1994, 161. The travertine cippi suggest the installation was understated.
186. See Intro., n.24 and Ch. 4, n.173.
187. *RIC*[2] I, Claudius no. 80 and 81, with legends AGRIPPINAE AVGVSTAE (in the dative) and TI CLAVD CAESAR AVG GERM P M TRIB POT P P, from 50–54 CE.

188. *RIC*[2] I, Claudius no. 75, with legends AGRIPPINAE AVGVSTAE and NERO CLAVD CAES DRVSVS GERM PRINC IVVENT, from 50–54 CE (see Ill. 4.1), visually similar to *RIC*[2] I, Claudius no. 83 (*denarii*). An issue of *aurei* portrays Claudius with Nero "Leader of the Youth," *RIC*[2] I, Claudius no. 82.
189. *RIC*[2] I, Gaius no. 55, dated 37–41: obv.: AGRIPPINA M F MAT C CAESARIS AVGVSTI; rev.: S P Q R MEMORIAE AGRIPPINAE (Agrippina, daughter of Marcus [Agrippa], mother of Gaius Caesar Augustus; The Senate and People of Rome in memory of Agrippina).
190. *RIC*[2] I, Claudius no. 103, dated 50–54 CE, with legend AGRIPPINA AVG GERMANICI F CAESARIS AVG in the nominative rather than the dative used in the other two issues.
191. Ginsburg 2006, 57; Rowan 2011, 244; Boatwright 2021, 125–27.
192. Sutherland 1986, 90; Levick 1982, 107–109; Noreña 2007, 302; see Duncan-Jones 2005, 262–63.
193. To judge from the publication in *OCRE* of coins centrally struck under Claudius.
194. See *Octavia* 164–65 (Claudius perished by his wife's doing); Plin. *HN* 2.92.4 (Claudius poisoned by his wife Agrippina with mushrooms); Cass. Dio 60.35.2; Suet. *Nero* 33.1, 39.3; Joseph. *AJ* 20.8.1–2 (couching it as a "report"). Tacitus' version is discussed in text. In a later outburst Tacitus' Agrippina herself admits responsibility for the poisoning: Tac. *Ann.* 13.14.3.
195. Aveline 2004.
196. For the poisoner trope, see, e.g., Santoro l'Hoir 2006, 111–95. Claudius' remarkable ill health while young improved when he became emperor, but he still suffered from stomach pains (Suet. *Claud.* 2.1, 31; cf. Sen. *Apocol.* 3.1, 6.1), making poison a convenient explanation of his death: Hurley 2001, 236–40; Levick 2015, 88–89.
197. Cass. Dio 60.33.9, discussed above.
198. Something referenced drolly in Sen. *Apocol.* 3.2, quoting Verg. *Georg.* 4.90.
199. Or of one's suffocation (as Tiberius) or butchering (as with Caligula: Suet. *Calig.* 58.3 adds the lurid detail that Caligula was stabbed in the groin).
200. Furneaux 2.114 *ad Ann.* 12.1.
201. Phlegon of Tralles, *Mir.* 7 (*FGrH* 2.1179, VII), tr. Hansen 1996, 39. The portent might have fit others reported by Tacitus, esp. if his *biformis hominum partus* refers to hermaphrodites rather than two-headed babies (cf. Woodman 2004, 242, n.89).
202. In contrast to other transformation entries in Phlegon's *Book of Marvels*, this one does not include an official report to the authorities or any expiation.
203. Tacitus uses the noun *flagitia*, connoting shame, disgrace, outrage. Cassius Dio (61.33.12) and Suetonius (*Claud.* 43) also report Claudius' anger at Agrippina, with Cassius Dio specifying motivation as her "exercising the same power as Claudius and desiring to have his title outright."
204. Tac. *Ann.* 12.64: *nec forma aetas opes multum distabant; et utraque impudica, infamis, violenta, haud minus vitiis aemulabantur quam si qua ex fortuna prospera acceperant.*
205. Here, Tacitus repeats his main point of Agrippina's responsibility for Nero's accession. Tac. *Ann.* 12.64: *Agrippina, quae filio dare imperium, tolerare imperitantem nequibat.*
206. Domitia Lepida would scarcely have been a supporter of Claudius, who was responsible for her daughter Messalina's death (see Ch. 3).
207. Tac. *Ann.* 12.65: *at novercae insidiis domum omnem convelli, maiore flagitio quam si impudicitiam prioris coniugis reticuisset. quamquam ne impudicitiam quidem nunc abesse Pallante adultero, ne quis ambigat decus pudorem corpus, cuncta regno viliora habere.*
208. Tac. *Ann.* 12.66; Cass. Dio 60.34.2–3. Agrippina and poisoned mushrooms are also noted in Juv. *Sat.* 6.620; Suet. *Nero* 33.1; Cass. Dio 60.35.4. For Locusta (also known as Lucusta), see Furneaux 2.145 *ad Ann.* 12.66.4; PIR[2] L 414.
209. Suet. *Claud.* 44.2: *... ubi autem et per quem dato, discrepant. Quidam tradunt epulanti in arce cum sacerdotibus per Halotum spadonem praegustatorem, alii domestico convivio per ipsam Agrippinam, quae boletum medicatum avidissimo ciborum talium optulerat.* See Hurley 2001, 238 ad loc. Suetonius does not name Locusta.
210. Suet. *Claud.* 44.3. Hurley 2001, 238–39, suggests Pliny the Elder as the probable source of the first alternative.
211. Tac. *Ann.* 12.67: the note of Xenophon's complicity underlines the deceitfulness of personal relationships at Claudius' court. Only five chapters earlier (*Ann.* 12.61), Claudius reportedly publicly extolled Xenophon, his skills, and their trusted relationship. Here, Xenophon is characterized as "not at all unaware that the worst crimes are begun with peril but achieved with a prize" (*ille tamquam nisus evomentis adiuvaret, pinnam rapido veneno inlitam faucibus eius demisisse creditur, haud ignarus summa scelera incipi cum periculo, peragi cum praemio*).

212. Tac. *Ann.* 12.67; Suet. *Claud.* 44.3; Sen. *Apocol.* 4. Suetonius adds Claudius' vomiting.
213. Sen. *Apocol.* 4; Aveline 2004, 454.
214. Suet. *Claud.* 45; Cass. Dio 60.34.3; Sen. *Apocol.* 1–3 allow us only to say it was before or on 13 October that year.
215. Tac. *Ann.* 12.68; Suet. *Claud.* 45. Antonia presumably had come from the home of her second husband, Faustus Cornelius Sulla Felix (Messalina's half-brother, whom Antonia married in 47; see PIR^2 C 1464). For parallels with literary accounts of Livia's delay in announcing Augustus' death to guarantee the accession of her own son and Tanaquil's delay in announcing that of Tarquinius Priscus until the accession of Servius Tullius, see Bauman 1994.
216. Tac. *Ann.* 12.69.3. It is left unclear who was the sponsor for the divinization: probably Nero. For the procedure of divinization see, e.g., Palombi 2014, Kierdorf 1986.
217. Tac. *Ann.* 13.21.3: *concilia.*
218. For the majority view, see, e.g., Barrett et al. 2016, 1–17 (with sources). Levick 2015, 84–91, admitting "on balance it looks as if Claudius' departure was brought about by Agrippina rather than due to her good luck" (89), argues that Claudius was preparing both boys as potential successors. See also Osgood 2011, 242–46.
219. Suet. *Nero* 33; Cass. Dio 60.35.4.

Chapter 5

1. See, e.g., Furneaux 2.155 *ad Ann.* 13.2.11.
2. In Tacitean fashion Agrippina is criticized in these chapters by intervening reports of deaths and court affairs (*Ann.* 13.1–2.2).
3. Tac. *Ann.* 12.69: *caelestesque honores Claudio decernuntur et funeris sollemne perinde ac divo Augusto celebratur, aemulante Agrippina proaviae Liviae magnificentiam*; "with Agrippina rivaling the magnificence of her great-grandmother Livia." When this chapter also notes Nero's promised donative to the praetorians and mentions Britannicus twice, it implies Agrippina's responsibility for both.
4. Tac. *Ann.* 13.2.3. *propalam tamen omnes in eam honores cumulabantur, signumque more militiae petenti tribuno dedit optimae matris. decreti et a senatu duo lictores, flamonium Claudiale, simul Claudio censorium funus et mox consecratio.*
5. The speech was on the day of the funeral: Tac. *Ann.* 13.3.1–2; Plin. *Pan.* 11.1.
6. Suet. *Vesp.* 9; Boatwright 2021, 200–201. We discuss below her over-life-size statue presumably once in this shrine.
7. Tac. *Ann.* 13.31 is the *locus classicus* for this political historian's dismissal of description of buildings in proper histories: see, e.g., Syme 1958, 292.
8. Boatwright 2021, 149–52. Antonia was promoted as *sacerdos divi Augusti* by her grandson Caligula in his first year (Cass. Dio 59.3.4; see Suet. *Calig.* 15.2), during which she died; she was celebrated as *sacerdos* under Claudius (e.g., *CIL* VI 921). Agrippina is the last imperial woman who was a priest of imperial cult.
9. Julia Augusta's freedman Cnidus is called *ab ornamentis sacerdotalibus* (in charge of her ceremonial dresses and outfits for religious occasions): *CIL* VI 8955 = EDCS-18900022, from after Livia's death: see Brännstedt 2015, 42, citing *CIL* VI 3992 as another possibility.
10. See Cass. Dio 56.46.1–2; Vell. Pat. 2.75.3; Ov. *Pont.* 4.9.107.
11. See Brennan 2022, 94–98.
12. The animosity against Tiberius (never consecrated) may have enabled the exoneration of Agrippina's first husband Ahenobarbus from treason and other charges reportedly encouraged by Tiberius in 37. See Ch. 1.
13. See Ch. 4; Eaton 2011, 63; n.4 this chapter.
14. *Prima novo principatu mors Iunii Silani proconsulis Asiae ignaro Nerone per dolum Agrippinae paratur.* In contrast, Pliny the Elder reports Nero poisoned Silanus (*HN* 7.58.5).
15. In a later reported outburst Tacitus' Agrippina admits her responsibility for this death and for the earlier one of L. Silanus: Tac. *Ann.* 13.14.3.
16. Cassius Dio (61.6.4), in an excerpt now placed somewhere in 54, has Agrippina personally send Marcus some of the same poison she had used for Claudius, because his goodness might contrast with "her son's manner of life." For Marcus Junius Silanus, see PIR^2 I 833.
17. Tac. *Ann.* 13.1: *nec minus properato Narcissus Claudii libertus, de cuius iurgiis adversus Agrippinam rettuli, aspera custodia et necessitate extrema ad mortem agitur, invito principe, cuius abditis vitiis per avaritiam ac prodigentiam mire congruebat.* Syme 1958, 289: "Tacitus... takes special care that Book XIII shall lead off as the exordium of a new section of the *Annales*."

18. Tac. *Ann.* 13.2: *quae cunctis malae dominationis cupidinibus flagrans habebat in partibus Pallantem, quo auctore Claudius nuptiis incestis et adoptione exitiosa semet perverterat.* Nero still does not appear as a subject, however, strengthening his lack of agency in these opening three chapters.
19. Tac. *Ann.* 13.2.3.
20. Nero's rupture from his mother in 55 included separating their homes: Tac. *Ann.* 13.18.3; Suet. *Nero* 34.1.
21. By Ov. *Pont.* 3.1.125, dated between 12 and 16 CE (Boatwright 2021, 40). Agrippina the Elder, too, was called a *femina princeps* because of her noble lineage: Tac. *Ann.* 2.75.1.
22. Cass. Dio 61.3.2. Suet. *Nero* 9.1 notes only the two being carried together in the same litter (see below). Reports of her public appearances with Claudius never mention litters. For Passienus and Caligula, see Ch. 3, and Suet. *Pass.*
23. Similarities of the two mother-son relationships seem to have been apparent to Nero, too, to judge from Suet. *Nero* 34.1, usually interpreted as a reference to Tiberius and Livia: when chafing against Agrippina's constant criticism Nero threatened "that he was going to give up the principate and go off to Rhodes" so as to make her unpopular (quoted in n.187, this chapter). Tiberius blamed his retreat to Capri in 27 on his mother's carping; the ill will for his earlier self-exile in Rhodes (6 BCE to 2 CE?) had actually been mitigated by her (Suet. *Tib.* 40, 51–52). Is Nero's Rhodes threat a note of his faulty history or simply his sarcasm (Warmington 1977, 91 ad loc.)?
24. See Eden 1984, 1–8. The *terminus post quem* is the death of Narcissus (Sen. *Apocol.* 13), probably by late October (Tac. *Ann.* 12.69–13.3; Eden, 4). The Menippean satire may have been produced for the Saturnalia beginning 17 December 54: Furneaux 2.23–24, n.11, 45, n.10, 171, n.1.
25. *Apocol.* 4.1–2, to modern sensibilities over-the-top. Smith 2021, 98–100, e.g., provides an excellent contextualized discussion of the similar immoderation of cameos.
26. For the murders and involvement of Narcissus, see, e.g., Sen. *Apocol.* 13; for the number killed, 14.1.
27. We hear nothing about Calpurnia (killed in 49; Tac. *Ann.* 12.22.3, 14.12.6; Cass. Dio 60.33.2[b]), Lollia Paulina (killed in 49; Tac. *Ann.* 12.22.1–4; Cass. Dio 60.32.3), or T. Statilius Taurus (killed in 53; Tac. *Ann.* 12.59.1).
28. In *Apocol.* 8.2 the incest charge against him and his sister is noted; in 10.4 Augustus points out that this victim of Claudius was his great-great-grandson; in 11.5 L. Silanus appears with Pompeius Magnus as sons-in-law whom Claudius killed.
29. Sen. *Apocol.* 13.5, listing family members Claudius killed, including the plural "mothers-in-law" (*socrus*); Tac. *Ann.* 12.64.4–65.2. For Agrippina and Domitia Lepida, see Ch. 4.
30. Sen. *Apocol.* 4.
31. Eden 1984, 7, discusses the political ramifications of mocking the official *consecratio*, arguing that the "governing class" was surely cynical about religious aspects, and the work was not publicized outside of the court.
32. For instance, the Acts of the Arval Brethren of 54 includes prayers for the safety and well-being of "Nero Claudius, the offspring of Agrippina Augusta wife of Tiberius Claudius Caesar Augustus Germanicus, *divus* princeps and public parent" (*CIL* VI 2034, p. 864, 3261 = *CIL* VI 32348 = *CFA* 22).
33. Eden 1984, 7–8, pictures some reactions of Agrippina, "not... whole-heartedly amused."
34. Tacitus remarks about Octavia at the death of her brother Britannicus in 55 that she, "though raw in years, had learned to hide pain, affection, and every emotion" (*Ann.* 13.16.7). Eden 1984, 8, suggests the three were kept unaware of the skit.
35. *RIC*[2] I, Nero no. 1–3 (Ill. 5.1 = no. 1): *Aurei* and *denarii*: obv., AGRIPP AVG DIVI CLAVD NERONIS CAES MATER; rev., NERONI CLAVD DIVI F CAES AVG GERM IMP TR P, with EX S C in the center. The single tribunician power of Nero dates the coin to his first year of rule, 13 October 54 to 12 October 55 (assuming 13 October as his first day as acknowledged princeps: Ch. 4, n.214). Inscriptions naming Agrippina "Mother of the Emperor" (*Agrippina Mater Augusti*) include EDCS-34500969 from Augusta Emerita (modern Mérida, Spain; text restored), the Acts of the Arval Brethren, *CIL* VI 2041 = *CFA* 27 (Rome), and *CIL* III 7107 = EDCS-28501031 (Smyrna). Coins of Caesarea in Cappadocia, e.g., also identify her as AGRIPPINA AVGVSTA MATER AVGVSTI: *RIC*[2] I, Nero no. 607–608 and 610–11, dated 54–60 CE.
36. See, e.g., Barrett 2017, 66. The legend (in the nominative, indicating action), "Agrippina Augusta, [wife] of *divus* Claudius, mother of Nero Caesar" (previous note), does not specify Nero as emperor. Coins struck in Rome generally use the nominative for the emperor or

issuing authority but an oblique case (usually dative) for someone else featured on the coin: *RIC* I, p. 92 and Ch. 4.

37. Nero's identification is in the dative, not nominative. The oak wreath surrounds EX S C, "In accordance with a senatorial decree."
38. *RIC*[2] I, Nero no. 6–7: Obv., NERO CLAVD DIVI F CAES AVG GERM IMP TR P COS; rev., AGRIPP AVG DIVI CLAVD NERONIS CAES MATER EX S C. Nero's name is on the obverse and in the more usual nominative, although Agrippina's name is also in the nominative. Our Ill. 5.2 is *RIC*[2] I, Nero no. 6.
39. Latham 2016, 113–28.
40. Smith 1987, 127–32; 172 × 142.5 (bottom) × 37.5.
41. Some tender that the figure was meant to be a personification, perhaps of Roma, with features assimilated to those of Agrippina: Barrett 2017, 67–68 (suggesting Concordia). The portrait is of the Ancona type: see Ch. 6.
42. Smith 1987, 129: Agrippina is slightly taller, however.
43. Smith 1987, 131.
44. Smith 1987, 129.
45. Smith 1987, 128–29, who points out that Nero does not wear military boots but shoes characteristic of senatorial (that is, civilian) dress.
46. Some consider her more dominant than Nero: see Barrett 2017, 67.
47. Somewhat continued by the *umbo*, or deep fold, of the toga on the figure to the viewer's right.
48. Smith 1987, 109, notes, however, that her ears of wheat assimilate her to Demeter.
49. Her maternal relationship may also be alluded to by the clinging thin chiton that exposes her midriff and navel and suggests fecundity. For Agrippina's "Neronianization," see Trillmich 2007, 46; Smith 1987, 129–31.
50. Smith 1987, 107–108: "to bestow a wreath implies higher rank than the recipient."
51. Smith 1987, 132.
52. For the three-layered sardonyx (8.0 cm H), see Smith 2021, 96, 125 no. 39 (with bibliography). Smith notes the execution as "surprisingly plain" and stresses that this allegorizing of Nero's coronation is independent of the scene in the Sebasteion.
53. Smith 2021, 96.
54. Smith 2021, 75–79, stressing the dominant presence of Agrippina and the cameo's dynamic mythological narrative.
55. *Anthologia Palatina* 6.329; Hemelrijk 1999, 114–15. The translation here differs slightly from Hemelrijk.
56. The size and finesse of the marble relief suggest it took months, if not at least a year, to carve.
57. Tac. *Ann.* 13.1.2: he was poisoned at a banquet by P. Celerius, a Roman equestrian, and Helius, a freedman, both installed to supervise the emperor's estate in Asia (see *IK, I. Eph.* 7,2,3043/44; *SEG* 39, 1172, for Celerius). In 57 the province of Asia accused Celerius in the senate of other crimes, but the trial dragged out until his death (*Ann.* 13.33.1).
58. *Ann.* 13.2: *Ibaturque in caedes, nisi Afranius Burrus et Annaeus Seneca obviam issent.... certamen utrique unum erat contra ferociam Agrippinae, quae cunctis malae dominationis cupidinibus flagrans habebat in partibus Pallantem.*
59. *Vesp.* 4: *Agrippinam timens potentem adhuc apud filium et defuncti quoque Narcissi amicos perosam*, with *amicos* (rather than *amici* in the better manuscripts): Jones 2000, 30 ad loc. For Vespasian's career, see PIR[2] F 398.
60. Tac. *Ann.* 13.1.4. Some presume Vespasian's personal antipathy to Agrippina (e.g., Barrett 1996, 67, 199), but Suetonius' note (in *Titus* 2) that Vespasian's son Titus was with Britannicus when the latter was poisoned at an imperial banquet (see below) suggests Vespasian was not totally detached from the court.
61. Despite Cassius Dio's statement (60.32.3) that Agrippina was training her son for the throne and was entrusting his education to Seneca, the boy was too young for military service and reputedly shirked "serious" subjects. Suet. *Nero* 52 notes Agrippina barring Nero's philosophical studies as not suitable for one who would rule.
62. Narcissus died within weeks of Claudius, and Claudius' confidant L. Vitellius died in 51.
63. Seneca's birthdate is given as 4 BCE to 1 CE (see, e.g., Wilson 2014); Burrus was born in 1 CE (PIR[2] A 441).
64. On this, see Barrett 2017, 70; Barrett 1996, 157–60; Ginsburg 2006, 37–42.
65. Cass. Dio 61.3.2–3.

66. Perhaps accounting for Seneca's silence about Agrippina in the *Apocolocyntosis*?
67. Tac. *Ann.* 13.3.1–2, 13.11.2. Cassius Dio (61.3.1) holds that Nero's acclamation speeches to praetorians and the senate were written by Seneca, who also was credited for Nero's announcement of Agrippina's death (Tac. *Ann.* 14.11.3).
68. *AE* 1927, 2 = *Corinth* VIII 2, no. 68; PIR² I 587. This is a unique instance of a woman sharing estates with a ruling emperor. The reference to Nero as *Caesar* alone suggests that Spartiaticus served in the first year of the possible span of 54–59.
69. E.g., Tac. *Ann.* 14.2 (though this is stated anonymously).
70. Cass. Dio 61.33.3 and 10.
71. Tac. *Ann.* 13.5.1.
72. Suet. *Aug.* 29.3. See Richardson 1992, 14 s.v. "Apollo Palatinus, Aedes."
73. See Ch. 1, n.28; Carandini 2018, tav. 10a–13; Carandini and Carafa 2017, Tab. 70, Tab. 282.
74. Tac. *Ann.* 13.5.1; for Claudius' motion in 47 CE, see Tac. *Ann.* 11.22.2. Quaestors designate were men who would serve the following year as quaestors, low-ranking financial officers.
75. Confusion comes because the anonymous life of Lucan holds that Lucan gave games "as was the custom" when quaestor designate. This occurred surely under Nero even though Suetonius, usually dependable about games, notes that it was Domitian who "reimposed the obligation" (*Dom.* 4): see Barrett et al. 2016, 27.
76. Now 61.3.2 in the Loeb edition.
77. Tac. *Ann.* 13.10: see Barrett 2017, 64, n.2. Suet. *Nero* 9.1 groups the statue with Nero's funeral and eulogy of Claudius as "display of filial piety," and Barrett et al. 2016, 33, n.28 holds that Suetonius antedates the honorific statue by a few months.
78. *CIL* VI 32352, 2041 (line 25), 2042 d (= *CFA* 24 *[...ex edicto(?)] / Neronis Claudi Caesaris Aug(usti) Germanici pr[incipis parentisque publici ante] / domum Domitianam ob memoriam Domi[tii patris eius*; *CFA* 27 and 28). Carandini and Carafa 2017, pl. 74 and 91 (cf. Sen. *Controv.* 9.4.18) has identified the ancestral house as the residence located beneath the later Temple of Venus and Roma. See also Barrett 1996, 165.
79. Her appearance alongside Claudius receiving homage from Caratacus and other British captives in 52 was staged outside Rome's pomerium (in the Praetorian Field). Similarly, her visual parity with Claudius (and Nero) at the Fucine Lake festivities showed her supervising enslaved combatants of a mock battle. See Ch. 4.
80. Tac. *Ann.* 13.5.2; Cass. Dio 61.3.3–4.
81. Cass. Dio 61.3.3 clarifies this: "Then... they [Burrus and Seneca, with Nero and Agrippina] did not re-ascend the tribunal, but made some excuse, so that the weakness in the empire should not become apparent to the foreigners; and thereafter they [Burrus and Seneca] labored to prevent any public business from being again committed to her hands." Tacitus also links the incident with the ambassadors to a diminished Rome by reporting in the next chapter (*Ann.* 13.5.2) worries that a threatened Parthian war could not be repelled by a mere 17-year-old ruled by a female or administered by "teachers" (Seneca and Burrus).
82. Cass. Dio 61.4.1–3, admiring the men's joint leadership and noting it suited Nero's indolence.
83. Cass. Dio 61.4.1, 4. He was similarly devious with Seneca and Burrus.
84. Cass. Dio 61.5.4. This Doryphoros, in charge of petitions (*a libellis*), seems to be the Doryphoros Nero subsequently "married" and then later removed because he opposed the princeps' marriage with Poppaea: PIR² D 194.
85. Tac. *Ann.* 13.13.1: *ceterum infracta paulatim potentia matris delapso Nerone in amorem libertae.*
86. Tac. *Ann.* 13.13.1: *liberta aemula, nurus ancilla.* Rome's prejudice against the enslaved and formerly enslaved ran deep: Nero suborned even consular men to swear that Acte was descended from a king (Suet. *Nero* 28). Agrippina would not have it: Cassius Dio adds the detail that when attempting to stop the affair, she even beat some of Nero's accomplices and got rid of others.
87. Besides Britannicus, Nero, and Agrippina, Octavia and her older stepsister Antonia seem to have been at the banquet (Tac. *Ann.* 13.17.2, *ad complexum sororum*), as well as "noble youths" including the later emperor Titus, who reportedly also tasted the poison and was long sick from it (Suet. *Titus* 2).
88. *Nihil rerum mortalium tam instabile ac fluxum est quam fama potentiae non sua vi nixa[e]*: Tac. *Ann.* 13.19.1. See, e.g., Furneaux 2.176 ad loc. for *nixae* rather than the *nixa* of the Medicean manuscript. Pallas was allowed to leave the court without further ado, which Oost 1958, 133–34, interprets as revealing the real desire of Nero and Seneca: to weaken Agrippina herself. Pallas died only in 62 (Tac. *Ann.* 14.65).

89. Tac. *Ann.* 13.20. For Fabius Rusticus, "the most eloquent of recent authors" (Tac. *Agric.* 10.3), see also Tac. *Ann.* 14.2.2, 15.61.3; Syme 1958, 289–94. Among the many works of C. Plinius is a now lost 31-book history of the later Julio-Claudian period (PIR[2] P 373; Tac. *Ann.* 15.53.3; Tac. *Ann.* 1.69.2). For Cluvius Rufus, a historian, *consul suffectus* before 65, and intimate member of the court, see PIR[2] C 1206; Tac. *Ann.* 14.2.1; Syme 1958, 289–94; Wiseman 2013, 109–14.
90. *Ann.* 13.13.1, in "womanly fashion" scorning "her freedwoman rival" before foully remonstrating with her son.
91. *Ann.* 13.13.2, *tum Agrippina versis artibus per blandimenta iuvenem adgredi, suum potius cubiculum ac sinum offerre contegendis quae prima aetas et summa fortuna expeterent*: "then Agrippina, in a sly volte-face, cajoled the boy, offering instead her bedchamber and lap for concealing what his first flush of youth and excess fortune desired." Furneaux 2.168 ad loc. interprets *cubiculum ac sinum* as hendiadys, the privacy of her own chamber where Nero might meet with Acte. But elsewhere, Tacitus uses *sinus* as an actual lap, often maternal (*Agr.* 4.2; *Dial.* 28.4; *Ann.* 6.45.5). *Sinus*, connoting intimacy, here may hint at Agrippina's rumored incest with Nero (see below). Woodman's translation (2004, 250) insinuates this: "offered her own bedroom and lap as an alternative for the concealment of what his young age and high fortune demanded." See also the goodbye kiss Nero gives Agrippina before having her killed (*Ann.* 14.4.5), noted at the end of this chapter.
92. *Ann.* 13.13.3: *quae mutatio neque Neronem fefellit, et proximi amicorum metuebant orabantque cavere insidias mulieris semper atrocis, tum et falsae.* Yet another instance of Tacitus expressing judgments through the thoughts and words of unnamed others, this is substantiated in the historian's own words, *praeceps posthac Agrippina ruere ad terrorem et minas* (*Ann.* 13.14.2); *volutare secum modo matris violentiam* (*Ann.* 13.15.1); *urgentibusque Agrippinae minis* (*Ann.* 13.15.3). Tacitus earlier used *atrox* to describe Agrippina the Elder: *Ann.* 4.52.1 (Ch. 1, n.24).
93. *Ann.* 13.13.4: *sed Agrippina non his instrui cultus suos, sed ceteris arceri proclamat et dividere filium, quae cuncta ex ipsa haberet.*
94. Tac. *Ann.* 13.14.2–4. Her speech, in indirect discourse, includes withering criticism of the "crippled" Burrus and "exile" Seneca. Other than Nero, Agrippina's listeners are not specified.
95. Tacitus devotes more than a long and detailed chapter to this (*Ann.* 13.15–16), presaging Agrippina's later murder at Nero's orders. Suetonius (*Nero* 33.2), although analogously detailing particulars of the poison, suggests Nero's motivation was envy of Britannicus' voice as well as fear of the boy as a political rival.
96. Tac. *Ann.* 13.16.4: *at Agrippina[e] is pavor, ea consternatio mentis, quamvis vultu premeretur, emicuit, ut perinde ignaram fuisse [quam] Octaviam sororem Britannici constiterit.* Suetonius omits Agrippina's presence when describing Britannicus' murder in Suet. *Nero* 33. Otherwise, his (shorter) presentation agrees with that of Tacitus. Only the *Octavia* (line 341) claims Agrippina's responsibility for Britannicus' death.
97. Tac. *Ann.* 13.18.2: *quasi quaereret ducem et partes.* Although by working with military officers and Rome's elite Agrippina acts like a powerful Republican man, by suggesting she was seeking a leader Tacitus notes that she herself could never command.
98. Tac. *Ann.* 13.18.3.
99. This section, Tac. *Ann.* 13.19–22 introduced by the gnomic statement noted above, is vividly substantiated: "Immediately Agrippina's doorstep was abandoned; no one consoled her, no one visited other than a few women who came in affection, or maybe in spiteful gloating."
100. Tac. *Ann.* 13.19.3. Even if a half-year had passed since Britannicus' death it could not be old news or "clichéd." Rubellius Plautus (PIR[2] R 115) was born after 33 to Julia (the daughter of Drusus the Younger and granddaughter of Tiberius: FOS #422; PIR[2] I 636) and her husband C. Rubellius Blandus (PIR[2] R 111).
101. Junia Silana, wed to C. Silius before he left her for Messalina, died at Tarentum probably in 59: FOS #474. Domitia, identified in this passage as Nero's aunt, had been wed to Crispus Passienus before he married Agrippina, which may explain her reported nasty rivalry with Agrippina (Tac. *Ann.* 13.19.4; FOS #319). For Iturius, see PIR[2] I 62; Calvisius, PIR[2] C 343; Paris, PIR[2] P 156. Atimetus is otherwise unknown.
102. Tacitus recounts a long and involved story of Silana's courtship by T. Sextius Africanus (PIR[2] S 659), adding the aside about the enduring and hateful rivalry between Agrippina and Domitia.

103. Tac. *Ann.* 13.20.2. It is unclear how we go from suspicion of Burrus through Burrus' support by Seneca to Burrus promising Nero he would deal with Agrippina were she found guilty. This is not the only time with Agrippina that outside sources are cited, though here Tacitus tarnishes Fabius by accusing him of bias for Seneca.
104. Tac. *Ann.* 13.21.
105. Rubellius Plautus similarly drops from Tacitus' narrative until the next book. He apparently continued living in Rome until 60 (Tac. *Ann.* 14.22), suggesting that he was not seen as any threat until after Agrippina's death.
106. Tac. *Ann.* 13.12.1: M. Salvius Otho (PIR^2 S 143; perhaps the host of Agrippina's last feast with Nero, and a short-lived emperor in 69); Claudius Senecio (imperial freedman; PIR^2 C 1016); 13.13.1; Seneca and his relative and friend Annaeus Serenus (PIR^2 A 618).
107. Tac. *Ann.* 13.16.1.
108. Tac. *Ann.* 13.18.1.
109. *Ann.* 13.15.3, e.g., sed *Nero lenti sceleris impatiens minitari tribuno, iubere supplicium venefi-cae.* The tribune, Julius Pollio, later became governor of Sardinia: PIR^2 I 473.
110. Tac. *Ann.* 13.13.4.
111. *Ann.* 13.18.4, although the Latin is difficult: *excubiasque militares, quae ut coniugi imperatoris olim, tum ut matri servabantur, et Germanos nuper eundem [in] honorem custodes additos digredi iubet.* Suetonius (*Nero* 34.1) and Cassius Dio (61.8.4) also note her being stripped of her guards, who included Germans.
112. Tac. *Ann.* 13.13.4.
113. *Ann.* 13.17.1–2. Tacitus gives greater credence to the rumor by attributing it to (unnamed) writers.
114. *Ann.* 13.20.1.
115. *Ann.* 13.15.3.
116. *Ann.* 13.20.2: *Nero trepidus et interficiendae matris avidus.*
117. Ann. 13.22.2: *Plautus ad praesens silentio transmissus est.* His later exile and death are reported in *Ann.* 14.22.5 and 14.59.3.
118. Suet. *Nero* 34.1 (n.187, this chapter).
119. Cf. Tac. *Ann.* 14.2, set in 59, in which Nero praises Agrippina's retreats into "her gardens or her villas at Antium and Tusculum." Maevania: Ch. 2, n.118.
120. Tac. *Ann.* 14.13.3: *seque in omnes libidines effudit, quas male coercitas qualiscumque matris reverentia tardaverat.*
121. Warmington 1977, 92 ad loc.
122. *CIL* X 1574 = *AE* 2016, +00265, cf. Tac. *Ann.* 14.27. Both names, Nero and Agrippina, were later erased. Agrippina does not have the epithet *Mater Augusti* or *Mater Neronis Caesaris* (cp. nn.35, 38, this chapter).
123. For 57 CE, *CIL* VI 2039 (p. 3270, 4175) = *CFA* 25b; for 58, *CFA* 27. Barrett 1996, 179, notes that the November entries for the years 56 and 59 have not survived, and the relevant text for Nero's birthday in 57 is missing.
124. *CIL* VI 32357 = *CFA* 31.
125. The spot, excavated in 1992/93, is near the later southwestern pier of the Arch of Constantine between the Palatine and Caelian: Morizio 1996; Carandini and Carafa 2017, Tab. 74 (esp. B). The aedicula there was built soon after Claudius' accession in January 42.
126. Di Brino 2016, 268, and Morizio 1996, 213, venture that the shrine once housed a statue of Messalina that was removed after her downfall in 48.
127. As well as for the military, where they helped provide tactical signaling and marching music.
128. Fejfer 2008, 82, notes that a portrait head, which cannot be identified as any of the members of the Julio-Claudian family, was also found in the area; we do not discuss that here.
129. *CIL* VI 40334 = EDR092834 (7 BCE to 4 CE): once bronze-lettered, *Ti(berio) Cla[ud]io Ti(beri) f(ilio) / [Ne]roni / pon[t(ifici) co(n)s(uli) II i]mp(eratori) II / [ae]n(e)ator[e]s tubicines / l[iti]cines cornicines / Romani.* Tiberius was remarkably generous to those on the Caelian after a devastating fire there in 27: Tac. *Ann.* 4.64. Di Brino 2016, 268, suggests there may also have been a statue of Caligula that was removed after 41.
130. *CIL* VI 40307 = EDR092818: *Imp(eratori) Ca<e=I>sari divi f(ilio) / Augusto / pontifici maximo co(n)s(uli) XI / tribunicia potestat(e) XI // Neroni Claudio divi / Claudii f(ilio) / Germanici Ca<e=I>saris n(epoti) / Ti(beri) Ca<e=I>saris Aug(usti) pron(epoti) / divi Augusti abn(epoti) / Ca<e=I>sari Aug(usto) Germanico pont(ifici) / max(imo) trib(unicia) potest(ate) II imp(eratori)*

co(n)s(uli) // Ti(berio) Claudio Drusi f(ilio) / Ca<e=I>sari Augusto / Germanico pontifici / maximo tribunicia pot(estate) / imp(eratori) co(n)s(uli) II // Iuliae Au[gustae] / Agri[ppinae] / Germanic[i Caisaris f(iliae)] / divi Cla[udi uxori] // Aen(e)atores tubicines liticines cornicines Romani / {Romani}.

131. *Aen(e)atores tubicines liticines cornicines Romani* (see previous note). Alexandrescu 2007 discusses and illustrates these different types of musical instruments.
132. *CIL* VI 40307 (Latin in n.130 above): "Imperator Caisar Augustus, son of a *divus*, pontifex maximus consul for the 11th time, with tribunician power for the 11th time." This inscription is what has suggested an original, freestanding honorific statue here in 12 BCE, replaced on the bench built in Claudius' reign (n.b. archaic spelling of Caisar).
133. *CIL* VI 40307 (Latin in n.130 above): "Nero Claudius Caisar Augustus Germanicus, son of *divus* Claudius, grandson of Germanicus Caisar, great grandson of Tiberius Caisar Augustus, great-great grandson of *divus* Augustus, pontifex maximus, with tribunician power for the second time, *imperator*, consul." Di Brino 2016, 268–69, emphasizes Nero's emulation of Augustus here.
134. *CIL* VI 40307 (Latin in n.130 above): "Tiberius Claudius, son of Drusus, Caisar Augustus Germanicus, pontifex maximus, with tribunician power, imperator, consul for the second time." Claudius may have helped fund the renovation of the collegial shrine.
135. *CIL* VI 40307 (Latin in n.130 above): note, however, that "daughter of Germanicus Caisar" is partially restored.
136. Morizio 1996, 211. The spelling of "Caisar" preserves Claudius' archaic orthography. The 55/56 renovation likely included the entire shrine.
137. See, e.g., Gallia 2022, 39.
138. Sen. *Apocol.* 12.1.
139. Morizio 1996.
140. Flower 2006, 193, and Varner 2004, 98–99, see this as a kind of *damnatio memoriae*, as memory sanctions often left obvious marks. But there was never a full *damnatio memoriae* sanctioned against her: see Ch. 6.
141. Suet. *Vesp.* 9. The shrine is called Claudium and Templum Claudii (respectively) by the *Curiosum* and *Notitia* of the Regionary Catalogues, Reg. II; *templum divi Claudi* in *CIL* VI 10251a = EDCS-16100479, Front. *Aq.* 1.20, and Suet. *Vesp.* 9; *LTUR* 1.277–78, s.v. "Claudius, Divus, Templum (reg. II)" (C. Buzzetti). Cf. Aur. Vict. *Caes.* 9 and *Epit.* 8.8.
142. Mart. *Spect.* 2.9–10. Recent excavations on the western Caelian indicate two phases of Neronian construction of the Claudium, consistent with an alteration of the plan after 59: Cioncoloni and Sorella 2019. Front. *Aq.* 1.20 indicates the finished rebuilding was in use by the end of the first century CE.
143. See, e.g., Carandini and Carafa 2017, Tab. 136; Wood 1999, 268.
144. See (most recently) *Claudio imperatore* 2019, 279–82 (F. Coarelli). Much of our understanding of the structure is due to its depiction on the Marble Plan of Rome.
145. In the early 2000s archaeologists explored tunnels running through the tuff of the platform: M. Gradozzi, "Sotterranei del Tempio di Claudio al Celio" (accessed 19 August 2023).
146. Along with other finds such as the "Victory of the Symmachi": Pavolini 2007, 310. Graywacke, a basalt stone also called *grovacca* or basanite, is a dense and prestigious green-gray stone from Wadi Hammâmât in Egypt's eastern desert. When polished, it resembles patinated bronze and stands out against white marble statues. Its quarries were under imperial control, and use of the stone may have been the prerogative of the imperial house in the first century CE: Belli Pasqua 1995, esp. 56–58; di Leo 1989, esp. 60.
147. See Moltesen 2007, 141. The head: Ny Carlsberg Glyptotek, Copenhagen, inv. no. 753.
148. Musei Capitolini, Centrale Montemartini, Rome, inv. no. 1882; Alexandridis 2004, cat. no. 106.
149. Head: 0.30 m H; statue body: 1.80 m H. Rose 1997, 74, notes that imperial statues of the Julio-Claudian period were usually 2.00–2.20 m H, slightly over life-size.
150. This suggests a date during Agrippina's short time as "imperial mother" from 54 to 59 CE; during her marriage to Claudius, Agrippina's image on coins and in Aphrodisias' Sebasteion had thin lips like those of Claudius.
151. Moltesen 2007, 143–47; Fisker's drawing from ibid., 147. Prominent jewelry on female portraiture seems post-Constantinian: Schade 2016, 251; Alexandridis 2004, 72.

152. E.g., the posthumous statue of Livia *orans* from Otriculum in central Italy. For this reworked statue, often dated to the second half of the first century CE and found in Otricoli in 1778–1779, see Alexandridis 2004, cat. no. 33.
153. Another fairly common type. A good example of it is another posthumous statue of Livia found in Veleia (now Velleia, Italy; currently in the Museo Nazionale di Antichità in Parma): Alexandridis 2004, cat. no. 30.
154. Moltesen 2007, 123–36.
155. Talamo 2011 identifies traces on the statue's head of pomegranate twigs entwined with a (white) wool thread, a symbolic decoration used by priestesses.
156. Moltesen 2007. That Agrippina's face was untouched contrasts the usual post-antique destruction of statues, especially their faces.
157. We return to the probable original location of the statue.
158. Højte 2005, 120; cp. the statue of Augustus that Agrippa wanted to put in the Pantheon but ended up placing in the porch (Cass. Dio 54.27.3).
159. Nero's "triumph" (see Champlin 2003, 212–13, 219–21) perhaps prompted removing Agrippina's statue from the shrine of the Aenatores, even closer to the route. Yet the proceedings missed at least one statue of Agrippina, which was later used to shame Nero: Cass. Dio 62.16.2[a].
160. Varner 2004, 99, suggests that Agrippina's Caelian statue and others were "warehoused" after her death. The remarkable Capitoline statue of Commodus as Hercules was preserved mostly intact by warehousing. A modern analogy might be the warehousing of some of the Confederate War Monuments in the United States.
161. After Agrippina's death Nero spent some months in Campania. The Fire of 64 started close to the Caelian and swept through the region (Tac. *Ann.* 15.38.2; Suet. *Nero* 38), severely damaging the shrine of the Aenatores.
162. Despite Vespasian's reported earlier fear of her (nn.59, 60, this chapter), Agrippina was integral to the principate. See Flower 2006, 193–94. A rehabilitation under the Flavians is suggested by the addition of Domitilla to her family monument at the Via Flaminia and her posthumous joint honor with Vespasian's wife on the Quirinal: Ch. 4, Ch. 6.
163. Pavolini 2007, 311, n.16, and Alexandridis 2004, 158 cat. no. 106, n.3, suggest the Isaeum, a shrine originating in the end of the Republic. For the palace, see HA, *Comm.* 16.3. Talamo 2007 suggests this location for both it and the "Victory of the Symmachi" statue also found in the wall.
164. Barrett 1996, 179, 238–40, suggests that after 55/56 Agrippina continued working politically, but more subtly than hitherto.
165. Trajan, a "good emperor" (r. 98–117), supposedly praised a *quinquennium* or five-year period in Nero's reign: Aur. Vict. *Caes.* 5.1–2 and *Epit. de Caes.* 5.1–3. Given the numerous setbacks Rome subsequently experienced, such as the rebellion in Britain in 60–61 and the Fire of Rome in 64, if this belief has any basis in reality, the reference would be to Nero's first five years. But many are cautious about the *quinquennium*: see Barrett et al. 2016, 22–24.
166. Tacitus introduces the year 56 with "inactivity abroad, disgusting immorality at home" (*Ann.* 13.25.1, *otium foris, foeda domi lascivia*, referring to Nero's actions). Famously, one of Nero's victims struck back: Tac. *Ann.* 13.25; Suet. *Nero* 26.
167. Nothing was as scandalous as those after 59, which included same-sex affairs and even "marriage" (e.g., Suet. *Nero* 28.1; Champlin 2003, 144–50), sexual abuse of elite women, public sexual violence against bound persons, and other acts the historians considered reprehensible. Acte, too, was said to be tolerated by Nero's advisors as a diversion from elite married women: Tac. *Ann.* 13.12.2. Compare the praise of Claudius' sexuality for his forbearance of adultery with elite women (see Ch. 4).
168. He reportedly recoiled from the noble and virtuous young woman: Tac. *Ann.* 13.12.2.
169. Wellebrouck 2017: Acte remained a trusted confidant, loyal (helping to bury Nero, Suet. *Nero* 50.1–3), esteemed (in 59 Seneca turned to her to dissuade Nero from incest with his mother: Tac. *Ann.* 14.2.1), and wealthy (18 freed and 14 enslaved dependents documented for her, contrasting Agrippina's at most 4 *liberti* and 14 enslaved: Chantraine 1980, 392, 394; Boatwright 2022).
170. Suet. *Nero* 28.2; Cass. Dio 61.11–12; Tac. *Ann.* 14.2. Cassius Dio has the Agrippina look-alike mistress provoke Poppaea to urge Nero to kill his mother.

171. Tac. *Ann.* 13.45–46, expatiating on her seduction of Nero. One husband was Otho, the later emperor. For this Poppaea Sabina, who would marry Nero only 12 days after Octavia's death in 62 (Suet. *Nero* 35.5), see FOS #646.
172. Tacitus later depicts her responsibility for the divorce and death of Octavia: *Ann.* 14.60–61.
173. Contra Messalina and Agrippina, she did not interfere with court cases or senatorial decisions (cf. Holztrattner 1995). For Poppaea, see (inter alia) Cass. Dio 62.28.1; Plin. *HN* 11.238, 28.183; Juv. 6.461–4.
174. Also named Rufrius Crispinus. He was one of Claudius' two praetorian prefects who flourished even after removal in 51 for Agrippina's substitute Burrus (see Ch. 4, n.125). For Poppaea's eponymous mother, see Ch. 3, n.120.
175. Tac. *Ann.* 13.42–43, *illum domus eius* (Germanicus) *adulterum fuisse...corrumpere cubicula principum feminarum.* The *cubicula principum feminarum* is ambiguous: it could be translated as I have above ("principes' women"), "of leading women," or simply as a rhetorical plural (pace Seita 1982, 316), so that both Tacitean references are to Julia Livilla (see Ch. 4). Suillius started with the charge that Seneca hated the friends of Claudius, under whom he had endured a most-deserved exile. Tacitus does not name Agrippina.
176. Cass. Dio 61.10.1, 6, with Barrett 1996, 162. Wilson 2014, 79, e.g., dismisses the allegation of adultery with Agrippina.
177. Cf. Cass. Dio 61.12; 61.20.3; 62.25.1–3.
178. Syme 1958, 308: removing someone from the narrative is a Tacitean way to build suspense.
179. Tac. *Ann.* 14.1; Cass. Dio 61.11.3 (cf. Suet. *Nero* 28.2). Cassius Dio adds that Seneca also urged Nero to rid himself of his mother.
180. At the very opening of Book 14: *cupientibus cunctis infringi potentiam matris et credente nullo usque ad caedem eius duratura filii odia*: Tac. *Ann.* 14.1, set in 59.
181. See Ch. 2 and the various omens at Nero's birth. Hug and Kelly 2022, 233–40, include a recent recapitulation of the "crisis" leading to Agrippina's death.
182. Tac. *Ann.* 14.9.3; Cass. Dio 61.2.2.
183. Tac. *Ann.* 13.21.4.
184. See Suet. *Nero* 33; Cass. Dio 60.35.4.
185. E.g., Barrett 2017, 69–70, citing Tac. *Ann.* 12.42.1 (appointment of Burrus as sole prefect), 13.18.2–3 (her welcoming tribunes and centurions into her house until Nero removed her guard), and 15.50.4 and 15.67.3 (still in 65, the praetorian prefect Faenius Rufus resented Agrippina's murder).
186. Tac. *Ann.* 14.7.5.
187. Suet. *Nero* 34.1: *Matrem facta dictaque sua exquirentem acerbius et corrigentem hactenus primo gravabatur, ut invidia identidem oneraret quasi cessurus imperio Rhodumque abiturus, mox et honore omni et potestate privavit abductaque militum et Germanorum statione contubernio quoque ac Palatio expulit; neque in divexanda quicquam pensi habuit, summissis qui et Romae morantem litibus et in secessu quiescentem per convicia et iocos terra marique praetervehentes inquietarent. Verum minis eius ac violentia territus perdere statuit.*
188. Tac. *Ann.* 14.1; Cass. Dio 61.11.3, adding (61.12.1) that Seneca too encouraged Nero to rid himself of Agrippina.
189. Artemidorus, *Oneirocritica* 1.79.3; translation in Hammond 2020. See Thonemann 2020, 73, 78, 84.
190. Tac. *Ann.* 13.20; see Syme 1958, 289–91; Martin 1981, 208–209. I return to *Ann.* 14.2.
191. Tac. *Ann.* 14.2.2: *sed quae Cluvius, eadem ceteri quoque auctores prodidere, et fama huc inclinat, seu concepit animo tantum immanitatis Agrippina, seu credibilior novae libidinis meditatio in ea visa est, quae puellaribus annis stuprum cum [M.] Lepido spe dominationis admiserat, pari cupidine usque ad libita Pallantis provoluta et exercita ad omne flagitium patrui nuptiis.* The whole exemplifies Tacitus' "weighted alternative" (Sullivan 1976, 318), in which piled-up details help convince the reader of the truth of one alternative over the other.
192. 61.11.3: "As if it were not notoriety enough for her that she had used her blandishments and immodest looks and kisses to seduce her uncle Claudius, she undertook to enslave even Nero in similar fashion" (Loeb tr.).
193. Suet. *Nero* 34 reports Agrippina's death; *Nero* 27–29 reports Nero's sexual practices.
194. Suet. *Nero* 27–29. Meister 2014, 67, notes this as one example of how "the same rumor could serve to discredit different persons—now Nero, now Agrippina, now both—according to received conceptual categories."

195. For Nero's pansexuality: e.g., Suet. *Nero* 28. Agrippina was only 44 at her death; her stamina is clear in the report that even though wounded she swam away from the contrived shipwreck in Baia (as we see at the end of this chapter).
196. Tac. *Ann.* 14.2, 4, 7, 8, 9, and 13; cp. Suet. *Nero* 34.4 and Cass. Dio 61.11.3–4; 61.12.1, discussed below. *Octavia* 125, 310–57, 955, the other major source for the death, is congruent; cf. Philostr. *Vit. Apoll.* 4.38.
197. See, e.g., Devillers 1995, Questa 1967. Also shared is Nero's final, prolonged embrace of his mother before she boarded the trick boat (Tac. *Ann.* 14.4.4; Suet. *Nero* 34.2; Cass. Dio 61.13.2).
198. Suetonius does not name the assassins. Tacitus and Cassius Dio, but not Suetonius, report Agrippina's last words, her command to her assassins to strike her first in her womb (Tac. *Ann.* 14.8.5, Cass. Dio 61.13.5; see end of this chapter).
199. Tac. *Ann.* 14.10 and 13; Suet. *Nero* 34.4; Cass. Dio 61.14.4.
200. Barrett et al. 2016, 56–57, compiles contradictions. For the shipwreck, whose far-fetched account raised skeptical laughter even when first reported to the senate (Tac. *Ann.* 14.11), see n.233, this chapter; Ash 2021.
201. Tac. *Ann.* 14.3.2; Suet. *Nero* 34, 2; Cass. Dio 61.12.2: In Suetonius (*Nero* 34.2) poison is unsuccessfully tried three times; in the other two authors its proposal is rejected (see further following note).
202. Tac. *Ann.* 14.3: poison would also be suspect because Britannicus had died that way.
203. Cass. Dio 61.12.2: Nero "did not dare to do anything in Rome, however, for fear the crime should become generally known." Tacitus' opening of Book 14, *Gaio Vips[t]ano [C.] Fonteio consulibus diu meditatum scelus non ultra Nero distulit*, suggests that Nero began actively plotting only in January 59.
204. Her relative insignificance in Suetonius' narrative fits the biographical focus on Nero.
205. See (e.g.) Ash 2021; Boatwright 2008; Baltussen 2002. Complications and deceptions include Agrippina's feigning not to understand her son's attempt to kill her (*Ann.* 14.16.1); poeticisms are notable in *noctem sideribus inlustrem et placido mari quietam quasi convincendum ad scelus dii praebuere*, and the hyperbolic description of public reaction to Agrippina's peril (14.5.1 and 8); paradoxes surface in the death of Acerronia and in Nero's statement that a "freedman [Anicetus] secured the empire for him" (14.5.3 and 14.7.5).
206. Keppie 2011.
207. A traditionally laudable combination, as in Thucydides' praise of Themistocles: 1.138.3.
208. Tac. *Ann.* 14.4.1, adding the misogynistic remark that Agrippina would swallow any rumor of reconciliation "with the gullibility of a woman receiving good news" *illuc matrem elicit, ferendas parentium iracundias et placandum animum dictitans, quo rumorem reconciliationis efficeret acciperetque Agrippina, facili feminarum credulitate ad gaudia.* Cass. Dio (61.12.3, 61.13.1) reports a long period of Nero's attentions to his mother as well as multiple shared feasts at Bauli, rendering Nero's matricide even ghastlier.
209. He did not invite her to his own residence. Bauli is not securely transmitted but generally agreed. Tiberius had died at Misenum in 37 (Suet. *Tib.* 72–73).
210. Underwater archaeology has recently revealed the villa and its refinements, some of which are exhibited in the Parco Archeologico dei Campi Flegrei in Baia, Italy.
211. According to Tacitus. Suet. *Nero* 34.2 has her go to the feast on a vessel that Nero has damaged during the dinner to substitute for it the booby-trapped ship.
212. Suet. *Otho* 3.1: Otho hosted this dinner. He was five years older than Nero.
213. Tac. *Ann.* 14.4, Suet. *Nero* 34.2, "kissing her breasts at their parting" (*atque in digressu papillas quoque exosculatus*)—stark contrast to his brief and perfunctory kisses after 55. See Davenport 2022, 304–306 (cf. Fronto, *Ad Antoninum Pium* 5 (ed. vdH 164 = Haines 1.226–8), for the "imperial kiss," the emperor's ceremonious kiss of senators and other high-ranking individuals on the lips to demonstrate that he was first among equals.
214. For Crepereius, see Levick and Jameson 1964. Acerronia (Polla) is the daughter of Cn. Acerronius Proculus (*cos.* 37) and sister of his same-named son who was governor of Achaea sometime after 44 (FOS #2; PIR^2 A 32–34; Barrett et al. 2016, 64, n.70, suggest the latter appointment came "possibly with Agrippina's support").
215. Cass. Dio 61.13.3 also indicates that the nighttime sea was trouble-free. The *Octavia* (309–76, 598–613; cf. Martial 4.63) anomalously depicts a turbulent sea: Ginsberg 2019.
216. Cass. Dio 61.13.3: the ship collapsed as planned, throwing Agrippina into the water; she then swam to shore unaided. Anicetus was on board to ensure the plot worked. *Octavia* 323–29 has everyone, including Agrippina, fall into the sea, wail, and strip off their clothes (to swim unencumbered?); Agrippina weeps profusely.

217. Cass. Dio 62.13.3 specifies the dark night and Agrippina's state as "full of drink," disparaging her but making her feat all the more remarkable.
218. Tac. *Ann.* 14.6.1.
219. For Agermus, see Eck 2022.
220. Tacitus sarcastically remarks, "at least this not through pretense" (Tac. *Ann.* 14.6).
221. Tac. *Ann.* 14.7.1: *tum pavore exanimis et iam iamque adfore obtestans vindictae properam, sive servitia armaret vel militem accenderet, sive ad senatum et populum pervaderet.*
222. Tac. *Ann.* 14.7.1, underscoring her continued resources and authority and hinting here that both advisors were in on the matricide. Cass. Dio 62.12.5 does not implicate the two, noting only that Nero would not entrust her killing to the praetorians.
223. The description begins, *Interim vulgato Agrippinae periculo, quasi casu evenisset*, "as if it were an accident!" (Tac. *Ann.* 14.8.1).
224. Tacitus puts the query into direct speech, rendering it the more poignant. Herculeius was a trierarch and Obaritus a fleet centurion (Tac. *Ann.* 14.8.2–4).
225. The *uterum* (uterus) of Tac. *Ann.* 14.8.5 succinctly expresses what others make explicit: "Strike here, Anicetus, strike here, for this bore Nero" (Cass. Dio 61.13.5); "This, this that bore such a monster, the sword should pierce" (*Octavia* 369–72). The scene echoes Clytemestra baring her breast and inviting her son Orestes to strike it (Aesch. *Cho.* 896).
226. Cass. Dio 61.14.1; not in Tacitus. For other expressions of this irony, see Ch. 6.
227. We have seen other ghastly bodily inspections, such as Agrippina checking Lollia Paulina's teeth (Ch. 4). Cassius Dio (62.14.1) holds that when told of Agrippina's death, Nero was overcome with disbelief, "because of the enormity of the crime." An individual claiming to be Nero gained popularity 20 years after his death in 68 (Suet. *Nero* 57).
228. Respectively, Tac. *Ann.* 14.9.1; Suet. *Nero* 34.4; Cass. Dio 62.14.2.
229. For these details of Tacitus' presentation (Tac. *Ann.* 14.9.1–2, including *incertum caritate in patronam an metu exitii*), not echoed in other accounts, see Boatwright 2008.
230. Tac. *Ann.* 14.9.1. The tomb has never been located, although Roman remains in Bacoli have long been called the "Sepolcro di Agrippina": Keppie 2009, 30, 62.
231. Tac. *Ann.* 14.10.1; Suet. *Nero* 34.4; *Octavia* 593–645; Cass. Dio 62.14.4, who adds that imagined military trumpet songs made him repeatedly move, a report Tacitus echoes (Tac. *Ann.* 14.10.3).
232. Cass. Dio 62.14.3 is the only source specifying that Nero gave money to the praetorians. This was crucial in light of their loyalty to Agrippina as Germanicus' child and their part in the assassination of Caligula (see above, Ch. 2)
233. Cass. Dio 62.14.3; Tac. *Ann.* 14.10.3–11.3. Tacitus holds that the latter incredible point raised the senators' sardonic laughter: no shipwrecked woman would ever send a lone man against the emperor. The historian adds that this part of the letters turned attention to Seneca, considered the author of Nero's official line. Quint. *Inst.* 8.5.18 identifies this letter as Seneca's work.
234. Tac. *Ann.* 14.12.1.
235. Suet. *Nero* 34.4 (soldiers, senate, and the people); Tac. *Ann.* 14.10.2 (centurions and tribunes commanded by the praetorian prefect Burrus; towns of Campania) and 14.12.1 (Rome's nobles and senate, other than Thrasea Paetus). For P. Clodius Thrasea Paetus, see PIR^2 C 1187.
236. Tacitus also here notes the removal of Agrippina as the last curb of Nero's depravity (*Ann.* 14.13).
237. For the route, see Champlin 2003, 212–13, 219–21.

Chapter 6

1. *Oct.* 598–600, 609–13: *manet inter umbras impiae caedis mihi / semper memoria, manibus nostris grauis / adhuc inultis…saeuit in nomen ferus /* (610) *matris tyrannus, obrui meritum cupit. / simulacra, titulos destruit mortis metu / totum per orbem, quem dedit poenam in meam / puero regendum noster infelix amor.* For this work, written soon after Nero's death in 68, see Intro., n.7.
2. See Kragelund 2007, 34; Ginsberg 2017, 172. The senatorial decrees, that Agrippina's birthday be among the *dies nefasti* and that the Quinquatrus be celebrated by annual games (Tac. *Ann.* 14.12.1; Ch. 5, n.234), ironically perpetuated her memory.
3. Kragelund 2007, 27; Flower 2006, 189–94.
4. Alexandridis 2004, Table 1. The next-highest numbers in Alexandridis' catalog are 17 for Sabina and 16 for Julia Domna. Ginsburg 2006, 79, identifies 15 statue groups with Agrippina.

5. The notable paucity of her attested *familia*, however, resembles that of Livilla and Messalina, both of whom suffered official memory sanctions: see Boatwright 2022. Agrippina's removal from the Shrine of the Aenatores (Ch. 5) may simply have been one group's reaction to her defamation. Varner 2001 surveys memory sanctions against imperial women.
6. For Agrippina in film, see Bell 2015 and Pucci 2007.
7. Wilhelm Xylander's Latin translation of Cassius Dio appeared in 1558: Millar 1964, 1–3; Manuwald 2013, 20.
8. For the events leading to Britannicus' death, which Tacitus holds were triggered by Agrippina's threats to favor him over Nero (Tac. *Ann.* 13.14.2–17), see Ch. 5.
9. Tac. *Ann.* 13.21.5: see Ch. 5. Apparently, nothing happened to Rubellius Plautus until three years after Agrippina's death, indicating his innocence of any plot with her.
10. Tac. *Ann.* 14.11.3. Ash 2021, 220, stresses how Tacitus' "theatricality" in narrating Agrippina's murder emphasizes Nero's transgressive acts.
11. There is no mention of any in Suetonius or Cassius Dio.
12. Neither Suetonius nor Cassius Dio relate anything about Agrippina after her death.
13. Faenius Rufus, a supporter of Agrippina whom she had rewarded with the grain supply prefecture in 55 and who was later defamed by Nero's minion Tigellinus as an adulterer of Agrippina keen to avenge her, was in the Pisonian conspiracy (Tac. *Ann.* 13.22.1, 15.50.3); the wealthy P. Anteius, whom Nero hated for his affection of Agrippina, was brought down in 66 (Tac. *Ann.* 16.14); Thrasea Paetus' refusal to participate in senatorial debates about Agrippina in 59 contributed to his unjust death in 66 (Tac. *Ann.* 16.21). For the Pisonian conspiracy, see Tac. *Ann.* 15.48–74.
14. For the history of Nero's later reign, see various works cited in Intro., n.46.
15. See, e.g., the Juvenalia in 59 (Cass. Dio 61.19.1; Suet. *Nero* 12.3); the Neronia (Tac. *Ann.* 20–21); Tiridates' crowning (Suet. *Nero* 13.1–2, 30; Cass. Dio 63.1–4, 63.6; Plin. *HN* 33.54).
16. See, e.g., Tac. *Ann.* 15.38- 41, 44–45; Suet. *Nero* 38, 16.2.2; Cass. Dio 62.16–17; Lactant. *De mort. pers.* 2.5–7; Euseb. *Hist. eccl.* 2.25.1–5.
17. Ginsberg 2017, 25–26, 172–75.
18. Manuwald 2013, 1–7, noting Busenello and Monteverdi's *L'incoronazione di Poppea* (1642–1643) as the first historical opera.
19. Plin. *HN* 1.7b.3: "Agrippina Claudi" as a source; her *commentarii* noted also in *HN* 7.46. The first 10 books of Pliny the Elder's *Historia Naturalis* were published in 77 and the rest after his death in 79. References below are from the database *Classical Latin Texts* of the Packard Humanities Institute, https://latin.packhum.org/.
20. Respectively, *HN* 7.71.6, 10.84.40, 10.120.2. I group here also Pliny's notes that Crispus Passienus, already eminent, became more famous through his marriage to Agrippina and his stepson Nero (16.242.5) and that she wore a gold *paludamentum* at the celebrations for the Fucine Lake's drainage (33.63.3).
21. *HN* 35.201; see Ch. 4, n.135.
22. *HN* 22.92.4.
23. *HN* 7.45.7 criticizes the two Agrippinas for bearing Caligula and Nero, who were so injurious to the world; 7.46.6 notes her breech birth of Nero, "the enemy of the human race during his entire principate."
24. Joseph. *AJ* 20.6.3; 20.8.1–2; *BJ* 2.12.8. His *Jewish War* appeared in 75–79; *Jewish Antiquities* was published around 93/94. Also notable is Josephus' report (*AJ* 20.154–57) that some historians actually praised Nero: see Champlin 2003, 24–25.
25. 5.146–48; 6.620–23 by name. His *Satires* were published in the 110s and 120s, but their relationship to Tacitus' *Annals* remains obscure: Syme 1958, 776–77.
26. 6.115–32; 10.329–45; 14.329–31, respectively.
27. Suet. *Vesp.* 9.
28. *CIL* VI 40452 = EDCS-00900157. Both women were dead.
29. Alföldy, Kolb, et al. (1996) at *CIL* VI.8.2 p. 4352, suggests the inscription implies rehabilitation of Agrippina in the new regime; W. Eck (personal communication) warns against arguing anything from this very uncertain inscription. Agrippina's enslaved *familia* had been transferred into the imperial fiscus (see Boatwright 2022, 112–13).
30. *CIL* VI 893 = EDCS-17301021, see von Hesberg and Panciera 1996, 148–61; and Ch. 4, n.184. For Titus, Suet. *Titus* 2; Tac. *Ann.* 13.16.
31. See, e.g., Eck 1993, 75–76; Boatwright 2021, 207–208.

32. Boatwright 1991.
33. Alexandridis 2004 catalogs only images with fairly secure provenances and adequate diagnostic remains.
34. Cristilli 2020 publishes a recent example from Lucus Feroniae north of Rome.
35. Personal communication from J. Dähner, 4/4/22, who kindly also told me that the head, sold to J. Paul Getty in Rome in 1939 and donated to the J. Paul Getty Museum in 1970, was found before or in 1933. It was identified as Livia Drusilla (Livia) until Hermine Speier re-identified it as Agrippina the Younger before sale to Getty interests.
36. See, e.g., Boschung 1993b, 8–10. Such typological studies also consider the rare busts and statues found with an identifying inscription or secure provenance. Ch. 4 and Ch. 5 discuss examples of sculptural installations in Rome epigraphically attested to have included images of Agrippina that are now lost.
37. Another complication is that at least in the first century, identified women on coins were shown in profile. See below for the assimilation of imperial women to others in their family, which also varies Agrippina the Younger's depicted physiognomy (see Ill. 4.3 and Ill. 5.3).
38. See, e.g., Trillmich 2007, 48, on the importance of hairstyles for identification of imperial women's portraits.
39. Tac. *Ann.* 14.10.3–11.3; cf. Cass. Dio 62.16.2ª. See the opening of this chapter.
40. Two of the four are derived from coin portraits; the other two are generally accepted for their physiognomic similarities to the first two. In the following I depend on Trillmich 2007, who provides a full bibliography. These four types are generally accepted (see, e.g., Alexandridis 2004; Boschung 1993a, 73–74).
41. Trillmich 2007, 49.
42. Trillmich 2007, 48–49; on each side there is more than one corkscrew curl. Wood 1988, 419–20, notes also that this group tends to show a "short, broad face with a low forehead, a small, thin-lipped mouth, and a distinct overbite which causes the lower lip to retreat slightly," and that all these are features of Germanicus' line. For coins, see, e.g., Ill. 4.1 = *RIC*² I, Claudius no. 75 (British Museum: 1844,0425.732). Didrachms from Caesarea also have this type: e.g., *RIC*² I, Nero no. 607.
43. Trillmich 2007, 49–51.
44. Wood 1999, 246–47, noting the rarity of the type, suggests the treatment of the hair in waves at the central part was due to recutting Messalina's portraits in 49.
45. Trillmich 2007, 51–52. The 2.03 m H standing statue of Ill. 6.2, now in the Museo Archeologico Nazionale of Parma, Italy, was found in the forum of ancient Velleia in 1761. See Alexandridis 2004, 162–63 cat. no. 114.
46. This contrasts with the flat treatment to either side of the middle part found in the three other types. For the "Stuttgart" head, see Wood 1999, 298 and fig. 138.
47. Trillmich 2007, 52–54; Wood 1988, 420.
48. Trillmich 2007, 55–57, dated from Caligula's reign to the adoption of Nero.
49. Pangerl 2019/1920.
50. Perhaps its first identification as a portrait of Livia (see n.35, this chapter) derives from the remains of the rolled-back hair, which looks as though it was to be gathered into Livia's characteristic chignon.
51. See, e.g., Smith 1987, 131; Trillmich 2007, 46.
52. See Zanker 1982, with discussion by, e.g., D'Ambra 2013, 518, and Fejfer 2008, 270–79. The concept holds that in their portraits non-imperial individuals mimicked imperial hairstyles, facial hair, and other physiognomic details such as treatment of the eyes and set of the mouth.
53. This conclusion rests partly on the slighter evidence for images of imperial women than of imperial men: even the highest estimate for known portraits of Livia, whose sculpted likeness is more common than that of other imperial women, is about 110: Brännstedt 2015, 44 (with epigraphic testimony for about 80 more now lost). The number of extant statues and busts of Augustus is calculated as some 250, with those of Hadrian about 150. Højte 2005 counts over 200 statue bases for Augustus and over 400 for Hadrian.
54. See, e.g., Davies 2008.
55. Dimensions: 128.27 × 33.02 × 26.67 cm. Marble. MIA, The William Hood Dunwoody Fund, inv. no. 32.16, now in Gallery 241. I thank the curator, Alyson Fulton-Kern, of the Minneapolis Institute of Art for information about this statue (1/22/24). The sculpture's entry in Kleiner and Matheson 1996, 145–46 no. 79, suggests this piece was from a civic or votive dedication rather than a funerary monument.

56. That the body type and dress (as well as hairstyle) here are idealized and youthful is common in female portraiture for older women (Matheson 2000, 126–28).
57. With very rare exceptions, Roman imperial women are not depicted with such signs of aging, not even Livia, who died at age 86: Matheson 2000, 130–32.
58. The piece, reportedly from Pompeii and once in the collection of the King of Naples, went through the Paris and then the New York art market: Kleiner and Matheson 1996, 145–46 no. 79.
59. 80 × 55 × 55 cm, face 62 cm from chin to top of head; no restorations. See Wood 1999, 302–304, figures 143–44; Fittschen and Zanker 1983, 6–7, no. 5, with earlier literature. Parisi Presicce et al. 2017, 438–39 cat. no. 43: "Testa ritratto fragmentaria femminile colossale" (L. Ungaro) dates this to 112. I thank Dott.essa Ungaro for discussion of this piece.
60. See, e.g., Fittschen and Zanker 1983, 6–7, no. 5, noting Trajanic characteristics.
61. See Boschung and Eck 1998, 473, n.1, citing earlier scholars about the vexed identification.
62. Boschung and Eck 1998. A squarish hole at the nape of the head earlier suggested that the head was once affixed to a shield (see, e.g., Wood 1999, 303); Parisi Presicce et al. 2017, 438 cat. no. 43 (L. Ungaro), holds that cleaning and re-examination of the piece indicates the head was attached to a statue.
63. Boschung and Eck 1998, 479–80.
64. Boschung and Eck 1998, 480–81.
65. Boschung and Eck 1998, 478–79. Ungaro 2017 discusses sculptures of Trajan's family from the Forum of Trajan.
66. See Trillmich 2007, 46. The argument incidentally relies on the concept of *Zeitgesicht*. Writing a decade earlier than Boschung and Eck but considering the same second-century context, Wood 1988, 424–25, argues that "Agrippina's presence in the sculptural program…must have been intended in part to demonstrate sympathy for the victim of Nero's most notorious political murder. Trajan…must have wished to encourage comparisons between his own *pietas* and Nero's lack of it."
67. See, e.g., Conte 1994, 542–43, noting traces of familiarity with the *Annals* only in the (fourth-century) Ammianus Marcellinus and in the Christian Sulpicius Severus, Orosius, Sidonius Apollinaris, and Cassiodorus. The two manuscripts are now known as the First and Second Medicean. For the Second, which begins in *Annals* 11, breaks off in *Annals* 16, and includes *Histories* 1 through part of 5, see Malloch 2013, 9–11.
68. W. Ryan 2012, xi–xii (in introduction by E. Duffy): ca. 1,000 manuscript copies in Latin, ca. 500 with vernacular translations of all or parts; at least 87 Latin editions, and 69 in various vernaculars printed between 1470 and 1500 alone. See also Park 2006, 155; Frazer 1971, 215.
69. Nero appears more incidentally in the *Golden Legend* in the lives of Saints Nazarius and Celsus and in the "Life of Saints Dionysius, Rusticus, and Eleutherius."
70. Translated in W. Ryan 2012, 346–47.
71. Nero is said to have died by sharpening a stake with his own teeth and driving it through his middle, or by being eaten by wolves.
72. In keeping with the era's general ignorance of Tacitus' later *Annals*.
73. Jacobus generally credits "a certain history, admittedly apocryphal" (W. Ryan 2012, 346–47; cf. ibid. xvii, Duffy's introduction), although he attributes to Orosius a detail on Nero's same-sex relationship. See also Frazer 1971, 215.
74. *Nero* 34: *atrociora…nec incertis auctoribus.*
75. *Cons.* 2.m6.3–7: *fratre qui quondam ferus interempto/matris effuse maduit cruore/*[5] *corpus et visu gelidum pererrans/ora non tinxit lacrimis, sed esse/censor exstincti potuit decoris.* Cropp 2007, 23–24, emphasizes the medieval elaboration of "Nero the Tyrant," tracing it in part to the earliest known French translation (c. 1230) of Boethius, *De Consolatione Philosophiae* 2.m6. See also Minnis 1981.
76. This also dates to the 13th century (Park 2006, 328, n.89; Minnis 1981, 319, 325–28).
77. See the Getty Museum ms. 33 (88.MP.70), fol. 226, a German manuscript illustration on parchment by Jansen Enikel created in Regensburg about 1400–1410 (leaf: 33.5 × 23.5 cm, or 13 3/16 × 9 ¼ in): https://www.getty.edu/art/collection/objects/2005/unknown-jansen-enikel-nero-giving-birth-to-a-toad-german-about-1400-1410/. The crowned and bearded Nero lies in his sickbed surrounded by attendants, and his "child" frog is in a basket at the bed's foot.
78. It appears even on an Italian majolica plate from the 16th century now in the National Museum of Ecouen, France (inv. no. ECL7529). By the 15th century, illustrations of other references to Agrippina and Nero reflect this story: for example, an illustration in Boccaccio's *De Mulieribus*

Claris now in the British Library, MS Royal 20 C V, f. 139 (ca. 1410), shows a robed and crowned Agrippina held up against a column by her hands (bound behind her) while a surgeon cuts into her womb in front of Nero (*non vidi*). This is not in Boccaccio's text.

79. Carlino 1988, 33: 1316 marks the appearance of the first didactic manual to deal with the technical details of anatomy, the *Anatomia* of Mundinus da Luzzi (Bologna); the earliest documented dissection of a human body took place at the University of Padua in 1341. *Andreae Vesalii suorum de humani corporis fabrica librorum epitome*, the abridgement of Vesalius' great work *De humani corporis fabrica libri septem*, appeared in 1543.
80. Carlino 1988, e.g. 34; Sawday 1995, e.g. 54–63, emphasizes the centrality of "the dignity [of] the anatomist" to public anatomical demonstrations up through the age of Vesalius.
81. Park 2006, 211–14; on 214 she notes that medical faculties perennially commented on and complained about the lack of female cadavers. Women were judged and punished at home.
82. Now in the Getty Museum: 96.MR.17.224v (object number); Ms. 63, fol. 224v (manuscript number). See https://www.getty.edu/art/collection/objects/105191/boucicaut-master-or-workshop-nero-pauses-for-a-drink-during-the-mutilation-of-his-mother's-body-french-about-1413-1415/. The leaf measures 42 × 29.6 cm (16 9/16 × 11 5/8 in.). I thank Getty Museum curators Elizabeth Morrison and David Brafman for alerting me to this image and discussing it with me.
83. Illustration from Ms. Harley 4425, f. 59r, ca. 1490 to ca. 1500, from south Netherlands (Bruges), now in the British Library, London. https://www.foliamagazine.it/en/nero-and-agrippina/.
84. To the left is even a basin for discarding parts cut away during a dissection.
85. Rebecca Messbarger has suggested to me that what is being lifted is the *omentum*, a layer of beaded fat that covers the organs of the lower abdomen, which themselves have the shape of a fertile womb. I thank her for formative discussions about dissection in this period.
86. Attendant personnel can include barber surgeons, an *ostentor* who directs the cutting, and students and discussants such as a teacher who explains the procedure: Carlino 1988.
87. Park 2006, 207–13.
88. Park 2006, 235–38: other such stories from Roman antiquity, such as that of Julius Caesar's birth by Caesarian section, served the same purpose.
89. Beard 2021, 265–69, with quotation from 268.
90. Conte 1994, 543; Reynolds 1983, 407–408 (R. J. Tarrant).
91. That Nero is beardless in these paintings corresponds to greater awareness of the actual history of this period, since in 59 he was not yet 22.
92. For the Prix de Rome, see https://eclecticlight.co/2021/07/04/creme-de-la-creme-winners-of-the-prix-de-rome-for-painting-2/. Beardsley's prints date from 1895 and 1896, when he was making his own translation of Juvenal, *Satire* 6.
93. Now in the Staatliche Gemäldegalerie, Kassel in Germany (inv. no. GK 581).
94. https://commons.wikimedia.org/wiki/File:Antonio_Zanchi_-_The_Death_of_Agrippina.jpg.
95. For the painting by Luca Ferrari (also called Luca da Reggio) in the Galleria Estense in Modena, see https://www.art-prints-on-demand.com/a/ferrari-luca-luca-da-regg/the-death-of-cleopatra-1.html.
96. Now in the Museo del Prado, Madrid, inv. no. P006371; 331 H × 500 W cm; painted in Rome.
97. This (407 × 277 cm) is now in Cremona, Palazzo del Comune, Sala della Consulta. In 1894 it won first prize in the History Painting section of the Fumagalli competition: https://www.lombardiabeniculturali.it/opere-arte/schede/CR160-00246/.
98. See https://www.christies.com/en/lot/lot-1664022, referring to A. Riccoboni, "Antonio Zanchi e La Pittura Veneziana del Seicento," *Saggi e Memorie di storia dell'Arte*, 5, 1966, pp. 83 and 97, fig. 87, and noting that the composition echoes the theme of the Rape of Helen.
99. See Ginsberg 2019.
100. The whole, 160 cm × 240.5 cm, is now in a private museum: https://commons.wikimedia.org/wiki/File:Gustav_Wertheimer_-_Der_Schiffbruch_der_Agrippina.jpg.
101. Boccaccio 2001, xi–xv, also detailing the stages of the work's composition and its dedicatee. In the following, I use the translation of *De Mulieribus Claris* by its editor and translator, V. Brown.
102. Dated 1355–1360, but with revisions until 1374: Boccaccio 2001, xi.
103. Boccaccio 2001, Praef. 4–5. Petrarch's *De viris illustribus* spurred Boccaccio's work: ibid., xii and Praef. 1.

104. Boccaccio 2001, Praef. 5–7.
105. Brown (Boccaccio 2001, 499) notes his sources for this *Life* as Suet. *Claud.* 44 and *Nero* 5.3, 28.2, 34.1–4, and Tac. *Ann.* 12.1–10, 64–69, 14.1–9. Malloch 2013, 12 (focusing on Claudius' era) lists parallels with Tac. *Ann.* 11.38, 12.1, 12.6, 12.9, 12.26, 12.42, 12.67, 14.3.
106. Reynolds 1983, 399–404 (M. Winterbottom), pointing out Boccaccio's fascination with Suetonius.
107. See, e.g., Conte 1994, 542–43.
108. Malloch 2013, 12–13; Reynolds 1983, 407–408 (R. J. Tarrant). The manuscript, Laurentianus Mediceus 68.2, now is in the Laurentian Library in Florence. Boccaccio turned to this manuscript for the four subsequent lives in *De Mulieribus Claris*, *Lives* 93–96 ("Epicharis, A Freedwoman," "Pompeia Paulina, Wife of Seneca," and "Sabina Poppaea, Wife of Nero" derive from the later *Annals*, and "Triaria, Wife of Lucius Vitellius," from *Histories* 2 and 3); see Boccaccio 2001, 499–500. Boccaccio used Tacitus' account of Seneca's death (*Ann.* 15.62–64) for his commentary on Dante's *Divina Commedia*: Conte 1994, 543; Manuwald 2013, 19.
109. Boccaccio 2001, *Life* 92.1: *genere, consanguinitate, imperio et monstruositate filii ac sua non minus quam claris facinoribus emicuit* (translation based on Brown, ibid. 385).
110. *Life* 92.3, cf. Suet. *Calig.* 24.1. In the report in *De Mulieribus Claris* Agrippina is "most beautiful" and Caligula a "disgusting man" (*formosissima*... *homo spurcissimus*). Boccaccio also calls her husband Ahenobarbus "austere and most haughty" (*fastidiosissimo atque gravi*, *Life* 92.2).
111. *Life* 92.3 and 92.4 (*decora pulchritudine sua*).
112. The reference to Lepidus and Pallas comes from Tac. *Ann.* 14.2.2.
113. *Life* 92.13.
114. Boccaccio calls her an *astutissima mulier* (*Life* 92.7).
115. For example, she is one of 302 women in Mary Hays, *Female Biography* (published in Latin in 1803; see Keegan 2018; Walker 2018). Agrippina the Elder, legendarily faithful to her husband Germanicus, makes it into Christine de Pizan, *Cité des Dames* (1405), but her daughter does not. "Agrippina" is included (as card S514) in the 1897 "Famous Women" trading card set available with Liebig's Meat Extract products. The military costume suggests that this famous woman is Agrippina the Elder.
116. Ketterer 2009, e.g., 15, noting the spread of Italian librettos to England, Spain, and Austria.
117. Manuwald 2013, 2; on p. 4 she also notes that this seems to be the first opera on a historical event.
118. Manuwald 2013, 4.
119. Ketterer 2009, 2; he also points out (ibid., 75) that by 1679 librettists and others clearly knew well Nero's reputation as a plundering, brutalizing, and raping tyrant.
120. Ketterer 2009, 7–14.
121. Ketterer 2009, 66; Manuwald 2013, 25, 170 (attributing the libretto definitively to Grimani).
122. Manuwald 2013, 34, notes that Agrippina's scheming "makes her often a significant figure in the plot" of Nero operas. From the 22 operas on the Nero theme catalogued by Manuwald 2013, 6–7, two earlier operas are also named for her: *Agrippina in Baia* (1687) and *L'Agrippina* (1703). In this book I do not treat Daniel Casper von Lohenstein's spoken drama *Agrippina* (1665).
123. For detailed synopsis of the opera's plot and history, see Manuwald 2013, 170–80; Ketterer 2009, 66–76.
124. One great exception is when Agrippina beguiles Poppea by promising the younger woman that she is trustworthy and has only Poppea's interests at heart.
125. In 43 Agrippina was not yet wed to Claudius, and Nero was six years old. See also van Zyl Smit 2019, 2–3.
126. Manuwald 2013, 171–72.
127. In 2020 it was staged with a contemporary setting (in 2000 McVicar had done the same in his production of the opera in Brussels), fitting the lack of agreement on any contextualized political interpretation of the opera (e.g., as criticism of the Vatican). See Manuwald 2013, 170–71; Ketterer 2009, 69; van Zyl Smit 2019, 5.
128. Van Zyl Smit 2019, especially 5.
129. See Boatwright 2021, 46 and passim.
130. E.g., Momigliano 1934, 76.
131. One can compare the later treatment of Messalina.

Bibliography

Alexandrescu, C.-G. 2007. "The Iconography of Wind Instruments in Ancient Rome: Cornua, Bucina, Tuba, and Lituus." *Music in Art* 32: 33–46.

Alexandridis, A. 2004. *Die Frauen des römischen Kaiserhauses: Eine Untersuchung ihrer bildlichen Darstellung von Livia bis Iulia Domna.* Mainz am Rhein.

Alföldy, G., A. Kolb et al., ed. 1996. *Corpus Inscriptionum Latinarum.* VI.8.2. *Titulos imperatorum domusque eorum thesauro schedarum imaginumque ampliato.* Berlin.

Ambühl, A. 2022. "The Flavians and Their Women: Rewriting Neronian Transgressions?" In *Flavian Responses to Nero's Rome*, ed. M. Heerink and E. Meijer, 55–86. Amsterdam.

Angelova, D. 2015. *Sacred Founders: Women, Men, and Gods in the Discourse of Imperial Founding, Rome through Early Byzantium.* Berkeley.

Argetsinger, K. 1992. "Birthday Rituals: Friends and Patrons in Roman Poetry and Cult." *Classical Antiquity* 11: 175–93.

Ash, R. 2021. "The Staging of Death: Agrippina the Younger and the Dramatic Turn." In *Usages of the Past in Roman Historiography*, ed. A. D. Poulsen and A. Jönsson, 197–224. Leiden.

Aveline, J. 2004. "The Death of Claudius." *Historia* 53: 453–75.

Baltussen, H. 2002. "Matricide Revisited: Dramatic and Rhetorical Allusion in Tacitus, Suetonius and Cassius Dio." *Antichthon* 36: 30–40.

Barbera, M. 2021. *Donne romane in esilio a Ventotene: L'opposizione politica femminile tra Augusto e Domiziano.* Genoa-Ventotene.

Barrett, A, A. 1990. *Caligula: The Corruption of Power.* New Haven.

Barrett, A. A. 1991. "Claudius' Victory Arch in Rome." *Britannia* 22: 1–19.

Barrett, A. A. 1996. *Agrippina: Sex, Power, and Politics in the Early Empire.* New Haven.

Barrett, A. A. 2002. *Livia: First Lady of Imperial Rome.* New Haven.

Barrett, A. A. 2005. "Aulus Caecina Severus and the Military Woman." *Historia* 54: 301–14.

Barrett, A. A. 2017. "Nero's Women." In *The Cambridge Companion to the Age of Nero*, ed. S. Bartsch, K. Freudenburg, and C. Littlewood, 63–76. Cambridge.

Barrett, A. A., E. Fantham, and J. C. Yardley, eds. 2016. *The Emperor Nero: A Guide to the Ancient Sources.* Princeton, NJ.

Barrett, A. A. and J. C. Yardley. 2023. *The Emperor Caligula in the Ancient Sources.* Oxford.

Bartman, E. 2001. "Hair and the Artifice of Roman Female Adornment." *AJA* 105: 1–25.

Bartsch, S., K. Freudenburg, and C. Littlewood, eds. 2017. *The Cambridge Companion to the Age of Nero.* Cambridge.

Barzano, A. 2011. "La politica dinastica di Caligola e la cosiddetta congiura del 39 d.C." *Aevum* 85: 65–80.

Bauman, R. 1994. "Tanaquil-Livia and the Death of Augustus." *Historia* 43: 177–88.

Beard, M. 2021. *Twelve Caesars. Images of Power from the Ancient World to the Modern.* Princeton, NJ.

Bell, B. 2015. "Agrippina im Film." In *Agrippina: Kaiserin aus Köln*, ed. M. Trier and F. Naumann-Steckner, 102–109. Cologne.

Bellemore, J. 1995. "The Wife of Sejanus." *ZPE* 109: 255–66.

Belli Pasqua, R. 1995. *Sculture di età romana in "basalto."* Rome.

Belli Pasqua, R. 2018. "Forme della propaganda imperial nel Dodecaneso: un ritratto di Agrippina minore da Kos." *Archeologia Classica* n.s. 8: 333–55.

Benoist, S. 2005. *Rome, le prince et la cité: Pouvoir impérial et cérémonies publiques (Ier siècle av.—début du IVe siècle apr. J.-C.* Paris.

Benoist, S., ed. 2013. "Autour de Germanicus." In *Cahiers du Centre Gustave Glotz* 24: 105–204.

Birley, A. 2007. "Sejanus: His Fall." In *Corolla Cosmo Rodewald. Monograph Series Akanthina* 2, ed. N. Sekunda, 121–50. Gdansk.

Boatwright, M. T. 1984. "Tacitus on Claudius and the Pomerium of Rome: *Annals* 12.23.1-24." *CJ* 80: 36–44.

Boatwright, M. T. 1991. "Imperial Women of the Early Second Century A.C." *AJP* 112: 513–40.

Boatwright, M. T. 2008. "Tacitus and the Final Rites of Agrippina: *Annals* 14, 9." In Vol. XIV of *Studies in Latin Literature and Roman History*, Collection Latomus vol. 315, 375–93.

Boatwright, M. T. 2021. *Imperial Women of Rome: Power, Gender, Context*. Oxford.

Boatwright, M. T. 2022. "The Missing *Familia* of Agrippina the Younger." In *Emperor, Army, and Society. Studies of Roman Imperial History for Anthony R. Birley*, ed. W. Eck, F. Santangelo, and K. Vössing, 107–16. Bonn.

Boccaccio, Giovanni. 2001. *Famous Women*. Edited and translated by V. Brown. Cambridge, MA.

Bodel, J. 2008. "From Columbaria to Catacombs: Collective Burial in Pagan and Christian Rome." In *Commemorating the Dead: Texts and Artifacts in Context*, ed. L. Brink and D. Green, 177–242. Berlin.

Boschung, D. 1993a. "Die Bildnistypen der iulisch-claudischen Kaiserfamilie. Ein kritischer Forschungsbericht." *JRA* 6: 39–79.

Boschung, D. 1993b. *Das römische Herrscherbild*. I, 2. *Die Bildnisse des Augustus*. Berlin.

Boschung, D. and W. Eck. 1998. "Ein Bildnis der Mutter Traians? Um Kolossalkopf der sogenannte Agrippina Minor vom Traiansforum." *AA* 3: 473–81.

Bradley, K. R. 1978. *Suetonius'* Life of Nero. *An Historical Commentary*. Brussels.

Brännstedt, L. 2015. "Livia on the Move." In *The Moving City: Processions, Passages and Promenades in Ancient Rome*, ed. I. Östenberg, S. Malmberg, and J. Bjørnebye, 37–46. London.

Brennan, T. C. 2022. *The Fasces. A History of Ancient Rome's Most Dangerous Political Symbol*. Oxford.

Bruno, V. T. and E. L. Will. 1985. "The Island of Pontia: A Nautical Survey." *Archaeology* 38: 40–47.

Buonocore, M. 2007. "Le iscrizioni ad Augusto e alla sua *domus* nelle città dell'Italia centro-appenninica (regio IV)." In *Contributi all'epigrafia d'età Augustea*, ed. G. Paci, 31–90. Tivoli.

Carandini, A. 2018. *Io, Agrippina. Sorella, moglie, madre d'imperatori*. Rome.

Carandini, A. and P. Carafa, ed. 2017. *The Atlas of Ancient Rome: Biography and Portraits of the City*. English language ed., tr. A. C. Halavais. Princeton, NJ.

Carlino, A. 1988. "The Book, the Body, the Scalpel: Six Engraved Title Pages from Anatomical Treatises of the First Half of the Sixteenth Century." *RES: Anthropology and Aesthetics* 16: 33–50.

Carlon, J. M. 2009. *Pliny's Women: Constructing Virtue and Creating Identity in the Roman World*. Cambridge.

Cenerini, F. 2010. "Messalina e il suo matrimonio con C. Silio." In *Herrschaftsstrukturen und Herrschaftspraxis. 2: "Augustae": machtbewusste Frauen am römischen Kaiserhof? Akten der Tagung in Zürich, 18.-20.9.2008*, ed. A. Kolb, 179–91. Berlin.

Champlin, E. 2003. *Nero*. Cambridge, MA.

Chantraine, H. 1980. "Freigelassene und Sklaven kaiserlicher Frauen." In *Studien zur antiken Sozialgeschichte. Festschrift Friedrich Vittinghoff*, ed. W. Eck, H. Galsterer, and H. Wolff, 389–416. Cologne and Vienna.

Chrol, E. D. and S. H. Blake. 2022. "Sexuality and the Court." In Kelly and Hug 2022, I.349–70.

Cioncoloni, R. and R. Sorella. 2019. "Un contesto di età giulio-claudia da scavi inediti all'Antiquarium del Celio." In *Claudio imperatore*, 283–85.

Claudio imperatore. 2019 = Parisi Presicce, C. and L. Spagnuolo, ed. 2019. *Claudio imperatore. Messalina, Agrippina e le ombre di una dinastia – Catalogo della mostra Ara Pacis 2019*. Rome.

Cogitore, I. 1992. "Séries de dédicaces italiennes à la dynastie julio-claudienne." *MEFRA* 104: 817–70.

Cogitore, I. 2002. *La légitimité dynastique d'Auguste à Néron à l'épreuve des conspirations*. Rome.

Cogitore, I. 2014. "Formes d'opposition sous Caligula: le role des femmes." In *Lo spazio del non-allineamento a Roma fra tarda repubblica e primo principato. Forme e figure dell'opposizione politica*, ed. R. Cristofoli, A. Galimberti, and F. Rohr Vio, 167–81. Rome.

Conte, G. B., tr. J. B. Solodow. 1994. *Latin Literature: A History*. Rev. D. Fowler and G. W. Most. Baltimore.

Corbier, M. 1994. "La maison des Césars." In *Épouser au plus proche. Incest, prohibitions et stratégies matrimoniales de la Méditerranée*, ed. P. Bonte, 243–91. Paris.

Corbier, M. 1995. "Male Power and Legitimacy through Women: The *domus Augusta* under the Julio-Claudians." In *Women in Antiquity: New Assessments*, ed. R. Hawley and B. Levick, 178–93. London.

Cramer, F. H. 1954. *Astrology in Roman Law and Politics*. Philadelphia.

Cristilli, A. 2020. "In der Villa der Volusii: Neue Überlegungen zum Porträt der Agrippina minor in Lucus Feroniae." *Antike Welt* 51.1: 68–73.

Cropp, G. M. 2007. "Nero, Emperor and Tyrant, in the Medieval French Tradition." *Florilegium* 24: 21–36.

D'Ambra, E. 2013. "Mode and Model in the Flavian Female Portrait." *AJA* 117: 511–25.

Davenport, C. 2022. "The Court and Ceremonial." In Kelly and Hug 2022, I.288–317.

Davies, G. 2008. "Portrait statues as models for gender roles in Roman society." In *Role Models in the Roman World: Identity and Assimilation*, ed. S. Bell, 207–20. Ann Arbor, MI.

De Caprariis, F. 1993. "Un monumento dinastico tiberiano nel Campo Marzio settentrionale." *BCAR* 95: 93–114.

Deline, T. 2015. "The Criminal Charges against Agrippina the Elder in A.D. 27 and 29." *CQ* 65: 766–72.

De Rossi, G. M., ed. 1986. *Le isole pontine attraverso i tempi*. Rome.

Dettenhofer, M. H. 2000. *Herrschaft und Widerstand im augusteischen Principat. Die Konkurrenz zwischen res publica und domus Augusta*. Stuttgart.

Devillers, O. 1995. "Tacite, les sources et les impératifs de la narration: le récit de la mort d'Agrippine (Annales XIV, 1-13)." *Latomus* 54: 324–45.

Di Brino, G. 2016. "La consacrazione del divo Augusto come forma di legittimazione del potere sotto i principati di Caligola e Nerone." In *Saeculum Aureum. Tradizione e innovazione nella religione romana di epoca augustea*. Vol. I: *Augusto, da uomo a dio*, ed. I. Baglioni, 261–72. Rome.

Di Leo, B. 1989. "Basalt." In *Radiance in Stone. Sculptures in Colored Marble from the Museo Nazionale Romano*, ed. M. L. Anderson, A. Giuliano, and L. Nista, 56–63. Rome.

Dixon, S. 1985. "The Marriage Alliance in the Roman Elite." *Journal of Family History* 10: 353–78.

Dixon, S. 1988. *The Roman Mother*. Norman, OK.

Drinkwater, J. F. 2019. *Nero: Emperor and Court*. Cambridge.

Drogula, F. K. 2011. "Controlling Travel: Deportation, Islands and the Regulation of Senatorial Mobility in the Augustan Principate." *CQ* 61: 230–66.

Dudley, D. 1959. "The Celebration of Claudius' British Victories." *University of Birmingham Historical Journal* 7: 6–17.

Duncan-Jones, R. P. 2005. "Implications of Roman Coinage: Debates and Differences." *Klio* 87: 459–87.

Eaton, J. 2011. "The Political Significance of the Imperial Watchword in the Early Empire." *Greece & Rome* 58: 48–63.

Eck, W. 1993. *Agrippina, die Stadtgründerin Kölns: Eine Frau in der frühkaiserzeitlichen Politik.* Cologne.

Eck, W. 2015. "Agrippina die Jüngere, die Namegeberin Kölns." In *Agrippina: Kaiserin aus Köln*, ed. M. Trier and F. Naumann-Steckner, 34–39. Cologne.

Eck, W. 2022. "Das angebliche Praenomen Lucius des Agermus, des Freigelassenen von Agrippina Augusta." *RhM* 165: 429–32.

Eck, W., A. Caballos, and F. Fernández. 1996. *Das senatus consultum de Cn. Pisone patre.* Munich.

Eden, P. T., ed. 1984. *Seneca, Apocolocyntosis.* Cambridge.

Edmondson, J. 2022. "Domestic Servants in the Imperial Court." In Kelly and Hug 2022, I.168–203.

Ehrhardt, C. 1978. "Messalina and the Succession to Claudius." *Antichthon* 12: 51–77.

Fagan, G. G. 2002. "Messalina's Folly." *CQ* 52.2: 566–79.

Fantham, E. 2006. *Julia Augusti, the Emperor's Daughter.* New York.

Fejfer, J. 2008. *Roman Portraits in Context. Image and Context.* Berlin and New York.

Fittschen, K. and P. Zanker. 1983. *Katalog der römischen Porträts in den Capitolinischen Museen und den anderen kommunalen Sammlungen der Stadt Rom.* Vol. 3: *Kaiserinnen und Prinzessinbildnisse, Frauenporträts.* Mainz.

Flory, M. B. 1988 [1997]. "The Meaning of 'Augusta' in the Julio-Claudian Period." *AJAH* 13: 113–38.

Flory, M. B. 1995. "The Deification of Roman Women." AHB 9.3/4: 127-34.

Flory, M. B. 1996. "Dynastic Ideology, the *Domus Augusta*, and Imperial Women: A Lost Statuary Group in the Circus Flaminius." *TAPA* 126: 287–306.

Flory, M. B. 1998. "The Integration of Women into the Roman Triumph." *Historia* 47: 489–94.

Flower, H. I. 1996. *Ancestor Masks and Aristocratic Power in Roman Culture.* Oxford.

Flower, H. I. 2006. *The Art of Forgetting: Disgrace & Oblivion in Roman Political Culture.* Chapel Hill, NC.

Foubert, L. 2016. "Crowded and Emptied Houses as Status Markers of Aristocratic Women in Rome: The Literary Commonplace of the *domus frequentata*." *Eugesta* 6: 129–50.

Frazer, R. M. 1971. "Nero the Singing Animal." *Arethusa* 4: 215–18.

Gallia, A. 2022. "Nero's Divine Stepfather and the Flavian Regime." In *Flavian Responses to Nero's Rome*, ed. M. Heerink and E. Meijer, 33–54. Amsterdam.

Gallivan, P. 1978. "The Fasti for the Reign of Claudius." *CQ* 28: 407–26.

Galsterer, H. 1990. "Von den Eburonen zu den Agrippinensern." *Kölner Jahrbuch für Vor- und Frühgeschichte* 23: 117–26.

Gascou, J. 1998. "Claude et Drusilla d'après une inscription d'Avignon (*CIL*, XII, 1026 = *ILS*, 195)." *ZPE* 121: 291–96.

Gasparri, C. 2014. "Marmi per l'imperatore. L'arredo del *Palatium*." In *Museo Palatino. Le collezioni*, ed. C. Gasparri and M. A. Tomei, 79–95. Milan.

George, M. 2022. "Imperial Villas." In Kelly and Hug 2022, I.239–66.

George, M. and B. Kelly 2022. "Court Spaces." In Kelly and Hug 2022, II.32–78.

Gibson, R. K. 2014. "Suetonius and the *uiri illustres* of Pliny the Younger." In *Suetonius the Biographer: Studies in Roman Lives*, ed. T. Power and R. K. Gibson, 199–230. New York.

Gill, C. 1983. "The Question of Character-Development: Plutarch and Tacitus." *CQ* 33: 469–87.

Ginsberg, L. D. 2017. *Staging Memory, Staging Strife: Empire and Civil War in the "Octavia."* Oxford.

Ginsberg, L. D. 2019. "A Tale of Two Waters: Agrippina's Death in Flavian Poetry." In *Campania in the Flavian Poetic Imagination*, ed. A. Augoustakis and R. J. Littlewood, 25–41. Oxford.

Ginsburg, J. 2006. *Representing Agrippina: Constructions of Female Power in the Early Roman Empire*. Oxford.

Gloyn, L. 2014. "Show Me the Way to Go Home: A Reconsideration of Seneca's *De Consolatione ad Polybium*." *AJP* 135: 451–80.

Grant, M. 1950. *Aspects of the Principate of Tiberius*. New York.

Griffin, M. T. 1976. *Seneca: A Philosopher in Politics*. Oxford.

Gues, E. B. 2019. "Valeria Messalina *partu potens*. La maternité de Messaline selon les auteurs anciens." *RH* 691: 509–40.

Hahn, U. 1994. *Die Frauen des römischen Kaiserhauses und ihre Ehrungen im griechischen Osten anhand epigraphischer und numismatischer Zeugnisse von Livia bis Sabina*. Saarbrücker.

Halfmann, H. 1986. *Itinera principum: Geschichte und Typologie der Kaiserreisen im Römischen Reich*. Stuttgart.

Halfmann, H. 2022. "Imperial Journeys." In Kelly and Hug 2022, I.267–87.

Hammond, M., tr. 2020. *Artemidorus: The Interpretation of Dreams*. With an introduction and notes by P. Thonemann. Oxford.

Hansen, W. 1996. *Phlegon of Tralles, Book of Marvels*. Translated, with introduction and commentary. Exeter, UK.

Harries, J. 2007. *Law and Crime in the Roman World*. Cambridge.

Hasegawa, K. 2005. *The* Familia Urbana *during the Early Empire: A Study of* Columbaria *Inscriptions*. Oxford.

Heil, M. 2013. "Agrippina und Kos. Eine Inschrift und ihre Geschichte." *ZPE* 184: 183–92.

Hemelrijk, E. A. 1999. *Matrona docta. Educated Women of the Roman Élite from Cornelia to Julia Domna*. London.

Hemelrijk, E. A. 2015. *Hidden Lives, Public Personae: Women and Civic Life in the Roman West*. Oxford.

Herz, P. 1981. "Die Arvalakten des Jahres 38 n.Chr. Eine Quelle zur Geschichte Kaiser Caligulas." *BJ* 181: 89–110.

Højte, J. M. 2005. *Roman Imperial Statue Bases: From Augustus to Commodus*. Aarhus.

Holztrattner, F. 1995. *Poppaea Neronis Potens. Die Gestalt der Poppaea Sabina in den Nerobüchern des Tacitus: mit einem Anhang zu Claudia Acte*. Graz.

Horster, M. 2011. "*Princeps iuventutis*: Concept, Realisation, Representation." In *Figures d'empire, fragments de mémoire: pouvoirs et identités dans le monde romain impérial (IIe s. av. n. è.—VIe s. de n. è.)*, ed. S. Benoist, A. Daguet-Gagey, and C. Hoët-Van Cauwenberghe, 73–103. Villeneuve-d'Ascq.

Horster, M. 2013. "Coinage and Images of the Imperial Family: Local Identity and Roman Rule." *JRA* 26: 243–61.

Houston, G. W. 1985. "Tiberius on Capri." *Greece & Rome* 32: 179–96.

Hug, A. and B. Kelly. 2022. "Narratives of Court Crises." In Kelly and Hug 2022, 2.228–48.

Hurlet, F. 2015. "The Roman Emperor and the Imperial Family." In *The Oxford Handbook of Roman Epigraphy*, ed. C. Bruun and J. Edmondson, 178–201. Oxford.

Hurley, D. W. 1993. *An Historical and Historiographical Commentary on Suetonius' "Life of C. Caligula."* Atlanta, GA.

Hurley, D. W., ed. 2001. *Suetonius: Divus Claudius*. Cambridge.

Jones, B. W., ed. 2000. *Suetonius: Vespasian*. With introduction, commentary and bibliography. London.

Joshel, S. R. 1995. "Female Desire and the Discourse of Empire: Tacitus's Messalina." *Signs* 21: 50–82.

Kantorowicz, E. 1957. *The King's Two Bodies: A Study in Mediaeval Political Theology*. Princeton, NJ.

Kaplan, M. 1979. "*Agrippina semper atrox*. A Study of Tacitus' Characterization of Women." In *Studies in Latin Literature and Roman History, I*, ed. C. Deroux, 410–17. Collection Latomus 164. Brussels.

Keegan, P. 2018. "Agrippina to Veturia: Ancient and Modern Companions to *Female Biography*." In *The Invention of Female Biography*, ed. G. L. Walker, 145–73. London.

Kelly, B. and A. Hug, ed. 2022. *The Roman Emperor and His Court c. 30 BC-c. AD 300*. Two volumes. Cambridge.

Keppie, L. 1984. "Colonisation and Veteran Settlement in Italy in the First Century A.D." *PBSR* 52: 77–114.

Keppie, L. 2009. *The Romans on the Bay of Naples: An Archaeological Guide*. Stroud.

Keppie, L. 2011. "'Guess Who's Coming to Dinner': The Murder of Nero's Mother Agrippina in its Topographical Setting." *G & R* 58: 33–47.

Ketterer, R. C. 2009. *Ancient Rome in Early Opera*. Urbana.

Kienast, D., W. Eck, and M. Heil. 2017. *Römische Kaisertabelle. Grundzüge einer römischen Kaiserchronologie*. 6th edition. Darmstadt.

Kierdorf, W. 1986. "*Funus* und *consecratio*. Zu Terminologie und Ablauf der römischen Kaiserapotheose." *Chiron* 16: 43–69.

Kleijwegt, M. 1996. "Caligula as Auctioneer." *AClass* 39: 55–66.

Kleiner, D. E. E. and S. B. Matheson, ed. 1996. *I, Claudia. Women in Ancient Rome*. New Haven.

Kokkinos, N. 2002. *Antonia Augusta: Portrait of a Great Roman Lady*. 2nd ed. London.

Kolb, A. 2010. "*Augustae* – Zielsetzung, Definition, prosopographischer Überblick." In *Herrschaftsstrukturen und Herrschaftspraxis. 2: "Augustae": machtbewusste Frauen am römischen Kaiserhof?: Akten der Tagung in Zürich, 18.-20.9.2008*, ed. A. Kolb, 11–35. Berlin.

Kragelund, P. 2007. "Agrippina's Revenge." In Moltesen and Nielsen 2007, 27–43.

Kragelund, P. 2018. *Roman Historical Drama. The* Octavia *in Antiquity and Beyond*. Oxford.

Kuhoff, W. 1993. "Zur Titulatur der römischen Kaiserinnen während der Prinzipatszeit." *Klio* 75: 244–56.

Latham, J. A. 2016. *Performance, Memory, and Processions in Ancient Rome: The* Pompa Circensis *from the Republic to Late Antiquity*. Cambridge.

Levick, B. M. 1982. "Propaganda and the Imperial Coinage." *Antichthon* 16: 104–16.

Levick, B. 2015. *Claudius*. 2nd edition. London.

Levick, B. and S. Jameson. 1964. "C. Crepereius Gallus and His Gens." *JRS* 54: 98–106.

Lindsay, H. 1995. "A Fertile Marriage: Agrippina and the Chronology of Her Children by Germanicus." *Latomus* 54: 3–17.

Lott, J. B. 2012. *Death and Dynasty in Early Imperial Rome. Key Sources, with Text, Translation, and Commentary*. Cambridge.

Malloch, S. J. V. 2009. "*Hamlet* without the Prince? The Claudian *Annales*." In *The Cambridge Companion to Tacitus*, ed. A. J. Woodman, 116–26. Cambridge.

Malloch, S. J. V., ed. 2013. *The Annals of Tacitus, Book 11*. Cambridge.

Malloch, S. J. V. 2020. *The Tabula Lugdunensis: A Critical Edition with Translation and Commentary*. Cambridge.

Manuwald, G. 2013. *Nero in Opera Librettos as Transformations of Ancient Sources*. Berlin.

Marshall, A. J. 1990. "Women on Trial before the Roman Senate." *EMC* 34: 333–66.

Martin, R. 1981. *Tacitus*. Berkeley.

Matheson, S. B. 2000. "The Elder Claudia." In *I Claudia II: Women in Roman Art and Society*, ed. D. E. E. Kleiner and S. B. Matheson, 125–38. Austin, TX.

Maxwell-Stuart, P. G. 1997. "Who were Pliny's *Caesares iuuvenes*?" *Latomus* 56: 824–28.

Meister, J. 2014. "Reports about the 'Sex Life' of Early Roman Emperors: A Case of Character Assassination?" In *Character Assassination throughout the Ages*, ed. M. Icks and E. Shiraev, 59–81. New York.

Millar, F. 1964. *A Study of Cassius Dio*. Oxford.
Millar, F. 1993. "Ovid and the *Domus Augusta*: Rome Seen from Tomoi." *JRS* 83: 1–17.
Minnis, A. J. 1981. "Aspects of the Medieval French and English Traditions of the *De Consolatione Philosophiae*." In *Boethius: His Life, Thought and Influence*, ed. M. Gibson, 312–61. Oxford.
Moltesen, M. 2007. "The Portrait Head and Its Reworking." In Moltesen and Nielsen 2007, 139–48.
Moltesen, M. and A. M. Nielsen, ed. 2007. *Agrippina Minor. Life and Afterlife*. Copenhagen.
Momigliano, A. 1934. *Claudius: The Emperor and his Achievement*. Oxford.
Moreau, P. 2002. *"Incestus" et "prohibitae nuptiae." L'inceste à Rome: Conception romaine de l'inceste et histoire des prohibitions matrimoniales pour cause de parenté dans la Rome antique*. Paris.
Moreau, P. 2009. "Domus Augusta: l'autre maison d'Auguste." In *L'expression du pouvoir au début de l'Empire. Autour de la Maison carrée à Nîmes*, ed. M. Christol and D. Darde, 33–43. Paris.
Morizio, V. 1996. "Le dediche ad Augusto e ai Giulio-Claudi." In *Meta Sudans*, ed. C. Panella, I.201–16. Rome.
Nicols, J. 1975. "Antonia and Sejanus." *Historia* 24: 48–58.
Nocchi, F. R. 2016. "*Femina mater, divinus adulescens*: i termini di una nascita controversa." In *Saeculum Aureum. Tradizione e innovazione nella religione romana di epoca augustea*. Vol. I: *Augusto, da uomo a dio*, ed. I. Baglioni, 81–90. Rome.
Noreña, C. F. 2007. "Hadrian's Chastity." *Phoenix* 61: 296–317.
Noy, D. 1991. "Wicked Stepmothers in Roman Society and Imagination." *Journal of Family History* 16: 345–61.
Noy, D. 2000. "'Half-Burnt on an Emergency Pyre': Roman Cremations Which Went Wrong." *G & R* 47: 186–96.
O'Neill, J. R. 2020. "Claudius the Censor and the Rhetoric of Re-Foundation." *CJ* 116: 216–40.
Oost, S. I. 1958. "The Career of M. Antonius Pallas." *AJP* 79: 113–39.
Osgood, J. 2011. *Claudius Caesar. Image and Power in the Early Roman Empire*. Cambridge.
Palombi, D. 2014. "*Inter divos relatus est*. La divinizzazione nella famiglia imperiale." In *Apoteosi da uomini a dei: Il mausoleo di Adriano*, ed. L. Abbondanza, F. Coarelli, and E. Lo Sardo, 188–99. Rome.
Pangerl, A. 2019–2020. "Ein neuer Porträttypus 'München-Antiochia' der Agrippina minor, bestimmt durch Münzporträts und eine Skulptur." *JNG* 69/70: 169–94.
Panoussi, V. 2018. "From Adultery to Incest: Messalina and Agrippina as Sexual Aggressors in Tacitus' *Annals*." In *Complex Inferiorities: The Poetics of the Weaker Voice in Latin Literature*, ed. S. Matzner and S. Harrison, 205–24. Oxford.
Parat, J. 2016. "Reconsidering the Traces of Scribonianus' Rebellion." *Radovi Zavoda za Hrvatsku Povijest* 48: 191–212.
Parisi Presicce, C., M. Milella, S. Pastor, and L. Ungaro, ed. 2017. *Traiano: Costruire l'impero, creare l'Europa*. Rome.
Parisi Presicce, C., and L. Spagnuolo, ed. 2019. *Claudio imperatore. Messalina, Agrippina e le ombre di una dinastia—Catalogo della mostra Ara Pacis 2019*. Rome.
Park, K. 2006. *Secrets of Women. Gender, Generation, and the Origins of Human Dissection*. New York.
Pavolini, C. 2007. "The Latest on the Caelian Hill." In Moltesen and Nielsen 2007, 113–14.
Pflug, J. and U. Wulf-Rheidt. 2022. "The Imperial Palaces on the Palatine Hill: Architecture as a Reflection of Social Practices and Imperial Authority." In Kelly and Hug 2022, I.204–38.
Possanza, D. M. 2004. *Translating the Heavens: Aratus, Germanicus, and the Poetics of Latin Translation*. Frankfurt am Main.
Potter, D. S. and C. Damon, ed., tr. 1999. "The 'Senatus Consultum de Cn. Pisone Patre.'" *AJP* 120: 13–42.
Power, T. 2014. "Suetonius' Tacitus." *JRS* 104: 205–22.

Pucci, G. 2007. "Agrippina sullo schermo." In Moltesen and Nielsen 2007, 160–69.
Purcell, N. 1986. "Livia and the Womanhood of Rome." *PCPS* 32: 78–105.
Questa, C. 1967. *Studi sulle fonti degli "Annales" di Tacito.* 2nd ed. Rome.
Raepsaet-Charlier, M.-T. 1987. *Prosopographie des femmes de l'ordre sénatorial (Ier-IIe siècles).* 2 vols. Louvain. (= FOS).
Reynolds, L. D., ed. 1983. *Texts and Transmission: A Survey of the Latin Classics.* Oxford.
Richardson, L. 1992. *A New Topographical Dictionary of Ancient Rome.* Baltimore.
Riess, W. 2012. "*Rari exempli femina*: Female Virtues on Roman Funerary Inscriptions." In *A Companion to Women in the Ancient World*, ed. S. L. James and S. Dillon, 491–501. Malden, MA.
Roller, M. B. 2022. "Dining and Hunting as Courtly Activities in the Roman Empire." In Kelly and Hug 2022, I.318–48.
Rose, C. B. 1997. *Dynastic Commemoration and Imperial Portraiture in the Julio-Claudian Period.* Cambridge.
Rowan, C. 2011. "The Public Image of the Severan Women." *PBSR* 79: 241–73.
Rutledge, S. H. 2001. *Imperial Inquisitions: Prosecutors and Informants from Tiberius to Domitian.* New York.
Ryan, F. X. 1993. "Some Observations on the Censorship of Claudius and Vitellius, A.D. 47-48." *AJP* 114: 611–18.
Ryan, W. G., tr. 2012. *Jacobus de Voragine: The Golden Legend. Readings on the Saints.* With an introduction by E. Duffy. 2nd edition. Princeton, NJ.
Saller, R. P. 1994. *Patriarchy, Property and Death in the Roman Family.* Cambridge.
Santoro L'Hoir, F. 1994. "Tacitus and Women's Usurpation of Power." *CW* 88: 5–25.
Santoro L'Hoir, F. 2006. *Tragedy, Rhetoric, and the Historiography of Tacitus'* Annales. Ann Arbor, MI.
Sawday, J. 1995. *The Body Emblazoned. Dissection and the Human Body in Renaissance Culture.* London.
Schade, K. 2016. "Women." In *The Last Statues of Antiquity*, ed. R. R. R. Smith and B. Ward-Perkins, 249–58. Oxford.
Seita, M. 1982. "Un'affare politico-giudiziaria dell'antica Roma: l'attacco di Suillio a Seneca." *Latomus* 41: 312–28.
Sheldon, R. M. 2018. *Kill Caesar! Assassination in the Early Roman Empire.* Lanham, MD.
Shotter, D.C.A. 2000. "Agrippina the Elder: A Woman in a Man's World." *Historia* 49: 341–57.
Simpson, C. J. 1980. "The 'Conspiracy' of A.D. 39." In *Studies in Latin Literature and Roman History*, ed. C. Deroux, 347–66. Brussels.
Simpson, C. J. 2008. "The Julian Succession and its Claudian Coda: A Different Perspective on the So-called 'Julio-Claudian Dynasty.'" *Latomus* 67: 353–65.
Smith, R. R. R. 1987. "The Imperial Reliefs from the Sebasteion at Aphrodisias." *JRS* 77: 88–138.
Smith, R. R. R. 2021. "*Maiestas Serena*: Roman Court Cameos and Early Imperial Poetry and Panegyric." *JRS* 111: 75–152.
Southon, E. 2019. *Agrippina: The Most Extraordinary Woman of the Roman World.* New York.
Späth, T. 2000. "Skrupellose Herrscherin? Das Bild der Agrippina minor bei Tacitus." In *Frauenwelten in der Antike: Geschlechterordnung und weibliche Lebenspraxis: mit 162 Quellentexten und Bildquellen*, ed. T. Späth and B. Wagner-Hasel, 262–81. Stuttgart.
Stafford, E. 2013. "'The People to the Goddess Livia': Attic Nemesis and the Roman Imperial Cult." *Kernos* 26: 205–38.
Strong, A. K. 2016. *Prostitutes and Matrons in the Roman World.* New York.
Sullivan, D. 1976. "Innuendo and the 'Weighted Alternative' in Tacitus." *CJ* 71: 312–26.
Sutherland, C. H. V. 1986. "Compliment or Complement? Dr Levick on Imperial Coin Types." *NC* 146: 85–93.
Swan, M. 1970. "Josephus, A. J., XIX, 251-252: Opposition to Gaius and Claudius." *AJP* 91: 149–64.

Syme, R. 1933. "M. Vinicius (Cos. 19 B. C.)." *CQ* 27: 142–48.
Syme, R. 1955. "Marcus Aemilius Lepidus, *Capax Imperii*." *JRS* 45: 22–33.
Syme, R. 1958. *Tacitus*. Oxford.
Syme, R. 1986. *The Augustan Aristocracy*. Oxford.
Talamo, E. 2007. "I ritrovamenti archeologici sul Celio e la scoperta della statua di Agrippina orante." In Moltesen and Nielsen 2007, 95–111.
Talamo, E. 2011. "Statua di Agrippina Minore come orante." In *Ritratti. Le tante facce del potere*, ed. E. La Rocca and C. Parisi Presicce, 230–31. Rome.
Talbert, R. J. A. 1984. *The Senate of Imperial Rome*. Princeton, NJ.
Temporini-Gräfin Vitzthum, H., ed. 2002. *Die Kaiserinnen Roms: von Livia bis Theodora*. Munich.
Thonemann, P. 2020. *An Ancient Dream Manual: Artemidorus' The Interpretation of Dreams*. Oxford.
Thorton, M. K. and R. L. Thorton. 1985. "The Draining of the Fucine Lake: A Quantitative Analysis." *AncW* 12: 105–20.
Treggiari, S. 1975. "Jobs in the Household of Livia." *PBSR* 43: 48–77.
Treggiari, S. 1991. *Roman Marriage.* Iusti Coniuges *from the Time of Cicero to the Time of Ulpian*. Oxford.
Treggiari, S. 2019. *Servilia and Her Family*. Oxford.
Trier, M. and F. Naumann-Steckner, ed. 2015. *Agrippina: Kaiserin aus Köln*. Cologne.
Trillmich, W. 1994. "Agrippina Minore." In *Enciclopedia dell'arte antica, classica, e orientale*. 2nd supplement, 1.115–16. Rome.
Trillmich, W. 2007. "Typologie der Bildnisse der Iulia Agrippina." In Moltesen and Nielsen 2007, 45–65.
Ungaro, L. 2017. "Il potere ritratto nel Foro di Traiano." In Parisi Presicce et al., 2017, 91–97.
Valentini, A. 2018. "*Ex ea nouem liberos tulit*: i figli di Agrippina Maggiore e Germanico." *Erga-Logoi* 6: 65–82.
Valentini, A. 2019. "*Puellae doctae*: l'educazione 'al femminile' nella *domus Augusta*." *Erga-Logoi* 7: 117–40.
Van Zyl Smit, B. 2019. "Agrippina as Prima Donna: The Reception of Agrippina, Mother of Nero, in Handel's Opera *Agrippina*." *In die Skriflig/In Luce Verbi* 53.2: a2506. https://indieskriflig.org.za/index.php/skriflig/article/view/2506.
Varner, E. R. 2001. "Portraits, Plots, and Politics: *Damnatio Memoriae* and the Images of Imperial Women." *MAAR* 46: 41–93.
Varner, E. R. 2004. *Mutilation and Transformation:* Damnatio Memoriae *and Roman Imperial Portraiture*. Leiden.
Vinson, M. P. 1989. "Domitia Longina, Julia Titi, and the Literary Tradition." *Historia* 38: 431–50.
von Hesberg, H. and S. Panciera, ed. 1994. *Das Mausoleum des Augustus. Der Bau und seine Inschriften*. Munich.
Walker, G. L. 2018. *The Invention of Female Biography*. London.
Wardle, D. 1998. "Caligula and his Wives." *Latomus* 57: 109–26.
Warmington, B. H. 1977. *Suetonius: Nero*. With introduction and notes. Bristol.
Weaver, P.R.C. 1972. *Familia Caesaris: A Social Study of the Emperor's Freedmen and Slaves*. Cambridge.
Webb, L. and L. Brännstedt. 2023. "Gendering the Roman Triumph: Elite Women and the Triumph in the Republic and Early Empire." In *Gendering Roman Imperialism*, ed. H. Cornwell and G. Woolf, 58–95. Leiden.
Weisser, B. 2017. "Germanicus als Mitglied der Augusteischen Familie und *Zwilling* des Drusus Minor: Lebenszeitliche Münzbilder zwischen 4 und 19 n. Chr." In *Augustus ist tot—Lang lehe der Kaiser! Internationales Kolloquium anlåasslich des 2000. Todesjahres des römischen Kaisers vom 20–22 November 2014 in Tübingen*, ed. M. Flecker et al., 71–90. Tübingen.

Welch, K. 2011. "Velleius and Livia: Making a Portrait." In *Velleius Paterculus: Making History*, ed. E. Cowan, 309–34. Swansea.

Wellebrouck, G. 2017. "Claudia Acte: le destin d'une affranchie." *Bulletin de l'Association Guillaume Budé* 1: 97–122.

Wilkes, J. 1972. "Julio-Claudian Historians." *CW* 65: 177–92, 197–203.

Wilson, E. 2014. *The Greatest Empire. A Life of Seneca.* Oxford/New York.

Winterling, A. 1999. Aula Caesaris. *Studien zur Institutionalisierung des römischen Kaiserhofes in der Zeit von Augustus bis Commodus (31 v. Chr.–192 n. Chr.).* Munich.

Winterling, A. 2009. *Politics and Society in Imperial Rome.* Malden, MA.

Wiseman, P. 1982. "Calpurnius Siculus and the Claudian Civil War." *JRS* 72: 57–67.

Wiseman, T. P. 2013. *The Death of Caligula: Josephus* Ant. Iud. *XIX 1–273. Translation and Commentary.* 2nd ed. Liverpool.

Wiseman, T. P. 2019. *The House of Augustus: A Historical Detective Story.* Princeton, NJ.

Wood, S. 1988. "*Memoriae Agrippinae*: Agrippina the Elder in Julio-Claudian Art and Propaganda." *AJA* 92: 409–26.

Wood, S. 1992. "Messalina, Wife of Claudius: Propaganda Successes and Failures of His Reign." *JRA* 5: 219–34.

Wood, S. 1995. "Diva Drusilla Panthea and the Sisters of Caligula." *AJA* 99: 457–82.

Wood, S. E. 1999. *Imperial Women: A Study in Public Images, 40 B.C.–A.D. 68.* Mnemosyne 194. Leiden.

Woodman, A. J., tr. 2004. *Tacitus: The Annals.* With introduction and notes. Indianapolis.

Zanker, P. 1982. "Herrscherbild und Zeitgesicht." *Wissenschaftliche Zeitschrift der Humboldt-Universität zu Berlin. Gesellschafts- und sprachwissenschaftliche Reihe.* 31.2–3: 307–12.

Index

Note: Agrippina the Younger is abbreviated as A.

For the benefit of digital users, indexed terms that span two pages (e.g., 52–53) may, on occasion, appear on only one of those pages.

Aenatores Romani, shrine of 92, 116–19, 123, 134, 197 n.159, 201 n.5
Agrippina the Elder (A.'s mother)
after Germanicus' death in 19 26–30, 48
on Arch of Germanicus 14–15, 26
birth in 14 BCE; early life; education 18–20, 25
criticized for masculine actions 23, 39
denied permission to remarry 29, 167 n.154, 177 n.50
exile on Pandateria; death in 33 29–33, 37–8, 40–1, 48–9
female friendships 4, 15, 27–9
granddaughter of Augustus 12–13, 15, 21–3, 27–30, 73–4, 191 n.21
honored posthumously by Caligula 36–41, 94–5
Julia Augusta's hostility 166 nn.130, 135
later reputation 154
marriage and children with Germanicus 12–13, 20–5, 27, 73–4, 205 n.115
model for A. 23, 60
Tiberius' hostility 15, 27–31, 39
visual depictions 5, 23, 37–8, 74, 94–5, 205 n.115
Ahenobarbus, Gnaeus Domitius (A.'s first husband)
charged under Tiberius in 37 34, 40–1, 44, 49–50, 52, 174 n.135, 190 n.12
consul in 32 32, 41, 57, 59
death in 40 49–50
family and wealth 31–2, 49–50, 57
marriage to A. in 28 30–4, 41, 46–7, 57, 110–11
member of Arval Brethren 32, 41, 110–11, 168 n.163
Nero's father 44–6, 49–50, 110–11, 168 n.163
political success 32, 41
Anthologia Palatina 107
Antonia the Younger (A.'s paternal grandmother)
A. and siblings' childhood residence 19, 25, 30–1, 167 n.161, 170 n.56
absent from Germanicus' funeral in 20 26–7
on Arch of Germanicus 14–15, 26
in Claudian family monuments 92–3
family 18–19, 21–2, 167 n.161, 169 n.31
honored by Caligula and Claudius 38–9, 55–6, 62, 82, 190 n.8
little public visibility but influential behind the scenes 19, 35, 38–9
Livilla's and Sejanus' deaths in 31 19, 180 n.145
model for A. 19
Nero moves A. into her house 113, 115–16
Palatine residence 16–17, 27–8
priest of *divus* Augustus 38–9, 100
refusal of Augusta title 38–9, 82
wealth and dependents 17
Arch of Claudius 62–3, 92–3
Arch of Germanicus 14–15, 26, 91–2
Arval Brethren
Ahenobarbus a member 32, 41, 110–11, 168 n.163
celebration of A.'s birthday 2, 116, 164 n.81
Claudius' divinization reflected in acta 191 n.32
thanksgiving for discovery of plot against Caligula 46
vows in 55/56 for the health of Nero, A., and Octavia 116
Augusta (title)
A. 61, 78, 82–4, 94–5, 141–3, 161 n.44, 185 n.108, 187 n.149
Antonia the Younger 38–9, 82
Julia Augusta (Livia) 19, 82
Messalina 56, 82

Augustus (Octavian) (A.'s maternal great-grandfather, princeps)
A. direct descendant 52–3, 82, 93–4, 99–101, 110–11, 132, 134
adoption of Tiberius 21
Agrippina the Elder emphasizes blood ties 15, 22–3, 27–30
claim to restore Republic 52
cult 15, 19, 27–9, 38–40, 43–4, 52–3, 55–6, 100
death in 14 18–19, 22–3, 52–3
education of grandchildren 18, 25
ideas of family 13–14, 21–2
image of modesty 16–17
Nero direct descendant 45, 49–50, 73, 110–11
Palatine residence 16–18, 28, 110
portrait statues 160 n.33, 202 n.53
posthumous adoption of Livia 13–14, 19
precedent for Claudius' adoption of Nero 78
regard for Agrippina the Elder 12–13, 22, 25, 27
in Shrine of the Aenatores Romani 116–19

birds, A.'s love of 49, 57, 138
birth and pregnancy
A. gives birth to Nero 44–5, 125–6, 164 n.80, 183 n.55
A.'s birthdate and birthplace 2, 9–10, 21–4, 82–3
Agrippina the Elder's fertility 12–13, 21–3, 27
childbearing as Roman ideal 21–2, 44
imperial women giving birth outside Rome 22–4
Nero said in later legend to want to give birth 147–8
omens at imperial births 44–5, 58
pregnant Agrippina the Elder facing mutinous troops 22–3
time between A.'s marriage and successful pregnancy 33, 44
travel by pregnant women 22–3
wet nursing 164 nn.79, 82, 165 n.97
Boccaccio, Giovanni 146, 148–9, 152–4, 172 n.88, 203 n.78
Boethius 147
Britannicus (A.'s stepson)
birth in 41 56
in Claudian family monuments 92–3
Messalina's son 56, 64, 67
murder by Nero in 55 80–1, 112–15, 133, 139, 167 n.140, 192 n.60, 199 n.202
name change 56, 62
not in Seneca, *Apocolocyntosis* 102–3
promoted by A. after she loses influence with Nero 112–13
supplanted by Nero as Claudius' heir 66–7, 73, 76–81, 84–5, 96–8, 112–13, 136–9

Caligula (Gaius) (A.'s brother, princeps)
assassination in 41 17–18, 36, 51–3, 59, 162 n.23, 189 n.199, 200 n.232
birth in 12; early life 21–6, 163 n.52, 172 n.93
burial by A. and Julia Livilla 55
coinage 37–40, 43–4, 91–2, 94–5
exile and seizure of property of A. and Julia Livilla 47–50, 54–5
eulogy for Julia Augusta in 29 31
favoritism for Drusilla 41–5, 50, 55–6, 73–4
honors for deceased family members 36–8
incest with A. and Julia Livilla 46–8, 73–4, 99, 170 n.56
incest with Drusilla 41–2, 46–7, 57, 73–4, 99
illness during first two years of reign 42–3, 45
later reputation 153–4
marriages arranged for female relatives 42, 56
move to Tiberius' Capri villa in 31 31, 33, 36, 40–1
multiple marriages and liaisons 34, 36, 41–2, 45–6, 49–50, 68, 81–2
Passienus' sycophancy 57, 101–2
plot against 3, 46–8, 50, 63
promotion of Claudius 38, 53
promotion of grandmother Antonia the Younger 38–9, 82, 190 n.8
promotion of sisters 35–7, 39–44, 62, 91–2, 99
rape of Drusilla 30–1, 153–4, 170 n.56
relationship with Nero 45, 49–50
in Seneca's dream about Nero 183 n.60
in Shrine of the Aenatores Romani 195 n.129
succeeded by Claudius in 41 53–5
succeeds Tiberius in 37 34–8, 53
supplants Gemellus as Tiberius' heir 36–7, 42, 45, 93–4, 184 n.77
cameos 4–6, 74, 98, 106–7, 143
carpentum (two-wheeled carriage) 37–9, 62, 87–8, 94–5, 182 n.44
Cassius Dio, *Roman History* 3–4, 136
Claudium (Temple of *divus* Claudius) 92, 99–100, 118–23, 134, 139

Claudius (A.'s paternal uncle and third husband, princeps)
- A. gets rid of female rivals 49–50, 81–2, 96, 98
- A. identified as wife 3–4, 8–9, 61, 138–9, 166 n.123, 177 n.58
- A.'s funeral for 19, 97–101, 104, 118
- A.'s priesthood of 99–100, 119, 121, 139
- A.'s public presence alongside 19, 74–6, 83–9, 101–2, 109–10, 138–9, 193 n.79
- acknowledgment of Drusilla's divinization 43
- adoption of Nero in 50 45, 78–82, 93, 138–9
- Arch in Rome 62–3, 92–3
- birth in 10 BCE 18–19, 22
- Caratacus' submission in 51/52 54–5, 72, 86–7
- children 34, 56, 67, 70, 88, 97, 102–3, 193 n.87
- Colonia Claudia Ara Agrippinensium established 82–4
- dangers of court during marriage to Messalina 57–60, 63–6, 72–3, 123
- death in 54 80–1, 95–8, 112–14, 125–6, 137–9, 153–4, 178 n.95
- eulogized by Nero 99–100, 109, 193 n.77
- family 14–15, 26, 53
- family monuments 62–3, 91–4
- Fucine Lake drainage in 51/52 88–9, 96–7
- honors for A. 75–6, 78, 82, 87–8, 94–5
- honors for Messalina 56, 62, 82, 87–8
- intellectual interests 71, 92–3, 118, 179 n.129
- Julia Livilla's exile; death in 41 57–8, 63, 73–4, 77
- marriage to A. in 49 68–74
- marriage to Messalina in 38 49–50, 56
- marriages to Plautia Urgulanilla and Aelia Paetina 34, 56, 68, 71–2
- Messalina's fall; death in 48 66–8, 71–2
- Nero supplants Britannicus as heir 66–7, 73, 76–81, 84–5, 96–8, 100–1, 112–13, 136–9
- portraits of A. resembling 8, 106, 196 n.150
- praetorian support 54–5, 61–2, 72–3
- promotion of family 55–8, 61–3, 82, 170 n.38
- rehabilitation of Caligula's exiles 49, 54–5
- Revolt of Scribonianus in 42 59–62, 65–6, 72–3, 176 n.27
- satirized in Seneca, *Apocolocyntosis* 65–6, 71, 97, 102–3, 118, 125–6
- in Shrine of the Aenatores Romani 118–19
- sickly and out of public life before principate 14–15, 38, 45, 53, 56
- succeeds Caligula in 41 51–5, 98
- Temple (Claudium) 92, 99–100, 118–23, 134, 139
- triumph of 44 62–3, 72, 86–8
- uncle-niece marriage 73–5, 99, 125–7
- visual depictions alongside A. 5, 74, 89–91, 94–5, 106

coins, *see also* portraits
- A. and family members on Caligula's coins 36–40, 43–4, 91–2, 94–5
- A. and family members on Claudius' coins 79–80, 82–4, 94–5, 141–3
- A. and sisters first living women on official coins 39–40
- A. first living woman with named numismatic portrait 6–7, 79–80, 94–5, 140
- A. on Nero's coins 99, 103–6
- Augustan Liberty on Claudius' coins 54–5
- Caligula's accession on his coins 168 n.2, 169 n.17
- circulation of imagery 5–6, 79–80, 94–5
- portraiture not controlled by imperial women 6–7, 94–5
- used for portrait typology 6–7, 104–6, 140–3

Cologne (Germany), *see* Oppidum Ubiorum

Commentarii, *see* memoirs

damnatio memoriae, *see* memory sanctions

domus, *see* family, imperial

Drusilla (A.'s sister)
- birth in 16; early life 21–4, 163 n.52, 165 n.102, 171 n.76
- Caligula's favoritism overshadows A. 42–3, 45, 50, 171 n.61
- death in 38; divinization 41–5, 50, 55–6, 70–1, 179 n.128
- depiction on coinage 36–7, 39–40, 91–2
- designated as heir by Caligula 42–3, 73–4
- incest with Caligula 41–2, 57, 73–4, 99
- marriages 32–3, 35–6, 41–3, 45, 56
- portraits identified as A.'s possibly hers 6–7
- public visibility under Caligula 36–7, 39–44, 62, 99
- rape by Caligula 30–1, 153–4, 170 n.56

Drusus Caesar (A.'s brother)
- birth in 8; early life 21, 165 n.102
- honored posthumously by Caligula 38, 40–1
- imprisonment; death in 33 30–3, 40–1, 171 n.67
- marriage to Aemilia Lepida 171 n.67
- potential heir to Tiberius 27, 29–30, 35, 39

Drusus the Elder (A.'s paternal grandfather)
on Arch of Germanicus 14–15, 26
in Claudian family 53, 55–6, 83, 92–3
death in 9 BCE 20–1
in *domus Augusta* 13–14
family and early life 18–19, 21–2, 163 n.59
Drusus the Younger (A.'s uncle, Livilla's husband)
in Claudian family monuments 93
death in 23 29–30, 163 n.54
family 29–30, 32, 93–4, 169 n.11
in Germanicus' funeral cortège 26
guardian of Nero Caesar and Drusus Caesar 27
heir apparent to Tiberius 29–30, 93
Palatine residence 16–17, 28

family, imperial (*domus Augusta*)
A. takes on new roles for women 35–40, 70
Antonia the Younger in 19, 21, 35, 38–9, 100
Caligula's promotion of relatives 35–40, 42–4, 91–2
Claudius' promotion of Claudian relatives 53, 55–8
dependents (*familia Caesaris*) 8–9, 17
education of children 25
endogamy 18–19, 73–4
evolution of women's role in A.'s time 1, 35–40, 62, 76, 100, 172 n.86
legally includes women 161 n.9
Livia (Julia Augusta) in 19, 35, 38–9, 55–6, 100
monuments 14–15, 91–4, 116–19
need for sons 21
religious veneration 15, 38–40, 43–4, 55–6, 99–100, 102–3, 119–23, 190 n.216
representation of princeps outside Rome 22
residences 12–13, 16–18, 27–9, 114–15
terminology 13–15
visual depictions 8
women barred from *imperium* 39, 42–3, 70
Forum of Trajan 145–6

Germanicus (A.'s father)
A. identified as daughter 26, 60–1, 68, 87, 92–5, 118, 124–5, 132, 139
adoption by Tiberius in 4 12–13, 18–19, 21, 35
Arch in Rome 14–15, 26, 91–2
birth in 16/15 BCE; family 14–19, 21, 26
in Claudian family 53, 83, 92–3, 169 n.29
death in 19 12–13, 26–7, 48
in *domus Augusta* 13–15
Gemma Claudia cameo 5, 74
honored posthumously by Caligula 36–8
learning and culture; authorship of *Aratea* 25
marriage to Agrippina the Elder in 5 12–13, 20–4, 27, 73–4, 205 n.115
military commands 22–5, 83
Nero as grandson 66–71, 73, 196 n.133
Palatine residence 16–17, 27–8, 30
popularity 26–7, 30, 37, 60–1, 66–7, 124–5
praetorians' loyalty to A. 100–1, 112–13, 125–6, 131, 200 n.232
praetorians' loyalty in Claudius' accession 53, 72–3
in transition from Augustus to Tiberius 12–13, 21–3
triumph of 17 24, 62
greeting ritual (*salutatio*) 17–19, 75–6

incest accusations
Ahenobarbus and Domitia Lepida 34, 49–50, 170 n.51
Caligula and sisters 41–2, 46–8, 73–4, 99
Claudius and Julia Livilla 57–8, 73–4
Nero and A. 46–7, 99, 126–8, 130, 153–4, 194 n.91, 197 n.169
Silanus and Junia Calvina 76–7, 191 n.28
uncle-niece marriage 3, 68–9, 73–5, 99, 101

Jacobus de Voragine, *Golden Legend* 146–8
Jean de Meun, *Roman de la Rose* 147–9
Josephus 3, 27, 51–2, 76, 138–9
Julia Augusta, *see* Livia
Julia Livilla (A.'s sister)
in A.'s funerary monument 58, 93–4
associated with deities in the East 43–4
betrothal to Quinctilius Varus 166 n.136, 167 n.153
birth in 17/18; early life 21–2, 25–6, 163 n.52, 165 n.102, 177 n.63
burial with A. of Caligula 55
Caligula's favoritism for Drusilla marginalizes 45, 171 n.61
closeness to Claudius 57–8, 73–4
depiction on coinage 36–7, 39–40, 91–2
exile under Caligula from 39 to 41 47–9, 51, 54–5
exile under Claudius; death in 41 57–60, 64–5, 81–2, 174 n.125, 179 n.110
incest with Caligula 46–8, 73–4, 99, 170 n.56
marriage to Marcus Vinicius in 33 32–3, 35–6, 47–8, 53–4, 56
portraits identified as A.'s possibly hers 6–7

plot against Caligula 46–8
plot against Claudius 57–60, 63
public visibility under Caligula 36–7, 39–42, 62, 99
relationship with Lepidus 42, 173 n.117
relationship with Seneca 57–8, 77, 198 n.175
Junia Claudilla (Caligula's first wife) 34, 36, 41
Juvenal 64, 138–9, 179 n.112, 204 n.92

Kos, inscriptions honoring A. and relatives 60–1, 181 n.25

Leonidas of Alexandria 107
Livia (Julia Augusta) (A.'s paternal great-grandmother)
A. and siblings' childhood residence 30–1, 163 n.52
absent from Germanicus' funeral in 20 26–7
adopted posthumously by Augustus with name change 13–14, 19, 38–9, 82
assistance to exiled Julia the Younger 167 n.156
death in 29 30–3, 167 n.141
dependents (*familia*) 17
divinization 43–4, 55–6
family 12, 18–19, 21, 73–4
female friendships 4, 25, 27
higher profile after Augustus' death 19, 31, 38–9, 55–6
honors and titles 17–19, 37–9, 82, 87–8, 182 n.45
honors later granted to Antonia the Younger, Drusilla, and A. 38–9, 43, 84
imperial woman with most visual representations 4–5, 135–6, 202 n.53
limited public visibility while alive 35, 38–9, 84, 110, 156, 182 n.39
marriage to Augustus in 38 BCE 159 n.3, 182 n.37
model for A. 19, 97–102
Palatine residence 16–17, 28
pivotal in development of imperial house 13–15
priest of *divus* Augustus 19, 38–9, 100
princeps femina 101–2
relationship to Tiberius compared to A.'s to Nero 191 n.23
rivalry with Agrippina the Elder 166 n.135
will suppressed by Tiberius and honored by Caligula 37–9
Livilla (Livia Julia, A.'s paternal aunt)
on Arch of Germanicus 14–15, 26
birth ca. 13 BCE; family 16–19
death in 31 19, 167 n.145
marriage to Drusus the Younger 14–17, 163 n.54, 167 n.143, 169 n.11
memory sanctions 169 n.11, 201 n.5
mother of Gemellus 169 n.11
part of wider imperial family 14–15
relationship with Sejanus 19, 29–30
rivalry with Agrippina the Elder 164 n.73
Tiberius forbids remarriage 177 n.50
Lollia Paulina (Caligula's third wife) 41–2, 45–6, 68, 81–2

marriage
A.'s first, to Ahenobarbus 31–2, 35, 110–11, 167 n.142
A.'s second, to Passienus 56–7, 201 n.20
A.'s third, to Claudius 8–9, 61, 67–74, 196 n.150
frequency of divorce 21–2
Messalina's and Silius' "marriage" 63–4, 66–8, 71–2, 138–9, 173 n.110
minimum age for women 30–1, 76–7
model of Agrippina the Elder and Germanicus 12–13, 20–5, 27, 73–4, 205 n.115
politically arranged for elite women 21, 33, 35, 42, 56, 73–4, 100–1, 182 n.37
Roman ideal 21–2
uncle-niece 68–9, 73–5
Martial 119, 138–9
Mausoleum of Augustus 13, 26–7, 37–8, 58, 92–4, 139, 163 n.58
memoirs (*Commentarii*), A.'s lost 2, 25, 30–1, 44–5, 49, 71, 138, 166 n.138
memory sanctions (*damnatio memoriae*)
against A. 8–9, 89, 119, 121–3, 135–6, 140
against Livilla 169 n.11, 201 n.5
against Messalina 70–1, 92–3, 179 n.104, 201 n.5
Messalina (Claudius' third wife)
birthdate 177 n.63
in Claudian family monuments 62–3, 92–3, 195 n.126
daughter of Domitia Lepida 49–50, 59, 96
death in 48 3, 67–8, 71–2, 77–8, 84–5
later reputation 138–9, 150
"marriage" to Silius in 48 63–4, 66–8, 71–2, 138–9, 173 n.110
memory sanctions 70–1, 92–3, 179 n.104, 201 n.5
mother of Britannicus and Octavia 56, 70, 77–8, 84–5, 181 n.29
parallels to A. 81–2, 86

Messalina (Claudius' third wife) (*cont.*)
portraits identified as A.'s may be hers 6–7, 202 n.44
public visibility, privileges, and honors 56, 61–3, 71, 82, 86–8
responsibility for deaths, including Julia Livilla, Junius Silanus, and Poppaea Sabina 57–9, 63–5, 72–3, 76, 81–2, 124
Revolt of Scribonianus in 42 59–60, 72
in Seneca, *Apocolocyntosis* 102
Tacitus' comparison to A. 75
threat to A. and Nero 58, 63–7
monuments, *see also* Aenatores Romani, shrine of; Arch of Claudius; Arch of Germanicus; Claudium; Forum of Trajan; Mausoleum of Augustus
A.'s funerary, for her siblings 58, 93–4, 139, 163 n.58, 181 n.25, 197 n.162
Claudian family 62–3, 91–4, 178 n.93

Nero (Lucius Domitius Ahenobarbus) (A.'s son, princeps)
A. identified as mother 3, 8–9, 152–4, 188 n.182
A. taking on male roles at beginning of reign 110–11
A.'s influence after 55 115–26, 128, 131–2
A.'s influence at beginning of reign 99–110
advisers 108–10
after A.'s death in 59 132–7, 185 n.100
attempted assassination by Messalina 58–9
birth in 37 44–5, 125–6, 164 n.80, 183 n.55
in Claudian family monuments 92–3, 118–19
Claudius' death in 54 95, 98, 125–6
on coinage 79–80, 94–5, 103–4
death in 68 3, 135–7, 156
Domitia Lepida's influence 49–50, 96
education 49–50, 57–8, 77, 108–9, 159 n.9
honors for father Ahenobarbus 110–11, 168 n.163
hostility to A. 108–16
hostility to A.'s supporters after her death 137
impact on A.'s posthumous reputation 137–9, 203 n.66
incest with A. 46–7, 99, 126–7, 132–3, 182 n.33, 194 n.91, 197 n.169, 199 n.213
inspection of A.'s body 132–3, 147–51, 204 n.91
later reputation 146–8, 154–5, 172 n.88
marriage to Octavia in 53 76–80, 95, 100–2, 124, 186 n.119
memory sanctions against A. 8–9, 89, 119, 121–3, 135–6, 140
murder of A. in 59 115–16, 121–3, 125–6, 128–34, 197 n.170, 198 n.179
murder of Britannicus in 55 80–1, 112–15, 133
Octavia's exile; death in 62 124, 137–8, 173 n.117
portraits of A. resembling 8, 106, 120–3
potential heir to Caligula 46–7, 49–50, 172 n.94
in sculpture 104–7, 188 n.169
in Seneca, *Apocolocyntosis* 3, 102–3
snake bracelet 58
succeeds Claudius in 54 99, 114, 156
supplants Britannicus as Claudius' heir 45, 66–7, 73, 76–82, 93, 97–8, 100–1, 112–13, 138–9
treason charge against A. in 55 112–15, 136–7
Nero Caesar (A.'s brother)
birth in 6; early life 21, 165 n.102
in Claudian family monuments 93
exile on Pontia; death in 31 30–3, 37–8, 40–1, 48, 167 n.141
honored posthumously by Caligula 37–8, 40–1
marriage to Julia, daughter of Livilla and Drusus the Younger 179 n.117
potential heir to Tiberius 27, 29–30, 35, 39

Octavia (anonymous drama) 3, 135–8, 154
Octavia (A.'s stepdaughter and daughter-in-law)
adoption into another family at betrothal to Nero 78–9
in Arval Brethren's vows 116
attempt to deflect Claudius' anger from Messalina 67
betrothal to Lucius Junius Silanus 56, 76–7, 101–2
in Claudian family monuments 92–3
exile on Pandateria; death in 62 48–9, 124, 137–8, 173 n.117, 185 n.99
grief for Britannicus 113–14, 191 n.34, 193 n.87
marriage to Nero in 53 76–80, 95, 100–2, 124, 186 n.119
not in Seneca, *Apocolocyntosis* 102–3
not reported at Fucine Lake 88
in *Octavia* (drama) 137–8
prevented from entering Claudius' bedchamber at his death 97

Octavia (Augustus' sister)
children 13, 164 n.67, 177 n.55, 181 n.12, 182 n.31
early remarriage 182 n.37
grandmother of Ahenobarbus 31–2, 49–50, 177 n.55
limited public role after triumviral period 35, 172 n.86, 186 n.131
privileges 170 n.33
Octavian, *see* Augustus
opera 137–8, 150–1, 154–5
Oppidum Ubiorum (modern Cologne) 9–10, 18–19, 22–4, 82–3
Ovid 13–14

paintings, history 150–2
Passienus, Gaius Sallustius Crispus (A.'s second husband)
consul in 27 and 44 57, 61, 63–4, 187 n.139
death 63
family and wealth 57, 63
friendship with Seneca 177 n.65
marriage to A. in 41 56–7, 201 n.20
marriage to Domitia 57, 160 n.20, 194 n.101
proconsul of Asia in 42/43 60–1, 66
Suetonius' *Life* 3, 63
sycophancy 57, 64–5, 101–2
Pliny the Elder, *Historia Naturalis* 4, 23, 44–5, 112, 138
portraits
A. second most frequently represented imperial woman 4–5, 135–6, 140
A.'s 94–5, 103–4, 119–23
Augustus' 60–1, 202 n.53
Caligula's 39–40
Claudius' 79–80, 94–5, 188 n.169
display contexts 5–6
identified as A.'s may be of other women 6–7, 140, 143–6, 192 n.41
imperial family members made to resemble one another 8, 106, 120–3, 141–3
Livia most frequently represented imperial woman 4–5, 135–6, 202 n.53
Nero's 79–80, 103–4
period face (*Zeitgesicht*) 143–4
typology of A.'s 6–7, 140–6, 188 n.168, 192 n.41
variety of A.'s 4–8, 89–90, 106, 121, 140–6
pregnancy, *see* birth and pregnancy

salutatio, *see* greeting ritual
Senatus Consultum de Cn. Pisone patre (SCPP) 14–15, 21–2, 27
Seneca the Younger, Lucius Annaeus
Apocolocyntosis 3, 10–11, 65–6, 71, 97, 102–3, 118, 125–6, 162 n.23, 181 n.27, 193 n.66
authors Nero's speech eulogizing Claudius 99–100, 109
birthdate 192 n.63
Consolatio ad Polybium 10–11, 65–6
exile in Corsica 57–8, 65–6, 77, 108–9, 194 n.94
later reputation 151, 205 n.108
on Nero's incest with and murder of A. 126–7, 131, 193 n.67, 197 n.169, 198 n.179, 200 n.233
plot against Claudius 57–8, 77
relationship with A. 10–11, 57–8, 65–6, 77, 108–9, 124–5, 194 n.94
relationship with Julia Livilla 57–8, 77, 124–5
sidelines A. under Nero 77, 102–3, 108–9, 111, 114, 123, 193 n.88
supports accused Burrus 195 n.103
tutor of Nero 57–8, 77, 108–9, 174 n.140
statues and sculpture, *see also* portraits
Caelian graywacke statue 4–5, 10, 116–23, 135–6, 139, 141–3
Getty head 4–8, 140, 143
Sebasteion relief of A. and Claudius 8, 89–91, 106, 143, 196 n.150
Sebasteion relief of A. and Nero 8, 89–90, 98, 104–6, 108, 141–3
Suetonius, *Lives* 3–4, 132–3, 136, 146–8, 152–4

Tacitus, *Annals*
date 1–2, 4, 146
first printed edition 149–50
influence on other authors 2–3, 136, 146, 152–4, 160 n.16
missing sections 46, 51, 66, 99–100, 170 n.56, 172 n.92, 177 n.72
sources 4, 112–14, 126–7, 166 nn.127, 138, 167 n.154, 195 n.113
Temple of *divus* Claudius, *see* Claudium
Tiberius (A.'s paternal great-uncle and adoptive grandfather, princeps)
absent from Germanicus' funeral in 20 26–7
adoption of Germanicus in 4 12–13, 18–19, 21, 35
Agrippina the Elder's exile; death in 33 29–33
arranges marriages of A. and sisters 31–3, 56, 167 n.142
Caligula moves to reside with in 31 31

Tiberius (*cont.*)
charges against Ahenobarbus in 37 34, 40–1, 44, 52, 174 n.135, 190 n.12
in Claudian family monuments 93
death in 37 34–5, 40–1, 44, 52, 189 n.199, 199 n.209
denial of honors to Livia and suppression of her will 19, 37–9
in *domus Augusta* 13–15
Drusus Caesar's imprisonment; death in 33 30–3, 170 n.52
family and early life 18–19, 163 n.59
grandson Gemellus supplanted as heir by Caligula 15, 34–8
hostility to Agrippina the Elder 15, 23, 27–9, 39
marriage to Julia the Elder 20, 22
Nero Caesar and Drusus Caesar as potential heirs 29–30, 35, 166 n.132
Nero Caesar's exile; death in 31 30–3, 170 n.52
never consecrated 190 n.12
opposition to women in public sphere 15, 23, 39, 84, 162 n.41, 170 n.35
Palatine residence 16–17, 25, 28
Passienus' sycophancy 57
precedent for Claudius' adoption of Nero 78
relationship to Livia compared to A.'s to Nero 191 n.23
Sejanus' and Livilla's plot and deaths 19, 169 n.11
in Shrine of the Aenatores Romani 116–18
succeeds Augustus in 14 12–19
Titus (princeps) 93–4, 139, 185 n.90, 192 n.60, 193 n.87

Vespasian (princeps) 108, 119, 123, 137–9, 159 n.7, 161 n.42